US   UK   USSR   Third Reich   Japan   Italy   France   Czechoslovakia   Sweden   Australia   Canada   Belgium   Netherlands   Hungary   Romania   Poland

Kyushu J7W Shinden

Boeing B-17 Flying Fortress

Vickers Wellington

Northrop P-61B Black Widow

de Havilland DH.98 Mosquito

Hawker Sea Fury

Focke-Wulf TA-152 Dora

IAR-80

Yokosuka D4Y Suisei Judy

Polikarpov Po-2

Fiat CR.32

Avia B534

Carro Veloce L3/35

CANT Z.501 Gabbiano

Hotchkiss 10.5 cm leFH16 (Sf) auf Gesch. 39H(f)

Henschel Hs-129B-3

Vickers Valentine Archer

T13 B3

Schneider AMC P16 RC

M3 Half-Track Car

SdKfz-234 Puma

Semovente 75/34

Kangaroo

M20 Utility Car

T-34/76

T-28A

M1931 B-4

Dodge WC54

Motor Torpedo Boat PT-109

Armoured car/ light tank   Medium/heavy tank   Tank destroyer   Howitzer   Anti-aircraft   Artillery   Missiles/ rockets   Rail   Fighter   Night fighter   Fighter-bomber   Bomber   Torpedo   Ship

WORLD WAR II
INFOGRAPHICS

JEAN LOPEZ   NICOLAS AUBIN   VINCENT BERNARD   NICOLAS GUILLERAT

GENERAL EDITOR   DATA DESIGN

WORLD WAR II
INFOGRAPHICS

WITH A FOREWORD BY JONATHAN FENBY

Thames & Hudson

CONTENTS

FOREWORD

World War II was the most devastating conflict ever fought on our planet, with consequences felt to the present day. The previous confrontation between the great powers from 1914 to 1918 had been dubbed 'the war to end all wars'; but the struggle which followed two decades later between the Axis nations headed by Germany, Italy and Japan and the Allies led by the United States, Soviet Union and Britain was far wider, more destructive more ideological and more world-changing, not only on its military fronts but also in its effect on both the global balance and on society and human relationships.

The battlegrounds themselves stretched from the far north of Europe to the South Pacific, with fighting of a scale not seen before on land, sea and in the air. The combined armed forces of the 30 belligerent nations numbered 130 million, topped by 34 million in the Soviet Union, 18 million in Germany and 16 million in the United States. Between 20 and 25 million military personnel were killed, but the civilian toll was even larger in total warfare in which indiscriminate killing rode roughshod over old conventions as ideology and doctrines of racial superiority added a deadly edge to the military struggle. In all, anywhere from 70 to 85 million people lost their lives as a result of the struggle for mastery between Fascism, Communism and Democracy in which victory was the only option.

The material destruction was unparalleled. Warfare became industrialized as never before as the economic weight of the Allies grew and the Axis powers sought desperately to augment their resources. Leading combatant nations mobilized their entire populations using propaganda on an unprecedented level. The deployment of new weapons changed the nature of conflict – heavy bombers, tanks, rockets and aircraft carriers amongst them, and then the atom bombs dropped by the United States on Hiroshima and Nagasaki. At the same time, governments boosted technological advances in radar, computing, communications, medicine and other fields, which would held to shape the post-war world.

In many nations, morality broke down and social cohesion fragmented, even as state control was increased. Occupation by foreign armies imposing their political systems set resistance partisans and collaborators with the invaders against one another. Terror was used on an often indiscriminate scale and the Nazis made their concentration camps into factories of death in pursuit of the Final Solution to eliminate Jews and others they classed as 'sub-human'. The struggle for survival predominated. Human life became cheap. Powerful leaders set on ultimate victory had no time for compromise. When the fighting finally ended, old empires were on their knees and two great powers new to global leadership faced one another in a fresh confrontation that would last for almost another half-century.

The driving forces of the war were both simple and complex. The Axis powers were intent on expansion, on challenging the Western victors of World War I, and saw force as the way to achieve that. They were greatly aided by the reluctance of other nations to oppose them, whether from weakness or from fear of re-igniting the bloodbath of the earlier conflict. Peace-keeping organizations set up after 1918 to police the globe proved ineffective in a world in which nationalism took the upper hand. At several points, the geo-political equation that led to full-scale global war might have gone in another direction had the political calculus between Berlin, London, Paris, Moscow, Washington and Tokyo taken on a different dimension. But, given the nature of the principal protagonists and the interests they championed, conflict was virtually inevitable.

In Europe, it is common to focus as a starting date on September 1939, when Britain and France declared war on Germany after its forces had invaded their treaty partner, Poland, and then on the Nazi regime's all-conquering advance to the west the following summer that brought the defeat of France in the third war between the two countries in seventy years. But German resentment at the Versailles Treaty imposed on it after World War I and Hitler's ambitions to make his country master of the continent had pointed to war well before this as Germany reoccupied the demilitarized Rhineland, carried out the *Anschluss* with Austria and then dismembered Czechoslovakia after the Munich Agreement of 1938.

On the other side of the globe, Japan had seized China's most industrialized region of Manchuria in 1931 and established a puppet state there before expanding its zone of influence and then launching full-scale war against the Nationalist regime of Chiang Kai-shek in 1937. Mussolini's Italy, for its part, had invaded Ethiopia in 1935 while the civil war in Spain saw German, Italian and Soviet involvement. The USSR had concluded its pact with Germany in 1939 as Stalin and Hitler chose to put the chances of territorial expansion in eastern Europe ahead of their ideological differences, though the German invasion of the USSR two years later would show the Nazi leader's true intentions.

As war spread across Europe with the German *Blitzkrieg* of 1940, the defeat of France and the isolation of Britain facing a Nazi-dominated continent, the United States was still bound by the isolationism that it had embraced after the end of World War I. For all his domestic political strength, Franklin Roosevelt felt the need to move carefully towards committing his country to engage in the fight against Fascism. The Japanese attack on Pearl Harbor at the end of 1941, followed by

Hitler's declaration of war on the United States, brought the world's most powerful economy out of isolation to assume the international role it had previously refused and to engage in a two-front war as Tokyo's forces surged through South-East Asia, humiliating European colonial powers and making the conflict truly global.

This sequence of events – some connected, others the result of unilateral decisions by individual governments – ensured that the conflict, which would last until the summer of 1945, would be worldwide in nature. In keeping with that scale, it was marked on land by huge military campaigns in Europe and Asia, at sea by great maritime battles between aircraft carriers in the Pacific and the struggle between vital supply convoys to Britain and German U-boats in the Atlantic, and in the air by the deployment of bomber forces in mass raids on cities, culminating in the dropping of atomic weapons on Japan. The size and complexity of the armed forces involved required unprecedented levels of organization, which changed the nature of warfare. The backing of populations on the home front was vital as grand strategy was implemented by a unique cast of leaders, headed by Roosevelt, Stalin, Hitler and Churchill, each of whom sought to personify their nation as did resistance standard-bearers such as de Gaulle and Tito.

The course of events to the defeat of Germany and Japan in the summer of 1945 produced huge battles, stretching across Europe from the Red Army's advance on Berlin to the west of the continent after the D-Day invasion of Normandy, and raging across the Pacific as the imperial Japanese forces were pushed back towards their home islands. Germany's threat to North Africa and the Middle East had been beaten off, and success in the Battle of the Atlantic ensured that Britain would be able to fight on, though economically drained by six years of combat. In contrast to the Axis powers, which never coordinated policy to any significant degree, Roosevelt and Churchill met regularly and held two summits with Stalin at Tehran and Yalta to maintain their joint front, even if their ambitions for the post-war world increasingly diverged as the Soviet dictator pursued his goal of carving out a deep security zone in eastern and central Europe under Moscow's control.

Thousands of historical accounts have been devoted to the war, dealing with everything from detailed examination of individual battles to the sweep of grand strategy, from the politics of the opposing leaders to the plight of civilians caught in the bloodlands of Europe and Asia. In addition, there has been a stream of films, documentaries, novels and television dramas set in the war years, ensuring that the legacy of the conflict remains a potent force, be it in British pride at standing alone in 1940, Chinese antagonism towards Japan or the 'never again' horror of the Holocaust.

This volume presents a new approach using infographics to provide readers with an analytical picture of how the conflict took shape and how it was fought, with specific building blocks on the many different elements that contributed to that. That enables it to embody a massive amount of information in an easily accessible form which, taken together, offers a unique panorama of the most massive war the world has seen.

Jonathan Fenby

PREFACE

More books have been written about World War II than hours have passed since it ended. And that tidal wave of paper is nothing compared to the sea of data produced by institutions – including the armed forces, ministries, governments, embassies, commissions, agencies, committees, offices, missions, businesses and think tanks – that were involved in the greatest conflict of all time. War causes death, destruction and suffering, but above all it generates statistics. A complete list of data sources on the American oil industry between 1940 and 1945 alone would not fit into in this book. In the post-war period, these mountains of data were then used as a basis for further research on various aspects of the war and in turn were added to our stock of knowledge and so on, ad infinitum.

The aim of this book is to create a better understanding of World War II. In embarking on this project, we felt like geologists going down into an inexhaustible data mine to collect tiny but relevant samples. Once crosschecked, confirmed and calibrated, these were used to expand on the fifty-three topics covered here. We must point out that this was just one of the many possible choices. Many aspects of the war have been omitted, geographical areas ignored, major operations not mentioned. For instance, we have not always given as much attention as we should to Asia, Africa and the Middle East, to women, factory workers, neutral countries, or the world of intelligence and special operations. Regretfully, a long list of subjects had to be left out, but we were obliged to be selective, or else the volume of data collected by the three authors and processed by just one data designer within the three years we spent on our research would have been unmanageable.

The massive amount of data we gathered needed to be presented in an attractive, concise and intelligent way. My thanks are due to Nicolas Guillerat for his skill in designing the infographics and maps to flesh out the statistics. In this graphic form, economic, demographic and military data no longer appears dry and abstract. But this is not a picture book in which you are encouraged to skip from one illustration to the next. It is a real history book, designed to be read, albeit in a different way. Each of the 357 maps and graphs contains a mass of information representing different levels of understanding and analysis and the reader can choose between them. On the topic of aircraft production, for instance, you might simply read that the USA, Great Britain and the Soviet Union had overall superiority over the Axis countries. But if you want to go into the topic in more detail you can see the national specializations in each sector, production rates, technical choices, and transfers of equipment between the Allies. We hope this will make the book appealing to those new to the subject as well as those with a more specialized interest. And thanks to the research by my co-authors, Nicolas Aubin and Vincent Bernard, the sources quoted at the end of each section are international and very carefully chosen. Keeping track of such a mass of often incomplete or contradictory statistics is quite an achievement.

This book is more than just an aide-memoire or a database. It is also a source of deeper information, discoveries, surprises and challenges to our knowledge of the most horrific event of the twentieth century. Looking at the illustrations here of American, British and Soviet production or, to take another example, comparative losses in the Battle of Britain and the Battle of the Atlantic, you might well answer the question of whether World War II was 'a close-run thing' differently. Did Churchill exaggerate the risk of an Axis victory in his memoirs in order to inflate his own and his country's stature? Looking at the command diagrams might also make you reassess the view that a totalitarian dictatorship is necessarily more efficient at fighting a war than a liberal democracy. Issues like these are raised under most of the subject headings. By taking a fresh approach to this hugely significant event, we have tried to show it in a different light.

Jean Lopez

1. THE CONTEXT OF THE WAR

THE FALL OF DEMOCRACY IN EUROPE

The inter-war period was the darkest point in the history of European democracy. After a century of victories, it was under attack from authoritarian, military and totalitarian regimes. Democracy's downfall started in Hungary in 1920, followed by regime changes in Italy, Poland, Lithuania, Portugal and Yugoslavia. After 1930, the global economic crisis weakened and disorientated the middle classes, leading to a second wave of right-wing extremism in which national resentments and the radicalization of disaffected minorities also played a major role. Everywhere, the emergence of openly anti-democratic parties went hand in hand with the growth of ideologies and values that echoed those that had held sway until 1914: the cult of personality, militarism, aggressive nationalism, veneration of the all-powerful state, anti-individualism. The creation and apparent success of new types of state such

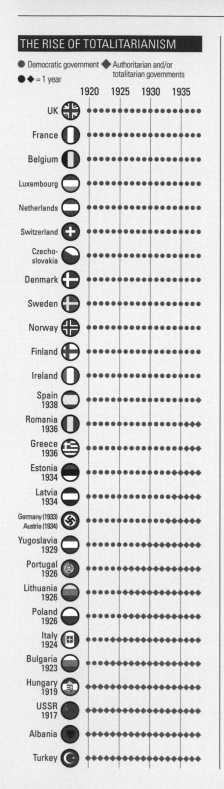

THE RISE OF TOTALITARIANISM

● Democratic government ◆ Authoritarian and/or totalitarian governments
●◆ = 1 year

1920 1925 1930 1935

UK
France
Belgium
Luxembourg
Netherlands
Switzerland
Czechoslovakia
Denmark
Sweden
Norway
Finland
Ireland
Spain 1938
Romania 1936
Greece 1936
Estonia 1934
Latvia 1934
Germany (1933) Austria (1934)
Yugoslavia 1929
Portugal 1926
Lithuania 1926
Poland 1926
Italy 1924
Bulgaria 1923
Hungary 1919
USSR 1917
Albania
Turkey

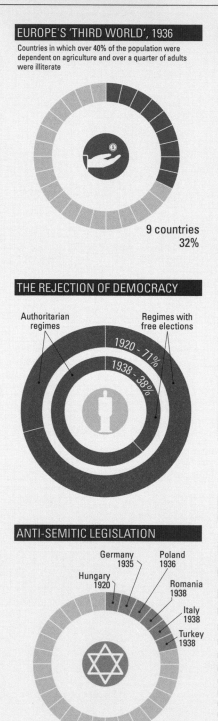

EUROPE'S 'THIRD WORLD', 1936

Countries in which over 40% of the population were dependent on agriculture and over a quarter of adults were illiterate

9 countries
32%

THE REJECTION OF DEMOCRACY

Authoritarian regimes

Regimes with free elections

1920 - 71%
1938 - 38%

ANTI-SEMITIC LEGISLATION

Hungary 1920
Germany 1935
Poland 1936
Romania 1938
Italy 1938
Turkey 1938

6 countries
21%

POLITICAL MAP OF EUROPE IN 1938

■ Parliamentary democracies
■ Territories under democratic control
■ Communist totalitarism regime
■ Nazi totalitarian regime
■ Fascist totalitarian regime
■ Authoritarian regimes
▨ Civil war

N
W   E
S

1 Belgium
2 Netherlands
3 Luxembourg
4 Denmark
5 Switzerland
6 Albania
7 Estonia
8 Latvia
9 Lithuania

Norway

Ireland

United Kingdom

Third Reich

France

Spain

Portugal

Italy

as the USSR, Fascist Italy and Nazi Germany encouraged the widespread rise of these 'anti-establishment' parties. Verbal and physical political violence became commonplace, an increasing number of anti-Semitic laws were passed, and wild territorial claims were staked, usually in military terms. Dollfuss, Erzberger, Rathenau, Matteotti, Pieracki, Alexander of Yugoslavia, Granjo, Duca and Stamboliyski were just a few of the hundreds of political figures that were assassinated. Around 1920, twenty-four European governments could be considered democratic. If the USSR and, for other reasons, the micro-states are left out of the picture, only Albania and Hungary did not have free elections. By 1938 the number of democracies had been reduced to eleven: Czechoslovakia, Finland, Belgium, France, the United Kingdom, Ireland, the Netherlands, Norway, Sweden, Denmark and Switzerland.

The abandonment of Czechoslovakia by the two major western democracies in the 1938 Munich Agreement was seen by all European democrats as a terrible betrayal, unforgivable in the context of this retreat into the past. Nonetheless, France and Britain could justifiably claim to be on the side of democracy when the war broke out in September 1939. Their enemy, Germany, was a totalitarian regime, backed by two other equally totalitarian states, Italy and the Soviet Union. Caught between the three, the countries of Central and Eastern Europe and the Balkans all gave up the ideals of free elections and a free press, the rule of law and equality for all their citizens. And the worst was yet to come. Six of the democracies surviving in 1938 succumbed in their turn in 1942. It was truly the 'midnight of the century'.

TERRITORIAL CLAIMS

7 countries
25%

MAJOR FASCIST AND COMMUNIST PARTIES

5 countries
18%

21 countries
75%

POWERFUL NATIONAL MINORITIES
opposed to the central government

5 countries
18 %

EUROPE'S NAZI & FASCIST PARTIES

PNF / Italy / 1919
National Fascist Party

NSDAP / Germany / 1920
National Socialist German Workers' Party

SP-NS / Slovakia / 1923
Slovakian Solidarity

Garda de Fier / Romania / 1927
Iron Guard

Geležinis Vilkas / Lithuania / 1927
Iron Wolves

Ustaše / Croatia / 1929
Revolutionary Movement

Vaps Movement / Estonia / 1929
Union of War of Independence Participants

NF / Switzerland / 1930
National Front

NSB / Netherlands / 1931
National Socialist Movement

BUF / United Kingdom / 1932
British Union of Fascists

FE de las JONS / Spain / 1933
Spanish Falange

NS / Norway / 1933
National Union

NSPA / Sweden / 1933
National Socialist Workers' Party

Perkonkrusts / Latvia / 1933
Thundercross

VNV / Belgium / 1933
Flemish National Union

Francisme / France / 1933
Francist Movement

ONR / Poland / 1934
National Radical Camp

REX / Belgium / 1935
Rexist Party

PPF / France / 1936
French Popular Party

Ratniks / Bulgaria / 1936
Warriors for the Advancement of the Bulgarian National Spirit

NP-HM / Hungary / 1939
Arrow Cross Party

SOURCES: 1. Dudley Kirk, *Europe's Population in the Interwar Years*, New York, 1969 • 2. Giovanni Capoccia, *Defending Democracy: Reactions to Extremism in Interwar Europe*, Baltimore, MD, 2005.

ECONOMIC FORCES

Does victory depend on economic strength? In the first phase of the war, from 1939 to mid-1942, military factors predominated. Surprise, speed, training, tactics, motivation and arms stockpiled before the war gave the advantage to the Axis. That did not mean, of course, that economic factors had no effect on their victories; after all, their combined GDPs were three-quarters the size of those of their enemies. At the end of 1940, after the victory over Western Europe and with the French empire out of the picture, the GDP of the Rome-Berlin Axis was even theoretically one-quarter higher than that of the British bloc. Everything changed when, after twenty-four months in the case of the Reich and six months in the case of Japan, the Axis countries proved unable to win and found themselves trapped in a war of attrition.

In the second phase of the war, the Allies had had time to remedy their most serious military weaknesses and economic power became crucial once again. The scale, quality and diversity of American and Soviet resources, combined with those of the British bloc and with the addition of those provided, willingly or otherwise, by Latin American and Middle Eastern countries, crushed everything that could be put in their way. In 1942, the GDP of the Allies was twice that of the enemy; in 1944, over three times; at the beginning of 1945, over five times. This economic imbalance was made worse by differences in the size of mobilizable populations, access to key strategic resources (energy, non-ferrous metals) and unexploited production reserves. In this regard, the figures opposite are slightly distorted by the reference year chosen, usually 1938. In that year, Roosevelt's America was going through another crisis after the improvements of the New Deal, with its GDP falling to $800 billion. Enormous agricultural, industrial and mining resources were underutilized, whereas those of Japan, Germany and Italy were working at full capacity. The mobilization of unused labour and production capacity, including 10.3 million unemployed, is made plain by a single figure: in 1945 the GDP of the United States was 84% higher than in 1938. Even with pillaging and forced labour, the Reich could only achieve an increase of 24%, and Japan 11%.

1 • LEVELS OF ECONOMIC DEVELOPMENT

The economic development of the two sides can be measured in various ways. In the Axis camp, only the German Reich rivalled Britain and the United States in the size of its industrial sector and the scale of its research and development, as evidenced by its ability to partly catch up in the field of radar and take the lead in developing jet aircraft and missiles. Italy, Japan and the USSR were considered developing countries, with a large and fairly unproductive agricultural population and limited technology. The British and the Americans could spend a quarter of their expenditure on aircraft, whereas the Soviets, Italians and Japanese still had enormous infantries.

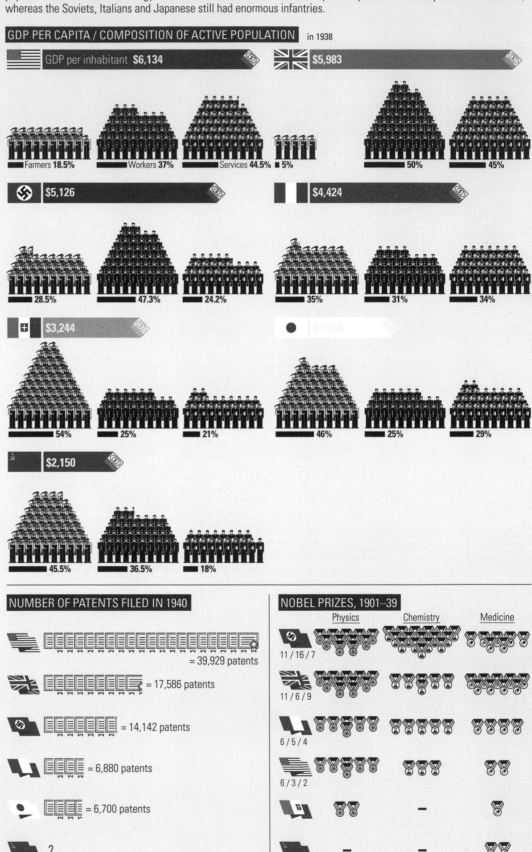

GDP PER CAPITA / COMPOSITION OF ACTIVE POPULATION   in 1938

GDP per inhabitant **$6,134** — Farmers **18.5%** · Workers **37%** · Services **44.5%**

$5,983 — 5% · 50% · 45%

$5,126 — 28.5% · 47.3% · 24.2%

$4,424 — 35% · 31% · 34%

$3,244 — 54% · 25% · 21%

$2,356 — 46% · 25% · 29%

$2,150 — 45.5% · 36.5% · 18%

NUMBER OF PATENTS FILED IN 1940

= 39,929 patents

= 17,586 patents

= 14,142 patents

= 6,880 patents

= 6,700 patents

?

?

2,000 = patents

NOBEL PRIZES, 1901–39

	Physics	Chemistry	Medicine
	11 / 16 / 7		
	11 / 6 / 9		
	6 / 5 / 4		
	6 / 3 / 2		
	–	–	–
	–	–	–

2 • GDP, AREA, POPULATION in 1938

Although on paper, the war might appear to have been a race for resources, with the Axis partly managing to make up for its deficits, this is misleading. The Axis powers had very little success in exploiting the reluctant populations and the economies of the countries they controlled, crippled by blockades. Hitler believed that, in order to win, he needed to take over all the Soviet Union's resources, which did not happen. He also saw this as the key to continental expansion, with its associated strategic advantages. The Japanese were of the same mind. It was strange that the two major Axis allies nevertheless did not make it a priority to unite for this purpose.

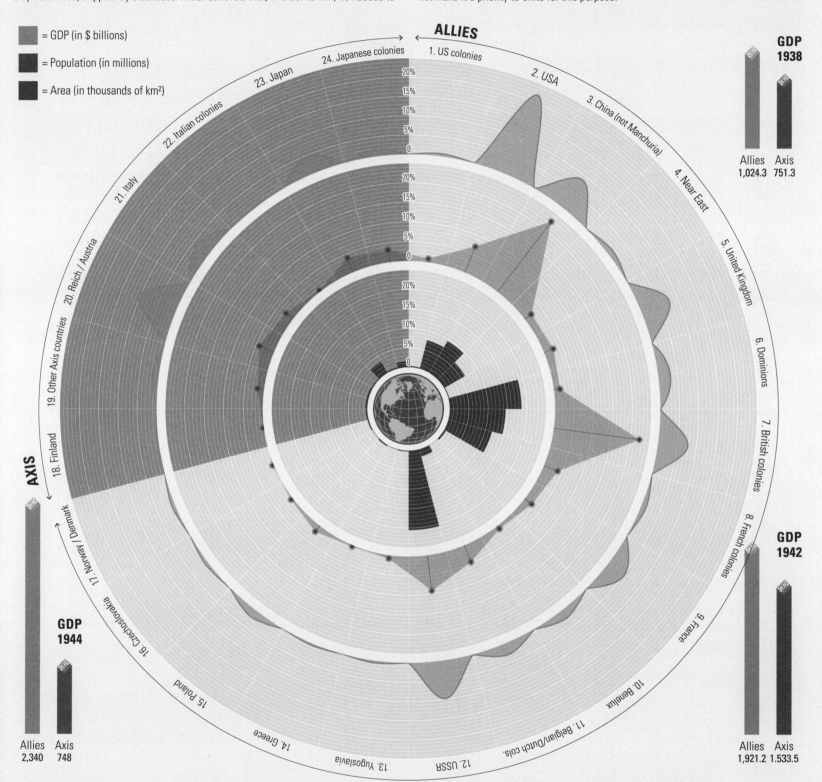

= GDP (in $ billions)

= Population (in millions)

= Area (in thousands of km²)

ALLIES

AXIS

GDP 1938
Allies 1,024.3   Axis 751.3

GDP 1942
Allies 1,921.2   Axis 1.533.5

GDP 1944
Allies 2,340   Axis 748

1. US colonies • 2. USA • 3. China (not Manchuria) • 4. Near East • 5. United Kingdom • 6. Dominions • 7. British colonies • 8. French colonies • 9. France • 10. Benelux • 11. Belgian/Dutch cols. • 12. USSR • 13. Yugoslavia • 14. Greece • 15. Poland • 16. Czechoslovakia • 17. Norway / Denmark • 18. Finland • 19. Other Axis countries • 20. Reich / Austria • 21. Italy • 22. Italian colonies • 23. Japan • 24. Japanese colonies

1. **US colonies:** $26.5 / 17.8 / 324 km² • 2. **USA:** $800.3 / 130.5 / 7,856 km² • 3. **China:** $320.5 / 411.7 / 9,800 km² • 4. **Near East:** $52.1 / 38.6 / 6,430 km² • 5. **UK:** $284.2 / 47.8 / 245 km²
6. **Dominions:** $114.6 / 30 / 19,185 km² • 7. **British cols.:** $284.5 / 406 / 14,995 km² • 8. **French cols.:** $48.5 / 70.9 / 12,099 km² • 9. **France:** $185.6 / 42 / 551 km² • 10. **Benelux:** $85.5 / 17.4 / 64 km²
11. **Belgian/Dutch cols.:** $5.5 / 77.4 / 14 / 68.1 / 240 km² / 1,904 km² • 12. **USSR:** $359 / 167 / 21,176 km² • 13. **Yugoslavia:** $21.9 / 16.1 / 248 km² • 14. **Greece:** $19.3 / 7.1 / 130 km² • 15. **Poland:** $76.6 / 35.1 / 389 km²
16. **Czechoslovakia:** $30.3 / 10.5 / 140 km² • 17. **Norway + Denmark:** $32.5 / 6.7 / 366 km² • 18. **Finland:** $12.7 / 3.7 / 383 km² • 19. **Romania + Hungary + Bulgaria:** $54.1 / 31.4 / 515 km²
20. **Reich + Austria:** $375.6 / 75.4 / 554 km² • 21. **Italy:** $140.8 / 43.4 / 310 km² • 22. **Italian cols.:** $2.6 / 8.5 / 3,488 km² • 23. **Japan:** $169.4 / 71.9 / 382 km² • 24. **Japanese cols.:** $62.9 / 59.8 / 1,602 km²

Situation in 1938: Axis (20+21+22+23+24): $751.3 / 258.9 / 6,336 km² • Allies (5+6+7+8+9+10+11+15+16+17): $1,225.2 / 748.5 / 50,433 km²
Situation in 1942: Axis (11+20+21+22+23+24+18+19 occupied territories): $1,533.5 / 622.5 / 13,973 km² • Allies (1+2+3+4+5+6+7+8+11+12): $2,256.5 / 1,271.2 / 89,658 km²

3 • KEY PRODUCTS   in % of world production, 1939

This list of fifteen products, not including oil, that were crucial to victory shows the imbalance between the two sides. Even in the case of basic materials such as steel, the German Reich and Japan did not have the means to achieve their ambitions. They were constantly required to decide between the demands of the three armed forces.

From 1942 onwards, the Reich survived on its stocks of some metal alloys. The Allies only had issues with access to natural rubber, after the Japanese took control of the rubber plantations in Asia. However, the US managed to develop a huge synthetic rubber industry in eighteen months, catching up on the lead the Reich had before the war.

Legend: USA · UK · Dominions · British colonies · France · French colonies · Europe (other) · USSR · Third Reich & Austria · Italy · Japan/Korea/Manchuria · Asia · Africa · Americas (other)

Coal 1,626,724,088 t
Iron 212,468,405 t
Steel 131,927,136 t
Ferroalloys 104,000,000 t
Manganese 6,051,779 t
Chrome 1,192,450 t
Tungsten 34,174 t
Nickel 117,065 t
Magnesium 1,238,585 t
Molybdenum 479,065 t
Bauxite 3,772,544 t
Aluminium 481,900 t
Copper 2,291,716 t
Rubber 1,005,254 t
Synthetic rubber 101,000 t

4 • AGRICULTURE

One of the majors concerns for leaders of countries at war is access to food, especially grains and cereals. In fact, Hitler could be said to have been obsessed with the threat of famine. Apart from Romania, all the countries with a surplus were on the Allied side.

Britain was much more dependent on wheat imports than any other country, hence the idea of causing a famine by waging a submarine war on its trade. The Reich fed its citizens by starving millions in the Soviet Union, Poland, France and Belgium.

THE FIVE MAJOR WHEAT PRODUCERS — from 1934 to 1938

Global wheat production (Danube region = Romania, Hungary, Bulgaria, Yugoslavia)

USA = 15% / Danube = 7% / Canada = 5% / Argentina = 5% / Australia = 3% / Rest of world = 65%

Global wheat exports

USA = 33% / Danube = 7% / Canada = 25% / Argentina = 20% / Australia = 15% / Rest of world = 0%

MAIN EUROPEAN WHEAT IMPORTERS — from 1932 to 1937 as % of total consumption

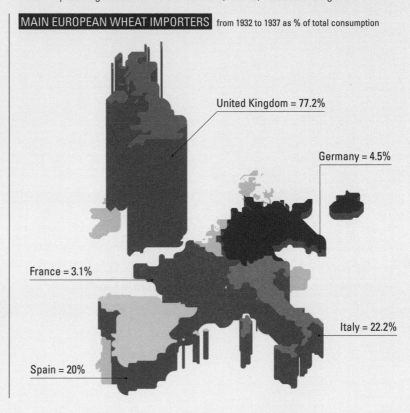

United Kingdom = 77.2%

Germany = 4.5%

France = 3.1%

Italy = 22.2%

Spain = 20%

5 • KEY INDUSTRIES

Germany's thriving chemicals industry enabled it to meet the demand for gunpowder and explosives until 1944. Japan and the USSR had greater difficulties. As well as having fewer chemical plants, they also lacked modern oil refineries. The ability to motorize and mechanize forces, critical in Europe where ground combat took place on a large scale, was directly dependent on a huge motor industry, as well as oil resources. Much of the German army was still horse-drawn, while its western opponents were extensively mechanized. The USSR only managed to make up for the shortfall by using American supplies.

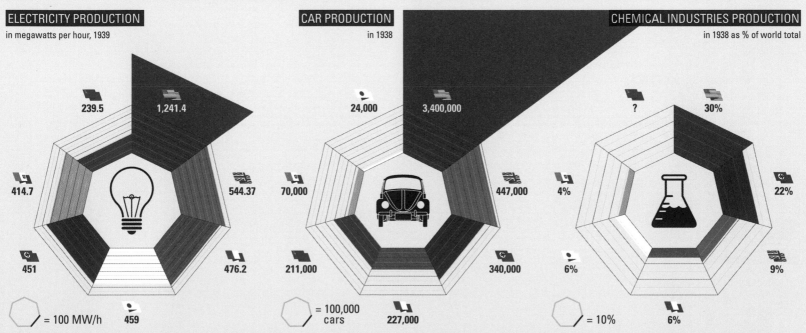

ELECTRICITY PRODUCTION in megawatts per hour, 1939

239.5 / 1,241.4 / 414.7 / 544.37 / 451 / 476.2 / 459

= 100 MW/h

CAR PRODUCTION in 1938

24,000 / 3,400,000 / 70,000 / 447,000 / 211,000 / 340,000 / 227,000

= 100,000 cars

CHEMICAL INDUSTRIES PRODUCTION in 1938 as % of world total

? / 30% / 4% / 22% / 6% / 9% / 6%

= 10%

SOURCES: 1. Tom Nicholas, 'The Origin of Japanese Technological Modernization', *Explorations in Economic History*, 48, 2011, pp. 272–91 • 2. François Caron, *Les Deux Révolutions industrielles du XXe siècle*, Paris, 1997 • 3. Mark Harrison (ed.), *The Economics of World War II*, Cambridge, 1998, p. 160 • 4. Max Rutzick & Sol Swerdloff, 'The Occupational Structure of US Employment, 1940–60', *Monthly Labor Review*, vol. 85, no. 11, November 1962 • 5. 'Évolution de la population active en France depuis cent ans d'après les dénombrements quinquennaux', *Études et conjoncture: Économie française*, vol. 8, no. 3, 1953 • 6. William H. Lockwood, *Economic Development of Japan*, Princeton, NJ, 1954 • 7. Imperial Institute, *The Mineral Industry of the British Empire and Foreign Countries, Statistical Summary 1936–1938*, London 1939 • 8. Johann Peter Murmann, 'Chemical Industries after 1850', *Oxford Encyclopedia of Economic History*, 2002 • 9. Gema Aparicio & Vicente Pinilla, *The Dynamics of International Trade in Cereals 1900–1938*, Murcia, 2015 • 10. Paul de Hevesy, *World Wheat Planning and Economic Planning in General*, Oxford, 1940.

ONE IN NINE MOBILIZED

Of the 2.2 billion people living in the world in 1939, nearly 130 million people (4% of them women) from 30 countries were mobilized in the Second World War. Around 70% of these were on the Allied side, with the rest on the Axis side. The largest numbers in absolute terms came from the USSR, the United States, China and the German Reich. The proportion mobilized relative to the total male population was highest in the Reich, Italy and the USSR. In Germany, the mass conscription of 18- to 50-year-olds was supplemented by nine million foreign workers (most of them not volunteers), prisoners of war and concentration camp prisoners. In the USSR, mobilization was too high, causing the civil economy to come close to collapse by 1942, especially

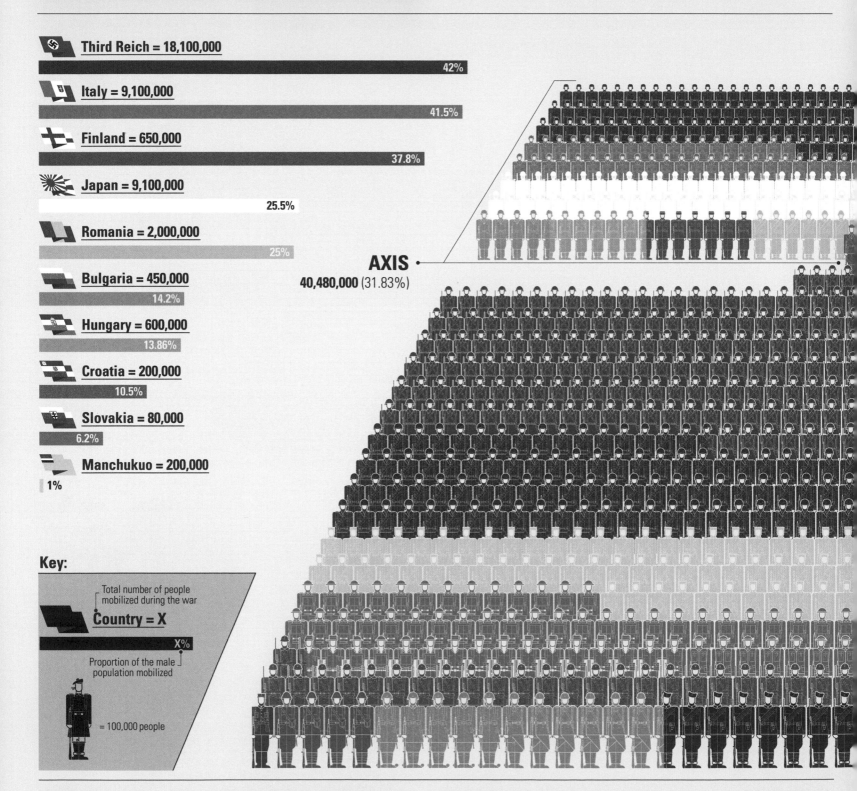

Third Reich = 18,100,000
42%

Italy = 9,100,000
41.5%

Finland = 650,000
37.8%

Japan = 9,100,000
25.5%

Romania = 2,000,000
25%

Bulgaria = 450,000
14.2%

Hungary = 600,000
13.86%

Croatia = 200,000
10.5%

Slovakia = 80,000
6.2%

Manchukuo = 200,000
1%

AXIS
40,480,000 (31.83%)

Key:

Total number of people mobilized during the war

Country = X
X%

Proportion of the male population mobilized

= 100,000 people

SOURCES: 1. Mark Axworthy, Cornel Scafes & Cristian Craciunoiu, *Third Axis, Fourth Ally: Romanian Armed Forces in the European War, 1941–45*, London, 1995 • 2. For Finland, personal communication from Louis Clerc • 3. G. F. Krivosheev (ed.), *Soviet Casualties and Combat Losses in the Twentieth Century*, London, 1997 • 4. James Nanney, *U.S. Manpower Mobilization for World War II*, Washington, DC, 1982

since 62 million of the population remained under German occupation. Troops were mustered from Romania twice, with 1.2 million Romanians fighting on the Axis side until September 1944. After that, nearly 600,000 fought on the Soviet side.

China was a special case. Some of the 14 million people mobilized between 1937 and 1945 never saw a weapon, let alone a Japanese opponent. Others disappeared as soon as they left the conscription office. Some only fought against other Chinese people – Communists. No record was kept of the forces mobilized by the Communists. The figures below only give a partial picture of the situation in Yugoslavia and in France. The Yugoslav army swept aside by the Wehrmacht in a few days in April 1941 theoretically

numbered one million men, but others were later called up to serve the Croatian state of Ante Pavelić or Tito's forces. How many of the five million mobilized in France in 1940 were also included in the 1.3 million recruited by Charles de Gaulle in 1944–45? There are no reliable figures. Conscription from the male population in Britain was limited from 1942 onwards in order not to paralyse the economy. From 1943 onwards, 10% of all British conscripts – known as the 'Bevin Boys', after the government minister Ernest Bevin – were sent to work in coal mines. To avoid the risk of military shortfall, Britain conscripted from its colonies; sometimes, as in the case of New Zealand and Australia, in higher proportions than those from the mother country.

127,171,000 men and women mobilized

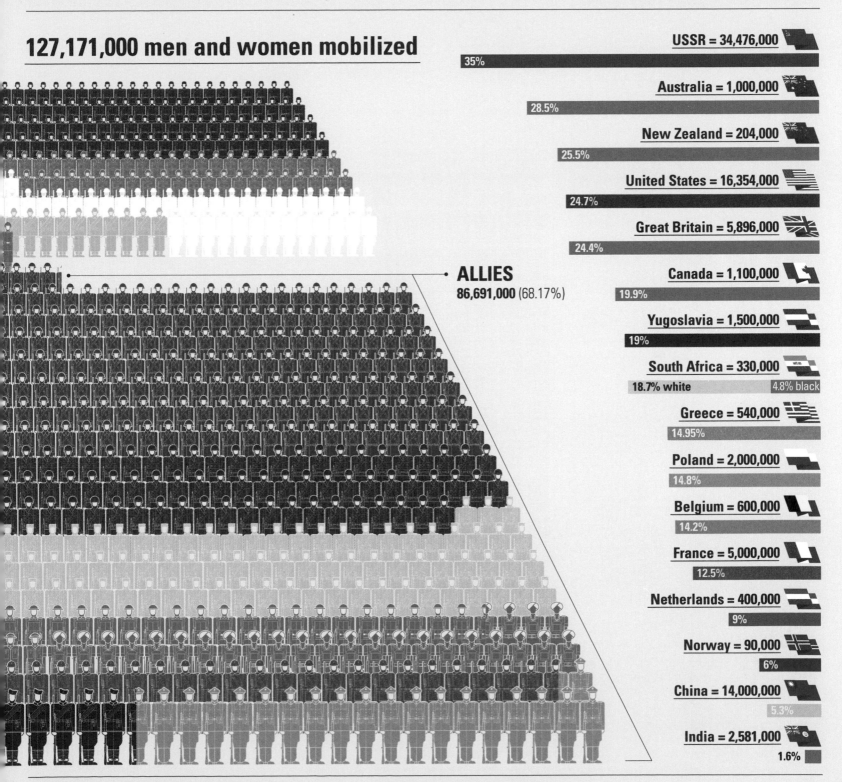

ALLIES
86,691,000 (68.17%)

USSR = 34,476,000
35%

Australia = 1,000,000
28.5%

New Zealand = 204,000
25.5%

United States = 16,354,000
24.7%

Great Britain = 5,896,000
24.4%

Canada = 1,100,000
19.9%

Yugoslavia = 1,500,000
19%

South Africa = 330,000
18.7% white   4.8% black

Greece = 540,000
14.95%

Poland = 2,000,000
14.8%

Belgium = 600,000
14.2%

France = 5,000,000
12.5%

Netherlands = 400,000
9%

Norway = 90,000
6%

China = 14,000,000
5.3%

India = 2,581,000
1.6%

• 5 Bernhard R. Kroener, *Das Deutsche Reich und der Zweite Weltkrieg*, vol. 5/1 & 5/2, *Organisation und Mobilisierung des deutschen Machtbereichs*, Stuttgart, 1988

THE ISSUE OF OIL

The oil power map for 1939 was the most unbalanced of all. The United States extracted almost two-thirds of crude oil worldwide. The major American, British and Dutch companies controlled resources in the rest of the world, in South America, the Middle East and the Dutch East Indies. Apart from the western Allies, the only power with enough crude oil to meet its needs was the USSR, whereas the Third Reich and Imperial Japan suffered shortages. In September 1939, Germany only had enough stocks for a few months' active operations. In 1940, stocks all over the Reich and across occupied Europe were supplemented by Romanian oil. Synthetic petrol from coal, which Hitler had made the main focus of his self-sufficiency policy, peaked in 1943, providing 40% of Germany's fuel requirements. The production-consumption balance, already fragile, collapsed in May 1944 when the American air offensive destroyed the synthesizing plants.

Japan was in an even more precarious position. In 1940, its national resources only covered 8.6% of its needs. The war could only continue because Japanese forces took control of the oil wells in the Dutch East Indies (Sumatra, Java) and Borneo, early in 1942. However, US submarines stopped these products from being taken back to Japan.

The 1941 German invasion did not affect the Soviet Union's oil potential and the damage caused by Hitler's second offensive in the summer of 1942 was not serious enough to jeopardize its motorized forces.

The position of Great Britain was extremely precarious. Since it was highly dependent on imports (99%), the booming demand for fuel for aircraft and ships had to be covered by massive imports from Caribbean and South American oilfields, as well as exports from the USA. This made protection of the transatlantic routes a constant worry. As for the United States, not only could it meet all its military and civilian needs, it also managed to increase exports to its allies. The oil situation was one of the most obvious factors behind the defeat of the Axis.

1 • CHANGING ENERGY NEEDS

The massive scale of the change in energy requirements during the inter-war period is apparent from just two figures. In 1918, an American soldier needed 15 kg of supplies every day, including 1.2 kg of fuel. In 1945 he needed 33.5 kg, including 16.5 kg of petroleum products.

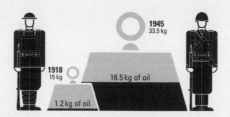

2 • WORLD CRUDE OIL PRODUCTION IN 1939

 = 1,000,000 tonnes

German and Japanese war leaders were well aware of the enormous imbalance in oil resources, which can be seen in the table below. But they based their plans on the hope of fast victories that would give them access to additional resources: Soviet oil for the Germans and Indonesian for the Japanese. However, the Germans had not expected to have to supply fuel for their Italian allies and the conquered economies.

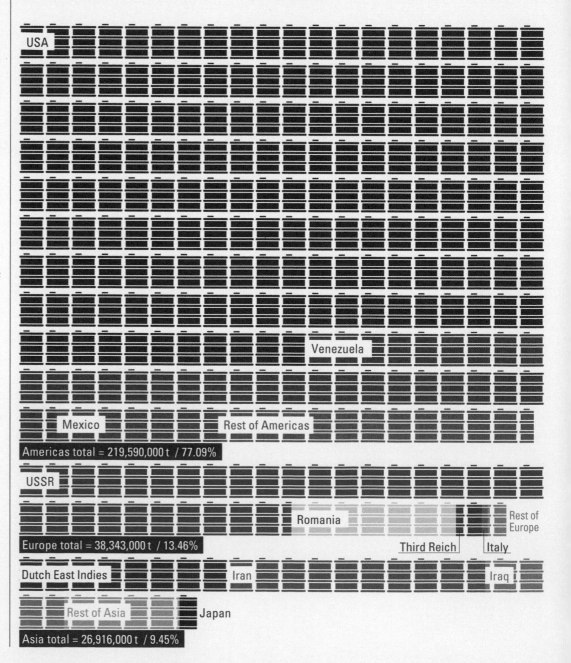

USA

Venezuela

Mexico   Rest of Americas

Americas total = 219,590,000 t / 77.09%

USSR

Romania   Rest of Europe

Third Reich   Italy

Europe total = 38,343,000 t / 13.46%

Dutch East Indies   Iran   Iraq

Rest of Asia   Japan

Asia total = 26,916,000 t / 9.45%

3 • THE ALLIES: MASTERS OF THE OIL GAME

The US oil industry achieved the unlikely feat of managing to supply civilian consumers (subject to some rationing), meeting the enormous demands of the armed forces (36 times higher in five years) and stepping up exports to its allies, chiefly Britain.

Both the British and the American situations illustrate the huge energy demands of a large navy and strategic bombing planes. By 1945, RAF consumption was 42 times higher than it had been in 1938 and that of the Royal Navy 10 times higher.

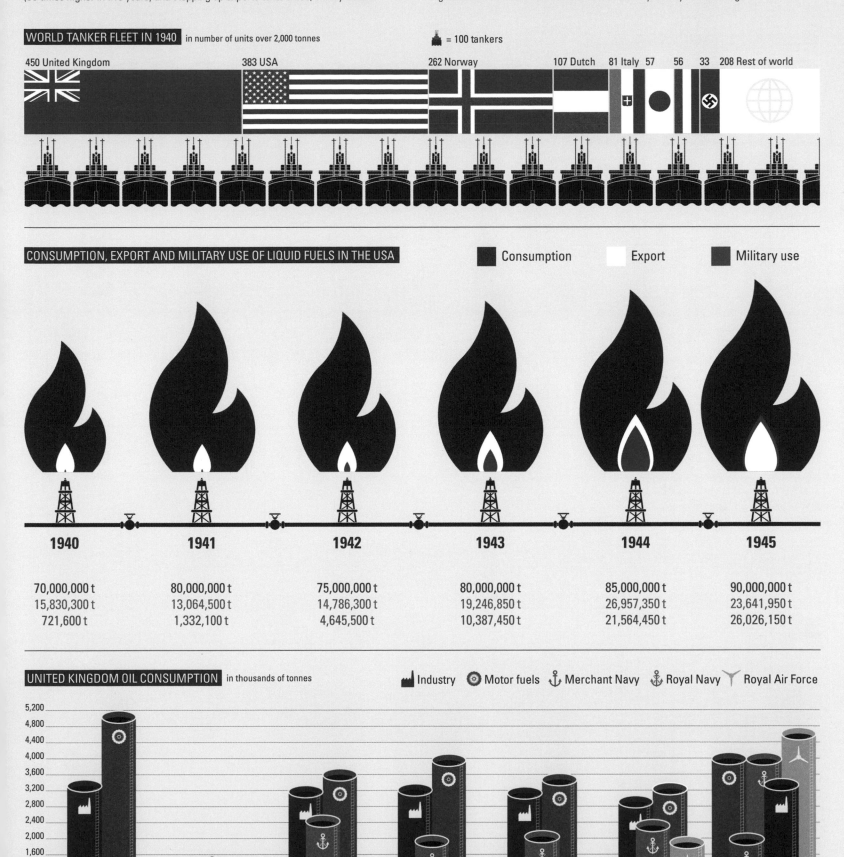

WORLD TANKER FLEET IN 1940 in number of units over 2,000 tonnes

🚢 = 100 tankers

450 United Kingdom · 383 USA · 262 Norway · 107 Dutch · 81 Italy · 57 · 56 · 33 · 208 Rest of world

CONSUMPTION, EXPORT AND MILITARY USE OF LIQUID FUELS IN THE USA

■ Consumption □ Export ■ Military use

	1940	1941	1942	1943	1944	1945
Consumption	70,000,000 t	80,000,000 t	75,000,000 t	80,000,000 t	85,000,000 t	90,000,000 t
Export	15,830,300 t	13,064,500 t	14,786,300 t	19,246,850 t	26,957,350 t	23,641,950 t
Military use	721,600 t	1,332,100 t	4,645,500 t	10,387,450 t	21,564,450 t	26,026,150 t

UNITED KINGDOM OIL CONSUMPTION in thousands of tonnes

🏭 Industry ⚙ Motor fuels ⚓ Merchant Navy ⚓ Royal Navy ✈ Royal Air Force

Y-axis: 0, 400, 800, 1,200, 1,600, 2,000, 2,400, 2,800, 3,200, 3,600, 4,000, 4,400, 4,800, 5,200

X-axis: 1938, 1939, 1940, 1941, 1942, 1943, 1944

4 • THE REICH'S QUEST FOR OIL, 1938—44 in thousands of tonnes

When Germany went to war, it had one asset – its synthetic fuel industry – and one ambition – to gain control of Romanian, Hungarian and Polish resources as quickly as possible. The map bottom right shows Germany's unrealistic strategic plan that was considered at the beginning of 1942: a wide-ranging dual movement around the eastern Mediterranean and the Black Sea, aimed at taking control of 20% of the world's oil resources in the Caucasus and the Middle East. By attacking Germany's synthetic fuel plants, American B-17 and Liberator bombers, accompanied by Mustang fighter planes, forced the Reich to survive precariously on its reserves.

THE REICH'S RESERVES, SEPTEMBER 1939 = 1 month of reserves

Industrial fuel = 3.2 months   Aviation fuel = 4.8 months   Motor fuel = 5.2 months   Naval fuel = 6.4 months

OIL PRODUCTION FOR THE REICH, 1938 TO 1944

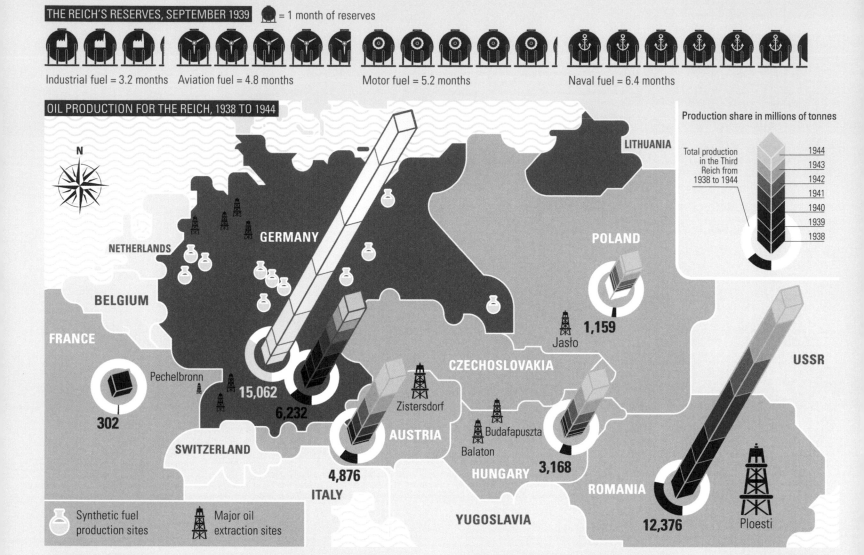

N

NETHERLANDS

GERMANY

BELGIUM

FRANCE

Pechelbronn

302

SWITZERLAND

15,062

6,232

ITALY

4,876

LITHUANIA

POLAND

1,159

Jasło

CZECHOSLOVAKIA

Zistersdorf

AUSTRIA

Budafapuszta

Balaton

HUNGARY   3,168

YUGOSLAVIA

ROMANIA

12,376

USSR

Ploesti

Production share in millions of tonnes

Total production in the Third Reich from 1938 to 1944

1944
1943
1942
1941
1940
1939
1938

Synthetic fuel production sites

Major oil extraction sites

GERMAN SYNTHETIC FUEL PRODUCTION UNDER ALLIED BOMBING IN 1944

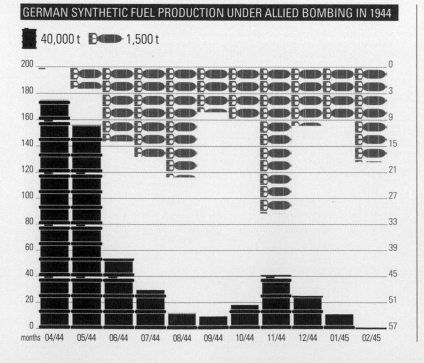

40,000 t   1,500 t

months 04/44 05/44 06/44 07/44 08/44 09/44 10/44 11/44 12/44 01/45 02/45

THE REICH'S FAILED GOAL OF OIL FROM THE CAUCASUS AND MIDDLE EAST

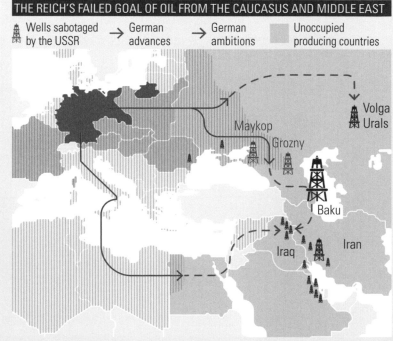

Wells sabotaged by the USSR → German advances → German ambitions   Unoccupied producing countries

Maykop   Volga Urals

Grozny

Baku

Iraq   Iran

5 • THE USSR: THE WORLD'S SECOND LARGEST PRODUCER UNDER ATTACK in thousands of tonnes

Part of the Reich's second strategic offensive in the USSR, Operation Edelweiss was a deliberate attempt to take over the oilfields of Maykop, Grozny and Baku. Maykop was taken but Soviet engineers rendered the wells unusable. Panzer troops came to within 30 km of Grozny and the Soviets set about widescale destruction in anticipation of a German takeover that ultimately did not occur. Preventive dismantling in Baku also explains the 45% drop in Soviet production in 1943. Nevertheless, what was left, supplemented by US supplies, was still enough to meet the Soviet Union's main military requirements.

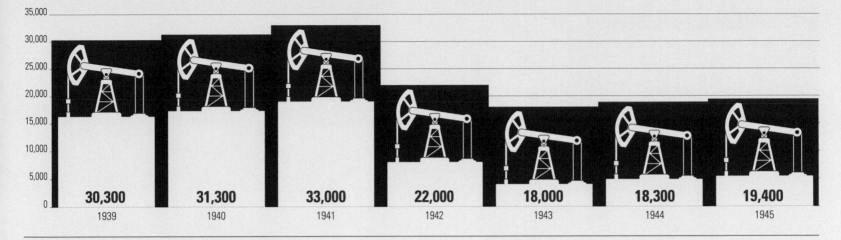

| 30,300 | 31,300 | 33,000 | 22,000 | 18,000 | 18,300 | 19,400 |
| 1939 | 1940 | 1941 | 1942 | 1943 | 1944 | 1945 |

6 • JAPAN: RELIANT ON DISTANT RESOURCES

When they took control of oil resources in the Dutch East Indies, the Japanese faced the problem of transporting crude oil 6,000 km back to Japan. Before the war, much of the shipping had been done by Western countries. A tanker building programme was started urgently, but its results were destroyed from 1943 by a US submarine and air offensive, whose spectacularly successful achievements are, paradoxically, less famous than those of the U-boats in the Atlantic.

JAPAN'S TRANSPORT ISSUES

USSR

CHINA

Tokyo

BRITISH
INDIA

BURMA

5,600 km

Palembang
DUTCH
EAST INDIES

AUSTRALIA

Japanese tankers   US submarines   US planes

OIL RESOURCES IN THE DUTCH EAST INDIES from Sumatra, Java and Borneo

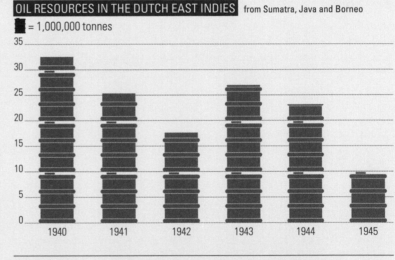

= 1,000,000 tonnes

| 1940 | 1941 | 1942 | 1943 | 1944 | 1945 |

TONNAGE OF JAPANESE-BUILT TANKERS SUNK BY US FORCES

in thousands of tonnes

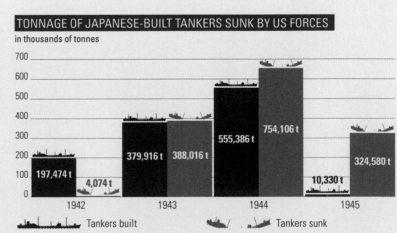

| 197,474 t | 4,074 t | 379,916 t | 388,016 t | 555,386 t | 754,106 t | 10,330 t | 324,580 t |
| 1942 | | 1943 | | 1944 | | 1945 | |

Tankers built   Tankers sunk

SOURCES: 1. DeGolyer & MacNaughton, 'Basic Data from Annual Reports of the US Bureau of Mines', *Twentieth Century Petroleum Statistics*, 1998 • 2. Dietrich Eichholtz, *War for Oil: The Nazi Quest for an Oil Empire*, Washington, DC, 2012 • 3. Dietrich Eichholtz, *Ende mit Schrecken. Deutsche Ölpolitik und Ölwirtschaft nach Stalingrad*, Leipzig, 2010, pp. 69–70 • 4. US Defense Fuel Supply Center • 5. *United States Strategic Bombing Survey*, February 1946 • 6. US Defense Fuel Supply Center and US Bureau of the Census • 7. *Velikaya Otechestvennaya Voyna*, vol. VII • 8. D. J. Payton-Smith, H.M. Stationery Office, 1971.

ARMS PRODUCTION COMPARED: 1939–45

The Reich, the Allies' main economic and technological opponent, lost the industrial battle in 1943, just as it mobilized all its resources and those of occupied Europe. Its belated efforts merely delayed its defeat by six months. Its three main opponents had assets that it did not possess. Their arms production was complementary, so that each could mass-produce what it was best at. Despite the issues that remained, particularly in the USSR and Britain, they were not short of raw materials and labour. They had top-quality equipment, especially transport, aircraft and combat ships, explosives, artillery and radar. Their production sites were protected from bombing from 1942 onwards.

The Americans had every advantage. They were leaders in all key areas of production, aircraft, ships, trucks and explosives, and could afford to equip all their allies, including China and France.

The Soviet arms industry had led the world until 1937. They focused on heavy equipment, tanks and artillery. In other areas (trucks, half-tracks, communication and detection equipment), they were generally weak.

The Germans were outclassed in volume in the field of explosives, artillery and means of transport, but they maintained their superiority in numbers of tanks, infantry weapons and submarines until the end. However, since they had to manufacture every type of weapon, they were constantly faced with the problem of taking from Peter to give to Paul. Their allies had too narrow an industrial base. Italy was totally unable to live up to the promise of 'millions of bayonets' boasted about by Mussolini. The Japanese made great strides with aircraft and ships but their technology, unlike that of the other fighting countries, did not improve during the war.

1 • PRODUCTION OF GROUND-BASED WEAPONS

The Allies manufactured five times more tanks than Germany, although this does not mean they always had five times more on the battlefield. A large part of their production was used to replace losses (four Allied tanks were destroyed for every German tank), making up for quality with quantity. The same was true of artillery, at least on the Eastern Front, where the Wehrmacht compensated for the lack of launch tubes by more effective firing, but that advantage was cancelled out by Britain and the USA. The German forces had no shortage of machine guns, machine pistols and

1 = 5,000 🚚 = Trucks/jeeps & light military vehicles   🚙 = Half-track vehicles

USA
🚚 = 2,382,311 / 62.5%
🚙 = 72,538 / 43.5%
🚜 = 88,610 / 32.4%
⚙ = 257,390 / 23.9%

UK
🚚 = 550,943 / 14.5%
🚙 = 57,000 / 34.2%
🚜 = 27,896 / 10.2%
⚙ = 124,877 / 11.6%

USSR
🚚 = 257,100 / 6.7%
🚙 = 0
🚜 = 105,251 / 38.4%
⚙ = 516,648 / 47.9%

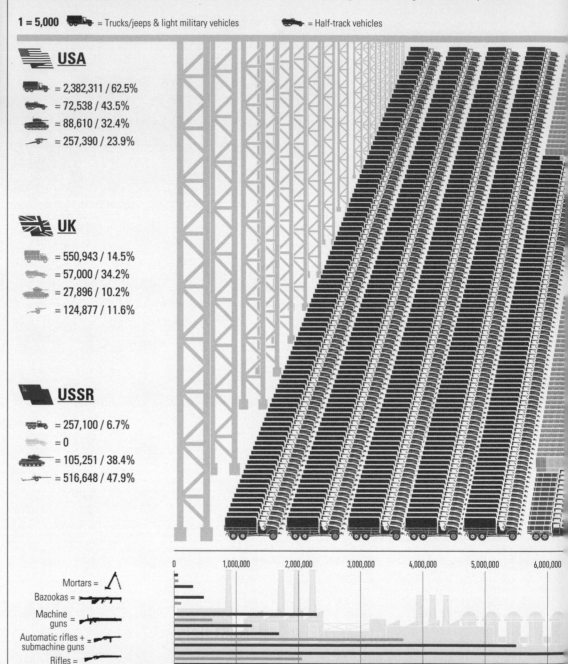

| | 0 | 1,000,000 | 2,000,000 | 3,000,000 | 4,000,000 | 5,000,000 | 6,000,000 |

Mortars =
Bazookas =
Machine guns =
Automatic rifles + submachine guns =
Rifles =

2 • MUNITIONS PRODUCTION

The Soviets were outstanding in the field of munitions production during the Second World War. Although Imperial Russia had only produced 10% of the shells made by the Kaiser's Germany, the USSR was on an equal footing with the Reich, despite its underdeveloped chemicals industry. The Allies' average volume of fire was three times higher than that of the Axis over the whole of the war, but in 1943 it was four times higher and in 1944 five times higher. The obstacle for Germany was a lack of steel and non-ferrous metals. By 1944, its artillery units were facing rationing. By the eve of Operation Bagration in June 1944, the situation was dire. The German Army Group Centre only had 70,000 rounds in reserve, compared with the one million of its Soviet opponents.

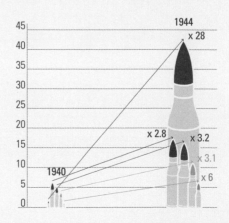

portable anti-tank weapons until 1945; in fact, their *Panzerfaust* was the envy of their opponents. The USA was far ahead of the rest of the world in the automobile industry and had been since the beginning. It supplied twice as many high-quality trucks, three times as many command cars, and five times as many tanker lorries, ambulances and radio cars as the rest of the world. The 102,251 tanks manufactured by the Soviets were

also an achievement, planned before the war. The idea was to create dual-use factories producing both tractors and tracked vehicles. For instance, the Chelyabinsk factory, built to make tractors (11,000 a year in 1939), gradually shifted to tanks between 1940 and 1941. In 1944, it produced 4,720 IS-2 and heavy assault guns, mobilizing 50,000 workers including 2,500 specialists evacuated from Leningrad and Stalingrad.

= Tanks & self-propelled guns   = Artillery / anti-aircraft guns / anti-tank guns

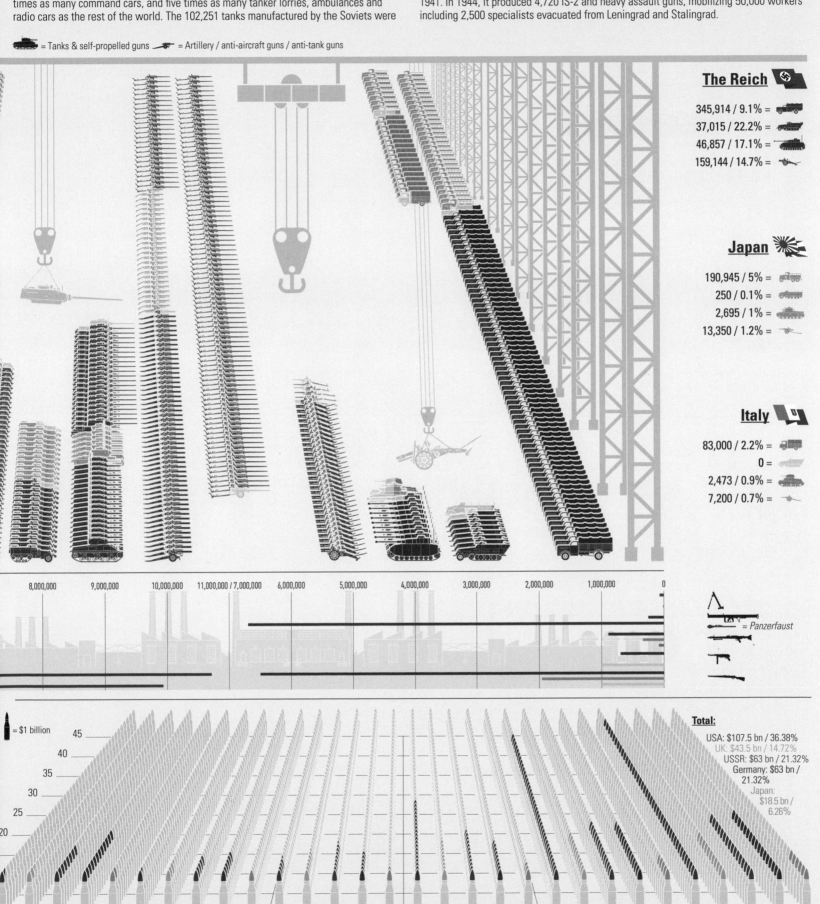

The Reich

345,914 / 9.1% =
37,015 / 22.2% =
46,857 / 17.1% =
159,144 / 14.7% =

Japan

190,945 / 5% =
250 / 0.1% =
2,695 / 1% =
13,350 / 1.2% =

Italy

83,000 / 2.2% =
0 =
2,473 / 0.9% =
7,200 / 0.7% =

= *Panzerfaust*

8,000,000   9,000,000   10,000,000   11,000,000 / 7,000,000   6,000,000   5,000,000   4,000,000   3,000,000   2,000,000   1,000,000   0

= $1 billion

45
40
35
30
25
20

Total:

USA: $107.5 bn / 36.38%
UK: $43.5 bn / 14.72%
USSR: $63 bn / 21.32%
Germany: $63 bn / 21.32%
Japan: $18.5 bn / 6.26%

1935–39   1940   1941   1942   1943   1944

3 • AIRCRAFT PRODUCTION

In 1938, the three Axis countries were manufacturing three times as many aircraft as their future adversaries, and often of better quality. This gave them a sense of power that helped to fuel their aggression. By 1940, they were producing no more than half as many aircraft as their opponents, then a quarter in 1942, rising to a third again in 1944. The stagnation of British and Soviet capabilities enabled the Germans and Japanese to catch up to a degree, but this was limited by the huge scale of US production. In two years, the US built or updated 30 massive factories, the top four of which produced more aircraft than Germany and Japan combined. The most productive was the North American Aircraft Corporation in Dallas, assembling 18,874 aircraft.

For the Germans, there were two hidden factors behind their increased production. Firstly, most of their budget was spent on fighter planes, at the expense of bombers and transport aircraft. Secondly, labour and energy were allocated to aircraft factories rather than to ground-based equipment. On the Allied side, since the USA could supply every type of aircraft required, the British were able to focus on producing fighters and strategic bombers. The Soviets withdrew from the latter sector, and instead concentrated their resources on tactical bombers, mainly the Ilyushin Il-2 Sturmovik (36,183 produced) and the Yakovlev Yak (31,000).

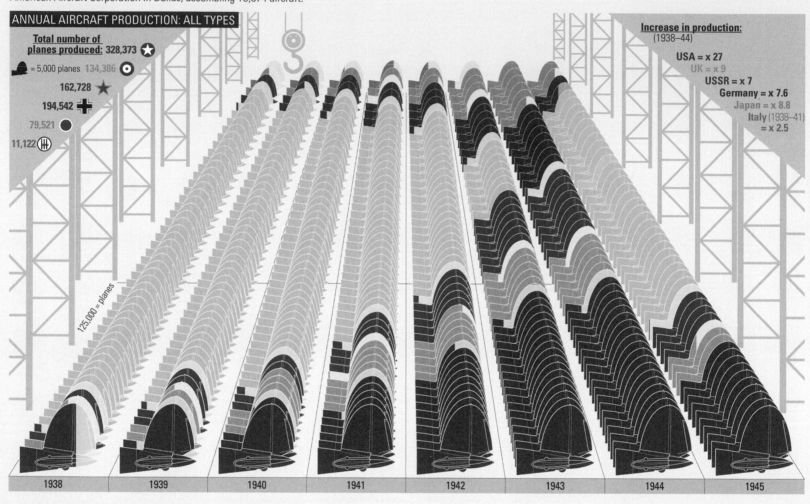

ANNUAL AIRCRAFT PRODUCTION: ALL TYPES

Total number of planes produced: 328,373 ★

= 5,000 planes 134,386 ◉

162,728 ★

194,542 ✚

79,521 ●

11,122 ⦿

125,000 = planes

1938 1939 1940 1941 1942 1943 1944 1945

Increase in production:
(1938–44)

USA = x 27
UK = x 9
USSR = x 7
Germany = x 7.6
Japan = x 8.8
Italy (1938–41) = x 2.5

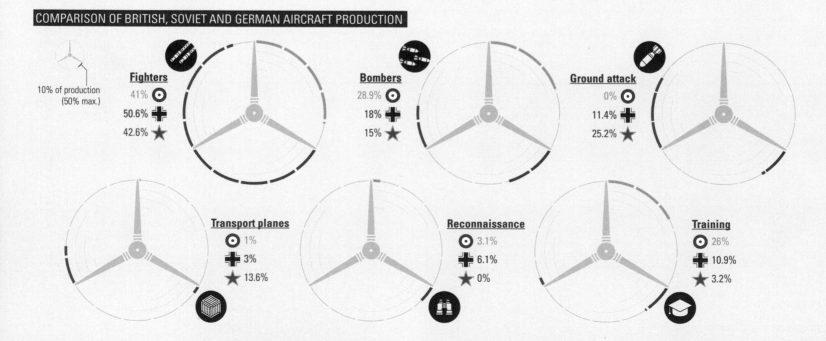

COMPARISON OF BRITISH, SOVIET AND GERMAN AIRCRAFT PRODUCTION

10% of production
(50% max.)

Fighters
41% ◉
50.6% ✚
42.6% ★

Bombers
28.9% ◉
18% ✚
15% ★

Ground attack
0% ◉
11.4% ✚
25.2% ★

Transport planes
◉ 1%
✚ 3%
★ 13.6%

Reconnaissance
◉ 3.1%
✚ 6.1%
★ 0%

Training
◉ 26%
✚ 10.9%
★ 3.2%

4 • SHIPBUILDING

It was in the shipbuilding industry that the disproportionate nature of war production was most marked. The Axis countries more or less stopped building battleships and cruisers in 1941, with Germany only manufacturing submarines and Japan building only destroyers, submarines and aircraft carriers. With their 1,141 U-boats, German shipyards launched three times as many submarines as all of the Allies combined, this specialization giving them the same qualitative advantage as the Americans had in the Pacific. Britain and the US stepped up production of escort ships and destroyers because of the need to watch over the thousands of convoys crossing the seas in all directions. The 141 aircraft carriers built by the United States more than made

up for the loss of 12 of them. With its heavy losses (6) and in spite of a few new launches, from 1943 onwards the Japanese imperial fleet was completely outclassed in quantity and quality, disappearing in 1944. A large part of America's naval efforts were dedicated to building 64,550 landing ships of all kinds, resulting in around 30 successful amphibious operations in Europe and Asia. Their number, variety (landing ships, smaller landing craft and landing vehicles) and complexity were such that the timing of operations partly depended on their production rate. If D-Day had not succeeded, it would have taken at least a year to begin again, purely because of the loss of several thousand of these specialized craft.

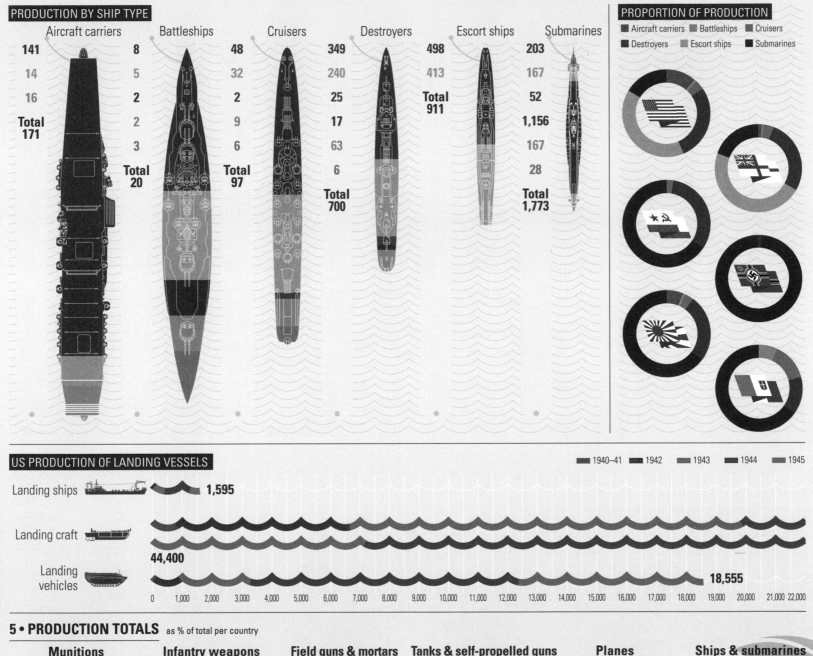

PRODUCTION BY SHIP TYPE

Aircraft carriers	Battleships	Cruisers	Destroyers	Escort ships	Submarines
141	8	48	349	498	203
14	5	32	240	413	167
16	2	2	25	Total 911	52
Total 171	2	9	17		1,156
	3	6	63		167
	Total 20	Total 97	6		28
			Total 700		Total 1,773

PROPORTION OF PRODUCTION

- Aircraft carriers
- Battleships
- Cruisers
- Destroyers
- Escort ships
- Submarines

US PRODUCTION OF LANDING VESSELS

1940–41 · 1942 · 1943 · 1944 · 1945

Landing ships **1,595**

Landing craft

Landing vehicles **44,400** ... **18,555**

0 1,000 2,000 3,000 4,000 5,000 6,000 7,000 8,000 9,000 10,000 11,000 12,000 13,000 14,000 15,000 16,000 17,000 18,000 19,000 20,000 21,000 22,000

5 • PRODUCTION TOTALS as % of total per country

Munitions	Infantry weapons	Field guns & mortars	Tanks & self-propelled guns	Planes	Ships & submarines
36.4% / 14.7% / 21.3%	30.3% / 16.5% / 34.1%	17.9% / 12.1% / 53.7%	32.4% / 10.2% / 38.4%	36.1% / 14.8% / 17.9%	34% / 23.7% / 2.2%
21.3% / 6.3% / ?	14.4% / 4.7% / ?	13.8% / 1% / 1.5%	17.1% / 1% / 0.9%	21.3% / 8.7% / 1.2%	31.6% / 7.2% / 1.2%

SOURCES: 1. John Ellis, *The World War II Databook*, London, 1993 • 2. Richard M. Leighton & Robert W. Coakley, *Global Logistics and Strategy, 1940–1943*, Washington, DC, 1995 • 3. Bernhard R. Kroener, *Das Deutsche Reich und der Zweite Weltkrieg*, vol. 5/2, Stuttgart, 1988 • 4. Hugh Rockoff, *America's Economic Way of War*, Cambridge, 2012 • 5. Mark Harrison (ed.), *The Economies of World War II*, 1998 • 6. Mark Harrison, *Soviet Planning in Peace and War, 1938–1945*, Cambridge, 2009 • 7. *Lexikon der Wehrmacht*: http://www.lexikon-der-wehrmacht.de

THE COST OF MANPOWER

Both sides faced the same formidable challenge: how could production be increased when 25 to 40% of the male population had been mobilized? There were three possible solutions: finding new sources of labour, reassigning manpower to factories, or increasing productivity, but not at the expense of agriculture and services. As far as the latter were concerned, the public sector workforce increased disproportionately as state control increased. The Reich had a shortage of manpower from 1939 onwards. Early rearmament had

forced it to redeploy its surplus manpower to the war effort back in 1935. With agriculture still relatively unmechanized, 8 million people were needed to work on the land, restricting movement from the countryside to the towns. Industry had difficulty increasing its production rates up to 1944, with the army demand for soldiers and manufacturers being slow to reorganize production (so that skilled male workers were kept in the factories). The UK was more efficient and encouraged subcontracting. Thousands of small

1 • NEW SOURCES OF MANPOWER

The Americans, unlike the Germans, had an inexhaustible pool of labour (the unemployed and women, as well as minorities blacklisted by industry). It is a cliché that German women stayed at home while American women were modelling themselves on Rosie the Riveter. In fact, 57% of German women, nine-tenths of them single, were working in 1944, compared with 43% in Britain and the US. Hitler took advantage of the Weimar Republic's feminist social policy. To assume that a million and a half were unproductive because they were classed as 'domestic workers' ignores the fact that the figure

included 96% agricultural workers. The misconception is due to the invisibility of many female German, Japanese and Soviet workers who were employed in agriculture, which siphoned off manpower, whereas in Britain and America it was mechanized. However, the Reich, unlike the USSR, failed to mobilize the remainder. In 1944, eight out of ten Soviet farm workers and one in every two manual workers were women. To compensate, Germany drew on forced labour by prisoners and subjugated civilians. By 1944, these represented one-fifth of the workforce, but German manpower was continuing to fall.

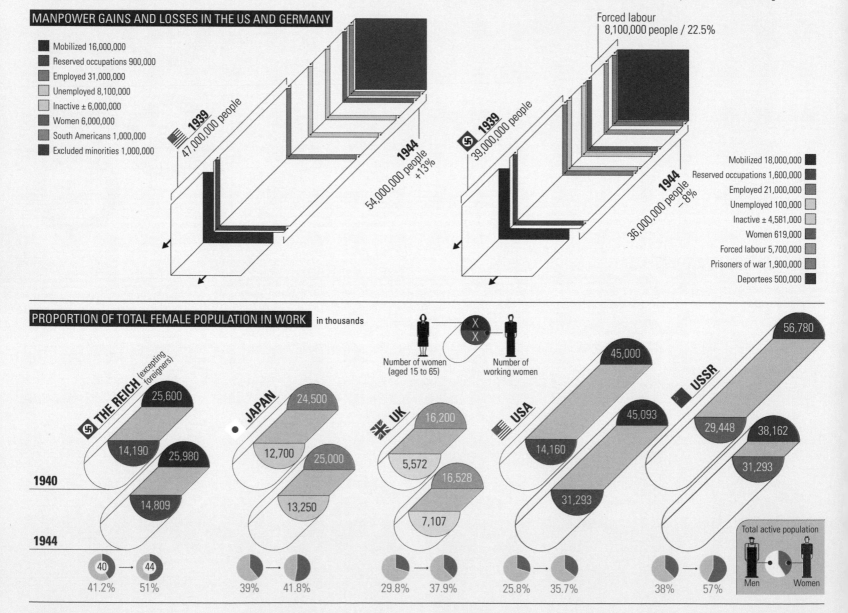

MANPOWER GAINS AND LOSSES IN THE US AND GERMANY

- Mobilized 16,000,000
- Reserved occupations 900,000
- Employed 31,000,000
- Unemployed 8,100,000
- Inactive ± 6,000,000
- Women 6,000,000
- South Americans 1,000,000
- Excluded minorities 1,000,000

1939 — 47,000,000 people
1944 — 54,000,000 people +13%

Forced labour 8,100,000 people / 22.5%

1939 — 39,000,000 people
1944 — 36,000,000 people −8%

- Mobilized 18,000,000
- Reserved occupations 1,600,000
- Employed 21,000,000
- Unemployed 100,000
- Inactive ± 4,581,000
- Women 619,000
- Forced labour 5,700,000
- Prisoners of war 1,900,000
- Deportees 500,000

PROPORTION OF TOTAL FEMALE POPULATION IN WORK in thousands

Number of women (aged 15 to 65)
Number of working women

THE REICH (excepting foreigners)
- 1940: 25,600 / 14,190
- 1944: 25,980 / 14,809
- 41.2% → 51%

JAPAN
- 1940: 24,500 / 12,700
- 1944: 25,000 / 13,250
- 39% → 41.8%

UK
- 1940: 16,200 / 5,572
- 1944: 16,528 / 7,107
- 29.8% → 37.9%

USA
- 1940: 45,000 / 14,160
- 1944: 45,093 / 31,293
- 25.8% → 35.7%

USSR
- 1940: 56,780 / 29,448
- 1944: 38,162 / 31,293
- 38% → 57%

Total active population
Men   Women

SOURCES: 1. R. Overy, *War & Economy in the Third Reich*, Oxford, 1992 • 2. R. Overy, *The Air War 1939–1945*, London, 2005 • 3. Adam Tooze, *The Wages of Destruction: The Making and Breaking of the Nazi Economy*, London, 2006 • 4. A. Aglan & R. Franck (eds.), *1937–1947. La guerre-monde*, vol. II, Paris, 2015 • 5. Mark Harrison, *The Economics of World War II*, 1998 • 6. Mark Harrison, *Accounting for War: Soviet Production, Employment, and the Defence Burden, 1940–1945*, Cambridge, 1996 • 7. Arthur Marwick, *The Home Front: The British and the Second World War*, London, 1976 • 8. Roger Chickering, Stig Förster &

firms – even telephone betting services – were switched to the war effort. But it too faced a shortage of manpower. In 1941, it began mobilizing men and women from the civilian population (which Hitler only did gradually). However, this was a difficult process. Fewer than 50% of women were recruited. And there were so many manufacturing orders that army conscription had to be restricted. The situation was different in the United States, which had a pool of 23 million people not in employment (the unemployed, women, and minorities). Taylorism, modelled on the motor industry, resulted in enormous productivity gains. The USA could afford to use staff carefully and increase internal consumption (3%). The USSR was in a serious situation. The invasion and mobilization had deprived

it of half its manpower, at a time when the Red Army needed mass recruitment to make up for the terrible losses. Salvation came from an extraordinary recovery plan with clever use of Stalinist mobilization and coercion, relying on basic equipment and inhuman sacrifices. Agricultural production was halved and reserved for the urban population and the armed forces (their rations were one-fifth the size of British rations), forcing the rural population to live in abject poverty. The standard of living, already very low, fell by 40%. It is still not clear why the system did not collapse in 1942, but it produced results. In 1943, the Soviet arms industry was twice as big as that of Germany, but at a huge cost. By 1945, Soviet society had been bled dry and was constantly haunted by the threat of famine.

2 • CHANGES IN THE WORKING POPULATION

In 1939, British economists divided industries into three categories. Group I was the war economy (steel, engineering, chemical); Group II was considered essential to the nation (agriculture, administration); and Group III was deemed 'less essential' (building and public works, trade, banking). However, these classifications did not fit Soviet society, which was fully militarized, even in the field of agriculture. They do show the ceiling quickly reached by German mobilization, the gradual optimization of the USA and the UK, the huge role of Russian and German agriculture, and the major changes in the USSR, sustainable for only a few months and then only with the help of the Lend-Lease Act.

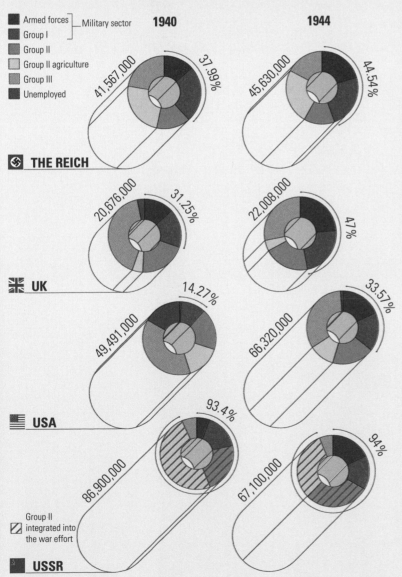

3 • PRODUCTIVITY: THE AERONAUTICS INDUSTRY

Allied superiority in this field was based on numbers. By 1944, the US had four times as many workers as the Germans working on engines and assembly. But productivity was also higher. They optimized every area of production, remembering that they were all closely interlinked (for instance, the disadvantage of a low-skilled workforce was remedied by the use of scientific management principles). The Axis still used 'workshop'-style facilities requiring skilled labour, with no assembly lines. They were hampered by military demands and, by 1944, facing difficulties due to a shortage of raw materials, Allied bombing raids, and sabotage by forced labourers.

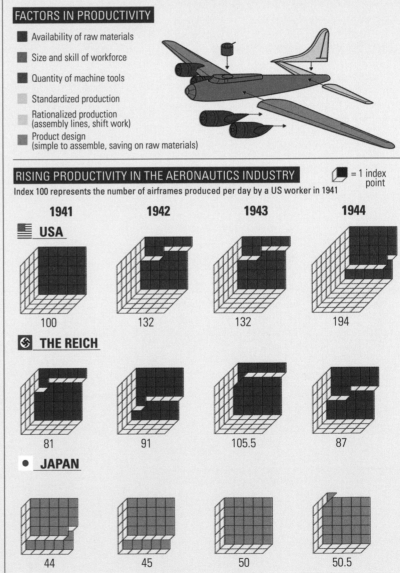

Bernd Greiner (eds.), *A World at Total War: Global Conflicts & the Politics of Destruction*, Cambridge, 2005 • 9. John Paxton, 'Myth vs. Reality: The Question of Mass Production in WWII', *Economics & Business Journal*, vol. 1, no. 1, 2008, pp. 91–104.

THE BRITISH EMPIRE AT WAR

From June 1940 to June 1941, Britain seemed to be alone in the war. But this was an illusion. Although the British Isles were set apart from the European mainland, Britain could rely on its colonial empire, a superpower that in 1939 controlled a third of the earth's surface and a quarter of its population, around 484 million people.

It is true that 70% of these were concentrated in India (the Raj, which at the time covered present-day India and Pakistan). This jewel in the crown had been destabilized by independence movements since the end of the 19th century. The situation was worsened when the Viceroy of India, Lord Linlithgow, declared war unilaterally without consulting local political leaders. Nehru was sympathetic to the Allied cause, but Gandhi refused to take part in the conflict. He was arrested on 9 August 1942 (and released for health reasons on 6 May 1944), while Subhas Chandra Bose raised an army for the Japanese. India nonetheless remained loyal and supported the Allied war effort. Despite the injustices and the huge human cost, local defence spending multiplied ninefold between 1939 and 1945. In 1945, the incompetence of the colonial powers caused a terrible famine in Bengal in which between 1.5 and 3 million people died. Despite all of this, however, Indian troops

1 • THE ECONOMY

Britain might have been a major industrial power but its gross domestic product (GDP) was still smaller than that of the Empire, which was a vital source of raw materials for the Allied cause, especially metals for alloys and rubber. The seizure of oil wells in Iraq and Iran in 1941 made up for the apparent shortage of crude oil. Support by ships from the Empire gave Britain control of 30% of the world's merchant ship tonnage. Britain's dependence on the Commonwealth explains why in 1941 and 1942 Churchill was particularly preoccupied by the war in the Atlantic.

GDP OF THE BRITISH EMPIRE IN 1939 in billions of dollars ⊞ = $10 billion

United Kingdom
$284.2 bn / 41.6%

Dominions
$114.6 bn / 16.77%

Colonies
$284.5 bn / 41.63%

Total: $683.3 bn

THE BRITISH EMPIRE'S STEEL PRODUCTION, 1939 in millions of tonnes 🏭 = 1,000,000 t

UK: 13,192,000 t
Canada: 1,407,000 t
Australia: 1,189,000 t
South Africa: 250,000 t
India: 1,035,000 t
Total: 17,073,000 t

2 • POPULATION OF THE BRITISH EMPIRE IN 1939 in millions of people

The combined populations of the United Kingdom and the Empire gave Britain a demographic power equalling that of China, the most highly populated country in 1939 (with 520 million inhabitants), far exceeding the USSR (168 million) and the USA (131 million). This was a world war and the Empire did not escape.

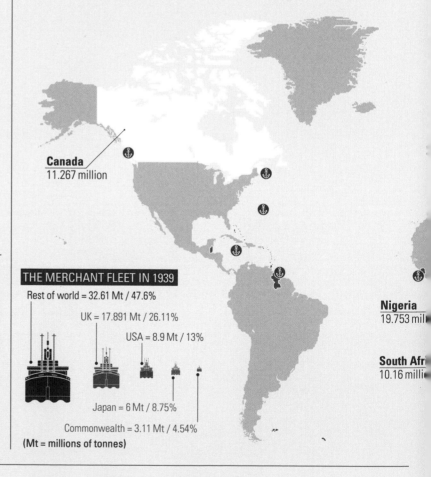

Canada
11.267 million

Nigeria
19.753 mil

South Afri
10.16 milli

THE MERCHANT FLEET IN 1939

Rest of world = 32.61 Mt / 47.6%

UK = 17.891 Mt / 26.11%

USA = 8.9 Mt / 13%

Japan = 6 Mt / 8.75%

Commonwealth = 3.11 Mt / 4.54%

(Mt = millions of tonnes)

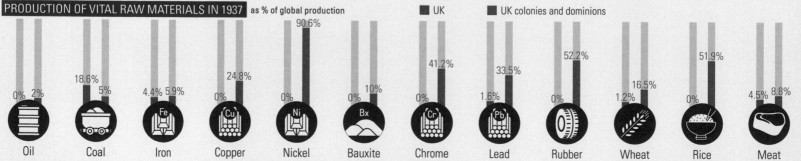

PRODUCTION OF VITAL RAW MATERIALS IN 1937 as % of global production
■ UK   ■ UK colonies and dominions

	Oil	Coal	Iron	Copper	Nickel	Bauxite	Chrome	Lead	Rubber	Wheat	Rice	Meat
UK	0%	18.6%	4.4%	0%	0%	0%	0%	1.6%	0%	1.2%	0%	4.5%
colonies	2%	5%	5.9%	24.8%	90.6%	10%	41.2%	33.5%	52.2%	16.5%	51.9%	8.8%

went to fight wherever the Empire needed them, not only in Burma and India but also in Africa, Syria, Italy, Greece and elsewhere.

Beyond the Indian subcontinent, the British could also call upon the Crown Dominions, former colonies to which the British government had granted virtually equal status. Theses made a vital contribution. Half the pilots in the Empire's air forces were trained overseas out of reach of the Luftwaffe, mainly in Canada. The Royal Canadian Navy helped to escort convoys in the Atlantic. Its fleet was increased from six escort ships and destroyers in 1939 to 193 in 1945, making it the third largest in the world.

Although the territories invaded by the Axis in Egypt and India were very sparsely populated, this was not true of Burma, Malaysia and Singapore (with its important naval base) and Hong Kong, which was under Japanese control from the end of 1941 to 1945.

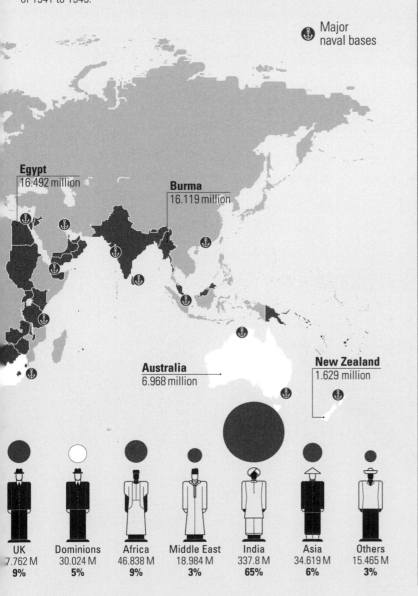

Major naval bases

Egypt
16.492 million

Burma
16.119 million

Australia
6.968 million

New Zealand
1.629 million

UK	Dominions	Africa	Middle East	India	Asia	Others
7.762 M	30.024 M	46.838 M	18.984 M	337.8 M	34.619 M	15.465 M
9%	5%	9%	3%	65%	6%	3%

3 • UNEQUAL MOBILIZATION

Although it relied increasingly on female workers (27% in 1939, 39% in 1944), Britain was forced to leave at least 10 million men working for the war economy, so it had to start conscripting from the Empire in 1939. India contributed the largest number of troops, but the majority of these were deployed locally. Only 11% of its ground forces were sent overseas, compared with 83% of New Zealanders (as its casualties reflect) and slightly over half of Canadians and Australians. The latter were a key part of the forces fighting in Africa from 1940 to 1942.

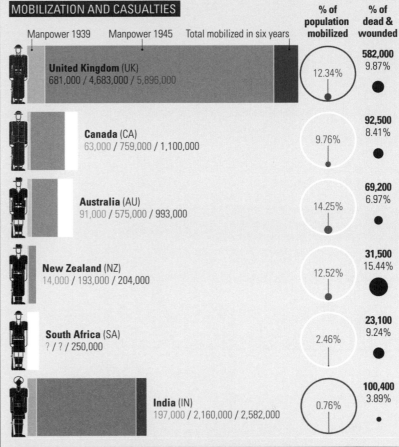

MOBILIZATION AND CASUALTIES

Manpower 1939 · Manpower 1945 · Total mobilized in six years · % of population mobilized · % of dead & wounded

United Kingdom (UK)
681,000 / 4,683,000 / 5,896,000 — 12.34% — 582,000 9.87%

Canada (CA)
63,000 / 759,000 / 1,100,000 — 9.76% — 92,500 8.41%

Australia (AU)
91,000 / 575,000 / 993,000 — 14.25% — 69,200 6.97%

New Zealand (NZ)
14,000 / 193,000 / 204,000 — 12.52% — 31,500 15.44%

South Africa (SA)
? / ? / 250,000 — 2.46% — 23,100 9.24%

India (IN)
197,000 / 2,160,000 / 2,582,000 — 0.76% — 100,400 3.89%

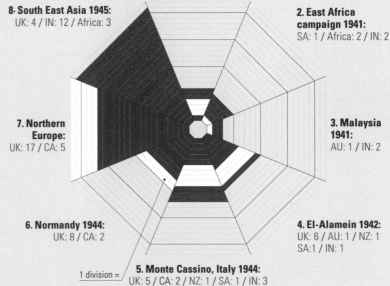

DIVISIONS FROM THE EMPIRE UNDER BRITISH COMMAND

1. Libya 1940:
UK: 1 / AU: 2 / NZ: 1 / IN: 1

2. East Africa campaign 1941:
SA: 1 / Africa: 2 / IN: 2

3. Malaysia 1941:
AU: 1 / IN: 2

4. El-Alamein 1942:
UK: 6 / AU: 1 / NZ: 1
SA: 1 / IN: 1

5. Monte Cassino, Italy 1944:
UK: 5 / CA: 2 / NZ: 1 / SA: 1 / IN: 3

6. Normandy 1944:
UK: 8 / CA: 2

7. Northern Europe:
UK: 17 / CA: 5

8. South East Asia 1945:
UK: 4 / IN: 12 / Africa: 3

1 division =

SOURCES: 1. Mark Harrison, *The Economics of World War II*, 1998, p. 3 • 2. John Ellis, *World War II: A Statistical Survey*, New York, 1995, pp. 249–73 • 3. R.A.C. Parker, *The Second World War: A Short History*, Oxford, 1989, p. 132 • 4. http://www.populstat.info • 5. John Ellis, *World War II: A Statistical Survey*, 1995, pp. 155–227.

US MILITARY AID: THE LEND-LEASE ACT

On 11 March 1941, after a vote in Congress, President Roosevelt passed the Lend-Lease Act, one of the most important acts of the Second World War. Its signing, which effectively revoked the Neutrality Act and the Cash and Carry Act of 4 November 1939, turned the USA into the arsenal of the Allies. The Act allowed the President to sell, transfer, rent or loan war equipment or any other goods to any country whose security was vital to the United States. Its original purpose was specifically to help Britain, which was on the verge of bankruptcy, and its dominions. It was extended to China in April 1941, to the USSR on 7 November, to the French Committee of National Liberation in November 1942 and eventually to some 40 other countries. Between March 1941 and September 1945, aid from the United States to its allies totalled $49 billion, 17% of their expenditure on the war. This was all the more generous in that it was given at the same time as the USA was rearming its own armed forces and often in competition with this. Over 47% of the aid was military

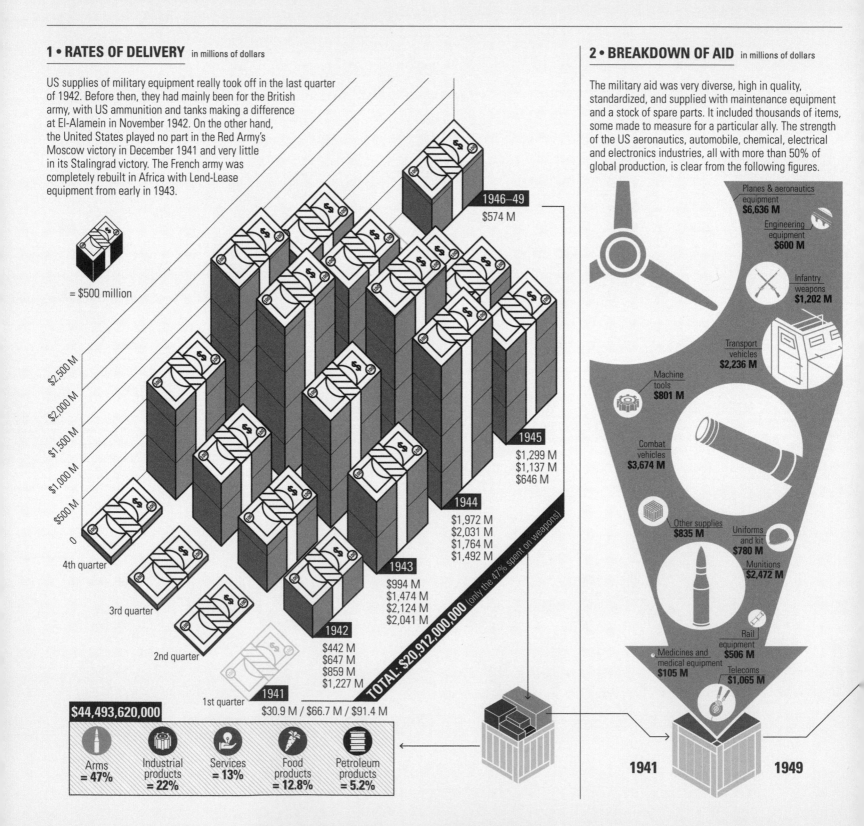

1 • RATES OF DELIVERY in millions of dollars

US supplies of military equipment really took off in the last quarter of 1942. Before then, they had mainly been for the British army, with US ammunition and tanks making a difference at El-Alamein in November 1942. On the other hand, the United States played no part in the Red Army's Moscow victory in December 1941 and very little in its Stalingrad victory. The French army was completely rebuilt in Africa with Lend-Lease equipment from early in 1943.

= $500 million

$2,500 M
$2,000 M
$1,500 M
$1,000 M
$500 M
0

4th quarter
3rd quarter
2nd quarter
1st quarter

1946–49
$574 M

1945
$1,299 M
$1,137 M
$646 M

1944
$1,972 M
$2,031 M
$1,764 M
$1,492 M

1943
$994 M
$1,474 M
$2,124 M
$2,041 M

1942
$442 M
$647 M
$859 M
$1,227 M

1941
$30.9 M / $66.7 M / $91.4 M

TOTAL: $20,912,000,000 (only the 47% spent on weapons)

$44,493,620,000

Arms = 47%
Industrial products = 22%
Services = 13%
Food products = 12.8%
Petroleum products = 5.2%

2 • BREAKDOWN OF AID in millions of dollars

The military aid was very diverse, high in quality, standardized, and supplied with maintenance equipment and a stock of spare parts. It included thousands of items, some made to measure for a particular ally. The strength of the US aeronautics, automobile, chemical, electrical and electronics industries, all with more than 50% of global production, is clear from the following figures.

Planes & aeronautics equipment **$6,636 M**
Engineering equipment **$600 M**
Infantry weapons **$1,202 M**
Transport vehicles **$2,236 M**
Machine tools **$801 M**
Combat vehicles **$3,674 M**
Other supplies **$835 M**
Uniforms and kit **$780 M**
Munitions **$2,472 M**
Rail equipment **$506 M**
Medicines and medical equipment **$105 M**
Telecoms **$1,065 M**

1941   **1949**

equipment, 22% industrial products, 12.8% food products, 13% services and 5.2% petroleum products. The lion's share, $30.7 billion (62% of the aid) went to the British Empire, followed by the USSR ($11 billion), France ($3.2 billion) and China ($1.6 billion). The British received nearly a quarter of their food from the US ($4.2 billion). The Soviets were second, with $1.7 billion's worth of flour, fats, tinned meat, sugar, powdered eggs and milk. Most of the machinery supplied also went to those two countries; the USSR received $1.5

billion out of the total of $2.4 billion, the British $0.8 billion. The figures below relate to the military items provided under the Lend-Lease Act. In the USSR, these were supplemented by British and Canadian equipment: 4,542 Matilda and Valentine tanks and nearly 7,000 Hurricane, Tomahawk and Kittyhawk aircraft. Although this equipment was inferior in quality and quantity to US equipment, it had the huge advantage of arriving quite early, in 1941 and 1942, when the Soviets had not yet managed to make up for their losses.

3 • SOME OF THE EQUIPMENT SUPPLIED in units

US-made aircraft and tanks represented a year's worth of British production and trucks two years' worth. In 1944, 20% of the weapons used by British forces were American. The equipment sent to the Red Army greatly improved its mobility (Studebaker trucks and Jeeps) and its command and control systems (radio, telephones) from 1943. The Marston

Mats enabled Soviet aircraft to cope with mud and take off more frequently. While the 10,000 flat wagons speeded up the transport of tanks to the front, the 1,955 locomotives made up for almost all the suspended production of rail engines. Like corned beef, US-made boots remained an emotive reminder for Soviets who lived through the war.

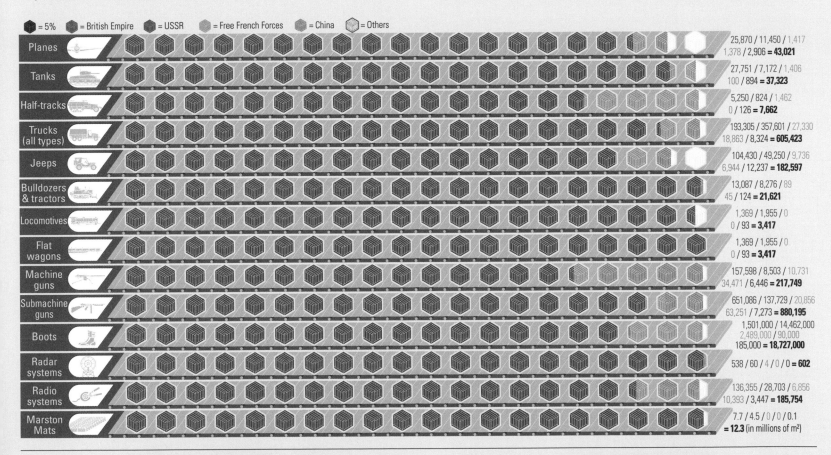

= 5% | = British Empire | = USSR | = Free French Forces | = China | = Others

	Breakdown	Total
Planes	25,870 / 11,450 / 1,417 1,378 / 2,906	**43,021**
Tanks	27,751 / 7,172 / 1,406 100 / 894	**37,323**
Half-tracks	5,250 / 824 / 1,462 0 / 126	**7,662**
Trucks (all types)	193,305 / 357,601 / 27,330 18,863 / 8,324	**605,423**
Jeeps	104,430 / 49,250 / 9,736 6,944 / 12,237	**182,597**
Bulldozers & tractors	13,087 / 8,276 / 89 45 / 124	**21,621**
Locomotives	1,369 / 1,955 / 0 0 / 93	**3,417**
Flat wagons	1,369 / 1,955 / 0 0 / 93	**3,417**
Machine guns	157,598 / 8,503 / 10,731 34,471 / 6,446	**217,749**
Submachine guns	651,086 / 137,729 / 20,856 63,251 / 7,273	**880,195**
Boots	1,501,000 / 14,462,000 2,489,000 / 90,000 185,000	**18,727,000**
Radar systems	538 / 60 / 4 / 0 / 0	**602**
Radio systems	136,355 / 28,703 / 6,856 10,393 / 3,447	**185,754**
Marston Mats	7.7 / 4.5 / 0 / 0 / 0.1	**12.3** (in millions of m²)

British Empire
$12,547,200,000
60%

USSR
$4,809,760,000
23%

Free French
$1,673,000,000
8%

China
$1,464,000,000
7%

Others
$418,000,000
2%

4 • WHO RECEIVED AID?

The British Empire (68%) and the USSR (26%) were by far the biggest recipients of US military aid and of industrial, mining and food aid. Britain monopolized 80% of the aid for the Empire because of the close strategic relationship between Britain and the USA and the need to prepare infrastructure in Britain that the US Army and Air Force would require when planning for D-Day. The equipment sent to Chiang Kai-shek's China did little to improve the performance of his forces. Some of it was reappropriated by the Communist forces.

SOURCES: 1. *21st Report to Congress on Lend-Lease Operations* 1946 • 2. *United States Army in World War II, Statistics: Lend-Lease*, Washington, DC, 2015 • 3. David Edgerton, *Britain's War Machine*, London, 2012 • 4. Albert L. Weeks, *Russia's Life-Saver: Lend-Lease Aid to the USSR in World War II*, Lanham, MD & Oxford, 2004.

THE PILLAGING OF EUROPE BY THE THIRD REICH

Between 1940 and 1944, the Third Reich forced all of its occupied European territories to work for the war economy. Some 7.6 million Europeans were put to work, voluntarily or by force, in Germany itself. Over half of them were Soviet or Polish, a quarter were women and another quarter were prisoners of war. Besides them, at the end of 1944, around 500,000 concentration camp prisoners were hired out to German firms by the SS or employed in SS businesses. Without this foreign labour to replace German manual and agricultural workers, representing 20% of the total workforce, it would have been impossible to raise the 17.3 million men recruited to the Wehrmacht. In addition to this levy of active forces, there was an enormous financial drain, mainly through the imposition of an unfair exchange rate and enormous occupation costs. Some of the huge sums raised were spent locally by Wehrmacht soldiers, partly on the black market. Most of the capital came back to the occupied countries in the form of military orders for local firms, known as 'S businesses' (S for Speer, one of Hitler's top ministers), which were then guaranteed manpower and raw materials. Over four million European workers were thus yoked to the German war machine, providing between a fifth and a quarter of its needs.

The exchange rate and the availability of unlimited funds also enabled the Reich to import any food products, raw materials and semi-finished products that it required, including 12% of its steel, 20% of its coal, leather, sulphuric acid, cereals, a third of its iron and meat, and half of its aluminium. Germany's heavy food imports led to chronic malnutrition throughout Europe. Daily calorie intake fell by half in France, 60% in Poland and three-quarters in the USSR to allow German rations to be maintained on Hitler's express orders. Actual looting also accounted for large sums: works of art, goods requisitioned without payment in the USSR, the theft of patents, seizure of stocks and equipment, and transfer of holdings at very low prices. The German war effort was also financed by dispossessing European Jews of their property, in proportions that are difficult to estimate but were certainly substantial. Perhaps it would have been more profitable for Germany if they had been put to work rather than slaughtered, just as the 3 million Soviet prisoners who died of hunger in 1941–42 would have provided 8% more manpower. But economic practicality often came second to ideology in the Reich.

SOURCES: 1. Bernhard R. Kroener, *Das Deutsche Reich und der Zweite Weltkrieg*, vols. 5/1 & 5/2, 1988 • 2. Hans-Erich Volkmann, *Ökonomie und Expansion: Grundzuge der NS-Wirtschaftspolitik*, Munich, 2003 • 3. Christoph Buchheim & Marcel Boldorf (eds.), *Europäische Volkswirtschaften unter deutscher Hegemonie, 1938–1945*, Munich, 2012 • 4. Adam Tooze, *The Wages of Destruction*, 2006.

1 • ARMAMENTS PRODUCED BY OCCUPIED COUNTRIES

The Reich organized the division of labour in occupied countries according to the industries they specialized in before the war. For instance, this table reflects France's strength in the aeronautics and automotive industries, as well as the role of Philips and the Dutch shipyards. However, armaments remained a very small part of this total, aside from additional orders for captured equipment (French tanks) and equipment supplied to Axis allies (French aircraft for Romania).

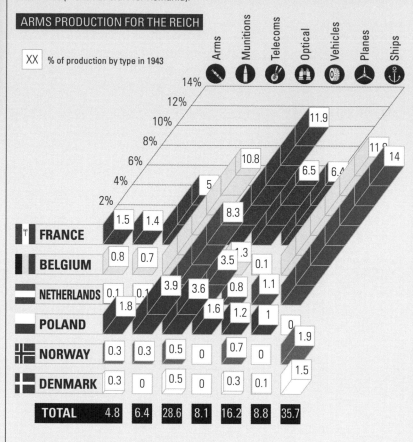

ARMS PRODUCTION FOR THE REICH

XX % of production by type in 1943

	Arms	Munitions	Telecoms	Optical	Vehicles	Planes	Ships
FRANCE	1.5	1.4	5	8.3	10.8	6.5	11.9
BELGIUM	0.8	0.7	3.5	1.3	0.1	6.4	11.9
NETHERLANDS	0.1	0.1	3.9	3.6	0.8	1.1	14
POLAND	1.8		1.6	1.2	1	0	1.9
NORWAY	0.3	0.3	0.5	0	0.7	0	1.5
DENMARK	0.3	0	0.5	0	0.3	0.1	
TOTAL	4.8	6.4	28.6	8.1	16.2	8.8	35.7

3 • THE LOOTING OF FRANCE

Of the occupied countries, France had the strongest and most diversified economy, the richest heritage and the largest monetary reserves. The desire to take revenge for the inter-war demands for reparations partly accounted for the widespread looting of the country. Refineries demolished, raw materials and rolling stock confiscated, machinery

EFFECT ON DAILY CALORIE INTAKE

■ Germany
■ France

In 1943–44, France supplied the Reich with
- **4.4% of its bread grain**
- **6% of its feed grain**
- **12% of its meat**
- **2% of its fats**
Two-thirds of these goods were consumed locally by the occupying forces.

c = calories

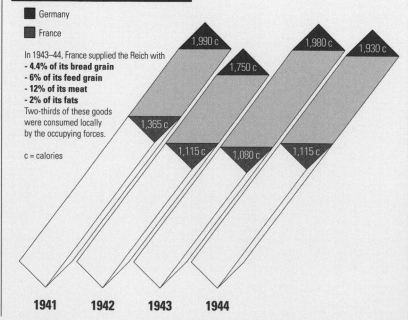

1941	1942	1943	1944
1,990 c	1,750 c	1,980 c	1,930 c
1,365 c	1,115 c	1,080 c	1,115 c

2 • FOREIGNERS AND THE GERMAN ECONOMY IN AUGUST 1944

Propaganda, high wages, deportations, raids, forced labour, prisoner-of-war camps: every possibility was exploited to secure manpower for the Reich. Over 80% of the workforce was completely or relatively unskilled. Women from Russia and Poland were forced to work in agriculture, while men from those countries were given the most dangerous work, in mining, the chemicals industry, metallurgy and mine clearance. Skilled workers from Western Europe worked in the aeronautics industry and motor factories. So great was the obsession with labour that the Kursk offensive in the summer of 1943 was planned with the specific aim of capturing one million Soviet soldiers, in order to put them to work.

FOREIGNERS AND THE GERMAN ECONOMY IN AUGUST 1944

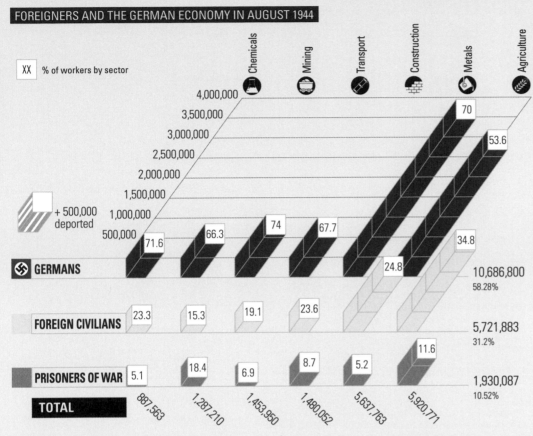

XX   % of workers by sector

+ 500,000 deported

	Chemicals	Mining	Transport	Construction	Metals	Agriculture	
GERMANS	71.6	66.3	74	67.7	24.8	34.8	10,686,800 / 58.28%
FOREIGN CIVILIANS	23.3	15.3	19.1	23.6			5,721,883 / 31.2%
PRISONERS OF WAR	5.1	18.4	6.9	8.7	5.2	11.6	1,930,087 / 10.52%
TOTAL	887,563	1,287,210	1,453,950	1,480,052	5,637,763	5,920,771	

(Metals: 53.6, 70; Agriculture: 34.8)

and patents stolen, occupation costs, an unfair exchange rate, deportation of workers: all these factors explain how the Reich drained France of between a third and a half of its GDP. The results were widespread poverty, the growth of the black market and prostitution, and a drastic fall in average calorie consumption. It is clear from these figures that it was mainly because of France's defeat in 1940 that the Reich was able to continue the war for so long.

OCCUPATION COSTS

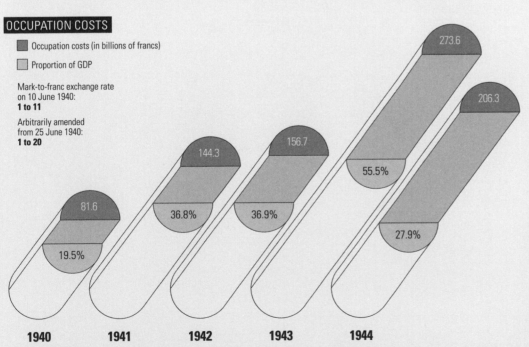

- Occupation costs (in billions of francs)
- Proportion of GDP

Mark-to-franc exchange rate on 10 June 1940:
1 to 11

Arbitrarily amended from 25 June 1940:
1 to 20

	1940	1941	1942	1943	1944
Occupation costs	81.6	144.3	156.7	273.6	
Proportion of GDP	19.5%	36.8%	36.9%	55.5%	

(1944: 206.3 / 27.9%)

CIVILIAN LABOUR BY COUNTRY IN THE GERMAN ECONOMY

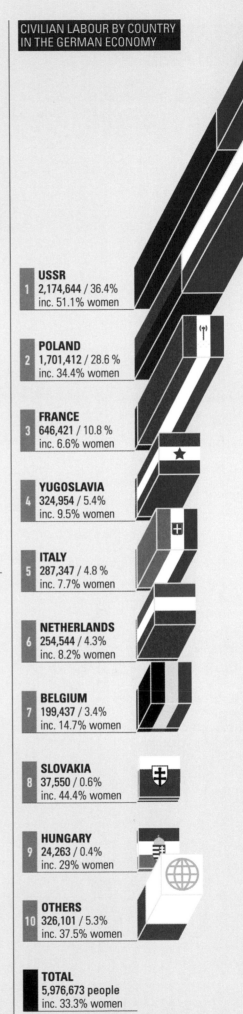

1. **USSR** 2,174,644 / 36.4% inc. 51.1% women
2. **POLAND** 1,701,412 / 28.6% inc. 34.4% women
3. **FRANCE** 646,421 / 10.8% inc. 6.6% women
4. **YUGOSLAVIA** 324,954 / 5.4% inc. 9.5% women
5. **ITALY** 287,347 / 4.8% inc. 7.7% women
6. **NETHERLANDS** 254,544 / 4.3% inc. 8.2% women
7. **BELGIUM** 199,437 / 3.4% inc. 14.7% women
8. **SLOVAKIA** 37,550 / 0.6% inc. 44.4% women
9. **HUNGARY** 24,263 / 0.4% inc. 29% women
10. **OTHERS** 326,101 / 5.3% inc. 37.5% women

TOTAL 5,976,673 people inc. 33.3% women

ALLIED CONFERENCES:

Never before had countries so geographically and ideologically remote from each other cooperated as successfully as the Allies did between 1941 and 1945. Operations were planned at meetings between heads of state. They also cooperated on the new world order, partly a consequence of the balance of power between the victors states (Yalta, Potsdam), but also decided in around a hundred more wide-ranging multilateral negotiations (which included neutral countries). The conferences were the backbone of the war and its conclusion, with repercussions that are still being felt. However, this activity did not mean that there was always a coherent programme.

The system lacked structure and the conferences were of two kinds. The superpowers (a term used from 1944 onwards) dominated the conferences with military aims, those that determined the future of the defeated side and defined the new world order. This experience of a condominium led Roosevelt to alter his position on how peace could be guaranteed in the future. In 1943, he abandoned collective security in favour of an oligarchic world order under the 'Big Four' or 'Four Policemen' (the USA, UK, USSR and China), who each had a veto and a sphere of influence. At the same time, in Washington, players with different world views worked on reshaping

1 • THE ANGLO-AMERICAN AXIS

The conferences were planned and run by Britain and the USA. Churchill was the most active participant, keen to preserve the British Empire, but Roosevelt was the dominant figure. Together they set the timetable for the war, while Stalin stayed in the background. He did not meet Roosevelt and Churchill until November 1943. France and China were allowed no influence. They were merely assigned a minor role for the future.

Churchill

Conferences attended*
18

Number of meetings**

13 · 1 · 1 · 5

14 · 3 · 7

Roosevelt · Stalin

2 · 1 · 1

3 · 1

De Gaulle · Chiang Kai-shek

* Statistics based on 18 official conferences
** Statistics based on 24 official conferences

2 • 17 CONFERENCES: PLANNING FOR VICTORY AND THE FUTURE

Although conferences were held more frequently at the end of the war, the ground was already being prepared in 1941. Even before Pearl Harbor, when the USA was still isolationist, the visionaries Roosevelt and Churchill promoted the Atlantic Charter on which the new world order was based. These two were also prominent in deciding the focus of the conferences: 17 in the Empire, 14 in the USA. However, British influence started to decline after 1943 and the USSR began to exert more influence, after initially being marginalized due to mutual mistrust. In two other respects, 1943 was a turning point. It was the year when the major military decisions had already been taken and there was a shift to more political considerations.

1. **ABC-1:** plan for cooperation if the USA enters the war
2. **Atlantic Charter:** post-war goals of the democratic nations
3. **First Moscow Conference:** principle of aid to the USSR
4. **ARCADIA:** war goal of 'Germany first', United Nations Declaration
5. **Second Washington Conference:** North African landing
6. **SYMBOL/Anfa:** landing in Italy, French rearmament, unconditional Axis surrender
7. **TRIDENT:** general strategy in Europe and Asia, including landing in France in May 1944
8. **QUADRANT:** general strategy in Asia, deciding location of Normandy landing
9. **Third Moscow Conference:** reversal of German annexation (Austria, Czechoslovakia, Poland, etc.), decision to set up an international court, Stalin supports the idea of the UN
10. **SEXTANT:** reversal of Japanese annexations
11. **EUREKA:** landing in south of France, USSR agrees to declare war on Japan, discussions on Germany's future
12. **Bretton Woods Conference:** new world economic order, creation of IMF and IBRD
13. **Dumbarton Oaks Conference:** structure of UN
14. **OCTAGON:** Morganthau Plan, principle of occupying Germany
15. **Yalta:** date set for USSR to enter war against Japan, principle of 4 occupation zones in Germany, composition of UN
16. **San Francisco Conference:** establishment of UN
17. **TERMINAL (Potsdam):** defined German borders and division into 4 zones, adoption of 5 Ds (disarmament, denazification, decartelization, democratization and decentralization), no separate agreement on reparations, ultimatum to Japan

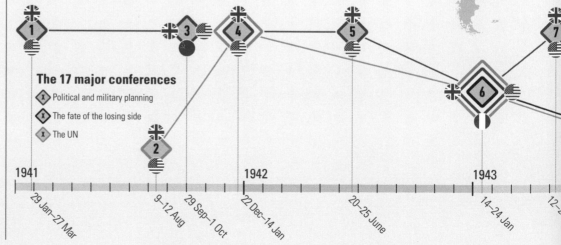

Quebec

San Francisco · Washington · Argentina

The 17 major conferences

- Political and military planning
- The fate of the losing side
- The UN

1941 · 1942 · 1943

29 Jan–27 Mar · 9–12 Aug · 29 Sep–1 Oct · 22 Dec–14 Jan · 20–25 June · 14–24 Jan · 12–

SOURCES: 1. Dan Plesch, *America, Hitler & the UN: How the Allies Won World War II and Forged a Peace*, London, 2011 • 2. Maurice Bertrand & Antonio Donini, *L'ONU*, Paris, 2015 • 3. David Reynolds, *From World War to Cold War: Churchill, Roosevelt, and the International History of the 1940s*, Oxford, 2007 • 4. Jean-François Muracciole & Guillaume Piketty (eds.), *Encyclopédie de la Seconde Guerre mondiale,*

PLANNING FOR THE POST-WAR WORLD

the global system, bringing together as many countries as possible. The Western countries believed that the causes of the war could be traced back to the 1929 crisis and the failure of existing structures (League of Nations, Economic and Financial Organization, Bank for International Settlements). They took the view (pioneered by David Mitrany) that participation by states in functional agencies would encourage the peaceful growth of international society. The emphasis was on a sector-based approach with more regulatory bodies. Old structures were maintained, while others, more influential, were formed earlier than the UN, via piecemeal initiatives.

This dichotomy led to the United Nations 'non' system. The San Francisco Conference established the condominium that the major powers wanted, creating an oligarchical Security Council, but it also ratified the UN's fragmentary structure. Independent organizations were linked to the UN without being subordinate to it. This autonomy meant that the UN was not a true umbrella organization; it did not have the last word on economic, social, cultural and humanitarian policies. For some time, there was only cohesion because of the dominant position of the United States in the various organizations.

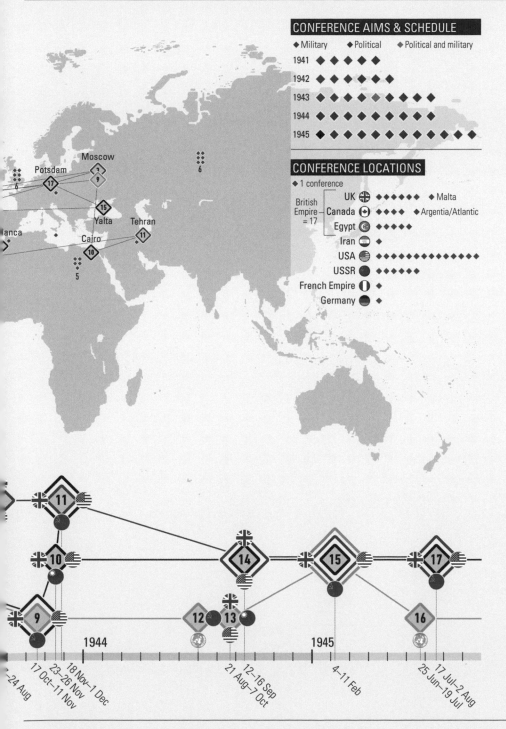

CONFERENCE AIMS & SCHEDULE

◆ Military ◆ Political ◆ Political and military

1941	◆ ◆ ◆ ◆ ◆
1942	◆ ◆ ◆ ◆ ◆
1943	◆ ◆ ◆ ◆ ◆ ◆ ◆ ◆ ◆
1944	◆ ◆ ◆ ◆ ◆ ◆ ◆ ◆
1945	◆ ◆ ◆ ◆ ◆ ◆ ◆ ◆ ◆ ◆ ◆ ◆

CONFERENCE LOCATIONS

◆ 1 conference

British Empire = 17

UK	✚	◆ ◆ ◆ ◆ ◆	◆ Malta
Canada	◆	◆ ◆ ◆ ◆	◆ Argentia/Atlantic
Egypt	◆	◆ ◆ ◆ ◆	
Iran	◆	◆	
USA	◆	◆ ◆ ◆ ◆ ◆ ◆ ◆ ◆ ◆ ◆ ◆ ◆ ◆ ◆	
USSR	●	◆ ◆ ◆ ◆ ◆ ◆	
French Empire	◐	◆	
Germany	◐	◆	

3 • THE UN 'NON' SYSTEM

The first UN conferences were held in 1942 (UNESCO education conferences; 44-nation FAO conference in Hot Springs) and its first agency (UNRRA) was set up in 1943. By the time the General Assembly was founded in October 1945 on the initiative of the 'Big Four' (USA, UK, USSR and China), most of the specialized agencies were already established. But they objected to being placed under the UN banner, so the General Assembly was only able to make recommendations to them, dashing hopes of a world government.

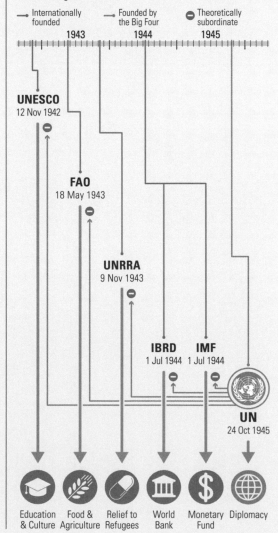

Paris, 2015 • 5. Dan Plesch & Thomas G. Weiss (eds.), *Wartime Origins and the Future United Nations*, Abingdon & New York, 2015

2. ARMS AND ARMED FORCES

HIGH COMMANDS:

The waging of a war on a global scale is an unimaginably complex task. The high command has to manage millions of people, organize their movements and schedules and take account of political and economic factors in order to coordinate the mobilization of manpower and industry. It defines overall strategies and runs military operations, sometimes from thousands of miles away. The Americans had faced challenges of this kind for centuries, but it was not until the 19th century, when armies expanded and operations tended to last longer, that a proper high command structure was needed, with

multiple sub-branches. Initial experience was gained in the First World War but this could not be replicated for the countries defeated in 1918 or for the United States and Japan, whose engagement came too little or too late. The Pentagon, established in 1942 to bring together the 30,000-strong staff of the US Department of War, illustrates the changing scale of world conflict.

Command structures were all the more complex because every attempt at rationalization met with resistance from existing bodies, leading to battles for influence and the preservation of

1 • THE USSR: RULING THE RED ARMY

On 22 June 1941, Soviet command of the war was disorganized. Two key institutions were not established for over a month. The first, the State Defence Committee (GKO), had a monopoly over political and economic power, which was exercised by the state apparatus presided over by Stalin. The armed forces high command, Stavka, only became effective when Stalin became its commander on 9 August 1941. It was under his personal control, with operations overseen via his representatives at the fronts or through the General Staff (Genshtab). The latter was excluded from some key functions, which were entrusted to those close to Stalin. The system operated without excessive bureaucracy, but Stalin disrupted it by constantly bypassing military hierarchies.

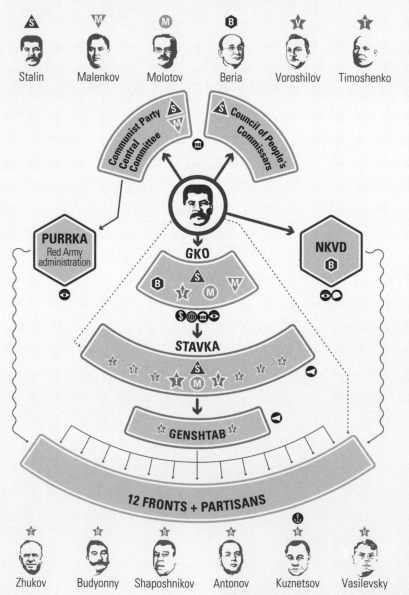

2 • THE FEUDAL NAZI NETWORK

After 1938, the once all-powerful Prussian command was replaced by a vaguer structure with poorly defined roles in which closeness to the Führer counted for more than function. This feudal polycracy, in which Goering, Speer and Himmler were leading figures, stirred up tensions and created overlapping purviews. No one except Hitler had access to all information. Everyone worked in the dark and competed with each other, while Hitler held the reins of control and provoked serious friction. The authority of the army high command (OKH), now confined to the Eastern Front, was constantly undermined. The OKW, although nominally overseeing all the German armed forces, was simply a communication channel with no thinkers or skills qualifying it to oversee war strategies. By 1942 there had ceased to be any kind of strategic planning.

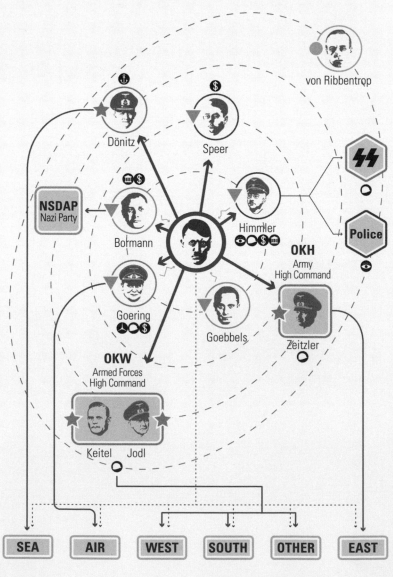

PLANNING THE WAR

anachronistic departments. Structures were built up gradually in layers, evolving from compromises, schisms and continuity. Of the examples shown here, only the British had a command structure before the war. All the others were radically altered just before or during the conflict. It is clear from the descriptions how much they reflected the type of society and ideology for which they were fighting. In that respect, the three dictatorships were similar, especially when compared to the Anglo-American democracies.

Key:

Functions
- → Command
- ∿ Surveillance
- ┄→ Interference
- ∨∨ Influence
- ⚡ In conflict
- ⌇ Circle of influence

- ▲ Head of State
- ▼ Politician
- ⬤ Diplomat
- ⬣ State Police
- ★ Military
- ★ Military

Means of control
- Political
- Diplomatic
- $ Economic/industrial
- State police
- All armed forces
- Land forces
- Naval forces
- Air forces

Organizations
- ○ Decision-making
- ▢ Military
- ▢ Political
- ▢ Repression
- ▢ Fronts

3 • THE ANGLO-AMERICAN ALLIANCE

The Allies had difficulties with cooperation, controlling distant theatres of war and the overlapping of army, navy and air force roles. National structures were backed by inter-service and international committees centred on the Combined Chiefs of Staff. The committee coordinated the war based on decisions made by politicians at Allied conferences, and distributed resources. Planning and oversight of the campaigns were delegated to high commands in the theatre of operations. Although not perfect, these structures arbitrated effectively on disputes, such as disagreements between the navy and the army on priorities in the Pacific. Another effective choice was to confine military minds to battle issues, while protecting them from intrusion by arch-strategist Churchill.

4 • JAPAN: A FRACTURED HIGH COMMAND

Ostensibly well-organized, with a committee responsible for overseeing the war and an emperor with absolute decision-making power, the Japanese command structure was actually undermined by Hirohito's refusal to arbitrate. The emperor allowed friction to build between the army and the navy, which had different aims. Consequently, strategy fluctuated according to the relationship between internal forces. In a fascistic move, General Tojo tried to concentrate power, merging the positions of prime minister, minister for the army and chief of staff in the spring of 1944. However, he came into conflict with the navy and the emperor dismissed him in July 1944. On the fronts, although the army was in control on the mainland, elsewhere operations and positions were assigned to each of the two services on a case-by-case basis and the command basically split in two.

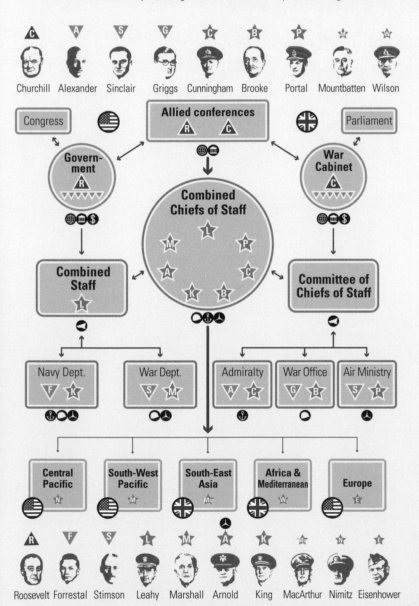

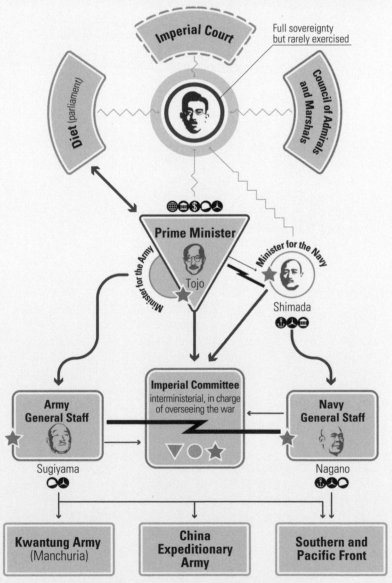

THE INFANTRY: THE MAINSTAY OF OPERATIONS

Infantry divisions, first established in 1759, were the mainstay of combat. Groups of 8,000 to 16,000 men, they were actually the first inter-unit level with a staff and a supply corps, making them a 'mini-army'. An infantry could be deployed on its own or as a team within a corps. It even became a benchmark for state power. Stalin is said to have asked disparagingly: 'How many regiments does the Pope have?' It owed its success to the fine balance between size, flexibility and versatility, able to function offensive or defensively and operate in open country, in towns or in the mountains. Creating smaller units for greater flexibility was more costly in terms of logistics and officers (an autonomous unit of 4,000 men needed almost as many services as one of 15,000 men). Establishing stronger divisions meant only having a few large unwieldy units. In 1939, an infantry division was an inexpensive structure that made optimum use of the demographic pool available. Poland raised 30, Belgium 22, and independent battalions could easily be added for reinforcement when necessary. In due course, 80% of the army was made up of infantry divisions and that figure remained constant throughout the war.

However, early battles caused considerable difficulties. Shattered by air strikes and armoured divisions, infantry divisions were unable to keep up with the new pace of operations. Too fragile and too slow, they could only be used to cover the huge fronts, a thankless but necessary task that required further mobilization. The number of Germany infantry divisions thus rose by 70% between 1939 and 1944. By 1943, it was over 200.

The difficulties were made even worse by shortages of men and equipment. German divisions had fewer and fewer vehicles and services and by 1944 their survival was only ensured theoretically by extra fire power, including assault rifles, MG 42 machine guns and cheap *Panzerfaust* anti-tank weapons. Lacking trucks and competent officers, Japan and the USSR opted for a downgraded structure, dependent for everything on the corps of which it was part. Finally, only the well-equipped British and US armies could afford to motorize their infantry divisions, reinforcing them with independent units. It wasn't rare to find divisions with a hundred tanks. Mechanically they became massive units of 20,000 men, or even 40,000, incorporating rear services. Only an efficient communication network and innovative strategies stopped them from grinding to a halt. Consequently, the number of divisions was limited. Although 11 million soldiers were called up, the US Army never fielded more than around 70 infantry divisions, and the British around 20. The infantry division was a forerunner of the enormous divisions of the Cold War, which had to be broken down into brigades to make them more flexible.

1 • POWER IN NUMBERS

Although somewhat overshadowed by the armoured divisions, infantry divisions were still the most common 'unit of account'. The vast Russian front required hundreds of them, often poorly equipped and trained, making tank units essential for penetration and operations, as well as for closing breaches. A Soviet infantry division only attacked if supported by extensive artillery and at the cost of terrible losses. In Western Europe, by contrast, infantry divisions were crucial to victory. Motorized and reinforced by a large number of independent battalions, they were versatile, penetrating the fronts and keeping pace with tanks during pursuits. In 1945, there were twice as many armoured vehicles supporting a British infantry division as there were in a Panzer division.

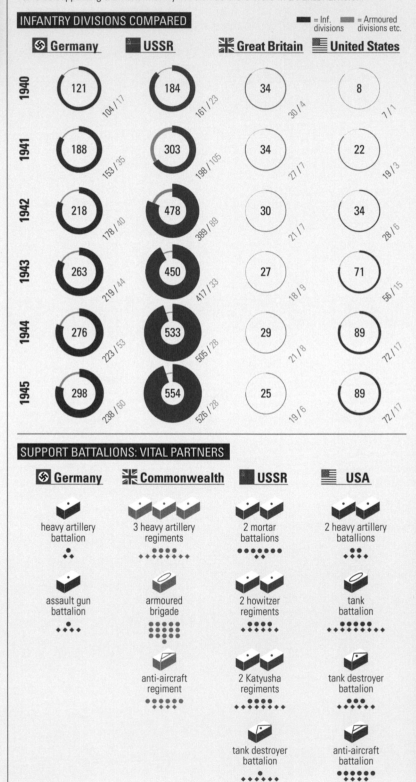

INFANTRY DIVISIONS COMPARED

■ = Inf. divisions   ▮ = Armoured divisions etc.

	Germany	USSR	Great Britain	United States
1940	121 / 104 / 17	184 / 161 / 23	34 / 30 / 4	8 / 7 / 1
1941	188 / 153 / 35	303 / 198 / 105	34 / 27 / 7	22 / 19 / 3
1942	218 / 178 / 40	478 / 389 / 89	30 / 21 / 7	34 / 28 / 6
1943	263 / 219 / 44	450 / 417 / 33	27 / 18 / 9	71 / 56 / 15
1944	276 / 223 / 53	533 / 505 / 28	29 / 21 / 8	89 / 72 / 17
1945	298 / 238 / 60	554 / 526 / 28	25 / 19 / 6	89 / 72 / 17

SUPPORT BATTALIONS: VITAL PARTNERS

Germany	Commonwealth	USSR	USA
heavy artillery battalion	3 heavy artillery regiments	2 mortar battalions	2 heavy artillery batallions
assault gun battalion	armoured brigade	2 howitzer regiments	tank battalion
anti-aircraft regiment		2 Katyusha regiments	tank destroyer battalion
		tank destroyer battalion	anti-aircraft battalion
		anti-tank gun battalion	

◆ = 1 unit
● = 10 units

2 • INFANTRY EQUIPMENT COMPARED

There was a huge disparity between British and US infantry divisions and those of other countries. The former were fully manned and motorized, with logistics ten times heavier than the horse-drawn equipment of other forces. Boosting firepower could not always compensate for falling manpower, which was often more serious in practice than this diagram shows. Italy's infantry divisions fell from 10,000 to 6,000 men in three years, and Soviet divisions from 14,400 to 7,000 or 8,000 in a few months. Every German combat group (10 men) had a machine gun (MG) that was much more efficient than the opposing side's automatic rifles (AR). This gave the group a reactivity and firepower that was hard to offset, even by drawing on support units. Equipment was adapted to suit each theatre of operations. Since horses could not be used in the desert, the Italians brought in more anti-tank weapons. Jungle conditions and overseas logistics forced the Japanese to prioritize light weapons (short-barrelled 75 mm artillery, grenade-launching mortars).

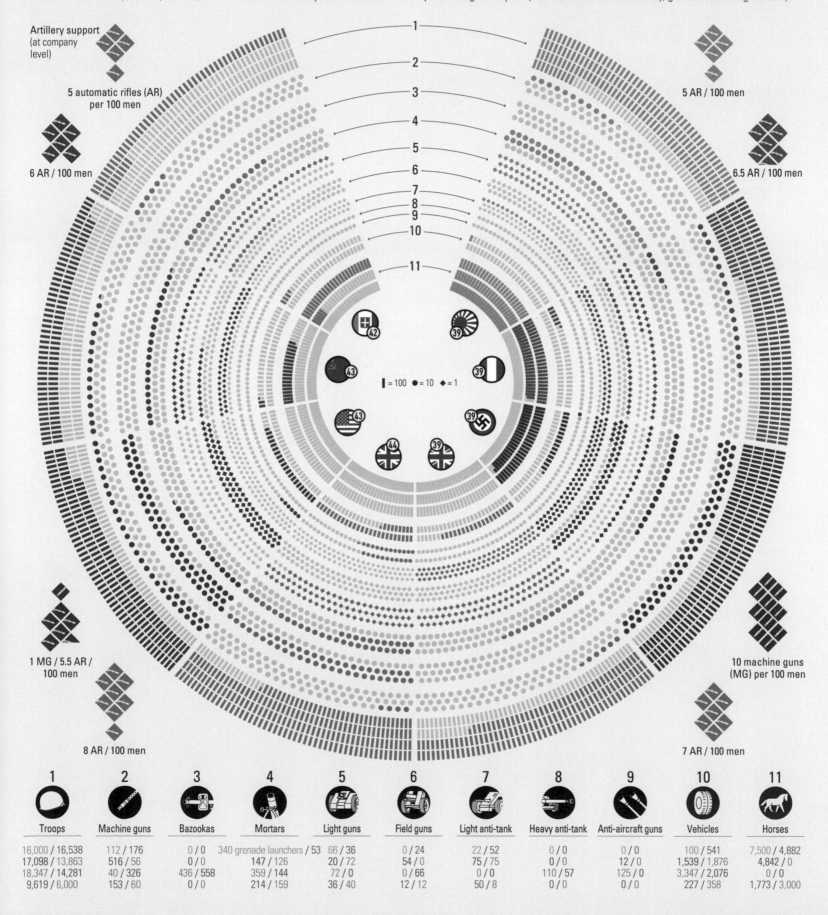

Artillery support (at company level)

5 automatic rifles (AR) per 100 men

6 AR / 100 men

1 MG / 5.5 AR / 100 men

8 AR / 100 men

5 AR / 100 men

6.5 AR / 100 men

10 machine guns (MG) per 100 men

7 AR / 100 men

| = 100 ● = 10 ◆ = 1

	1	2	3	4	5	6	7	8	9	10	11
	Troops	Machine guns	Bazookas	Mortars	Light guns	Field guns	Light anti-tank	Heavy anti-tank	Anti-aircraft guns	Vehicles	Horses
	16,000 / 16,538	112 / 176	0 / 0	340 grenade launchers / 53	66 / 36	0 / 24	22 / 52	0 / 0	0 / 0	100 / 541	7,500 / 4,882
	17,098 / 13,863	516 / 56	0 / 0	147 / 126	20 / 72	54 / 0	75 / 75	0 / 0	12 / 0	1,539 / 1,876	4,842 / 0
	18,347 / 14,281	40 / 326	436 / 558	359 / 144	72 / 0	0 / 66	0 / 0	110 / 57	125 / 0	3,347 / 2,076	0 / 0
	9,619 / 6,000	153 / 60	0 / 0	214 / 159	36 / 40	12 / 12	50 / 8	0 / 0	0 / 0	227 / 358	1,773 / 3,000

3 • THE STRUCTURE AND DEPLOYMENT OF GERMAN FORCES

The nucleus of the German fighting forces was the nine-man group with one machine gun, and sometimes with four *Panzerfäuste*. Like many others, the Germans adopted a triangular structure (3 groups to a section, 3 regiments to a division, etc.) that was flexible and made economical use of manpower. Usually two groups worked together,

while a third was kept in reserve. Specialist units were grafted on at division level. The staff drew on them as necessary to make up combat groups (*Kampfgruppen*), with the infantry as their core. The division looked impressive, with its anti-tank weapons and armoured vehicles, but it was no longer as effective as its predecessors. The support units had suffered 'demodernization' and were poorly kitted out with disparate equipment. In 1944, infantry battalions were reduced from 9 to 6, although the triangular

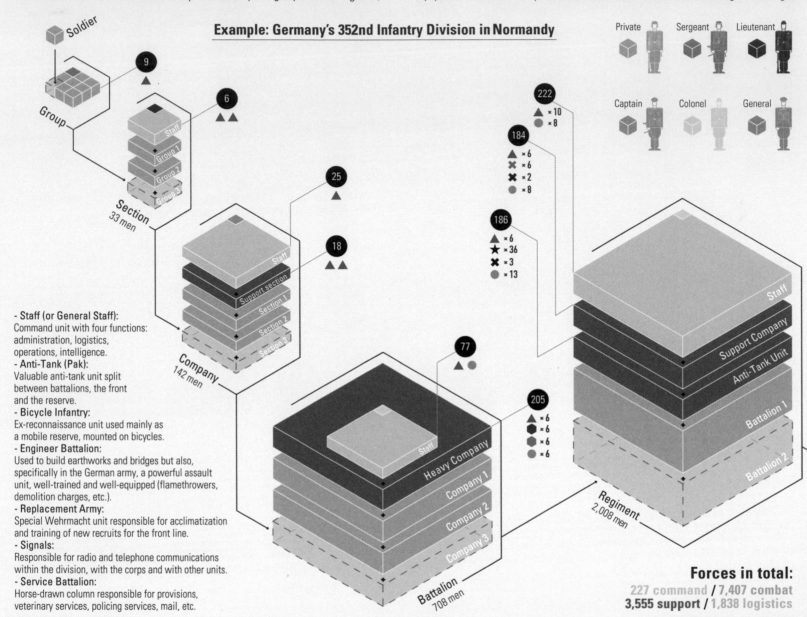

Example: Germany's 352nd Infantry Division in Normandy

- **Staff (or General Staff):**
Command unit with four functions: administration, logistics, operations, intelligence.
- **Anti-Tank (Pak):**
Valuable anti-tank unit split between battalions, the front and the reserve.
- **Bicycle Infantry:**
Ex-reconnaissance unit used mainly as a mobile reserve, mounted on bicycles.
- **Engineer Battalion:**
Used to build earthworks and bridges but also, specifically in the German army, a powerful assault unit, well-trained and well-equipped (flamethrowers, demolition charges, etc.).
- **Replacement Army:**
Special Wehrmacht unit responsible for acclimatization and training of new recruits for the front line.
- **Signals:**
Responsible for radio and telephone communications within the division, with the corps and with other units.
- **Service Battalion:**
Horse-drawn column responsible for provisions, veterinary services, policing services, mail, etc.

Forces in total:
227 command / 7,407 combat
3,555 support / 1,838 logistics

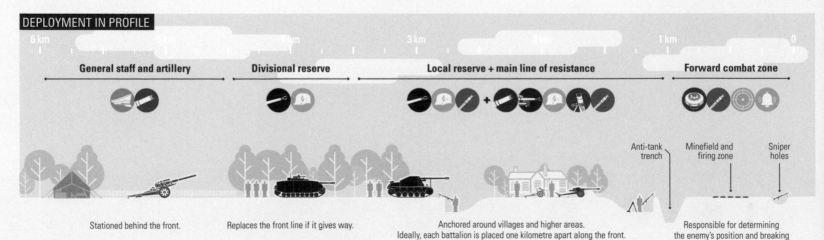

DEPLOYMENT IN PROFILE

SOURCES: 1. Alex Buchner, *The German Infantry Handbook, 1939–1945*, West Chester, PA, 1991 • 2 Shelby L. Stanton, *World War II Order of Battle: An Encyclopedic Reference to the US Army Ground Forces from Battalion through Division, 1939–1946*, Mechanicsburg, PA, 2006 • 3. Gordon L. Rottman, *Japanese Army in World War II*, Oxford, 2005 • 4. Steven J. Zaloga, *The Red Army Handbook*, Stroud, 1998 •

structure was maintained through bicycle infantry, engineer battalions and replacement armies (which trained reinforcements). However, their deployment as infantry was a disaster. By the end of 1944, each division had only 10,000 men, well below the 17,000 in 1939. But the worst problem was the shortage of officers, who were key to the German attack strategy. Even in defence, initiative was encouraged. In theory, a division defended a 6- to 12-km front with 6 battalions (from 1 to 2 km) and 3 in reserve. The main

line of resistance followed peaks or rivers, while farms and villages became defences. Failing that, the men dug in around the MG or Pak anti-tank gun. The strategy was not simply to hold the position but to retake any ground lost in improvised counter-attacks, requiring reactive and autonomous leadership at all levels. But in practice, a division was stretched across a double length of front, sacrificing the divisional reserve. Local counter-attacks then became decisive and the lack of officers was a very serious problem.

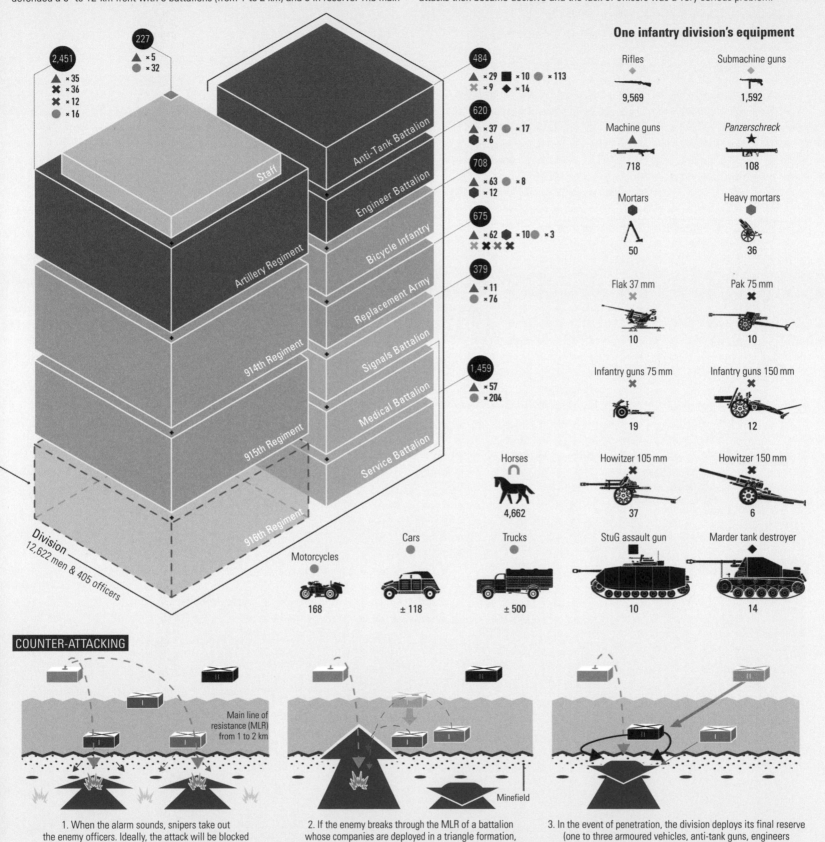

One infantry division's equipment

Rifles	Submachine guns
9,569	1,592

Machine guns	*Panzerschreck*
718	108

Mortars	Heavy mortars
50	36

Flak 37 mm	Pak 75 mm
10	10

Infantry guns 75 mm	Infantry guns 150 mm
19	12

Horses	Howitzer 105 mm	Howitzer 150 mm
4,662	37	6

Motorcycles	Cars	Trucks	StuG assault gun	Marder tank destroyer
168	± 118	± 500	10	14

Division
12,622 men & 405 officers

COUNTER-ATTACKING

Main line of resistance (MLR) from 1 to 2 km

Minefield

1. When the alarm sounds, snipers take out the enemy officers. Ideally, the attack will be blocked in no man's land where heavy artillery strikes will push the enemy into the minefields covered by machine gun fire.

2. If the enemy breaks through the MLR of a battalion whose companies are deployed in a triangle formation, a local counter-attack is improvised to repel it with the aid of the retreating company and one or two armoured vehicles.

3. In the event of penetration, the division deploys its final reserve (one to three armoured vehicles, anti-tank guns, engineers stationed on road crossings), supported by all available artillery. If possible, companies at the front attack the enemy flanks.

5. Stephen Bull, *World War II Infantry Tactics*, vols. 1 & 2, Oxford, 2004 & 2005 • 6. Martin van Creveld, *Fighting Power: German & U.S. Army Performance, 1939–1945*, London, 1983 • 7. Joseph Balkoski, *Beyond the Beachhead: The 29th Infantry Division in Normandy*, Mechanicsburg, PA, 2005 • 8. *Tableaux d'effectifs de guerre de l'armée française* (official archives) • 9. www.ATF40.fr • 10. www.niehorster.org

ARTILLERY: THE HAMMER OF THOR

Artillery was ultimately responsible for 60% of deaths and casualties. This statistic alone shows the importance of weaponry that was both underestimated and essential in supporting attacks and in crushing enemy assaults, in any theatre or season. The effectiveness of Second World War artillery depended on synergy between guns, personnel, motorization and radio.

In 1918, guns reached a pinnacle of development with high-quality barrels, ballistics and eventually ammunition. Twenty years later, they were reliable, strong, easy to make and deploy. American guns, modern versions of the French 75 and 155 MPF, were of a particularly high standard. German guns, being awkward to handle, were less successful. Equipment fell into two categories. The Germans and Americans favoured powerful 105

and 150 mm howitzers. But while the Americans built up a uniform stock, the Germans were forced to include thousands of captured weapons. Other combatants relied on lighter quick-firing field guns from 1918 stock (France, Italy, Japan), of which the versatile 25-pounder howitzer and the Soviet ZiS-3 were modern versions. But because they lacked punch, they needed an excessive amount of ammunition and heavy artillery was needed as soon as the enemy was entrenched. The Soviets and later the Germans also produced innovative rocket launchers (Katyushas and Nebelwerfers).

Artillery called for effective technical management, in which the Americans, British and Germans excelled, but it was lacking in the armies of Asia and Eastern Europe and in the Free French forces. The introduction of 6 x 6 cross-country

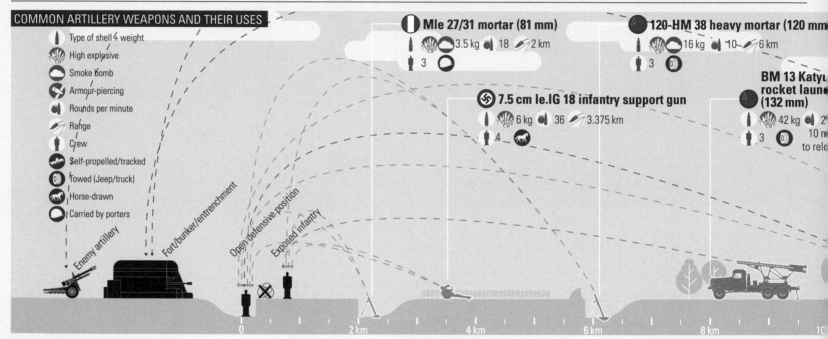

COMMON ARTILLERY WEAPONS AND THEIR USES

Type of shell & weight
High explosive
Smoke bomb
Armour-piercing
Rounds per minute
Range
Crew
Self-propelled/tracked
Towed (Jeep/truck)
Horse-drawn
Carried by porters

Enemy artillery
Fort/bunker/entrenchment
Open defensive position
Exposed infantry

Mle 27/31 mortar (81 mm)
3.5 kg · 18 · 2 km
3

120-HM 38 heavy mortar (120 mm)
16 kg · 10 · 6 km
3

7.5 cm le.IG 18 infantry support gun
6 kg · 36 · 3.375 km
4

BM 13 Katyu rocket laune (132 mm)
42 kg · 2
3 · 10 m to relo

0 · 2 km · 4 km · 6 km · 8 km · 10

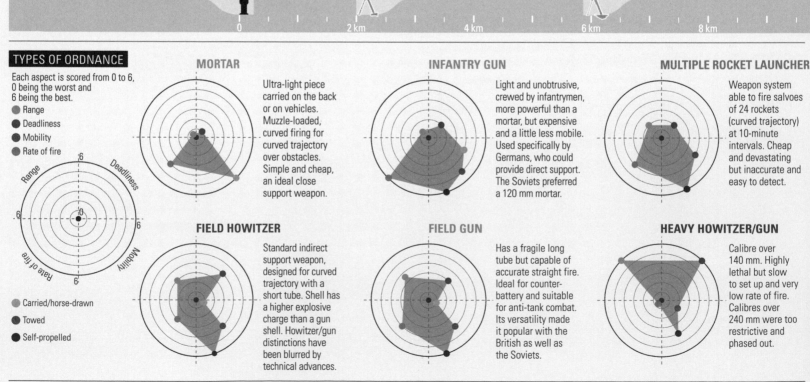

TYPES OF ORDNANCE

Each aspect is scored from 0 to 6, 0 being the worst and 6 being the best.
● Range
● Deadliness
● Mobility
● Rate of fire

Range · Deadliness · Mobility · Rate of fire
6 · 6 · 0 · 6 · 6

● Carried/horse-drawn
● Towed
● Self-propelled

MORTAR
Ultra-light piece carried on the back or on vehicles. Muzzle-loaded, curved firing for curved trajectory over obstacles. Simple and cheap, an ideal close support weapon.

INFANTRY GUN
Light and unobtrusive, crewed by infantrymen, more powerful than a mortar, but expensive and a little less mobile. Used specifically by Germans, who could provide direct support. The Soviets preferred a 120 mm mortar.

MULTIPLE ROCKET LAUNCHER
Weapon system able to fire salvoes of 24 rockets (curved trajectory) at 10-minute intervals. Cheap and devastating but inaccurate and easy to detect.

FIELD HOWITZER
Standard indirect support weapon, designed for curved trajectory with a short tube. Shell has a higher explosive charge than a gun shell. Howitzer/gun distinctions have been blurred by technical advances.

FIELD GUN
Has a fragile long tube but capable of accurate straight fire. Ideal for counter-battery and suitable for anti-tank combat. Its versatility made it popular with the British as well as the Soviets.

HEAVY HOWITZER/GUN
Calibre over 140 mm. Highly lethal but slow to set up and very low rate of fire. Calibres over 240 mm were too restrictive and phased out.

SOURCES: 1. Gilles Aubagnac, 'L'Artillerie terrestre de la Seconde Guerre mondiale: quelques aspects des grands tournants technologiques et tactiques et leur héritage', *Guerres mondiales et conflits contemporains*, no. 238, PUF, 2010/2, pp. 43–59 • 2. Paul Gaujac, *US Field Artillery in World War II: 1941–45*, Paris, 2009 • 3. Shelford Bidwell & Dominick Graham, *Fire Power: The British Army Weapons & Theories of War*

vehicles improved the mobility of weapons and supplies. Even so, only British and US artillery was fully motorized. Other nations still used horse-drawn ordnance, with the exception of armoured vehicle support artillery and heavy artillery. Mechanized artillery (fixed guns on an armoured vehicle chassis) or assault guns (tracked vehicles with gun turrets), which were even more mobile and reactive, followed the tanks.

The most revolutionary development was radio. One French regiment went from 15 radios in 1939 to 150 in 1943. Support was speeded up by virtually instantaneous passing of information between the front (forward observers and light aircraft) and the rear. British and US teams were connected to a fire direction centre (FDC) equipped with firing charts, realizing the dream of

decentralized artillery in the field but with centralized fire. Any enemy attacks could be stopped almost as soon as they began.

The use of artillery and its impact were determined by the balance between the four factors of guns, personnel, motorization and radio. The Germans, with fewer resources, favoured limited but reactive support; local artillery was integrated into combat groups. The Soviets opted for heavy support, grouped into artillery divisions or even corps, which made full use of specialists and radio, effective 'hammers' at the start of an offensive but quickly set aside. With their optimum synergy, British and US forces were by far the most efficient. Their accurate, heavy and rapid fire was closely coordinated with each manoeuvre so the Germans were hit hard, while fewer shells were used than in the previous conflict.

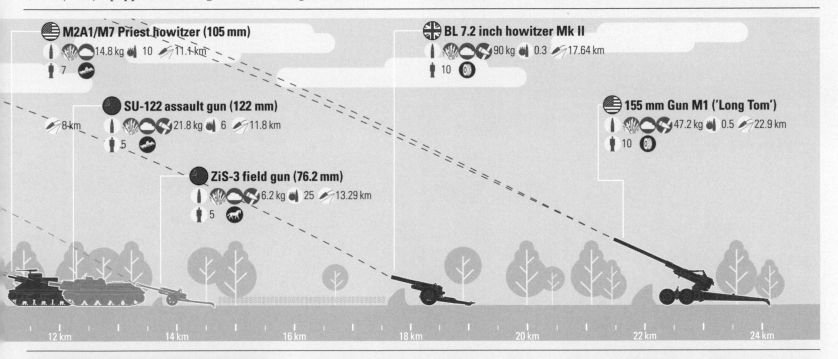

M2A1/M7 Priest howitzer (105 mm)
14.8 kg · 10 · 11.4 km · 7

SU-122 assault gun (122 mm)
8 km · 21.8 kg · 6 · 11.8 km · 5

ZiS-3 field gun (76.2 mm)
6.2 kg · 25 · 13.29 km · 5

BL 7.2 inch howitzer Mk II
90 kg · 0.3 · 17.64 km · 10

155 mm Gun M1 ('Long Tom')
47.2 kg · 0.5 · 22.9 km · 10

12 km   14 km   16 km   18 km   20 km   22 km   24 km

BRITISH ARTILLERY COMBAT TACTICS IN 1944

Artillery battalion · Command · Artillery · Troops · Observers · Observation aircraft · Radio · Front line

1. Break through the front line with a rolling barrage

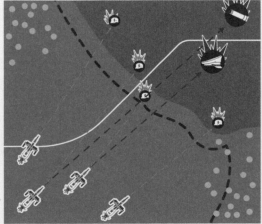

This preliminary assault lasts for several minutes:
1 Bomb the command centres.
2 Bomb artillery and anti-aircraft defence positions.
3 Hit enemy defences with explosive shells and smoke bombs with all available ordnance, often combined with air bombardment.

2. Sustain the assault

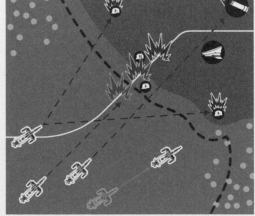

50% of resources used for planned strikes: counter-battery and rolling barrage (shelling along the front line precisely timed in 100-metre dashes).
25% of resources kept in reserve to meet unexpected requirements.
25% of resources redeployed to the front.

3. Break the enemy counter-attack

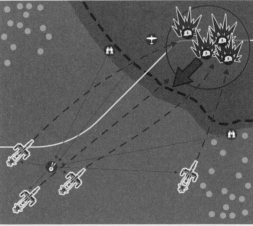

The British and US Time On Target (TOT) technique was the ultimate in defensive fire. Using forward observers and a centralized command, salvoes of artillery fire could be timed to hit the enemy at the same time, literally stunning them.

1904–1945, London, 1982 • 4. John Norris & Robert Calow, *Infantry Mortars of World War II*, Oxford, 2002 • 5. Chris Bishop, *The Illustrated Encyclopedia of Weapons of World War II*, London, 1984 • 6. John Ellis, *World War II: A Statistical Survey*, New York, 1995.

INSIDE AN ARMOURED DIVISION

The unstoppable Panzer divisions that had such a staggering impact in 1940 were not merely the culmination of a tank revolution but also a successful marriage between new technology and more traditional strategies.

The story begins in 1917. The Germans were hoping to break through the front using *Stosstruppen*, autonomous shock troops who could infiltrate and turn a battle into a multitude of small-scale skirmishes designed to disperse the enemy forces. In 1923, Hans von Seeckt's Reichswehr extended the concept, aiming to form a compact semi-professional army for limited warfare, with autonomous leaders skilled in inter-service combat. It would have motorized troops,

using speed to boost the shock effect and compensating for any lack of numbers with defensive mobility. The idea incorporated all the features of the future Panzer division. Tanks, radio and ground attack aircraft, made more reliable in the 1930s, all had a place in the strategy. Hitler made the plan a reality but also disrupted it. He provided the necessary funds for equipment but wanted a different model, insisting on a large army with only the forefront motorized.

In 1938 and 1939, the first Panzers began moving across Europe. They were autonomous multi-purpose vehicles designed for breakthrough and exploitation, passing over obstacles and crushing enemy attacks. They were queens of the battlefield, capable of quick

1 • RULING THE BATTLEFIELD

The high commands interpreted Germany's resounding victories of 1939–41 as proof that armoured divisions were the key to winning a war. The Americans formed 61 (one-third of its planned divisions), while the USSR raised the same number in 1940–41. Even Japan, Romania and Hungary, although they only had small automobile industries, bled themselves dry to produce two or three similar divisions. Not to be outdone, the Nazis doubled its total in 1940. The SS and even the Luftwaffe wanted their own. By 1945, Hitler was trying to fight back by creating new divisions that only existed on paper. Elsewhere, ambitions were more limited. Too complex, costly and logistically demanding, and ultimately less crucial outside the Wehrmacht, armoured divisions never again represented more than 20% of forces.

ARMOURED DIVISIONS AS A PERCENTAGE OF ARMIES IN THE EUROPEAN THEATRE

	1940	1941	1942	1943	1944	1945
USA	% of ID / % of AD	no. of ID / no. of AD —	100%	88.89% / 11.11% — 7	84.44% / 15.56% 18 / 2	82.8% / 17.2% 45 / 7 — 93 / 16
Commonwealth	94.74% / 5.26% 19 / 1	96.73% / 3.27% 27 / 1	85.71% / 14.29% 21 / 3	86.67% / 13.33% 30 / 4	79.59% / 20.41% 49 / 10	81.25% / 18.75% 48 / 9
France	94.23% / 5.77% 104 / 6	—	—	—	62.5% / 37.5% 8 / 3	80% / 20% 15 / 3
Italy	97% / 3% 66 / 2	95.16% / 4.84% 62 / 3	96% / 4% 75 / 3	100% 57	—	—
Third Reich	92.6% / 7.4% 121 / 9	89.9% / 10.1% 188 / 19	89% / 11% 218 / 24	89.3% / 10.7% 263 / 28	88.8% / 11.2% 276 / 31	88.3% / 11.7% 298 / 33

THE TIP OF A VERY MIXED ARMY The German army on 10 May 1940

9 territorial divisions

6 motorized divisions

5 divisions in training

127 infantry divisions, inc. 61 battle-ready

10 Panzer divisions

2 • THE HIGH COST OF PANZER DIVISIONS

To meet the needs of the Russian front, Hitler doubled the number of divisions, drawing on the stocks of conquered lands and reducing tanks by a third. The drop was offset by improvements in quality. But a Panzer's lifespan was short. Within weeks, half of them were out of commission, mainly due to breakdown. Industry could not compensate.

TANK TYPES AVAILABLE in armoured divisions in the east

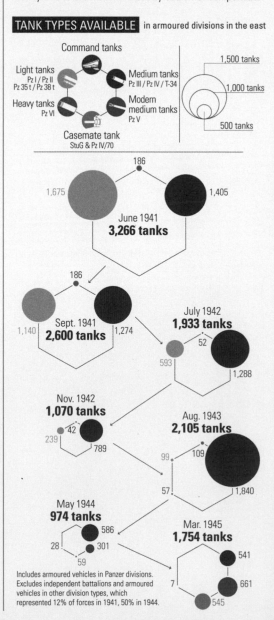

Command tanks

Light tanks
Pz I / Pz II
Pz 35 t / Pz 38 t

Medium tanks
Pz III / Pz IV / T-34

Heavy tanks
Pz VI

Modern medium tanks
Pz V

Casemate tank
StuG & Pz IV/70

1,500 tanks
1,000 tanks
500 tanks

186
1,675 — 1,405
June 1941
3,266 tanks

186
1,140 — 1,274
Sept. 1941
2,600 tanks

July 1942
1,933 tanks
593 / 52
1,288

Nov. 1942
1,070 tanks
239 / 42
789

Aug. 1943
2,105 tanks
99 / 109
57
1,840

May 1944
974 tanks
28 / 586
301
59

Mar. 1945
1,754 tanks
7 / 541
661
545

Includes armoured vehicles in Panzer divisions. Excludes independent battalions and armoured vehicles in other division types, which represented 12% of forces in 1941, 50% in 1944.

and decisive victories by encircling vast areas. The rest of the army cleaned up the mess. But these valuable vehicles were not robust. Serious maintenance issues and versatility that led to misuse caused them to come to grief on the Russian steppes. Elsewhere, the Panzer divisions drained the best officers and equipment from the rest of the army, which merely delayed their inevitable decline. Worn out and facing an enemy that now had solutions (Soviet anti-tank fronts, Allied air superiority), the Panzer began losing its power, becoming a crucial but overstretched firefighter and ending up scattered between outposts of resistance, outflanked by the enemy. A sad ending after it had struck en masse at lightning speed.

In 1939, the other armed forces had no strategy to combat Panzers and no equivalent weapon. Their armoured divisions were simply converted cavalry units or forces attached to the infantry. In Abbeville, three Franco-British armoured divisions were decimated by a weak infantry division. Soon everyone was trying to emulate the Wehrmacht. The genetically inflexible British army only managed to mimic it. The Soviets gave up and explored their own possibilities. Only the Americans had something akin to the Panzer in 1944. Less powerful, it was equally flexible but more mobile and benefited from being integrated into a homogeneous motorized army of the kind that von Seeckt had dreamed of.

Before the battle of Kursk, only half of the theoretical number of tanks remained and in some cases, only a quarter. The advent of Panther tanks did not hide the deteriorating situation. Even the privileged western divisions did not have the materiel needed for a mobile war. By 1945, fewer than thirty Panzers were operational.

3 • A STRONG AND BALANCED STRUCTURE

As well as being armoured, a Panzer division was a complex inter-unit structure with infantry and artillery as vital components. It was homogeneous and fully mechanized, able to recombine its battalions constantly in combat. Every leader was able to handle the *Kampfgruppen* (inter-unit combat groups) and was trained in *Auftragstaktik*: senior officers defined overall goals, but left it to their subordinates to decide how to achieve them. The Allies, focused on tanks, had trouble emulating this versatility until the Americans set up a triangular structure with three permanent Combat Commands. Without this structure and short on well-trained officers, British battle groups had a tougher time.

HOW MANY TANKS PER DIVISION? on the Eastern front

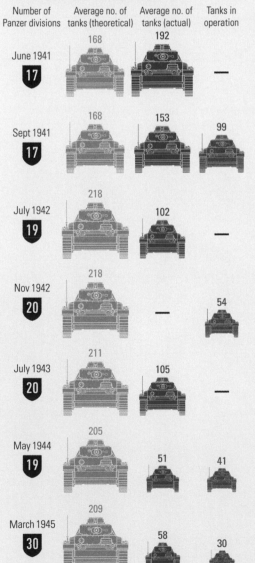

TANKS, INFANTRY AND ARTILLERY: FINDING THE RIGHT BALANCE

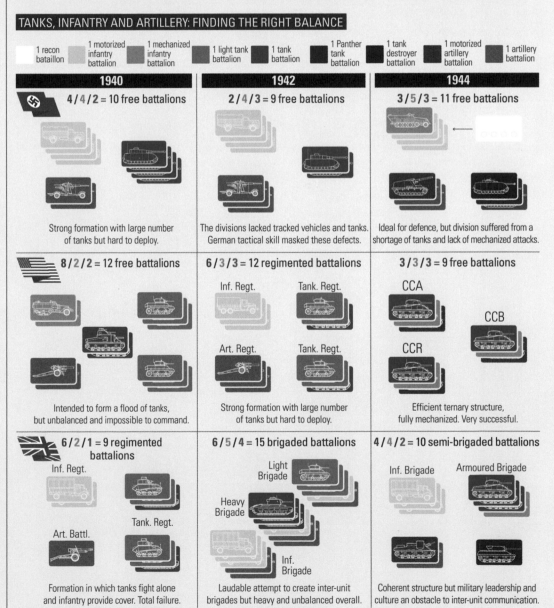

COMPOSITION OF A GERMAN PANZER DIVISION AND A US ARMOURED DIVISION

From 1940 onwards, the synergy of the Panzer divisions was improved. Weaponry was reinforced. An infantry battalion fought alongside tanks on half-tracks (*Schützenpanzerwagen* or SPW), while a third of the artillery was self-propelled, making it more reactive. Recon and engineer battalions were better equipped with combat vehicles and became formidable. The division was unequalled as a holding force. However, resources were not available for full mechanization and the shortage of tanks made itself felt when attacking. Resources allocated rarely matched those promised. This did not apply to the US Armored Division, which was more homogeneous but less versatile since it was designed for offensives.

×2 — Panzer battalion 98 tanks

×1 — mechanized infantry bn. 90 SPW

×3 — motorized infantry bn. 58 trucks

×1 — mechanized artillery bn. 12 × 105 mm guns & 6 × 150 mm

×2 — motorized artillery bn. 18 × 105 mm guns

×1 — recon battalion 124 armoured cars

×1 — logistics battalion 840 tonnes of equipment

×3 — anti-tank company 15 tanks/Marders

×3 — anti-air company 8 × 88 mm guns or 12 × 20 mm

×3 — engineer company 11 SPWs

×3 — signals company 6 SPWs + 22 trucks

×3 — medical company 18 trucks

16 385 troops / 207 tanks / 45 tank destroyers / 407 armoured cars & SPW / 2,943 vehicles / 36 field guns

10,610 troops / 293 tanks / 36 tank destroyers / 523 armoured cars & half-tracks / 1,028 vehicles / 54 heavy guns

×3 — tank battalions 76 tanks

×3 — mechanized infantry bn. 78 half-tracks

×3 — mechanized artillery bn. 18 × 105 mm guns

×1 — logistics battalion 480 tonnes of equipment

×3 — attached anti-tank company 12 M10 tank destroyers

×3 — attached anti-air company 12 × 40 mm + 12 × 4 × 12.7 mm

×3 — recon company 17 armoured cars

×3 — engineer company 5 half-tracks + 22 trucks

×3 — signals company 19 half-tracks + 43 trucks

×3 — medical company 48 trucks

KG 2

KG 1

KG 3

MOVEMENT 2

Engagement by an Armoured Division
(Evreux sector, August 1944)

The division had three Combat Commands (general staff with forces that varied according to mission). Each CC was broken down into Task Forces, also inter-unit. **1.** The CCB provided fire support, while **2.** the CCA surrounded the target. The target attained, **3.** the CCA became a barricade to break the inevitable counter-attack, aided by **4.** the CCR attacked its flanks. **5.** The CCB then took point on the next target.

RADIO CONTACT AT ALL TIMES

The radio communications system covered the whole division and allowed it to maintain cohesion when spread over a large area. It required hundreds of sets, ranging from the most basic, allowing tanks to communicate with each other, to very powerful, with a range of over 50 km for contact with army command. The Germans had a ground-air link allowing support in 45 minutes by 1940. The Allies could not match this until July 1944. Radio also enabled the US to assist their middle-rank officers on the front line, who were less autonomous than their German counterparts.

Infantry Division

CCB

Armoured Division

CCA

CORPS

CCR

Infantry Division

SOURCES: 1. Thomas L. Jentz, *Panzertruppen: The Complete Guide to the Creation & Combat Employment of Germany's Tank Force, 1939–1945*, 2 vols., Atglen. PA, 1996 • 2. Roman Jarymowycz, *Tank Tactics: From Normandy to Lorraine*, Boulder, CO, 2001 • 3. Yves J. Bellanger, *US Army Armored Division 1943–1945, Organization, Doctrine, Equipment*, Lulu.com, 2010 • 4. Pier Paolo Battistelli, *Panzer Divisions*, 3 vols.,

SUPERIOR POWER

● German infantry battalion ● *Panzergrenadier* battalion ● US infantry battalion ● US mechanized infantry battalion

The formidable firepower of an armoured division was not due solely to its tanks. It was better resourced than an infantry division at all levels.

Soldiers and officers: **708 men** / 928 men / 871 men / **1,037 men**

Rifles + submachine guns + automatic rifles: **477 + 127 + 0** / 552 + 208 + 0 / 763 + 0 + 27 / **872 + 126 + 0**

Machine guns: **55** / 150 / 20 / **103**

Armoured combat vehicles: **0** / 97 / 0 / **81**

Trucks: **8** / 60 / 69 / **48**

Mortars: **10** / 6 / 15 / **10**

Field guns: **0** / 14 × 75 mm / 0 / **3 × 75 mm**

Pak: **0** / 9 × 37 mm + 3 × 75 mm / 3 × 57 mm / **9 × 57 mm**

Flak guns: **0** / 0 / 0 / **0**

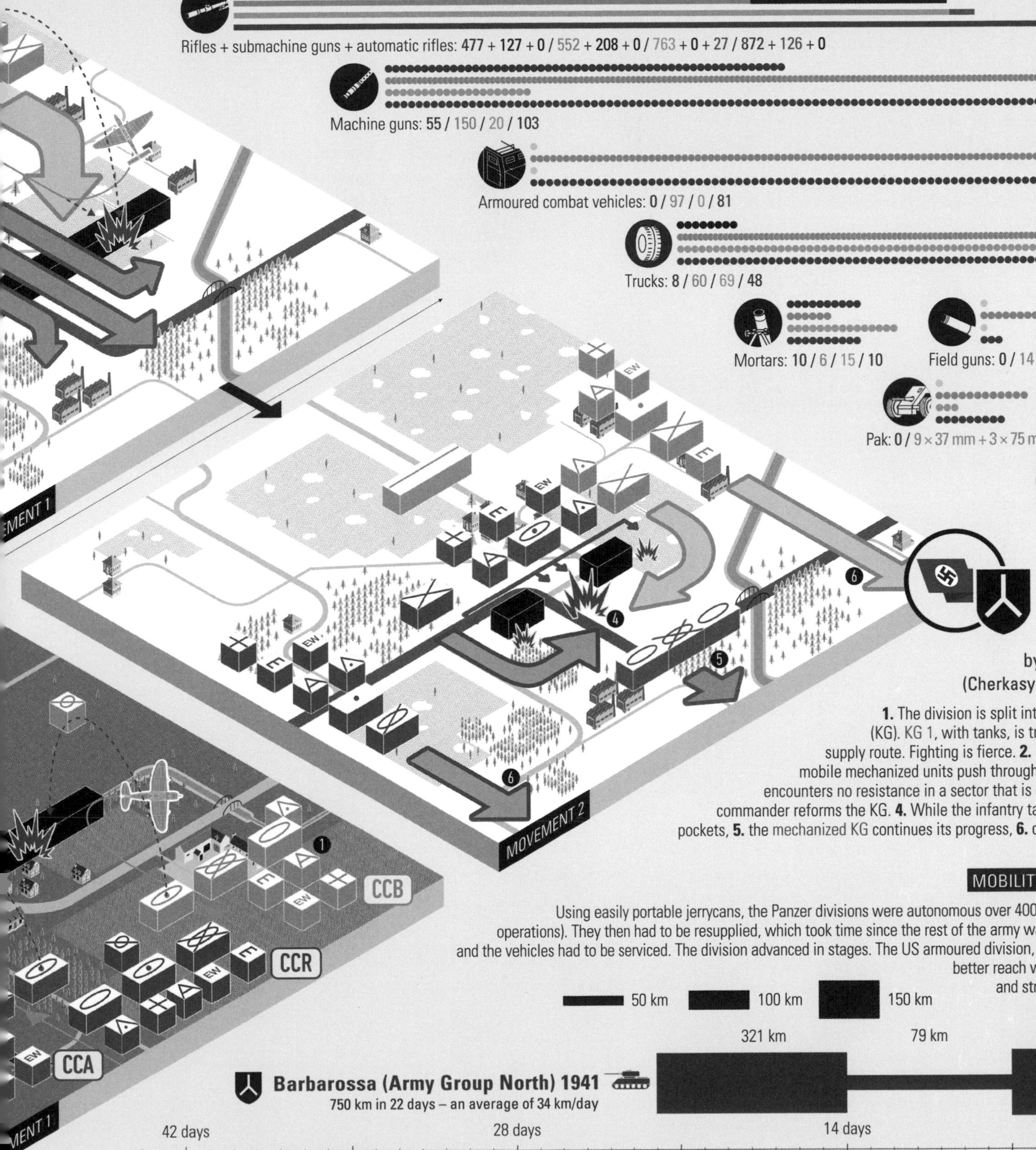

Engagement by a Panzer division (Cherkasy sector, early 1944):

1. The division is split into three *Kampfgruppen* (KG). KG 1, with tanks, is trying to open up a vital supply route. Fighting is fierce. **2.** KG 2 assists KG 1. The mobile mechanized units push through. **3.** To the south, KG 3 encounters no resistance in a sector that is difficult to access. The commander reforms the KG. **4.** While the infantry takes out any remaining pockets, **5.** the mechanized KG continues its progress, **6.** covered by light forces.

MOVEMENT 1

MOVEMENT 2

CCB

CCR

CCA

MOBILITY AND AUTONOMY

Using easily portable jerrycans, the Panzer divisions were autonomous over 400 km (approx. 10 days of operations). They then had to be resupplied, which took time since the rest of the army was some distance away and the vehicles had to be serviced. The division advanced in stages. The US armoured division, although slower, had a better reach with more reliable tanks and stronger theatre logistics.

— 50 km   — 100 km   — 150 km

Barbarossa (Army Group North) 1941
750 km in 22 days – an average of 34 km/day

321 km   79 km   350 km

42 days   28 days   14 days

35 days   21 days   7 days

Pursuit 1944
884 km in 40 days – an average of 22.1 km/day

190 km   181 km   126 km   138 km   180 km   69 km

Oxford, 2007–2009 • 5. James S. Corum, *The Roots of Blitzkrieg: Hans von Seeckt and German Military Reform*, Lawrence, KS, 1992 • 6. Matthias Strohn, *The German Army and the Defence of the Reich: Military Doctrine and the Conduct of the Defensive Battle, 1918–1939*, Cambridge, 2011 • 7. John Buckley, *British Armour in the Normandy Campaign, 1944*, London, 2004.

AN ALTERNATIVE APPROACH: THE SOVIET TANK ARMY

In 1941, the Red Army included huge mechanized corps, theoretically made up of 1,000 tanks. These lumbering juggernauts, which could scarcely move and fight, were swept away in a few weeks in Operation Barbarossa. Aware of the shortage of competent officers and efficient signals, General Zhukov had these early mechanized corps abolished in July and replaced them with 250-tank armoured divisions. These were still too heavy and in the autumn they were replaced by small brigades of 60 tanks. To combat the Panzer corps, in April 1942 the Soviets formed armoured corps of 200 tanks, then, from May, began to utilize a broader formation, the tank army. Five tank armies were quickly set up, all with different structures. Based on shaky compromises, they incorporated one or two infantry divisions and some of the logistics were horse-drawn. They were crushed when the Germans marched on the Volga.

On 26 January 1943, the Stavka ordered the creation of five new tank armies, this time fully motorized with a uniform structure. With a strength on paper of 46,000 men, they were made up of about 650 tanks divided between an armoured corps and a motorized corps, a motorcycle regiment, anti-tank defences, field artillery, rocket launchers, signals, liaison aircraft and a battalion of engineers. Services were doubled and motorized (one transport regiment, two maintenance battalions, two recovery, fuel and lubricant companies). In the field, the resources provided for these forces varied widely, depending on availability. Their composition was also gradually altered in an ongoing process of improvement. On 10 April 1943, artillery resources were increased to two anti-tank regiments (40 guns), two heavy mortar regiments (72 x 120 mm guns), two self-propelled gun regiments (42 guns) and two anti-aircraft defence regiments, which would become a complete division.

In 1944, the engineers' battalion became a powerful brigade. At the time, the order of battle was made up of six tank armies. These were involved in all the offensives following the Kursk Offensive in July 1943 and they led the Red Army to Berlin, Prague and Vienna. Although powerful and, from 1944 onwards, able to survive a 300- to 400-km advance using the 'deep operations' doctrine, they lacked mechanized infantry and their logistics were always precarious, so they would never be as flexible or versatile as the Panzer corps or the US armoured divisions. However, at the cost of terrible losses, they fulfilled their mission to penetrate deep into the enemy's lines and withstand its always dangerous counter-attacks, thus opening up the way for the 60 combined armies that made up the bulk of the Red Army.

SOURCES: 1. Charles C. Sharp, *Red Storm: Soviet Mechanized Corps and Guards Armored Units 1942 to 1945*, West Chester, OH, 1995 • 2. Igor Nebolsin, *Stalin's Favorite*, vols.1 & 2, Warwick, 2019 • 3. I. G. Drogozov, *Tankovyi Mech Strany Sovetov*, Moscow, 2003.

OVERVIEW: THE 2ND GUARDS TANK ARMY

■ Units within the armoured or mechanized corps
■ Army units
▬ 1 battalion (bn)
▬ 1 regiment / brigade (regt / bde)
■ 1 division (div.)

2 armoured corps

6 armoured bde
2 motorized inf. bde
1 infantry div.
1 armoured bde
2 heavy tank regt
2 anti-tank regt
1 rocket-launcher regt
1 signals regt
1 motorcycle bn
2 transport bn
1 pioneer bn
1 cavalry column

1 Feb 1943

30,000
408
1,311
24
113
73

Soldiers   Tanks   Tank destroyers   Armoured recon vehicles

Trucks   Katyushas   Anti-tank guns   Field guns   120 mm heavy mortars

CONSTANT IMPROVISATION, 1945

1st Guards Tank Army:

Armoured corps

Mechanized corps

2nd Guards Tank Army:

1 • THE EVOLUTION OF THE TANK ARMY

In 1942, the tank armies were formed primarily to counter breakthroughs by the Panzer corps. However, a lack of rifles and self-propelled artillery made it necessary to include a non-motorized infantry division, which slowed down the whole army. Tactically, too, Soviet commanders were no match for the enemy. After Stalingrad, which was won by the armoured corps and not the tank armies, the Soviet high command thought it was time to introduce the 'deep battle' doctrine devised by Triandafillov in 1929.

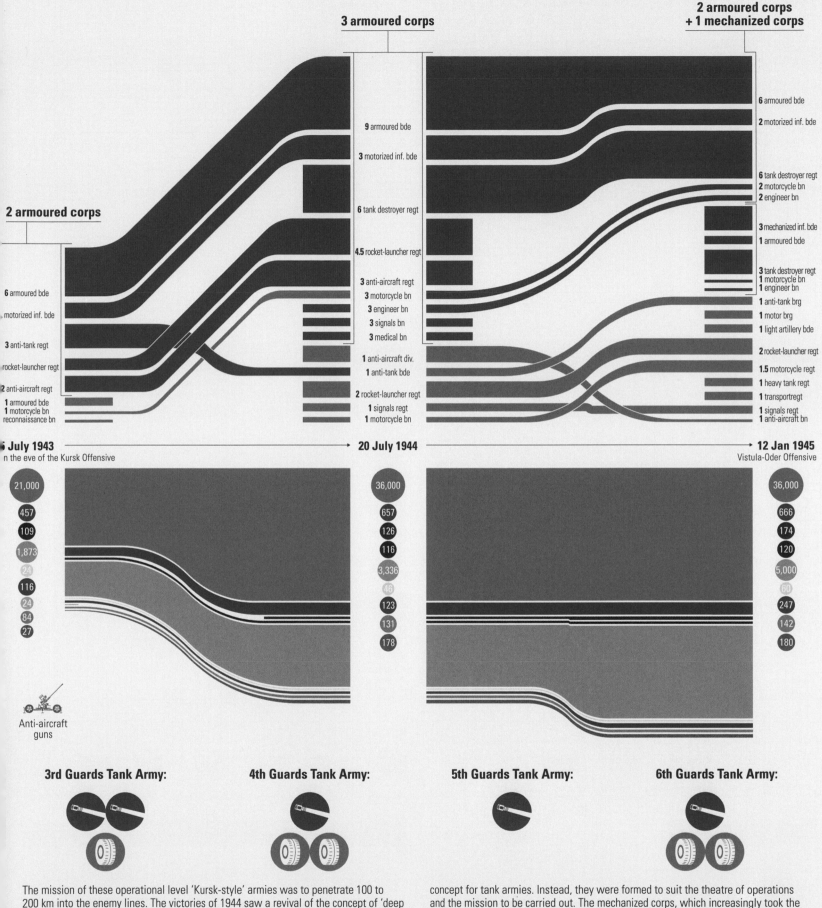

3 armoured corps

**2 armoured corps
+ 1 mechanized corps**

2 armoured corps

9 armoured bde

3 motorized inf. bde

6 tank destroyer regt

4.5 rocket-launcher regt

3 anti-aircraft regt

3 motorcycle bn

3 engineer bn

3 signals bn

3 medical bn

1 anti-aircraft div.

1 anti-tank bde

2 rocket-launcher regt

1 signals regt

1 motorcycle bn

6 armoured bde

motorized inf. bde

3 anti-tank regt

rocket-launcher regt

2 anti-aircraft regt

1 armoured bde
1 motorcycle bn
reconnaissance bn

6 armoured bde

2 motorized inf. bde

6 tank destroyer regt
2 motorcycle bn
2 engineer bn

3 mechanized inf. bde

1 armoured bde

3 tank destroyer regt
1 motorcycle bn
1 engineer bn

1 anti-tank brg

1 motor brg

1 light artillery bde

2 rocket-launcher regt

1.5 motorcycle regt

1 heavy tank regt

1 transportregt

1 signals regt
1 anti-aircraft bn

July 1943
n the eve of the Kursk Offensive

20 July 1944

12 Jan 1945
Vistula-Oder Offensive

21,000

457

109

1,873

24

116

24

84

27

36,000

657

126

116

3,336

46

123

131

178

36,000

666

174

120

5,000

60

247

142

180

Anti-aircraft
guns

3rd Guards Tank Army:

4th Guards Tank Army:

5th Guards Tank Army:

6th Guards Tank Army:

The mission of these operational level 'Kursk-style' armies was to penetrate 100 to 200 km into the enemy lines. The victories of 1944 saw a revival of the concept of 'deep operations' favoured by Tukhachevsky, which came to shape operations and strategy. The tank army, which could travel 400 to 500 kilometres, was increased by 50%. The final change added anti-tank guns, engineers and trucks to the formations, which no longer had to fear attack by a Panzer corps.

The Vistula-Oder Offensive of January 1945 is the best illustration of this strategy. As shown overleaf, on 8 May 1945, the Soviets had still not established a uniform

concept for tank armies. Instead, they were formed to suit the theatre of operations and the mission to be carried out. The mechanized corps, which increasingly took the place of the armoured corps, were not worthy of the name. They contained more tanks than the armoured corps and had no half-tracks to protect the forces on the battlefield. Eight to fifteen men were perched on each tank with no protection, so losses were heavy. It was not until the 1950s that the Soviet army managed to progress from a motorized corps to a mechanized corps, mainly thanks to the revolutionary design of the BMP-1 infantry vehicle.

2 • THE 2ND GUARDS TANK ARMY IN OPERATION: JANUARY 1945

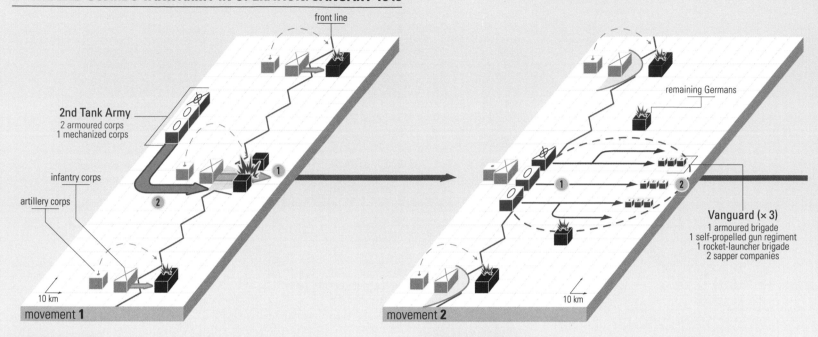

front line

2nd Tank Army
2 armoured corps
1 mechanized corps

infantry corps

artillery corps

10 km

movement **1**

remaining Germans

Vanguard (× 3)
1 armoured brigade
1 self-propelled gun regiment
1 rocket-launcher brigade
2 sapper companies

10 km

movement **2**

1. POSITIONING

Unlike Panzer divisions, the Soviet tank armies did not create breaches in the enemy defences. That was the task of the infantry armies, supported by artillery corps and a number of tanks and self-propelled gun brigades and regiments. (1) As soon as the German defence zone was penetrated to a depth of 8 to 15 km and a width of 15 to 30 km, sometimes less, (2) the tank army took up its departure positions, located in advance. Each corps was assigned a general direction and daily advance 'rules' and had to ensure that it remained in constant contact with its neighbours.

2. RAPID ADVANCE

The three corps lined up in parallel, occupying a front around 40 km long (1). Each corps sent an advance detachment (2) consisting of an armoured brigade, a self-propelled gun regiment, a rocket-launcher brigade and two companies of sappers. These were to take control of routes following the breakthrough. The army stretched out over 100 km of roads and the advance front widened to 100 km. Attack aircraft could be called in via the US-supplied radio vehicle if necessary.

3 • BRIGADES AS BASIC BUILDING BLOCKS structures in November 1943

Except in the Far East, the Soviets soon gave up the armoured division. The basic component of the corps was the armoured brigade, although hundreds of regiments of half the size remained in the form of infantry protection units (T-34 and SU-76) or shock units (KV then JS-2 heavy tanks). One brigade had no chance of facing a Panzer division on its own. It was only viable when combined with others in the corps and when it could call on specialized anti-tank units or a mechanized brigade, forming a 'front' that combined mines, guns and rocket-launchers with precision and saturation firing. Requiring few supply services, the brigades were easily expendable and replaceable.

A SOVIET ARMOURED BRIGADE

T-34 tank battalion

motorized infantry battalion
(4 anti-tank guns + 6 × 82 mm mortars)

anti-aircraft section

anti-aircraft company

anti-tank company

transport company

medical section

1,354

65 T-34 tanks

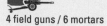 4 field guns / 6 mortars

 18 anti-tank guns

 120

A SOVIET MECHANIZED BRIGADE

motorized infantry battalion

artillery battalion

mortar battalion

anti-aircraft company

reconnaissance company

anti-tank company

sappers & miners company

machine gun company

transport company

medical section

3,500

0 tanks

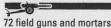 72 field guns and mortars

 54 anti-tank guns

 400

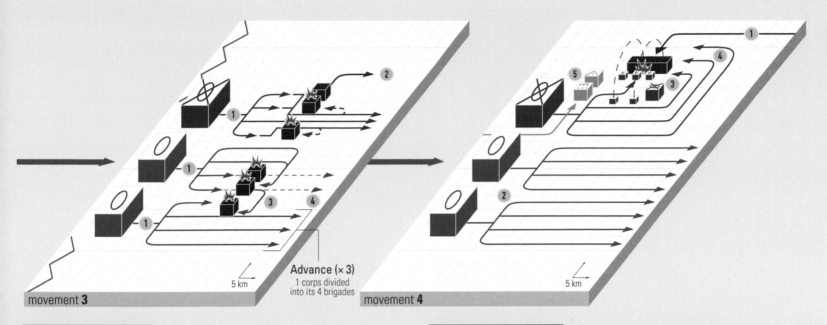

Advance (× 3)
1 corps divided
into its 4 brigades

5 km

movement **3**

5 km

movement **4**

3. ATTACK DEPLOYMENT

The aim was to penetrate an established line of defence. Each corps divided its four brigades into 'prongs' (1). Those that found a weak point cut into the enemy rear (2), forcing them to flee or fight back. Frontal attacks were gradually abandoned in favour of minimal 'German-style' manoeuvres. Towns were taken by swift surprise attacks (3), or bypassed if there was strong resistance. Then the corps regrouped and the advance continued (4).

4. DEFENCE DEPLOYMENT

(1) A Panzer division attacked the army flank. (2) The two corps not involved continued on their way. (3) The corps that had been attacked slowed down, positioning a motorized infantry brigade, its three assault gun regiments and all its rocket-launchers outwards, facing the enemy; (4) its other three brigades continued, then started turning. (5) The army also dispatched the motorized engineers brigade and the anti-tank artillery brigade. A total of 200 anti-tank artillery tubes and thousands of mines blocked the Panzer division's attack front.

4 • THE ROLE OF TANK ARMIES AND THEIR CASUALTY RATE

Although a crucial exploitation tool, tank armies made up only a small part of the Red Army, which was still dominated by heavy horse-drawn infantry. Unlike the Germans, who placed all their tanks in divisions, the tank armies never grouped together more than half the tanks available. The rest would go to the infantry armies in the form of independent corps, brigades and regiments that could fulfil multiple roles: infantry protection, penetration, short-distance exploitation. Losses remained high up right up to the end of the war. Between 1943 and 1945, 310,487 tank crew members were killed, most of them in combat. Of 131,000 tanks manufactured during the war, 96,500 were destroyed in battle. In 1941, the Soviets sacrificed 15 tanks for each German tank, but by 1944 the ratio was 4 to 1.

TANK ARMIES WITHIN THE RED ARMY in 1944

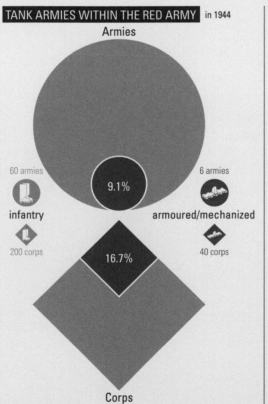

Armies

9.1%

60 armies
infantry

6 armies
armoured/mechanized

200 corps

16.7%

40 corps

Corps

SOVIET ARMOURED FORCES ON 8 MAY 1945

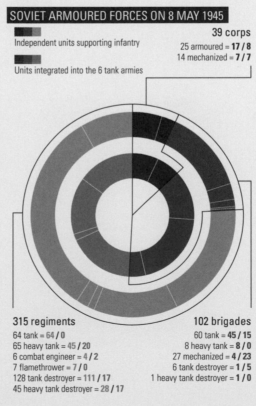

Independent units supporting infantry

Units integrated into the 6 tank armies

39 corps
25 armoured = **17 / 8**
14 mechanized = **7 / 7**

315 regiments
64 tank = **64 / 0**
65 heavy tank = **45 / 20**
6 combat engineer = **4 / 2**
7 flamethrower = **7 / 0**
128 tank destroyer = **111 / 17**
45 heavy tank destroyer = **28 / 17**

102 brigades
60 tank = **45 / 15**
8 heavy tank = **8 / 0**
27 mechanized = **4 / 23**
6 tank destroyer = **1 / 5**
1 heavy tank destroyer = **1 / 0**

SURVIVAL RATES IN THE 2ND TANK ARMY

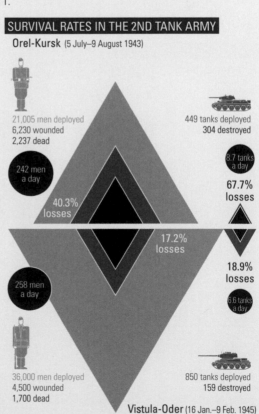

Orel-Kursk (5 July–9 August 1943)

21,005 men deployed
6,230 wounded
2,237 dead

242 men
a day

40.3%
losses

449 tanks deployed
304 destroyed

8.7 tanks
a day

67.7%
losses

17.2%
losses

258 men
a day

18.9%
losses

6.6 tanks
a day

36,000 men deployed
4,500 wounded
1,700 dead

850 tanks deployed
159 destroyed

Vistula-Oder (16 Jan.–9 Feb. 1945)

TANKS AND ANTI-TANK WEAPONRY

When tanks first appeared in the middle of the First World War, they were heavy, slow and unreliable. At the time, they were an attempted Allied response to the impasse of trench warfare and the inability of the infantry to pass unprotected through the wall of machine-gun fire with artillery support. Tanks played a key role in the 1918 offensives but quickly led to defensive counter-measures (obstacles, mines, use of direct fire artillery), which in turn called for greater protection. The small turreted French Renault FT, light and easy to manoeuvre for its time, was a real innovation and a model for all inter-war armoured vehicles. Although obsolete,

it was still in use in many countries, including France, in 1939. It was not until the 1920s in Soviet Russia and then the 1930s in other European countries that the concept of tank-on-tank warfare evolved, reaching its height in the Second World War in Europe.

At the start of the war, tanks came in vastly different models designed for very different functions and not all were capable of confronting their opposite numbers. They were often split into infantry tanks (heavy and slow, designed for support) and cavalry tanks (less protected but faster, designed for reconnaissance, exploitation and tank-on-tank combat). Light tanks weighed

1 • TANKS

The chief traits of WW2 tanks were protection (armour thickness and design), mobility (all-terrain tracked undercarriage, engine power, ground clearance), and an armed turret that could turn 360 degrees (calibre of main gun and shells). Except in the Red Army to 'scare' the enemy, firing while in motion was not common, since without a

gun stabilizer, it was not very accurate. Other key parameters were organization and tactical coordination (radio communication was rare in 1940, except in the Wehrmacht), composition and training of the crew (two or three men at the start of the war, four or five later) and inter-service environment (air cover, infantry support).

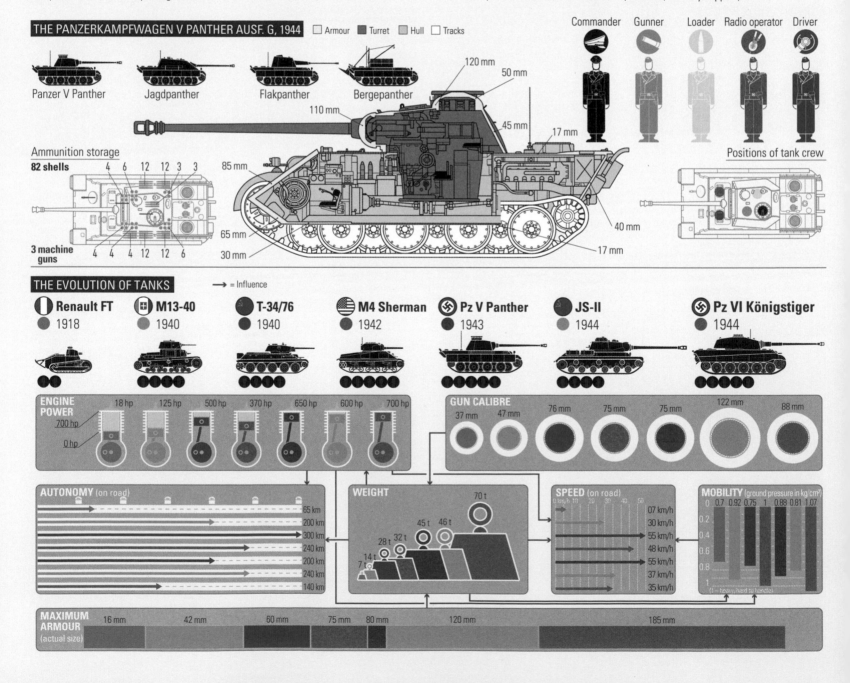

just over 10 tonnes, while heavy tanks could be 20 and in rare cases 30 tonnes (e.g. the French B1), with armour between 15 and 40 mm and often simple weapons (e.g. basic machine guns for the German Panzer, a 20 mm gun for the French R35). Within a few years, however, the evolution of tactics and progress in the fields of motorization (diesel), protection and armour (laminated, welded, moulded or add-on) resulted in increasingly powerful tanks (up to 60 or 70 tonnes, with high-speed guns, 75 mm or over), such as the Soviet T-34 and KV in 1941 and the German Tiger and Panther in 1942–43, designed for direct combat with other tanks.

Engines were generally diesel, except in the Wehrmacht, which opted for petrol as it was simpler and cheaper. By 1945, tank designs had gradually come closer to the modern concept of the main battle tank, a balanced vehicle suited to a variety of roles, mobile, heavily armoured and powerful, part of a complex inter-unit environment. Examples included the US Pershing tank, which prefigured the Patton tank family, the Soviet T34/85, predecessor to the T-54/55 family, the British Centurion and the German Panther.

2 • ANTI-TANK WARFARE

Whether carried (anti-tank rifles, later followed by hollow-charge rocket launchers), self-propelled, or mounted on a motorized vehicle, anti-tank weapons were linked closely to the evolution of tanks themselves. Logically, many of the best anti-tank guns in the war were based on anti-aircraft guns (German 88 mm, US 90 mm) designed for high-altitude firing. Their destructive power depended on:
• their calibre (20–50 mm early in the war; 75–90 mm later; up to 128–152 mm in 1945);
• the calibre length of the tube (L/21, L/43, L/70, etc), which determined the initial speed of the shells (up to 1,000 metres/second or more), with enough kinetic energy to penetrate armour (not applicable for hollow charges);

• the type of anti-tank shell (full AP shell, high-explosive AP-HE, AP capped shell, composite rigid shell with reinforced tungsten point, etc.), each with its own characteristics. The standard explosive shells (HE) that were formidable against infantry and light vehicles were generally ineffective against tanks, apart from the blast effect in the case of bigger calibres.

From 1943 onwards, hollow charges gradually revolutionized the battlefield by giving the infantry, whose anti-tank rifles had become useless by the start of the war, a portable weapon (bazooka, *Panzerschreck*, *Panzerfaust*) that was capable of penetrating the thickest tank armour, albeit only at short or very short range.

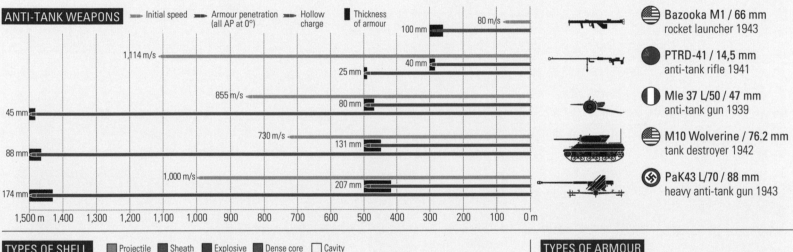

ANTI-TANK WEAPONS — Initial speed — Armour penetration (all AP at 0°) — Hollow charge — Thickness of armour

Bazooka M1 / 66 mm rocket launcher 1943
PTRD-41 / 14,5 mm anti-tank rifle 1941
Mle 37 L/50 / 47 mm anti-tank gun 1939
M10 Wolverine / 76.2 mm tank destroyer 1942
PaK43 L/70 / 88 mm heavy anti-tank gun 1943

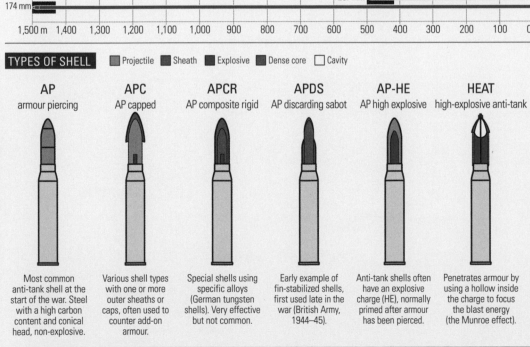

TYPES OF SHELL

■ Projectile ■ Sheath ■ Explosive ■ Dense core □ Cavity

AP armour piercing
Most common anti-tank shell at the start of the war. Steel with a high carbon content and conical head, non-explosive.

APC AP capped
Various shell types with one or more outer sheaths or caps, often used to counter add-on armour.

APCR AP composite rigid
Special shells using specific alloys (German tungsten shells). Very effective but not common.

APDS AP discarding sabot
Early example of fin-stabilized shells, first used late in the war (British Army, 1944–45).

AP-HE AP high explosive
Anti-tank shells often have an explosive charge (HE), normally primed after armour has been pierced.

HEAT high-explosive anti-tank
Penetrates armour by using a hollow inside the charge to focus the blast energy (the Munroe effect).

TYPES OF ARMOUR

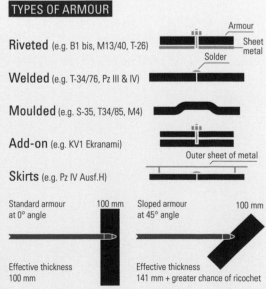

Riveted (e.g. B1 bis, M13/40, T-26)
Welded (e.g. T-34/76, Pz III & IV)
Moulded (e.g. S-35, T34/85, M4)
Add-on (e.g. KV1 Ekranami)
Skirts (e.g. Pz IV Ausf.H)

Standard armour at 0° angle — 100 mm
Effective thickness 100 mm

Sloped armour at 45° angle — 100 mm
Effective thickness 141 mm + greater chance of ricochet

SOURCES: 1. Thomas L. Jentz & Hilary L. Doyle, *Germany's Panzers in World War II: From Pz.Kpfw.I to Tiger II*, Atglen. PA, 2004 • 2. Jean Restayn, *Allied Tank Encyclopedia*, Paris, 2008 • 3. J. Salt, *WW2 Penetration Figures*, 1998 (annotated archive compilation) • 4. Laurent Tirone, *Panzer: The German Tanks Encyclopedia*, Aix-en-Provence, 2015 • 5. http://www.tanks-encyclopedia.com

THE EVOLUTION AND PERFORMANCE OF FIGHTER PLANES

Fighter and bomber planes were developed in the First World War from the nucleus of the flimsy unarmed observation aircraft of 1914. They evolved rapidly up to 1918 and continued to develop in the inter-war years, a period of intense research into the potential of the air force. Some theorists, like the Italian Giulio Douhet, even believed that planes could win the war on their own. On the eve of the Second World War, the technical limits of multiplanes and strut-braced monoplanes had been reached and their high manoeuvrability did not make up for their fragility and lack of speed. Canvas and wood structures were already being replaced by metal, while the low-wing cantilever monoplane with retractable undercarriage became standard, usually single-engined in the case of fighters or fighter-bombers, twin-engined or three-engined in the case of bombers and transport aircraft, and sometimes even four-engined with a very long operating range, like the US B-17 Flying Fortress.

1 • THE SEARCH FOR A VERSATILE COMBAT AIRCRAFT: VARIANTS OF THE JUNKER JU-88

The best aircraft, such as the Bf 109 and the Spitfire, were constantly improved and produced in multiple specialized variants throughout the war. One example of these changes and adaptations to different combat roles was the Junker JU-88 twin-engined plane, designed in the 1930s and in use in 1939 as a 'standard' medium bomber with a dive-bombing capability. Until 1945, a large number of different variants of the aircraft (of which about 15,000 were built) were produced to suit a range of missions; one version was even used as an airborne 'flying bomb' (the Mistel). These developments are representative of the quest for a truly effective and versatile fighter plane, which continued as technology progressed in the decades that followed and is still ongoing today with aircraft such as the Tornado, the F/A-18 and the Rafale.

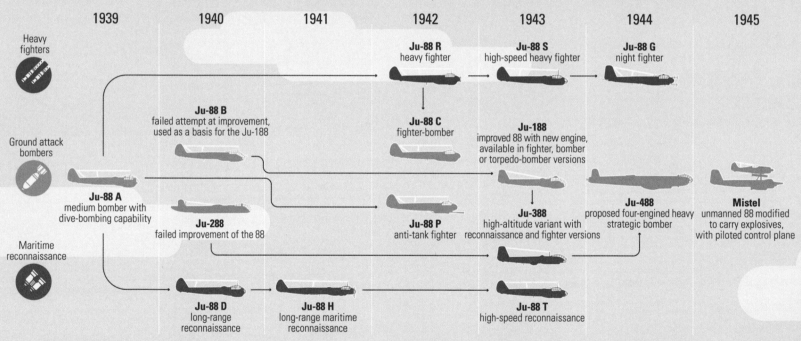

2 • PAYLOAD, OPERATIONAL CEILING AND RANGE OF BOMBERS IN STANDARD CONFIGURATION

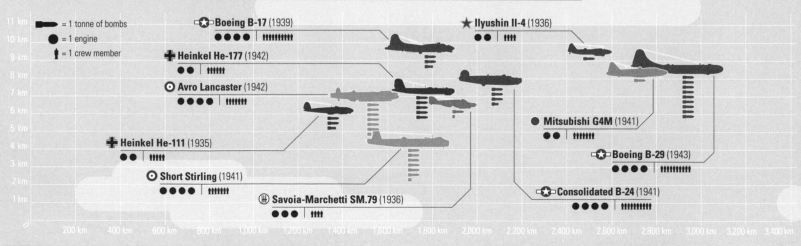

SOURCES: 1. Robin Higham & Stephen Harris (eds.), *Why Air Forces Fail: The Anatomy of Defeat*, Lexington, KT, 2016 • 2. R. Chamagne, *L'Art de la guerre aérienne*, Sceaux, 2006 • 3. W. Craven & J. Cate (eds.), *Men and Planes, AAF in WW2*, vol. VI, Chicago, 1955 • 4. W. Murray, *Strategy for Defeat: Luftwaffe 1933–1945*, Montgomery, AL, 1983 • 5. Richard Overy, *The Air War: 1939–1945*, Lincoln, NE, 2005.

3 • WHEN THE FIGHTER PLANE WAS KING

Many different aircraft were produced in the Second World War to serve a variety of roles, ranging from small observation planes (e.g. Fieseler Storch, Lysander) to enormous multi-engined bombers and transport planes (B-29 Superfortress, Me 23 Gigant) and including an impressive range of bombers, fighter-bombers and attack aircraft (Messerschmitt Bf 10, P-47 Thunderbolt, Il-2 Sturmovik) and specialized aircraft (reconnaissance, torpedo bombers, training, etc.). In the first part of the war, the quest was for the best formula and the optimum combination of fighter planes, attack planes (often dive bombers) and bombers against enemy forces and infrastructure. Although the 'horizontal' bomber carrying one to ten tonnes of bombs was the ideal offensive weapon, its intrinsic vulnerability meant that fighter aircraft were still central to the war in the air, whether in achieving air superiority or as escorts. The Luftwaffe went into the war with a slight theoretical advantage: the Messerschmitt Bf 109 and the Junker JU-87 Stuka (a dive bomber) were flown by pilots with experience in the Condor Legion in Spain. But that advantage, also to some extent enjoyed briefly by Japan with the light Mitsubishi A6M Zero navy plane, originally with superior piloting, was soon

challenged, first of all in 1940 in the Battle of Britain against the RAF's impressive Supermarine Spitfire. The growing power of the Allies led to a performance race in fields including engine design (radial or inline, from less than 1,000 to 1,500 horsepower), extra weaponry (6 to 8 heavy machine guns and/or automatic guns, rockets, etc. instead of 2 to 4), higher operational ceilings (pressurized cockpits, oxygen masks, etc.), and better navigation and detection (including onboard radar and direction finding).

Traditional dogfights, which required close-turning planes, were replaced by elaborate tactics calling for speed, firepower and aircraft that were robust rather than 'aerobatic'. In 1943–44, both sides came up against technological barriers with the German Fw-190 and the North American P-51, particularly as regards speed (from 650 to 700 km/h compared with 400 to 500 km/h in 1939). It was then that the first jet planes began to appear, notably the German Me 262 and the British Gloster Meteor. They promised to revolutionize air tactics but it was too late to change the established balances.

Another form of aircraft was also being developed at the same time. In 1945, its use was still small-scale, even confidential, but it had great potential: the helicopter.

1939–40: The Bf 109 E vs. the MS.406

The MS.406 was typical of the first generation of low-wing fighter planes in the second half of the 1930s. The Bf 109 E was superior in almost every area. In 1940, the only opponents that could match it were the Dewoitine D.520, although there were very few of these in service, and the Spitfire Mk. I over Britain.

1944: The Fw-190D vs. the P-51 D

The tapered wing P-51 D was the best prop fighter plane. Fast and manoeuvrable, it had a large range that could be extended with an external tank and a limited capability for use as a fighter-bomber. The 'long nose' Fw-190, made in several variants including a heavily armed attack bomber (*Sturmbocke*) was developed from German prop fighters. It was one of the finest aircraft of the war, outclassing most of its opponents apart from the P-51.

1945: The Jet Age

A duel that never happened: the Me 262 vs. the Gloster Meteor. The Me 262A, delayed at least a year, was the first operational jet-powered fighter-bomber of the war. It proved to be extremely dangerous because of its exceptional speed. Its British equivalent, the Gloster Meteor F.3, was slightly less high-performance but was very effective in fighting the V1s over England. Although both deployed in combat in 1944–45, the two aircraft never met.

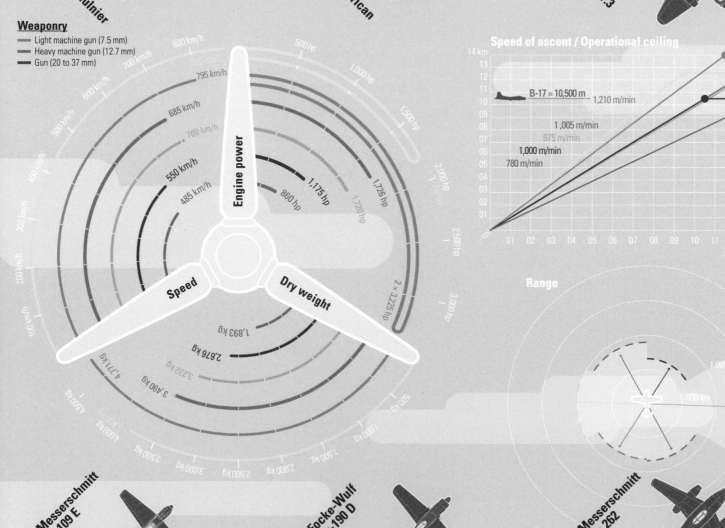

AIRBORNE OPERATIONS: EXPENSIVE AND RISKY

The idea of using a piece of fabric to slow down a fall dates back to antiquity, and the word 'parachute' and the earliest trials at least to the 19th century. Before the First World War, parachuting was pioneered by civilians. Its first military use was in 1918, as backup for French balloon pilots and German pilots who had been shot down, and for Italian 'commando' raids. The prospect of being able to drop thousands of infantrymen on the German rear guard by air appealed to some officers, especially the Americans and French, but it was shelved after the 1918 victory.

It was not until the 1930s, first in the USSR and then in Germany, that the use of parachutes by the military really started to expand. The USSR introduced extensive parachute training with parachute towers and trained thousands of soldiers in the 1930s. The Kiev manoeuvres in 1934 were the first demonstration of large-scale jumps from the wings of TB-3 aircraft (the paras had to exit via a hatch on the roof!) and the first para brigades were soon established. But this initial advantage did not last. At the start of the war, Germany was ahead in this field, setting up highly efficient elite units, especially during the Western campaign, in the Netherlands and Belgium. Other nations developed airborne resources on a more limited scale. It was a costly field, needing highly selective training, special lightweight equipment with limited strength and endurance (light vehicles and guns, sometimes tanks like the British Tetrarch or the 7.5 tonne American Locust) and a sophisticated fleet of aircraft. Only Britain and the USA truly embraced airborne operations, relying on the fact that their aeronautics production and superiority in the air were sufficient for them to risk large joint operations. The Germans and the Soviets no longer took risks of this kind after the heavy German losses in Crete in 1941 and the Soviet casualties in Bukrin in 1943.

1 • AIRBORNE UNITS IN THE WAR

Airborne forces were divided into three main categories:
• paratroopers, jumping from an aircraft to land in a drop zone,
• airborne troops on gliders, landing in a landing zone,
• light troops, specialist or non-specialist, which could simply be transported by air to captured airfields.
In most countries, the troops were organized into large specialist units (divisions), generally within the army, but more rarely the air force (Germany and France) or even the navy (Japan). By 1944–45, both the Germans and the Allies had airborne corps and even an airborne army, but only the Allies could deploy those troops for their intended purpose.

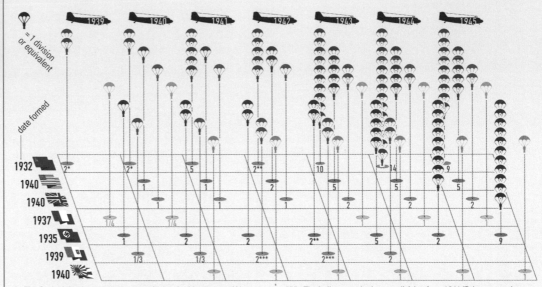

* The Soviet brigades were approx. equivalent in this case to a Western regiment, with the Soviet corps equivalent to a division (10,000 men).
** The German *Fallschirmjäger* divisions and Soviet parachute divisions (1942 on) were an elite infantry with no parachute equipment or training and no squadrons of aircraft for large-scale jumps.
*** The Italian army had a para division from 1941 (Folgore, mostly destroyed in Africa, then Nembo) and an airborne division (La Spezia). Plans for a new division (Ciclone) to invade Malta were aborted.
**** The British and US airborne divisions were based on a joint paratrooper/airborne structure.

2 • DEPLOYMENT OF AIRBORNE FORCES

There was a long path from the concept of vertical envelopment to its tactical implementation. An operational jump that was fast and accurate enough to drop or land troop units and then regroup them on the ground, in spite of navigational and meteorological hazards, was a much more complex undertaking than first imagined. An airborne operation also required a huge fleet of suitable aircraft for the men (10 to 20 per aircraft or glider) and equipment (weapons, ammunition etc.) and often had to make several trips under enemy fire. It was in this manner that the Luftwaffe lost several hundred JU-52s in the Netherlands in 1940, stuck on the ground at captured airfields or destroyed in combat.

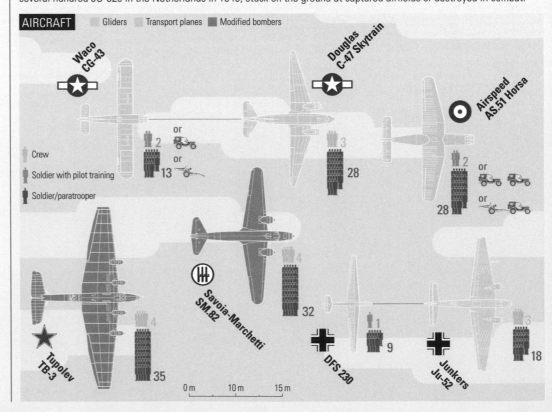

ESTABLISHING A BRIDGEHEAD WITH VERTICAL ENVELOPMENT

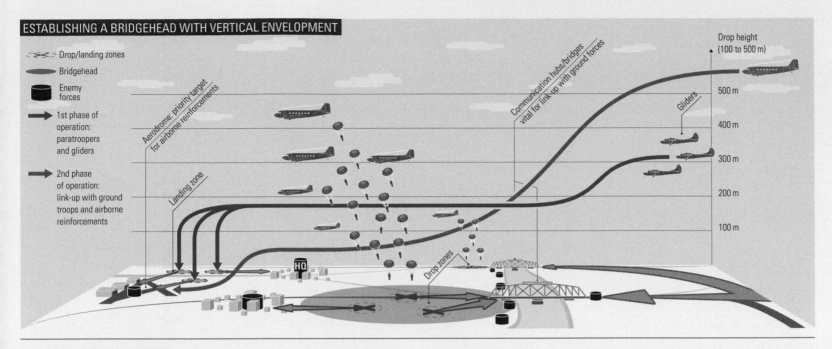

Drop height (100 to 500 m)

- Drop/landing zones
- Bridgehead
- Enemy forces
- 1st phase of operation: paratroopers and gliders
- 2nd phase of operation: link-up with ground troops and airborne reinforcements

Aerodrome: priority target for airborne reinforcements

Communication hubs/bridges vital for link-up with ground forces

Gliders

Landing zone

Drop zones

HQ

500 m
400 m
300 m
200 m
100 m

3 • MAJOR OPERATIONS

Taking place by day or more rarely by night, airborne operations were frequent, but very few of them involved more than several dozen or a few hundred men at most. Large operations involving thousands of airborne troops were mainly carried out by the Germans up to 1941 and by British and US forces between 1943 and 1945. Difficult to implement because they required at least temporary air superiority and a vulnerable fleet of hundreds of aircraft and gliders, these operations were tactically very risky, and could even be suicidal if a link with ground troops could not be quickly established. Even when successful, they always resulted in heavy losses of carefully selected and trained young troops. In fact, with the exception of British and US forces, troops of this kind were mainly utilized as shock infantry in the second half of the war; after 1942, many German *Fallschirmjäger*, for instance, were never even qualified to jump.

LARGE-SCALE AIRBORNE OPERATIONS IN EUROPE

1. Netherlands	**2. Crete**	**3. Vyazma**	**4. Normandy**	**5. Netherlands**	**6. Wesel**
10–14 May 1940	Operation Merkur 20–30 May 1941	Operation Jupiter Jan–Feb 1942	5–6 June 1944	Op. Market Garden 17–25 Sept 1944	Op. Varsity 24 March 1945
7th Flieger Division 22th Luftlande Div.	7th Flieger Division + reinforcements	Soviet 4th Airborne Corps	UK 6th Air. Div. US 82nd & 101st Air. Div.	UK 1st Air. Div./Pol. 1st Paras US 82nd & 101st Air. Div.	UK 6th Air. Div. US 17th Air. Div.
10,000 men 3,000† / 30%	11,000 men 4,500† / 41%	10,000 men = 50%	24,000 men 3,800† / 16%	34,000 men 12,000† / 35%	17,000 men 2,700† / 16%
400 planes 50 gliders	550 planes 70 gliders	500 planes -	1,200 planes 500 gliders	1,500 planes 500 gliders	1,700 planes 1,300 gliders

Successful
Failed to link up with other forces
Failed to capture main target, Arnhem
Night mission: successful
Heavy airborne losses
Successful, but heavy ground losses

AMERICAN PARATROOPERS ON D-DAY

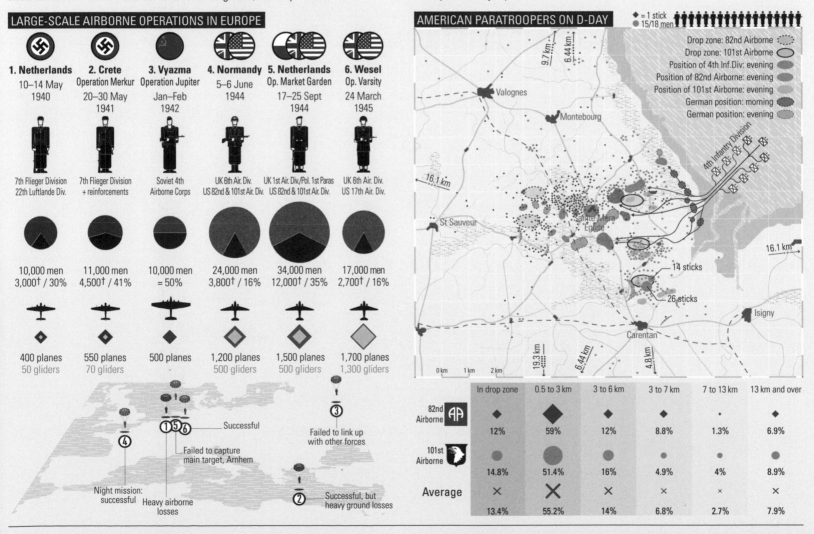

◆ = 1 stick
● 15/18 men

Drop zone: 82nd Airborne
Drop zone: 101st Airborne
Position of 4th Inf.Div: evening
Position of 82nd Airborne: evening
Position of 101st Airborne: evening
German position: morning
German position: evening

Valognes
Montebourg
St Sauveur
4th Infantry Division
Ste Mère Église
14 sticks
26 sticks
Isigny
Carentan

9.7 km 6.44 km 16.1 km 16.1 km 19.3 km 6.44 km 4.8 km

0 km 1 km 2 km

	In drop zone	0.5 to 3 km	3 to 6 km	3 to 7 km	7 to 13 km	13 km and over
82nd Airborne	12%	59%	12%	8.8%	1.3%	6.9%
101st Airborne	14.8%	51.4%	16%	4.9%	4%	8.9%
Average	13.4%	55.2%	14%	6.8%	2.7%	7.9%

SOURCES: 1. Gaston Erlom, *Les parachutistes soviétiques 1930–1945*, Paris, 2017 • 2. James M. Gavin, *Airborne Warfare*, Nashville, TN, 1980 (1947) • 3. G. A. Harrison, *Cross-Channel Attack*, Washington, DC, 2011 • 4. Bruce Quarrie, *German Airborne Troops, 1939–45*, Oxford, 1983 • 5. G. Rottman, *World War II Airborne Warfare Tactics*, Oxford, 2006 • 6. Steven Zaloga, *US Airborne Divisions in the ETO*, Oxford, 2007.

COMBAT FLEETS

Second World War combat fleets were made up of warships of several kinds. They had complementary roles according to their weaponry and armour, ranging from heavy battleships of 20,000 tonnes or more, down to torpedo boats of around 1,000 tonnes, and including many different types of cruisers, destroyers and submarines. The introduction of detection systems such as radar and Asdic (an early form of sonar) was a major technological advance in the war years, as was a rise in the various types of aircraft carriers developed in the inter-war period.

The term 'capital ship' referred to the most valuable ships in the fleet; it primarily applied to battleships but was soon also extended to aircraft carriers, which replaced battleships as key vessels, particularly in the huge theatre of operations in the Pacific.

Note: The tonnages given here are those used in international treaties, i.e. the displacement of the ships does not include war load. For example, the French battleship *Richelieu* displaced 35,000 tonnes but weighed 48,000 tonnes fully loaded.

Combat ship hull classifications

BB/BC: battleship, battle cruiser
CV/CVL/CVE: aircraft carrier (heavy/light/escort)
CVS/AV: seaplane carrier
CA/CL: cruiser (heavy/light)
DD/DE: destroyer, destroyer escort
SS: submarine

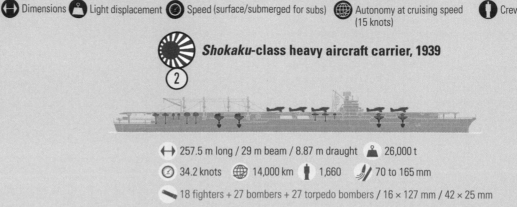

⟷ Dimensions ⬛ Light displacement ⊘ Speed (surface/submerged for subs) 🌐 Autonomy at cruising speed (15 knots) Crew Armour

Shokaku-class heavy aircraft carrier, 1939
2

⟷ 257.5 m long / 29 m beam / 8.87 m draught ⬛ 26,000 t
⊘ 34.2 knots 🌐 14,000 km 1,660 70 to 165 mm
18 fighters + 27 bombers + 27 torpedo bombers / 16 × 127 mm / 42 × 25 mm

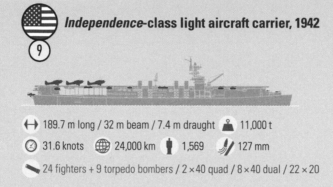

Independence-class light aircraft carrier, 1942
9

⟷ 189.7 m long / 32 m beam / 7.4 m draught ⬛ 11,000 t
⊘ 31.6 knots 🌐 24,000 km 1,569 127 mm
24 fighters + 9 torpedo bombers / 2 × 40 quad / 8 × 40 dual / 22 × 20

Ruler-class escort carrier, 1942
25

⟷ 151 m long / 21.2 m beam / 7.8 m draught ⬛ 15,390 t
⊘ 16.5 knots 🌐 48,700 km 646 0
12 fighters + 12 torpedo bombers / 2 × 127 / 8 × 40 twin
14 × 20 twin / 7 × 20

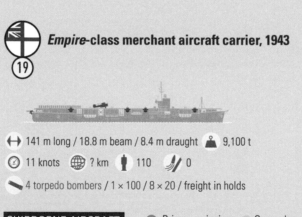

Empire-class merchant aircraft carrier, 1943
19

⟷ 141 m long / 18.8 m beam / 8.4 m draught ⬛ 9,100 t
⊘ 11 knots 🌐 ? km 110 0
4 torpedo bombers / 1 × 100 / 8 × 20 / freight in holds

Cdt Teste seaplane carrier, 1929
1

⟷ 167 m long / 27 m beam / 6.93 m draught ⬛ 10,000 t
⊘ 20.5 knots 🌐 11,112 km 686 30 to 50 mm
26 seaplanes / 12 × 100 / 8 × 37 / 12 × 13.2

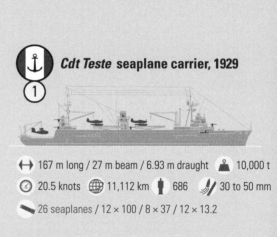

SHIPBORNE AIRCRAFT
● Primary mission ● Secondary mission ⟶ Targets

▨ Combat
◗ Dive bombing
◢ Torpedo bombing
ℍ Reconnaissance
➕ Rescue

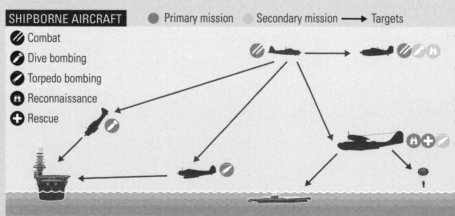

- **Fighter:** attacks other fighters and protects aircraft carrier and its squadron.
- **Torpedo bomber:** attacks other ships, especially heavy ships (aircraft carriers and battleships), may carry bombs instead of torpedoes (e.g. Avenger).
- **Dive bomber:** attacks ships.
- **Light seaplane:** mainly reconnaissance, sometimes attack.
- **Heavy seaplane:** operates from a base but may be supported by a seaplane tender; long-distance reconnaissance, possibly attacks on submarines or supply ships, rescues.

1 • AIRCRAFT CARRIERS: NEW RULERS OF THE WAVES

Introduced at the end of the First World War when it became clear that military aircraft would be playing an increasingly important role, aircraft carriers were for a long time experimental and their tactical importance was controversial. It was the oceanic powers, the United States, Britain and Japan, that first realized their potential, which was closely dependent on the number, type and performance of the aircraft aboard: fighters, dive bombers and torpedo bombers. After demonstrations at Taranto (1940), Pearl Harbor (1941) and Midway (1942), aircraft carriers truly became capital ships, essential to the fleet. The concept of the seaplane carrier, on the other hand, turned out to be a dead end. Aircraft carriers were divided into heavy carriers (20,000 tonnes and over, with 50–100 aircraft), light carriers (around 15,000 tonnes, 30–50 aircraft), and the smaller and slower escort carriers (around 10,000 tonnes, 15–30 aircraft). The latter played an important role, escorting sea convoys, supporting amphibious operations or tracking submarines.

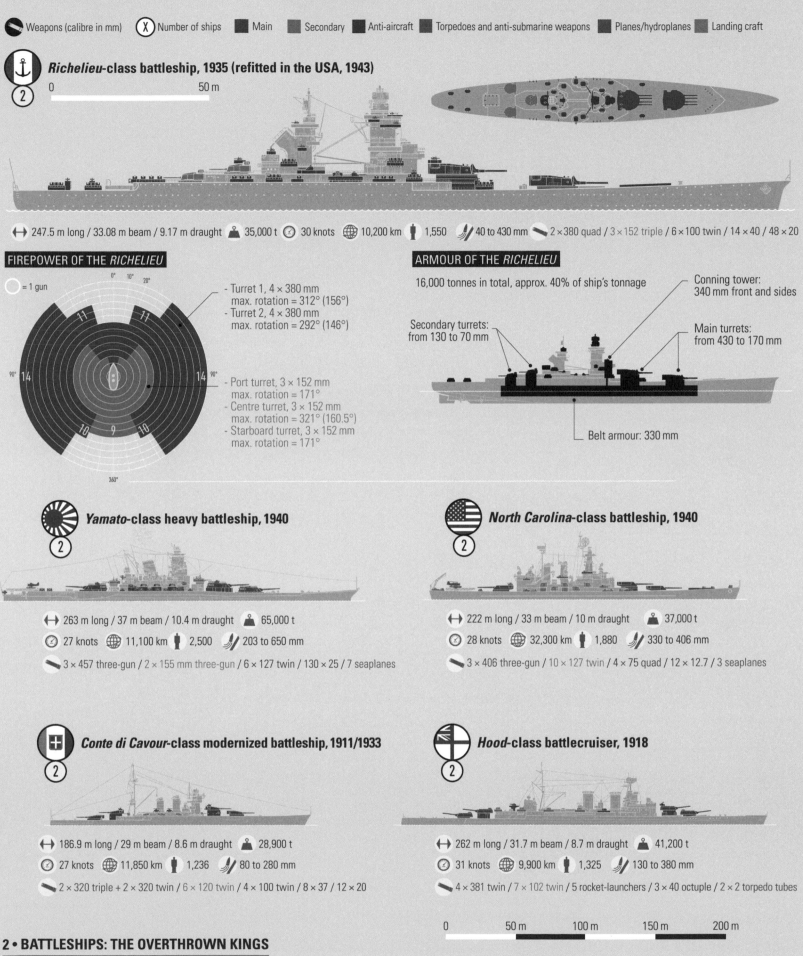

Weapons (calibre in mm) · **(X) Number of ships** · ■ Main · ■ Secondary · ■ Anti-aircraft · ■ Torpedoes and anti-submarine weapons · ■ Planes/hydroplanes · ■ Landing craft

Richelieu-class battleship, 1935 (refitted in the USA, 1943)

(2)

0 — 50 m

↔ 247.5 m long / 33.08 m beam / 9.17 m draught · ⚓ 35,000 t · ⏱ 30 knots · 🌐 10,200 km · 👤 1,550 · ⚔ 40 to 430 mm · 🔫 2 × 380 quad / 3 × 152 triple / 6 × 100 twin / 14 × 40 / 48 × 20

FIREPOWER OF THE *RICHELIEU*

○ = 1 gun

0° 10° 20°
11 · 11
90° 14 · 14 90°
10 · 9 · 10
360°

- Turret 1, 4 × 380 mm
  max. rotation = 312° (156°)
- Turret 2, 4 × 380 mm
  max. rotation = 292° (146°)

- Port turret, 3 × 152 mm
  max. rotation = 171°
- Centre turret, 3 × 152 mm
  max. rotation = 321° (160.5°)
- Starboard turret, 3 × 152 mm
  max. rotation = 171°

ARMOUR OF THE *RICHELIEU*

16,000 tonnes in total, approx. 40% of ship's tonnage

Conning tower:
340 mm front and sides

Secondary turrets:
from 130 to 70 mm

Main turrets:
from 430 to 170 mm

Belt armour: 330 mm

Yamato-class heavy battleship, 1940

(2)

↔ 263 m long / 37 m beam / 10.4 m draught · ⚓ 65,000 t
⏱ 27 knots · 🌐 11,100 km · 👤 2,500 · ⚔ 203 to 650 mm
🔫 3 × 457 three-gun / 2 × 155 mm three-gun / 6 × 127 twin / 130 × 25 / 7 seaplanes

North Carolina-class battleship, 1940

(2)

↔ 222 m long / 33 m beam / 10 m draught · ⚓ 37,000 t
⏱ 28 knots · 🌐 32,300 km · 👤 1,880 · ⚔ 330 to 406 mm
🔫 3 × 406 three-gun / 10 × 127 twin / 4 × 75 quad / 12 × 12.7 / 3 seaplanes

Conte di Cavour-class modernized battleship, 1911/1933

(2)

↔ 186.9 m long / 29 m beam / 8.6 m draught · ⚓ 28,900 t
⏱ 27 knots · 🌐 11,850 km · 👤 1,236 · ⚔ 80 to 280 mm
🔫 2 × 320 triple + 2 × 320 twin / 6 × 120 twin / 4 × 100 twin / 8 × 37 / 12 × 20

Hood-class battlecruiser, 1918

(2)

↔ 262 m long / 31.7 m beam / 8.7 m draught · ⚓ 41,200 t
⏱ 31 knots · 🌐 9,900 km · 👤 1,325 · ⚔ 130 to 380 mm
🔫 4 × 381 twin / 7 × 102 twin / 5 rocket-launchers / 3 × 40 octuple / 2 × 2 torpedo tubes

0 — 50 m — 100 m — 150 m — 200 m

2 • BATTLESHIPS: THE OVERTHROWN KINGS

Battleships were the heaviest and most powerful ships in the fleets, originating from the early ironclads and other frigates of the second half of the 19th century, then developed in the early 20th century into the first modern dreadnoughts. Heavily armoured, with artillery turrets each carrying two to four of the most powerful guns (standard calibre 280 to 381 mm, rising to 406 or even 460 mm), battleships ruled the waves until aircraft with a capability to strike beyond the horizon became more important. They were then reduced to the rank of vulnerable floating artilleries. At first, there were two main types: battleships (heavily armoured but slow) and battle cruisers (less heavily armoured but faster). At the end of the 1930s, another generation appeared: fast super-battleships that were even heavier and more heavily protected. Despite their heavily reinforced shipborne anti-aircraft defences, they too were permanently replaced by aircraft carriers.

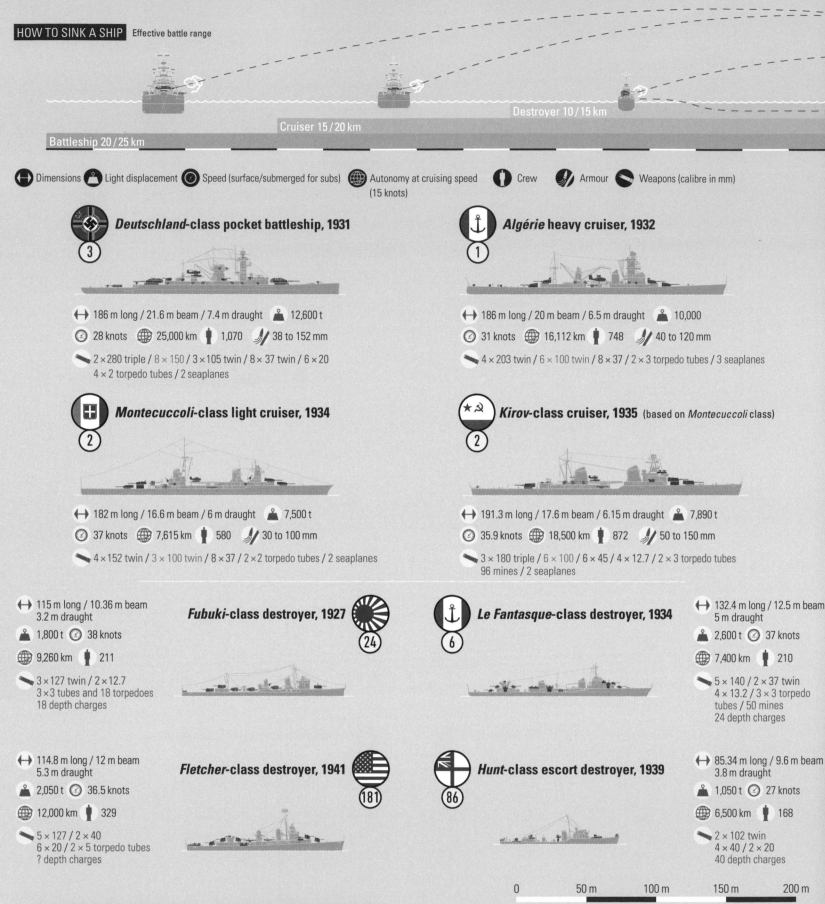

HOW TO SINK A SHIP Effective battle range

Destroyer 10 / 15 km

Cruiser 15 / 20 km

Battleship 20 / 25 km

Dimensions ⊙ Light displacement ⊙ Speed (surface/submerged for subs) ⊙ Autonomy at cruising speed (15 knots) ⊙ Crew ⊙ Armour ⊙ Weapons (calibre in mm)

Deutschland-class pocket battleship, 1931 ③

186 m long / 21.6 m beam / 7.4 m draught | 12,600 t
28 knots | 25,000 km | 1,070 | 38 to 152 mm
2 × 280 triple / 8 × 150 / 3 × 105 twin / 8 × 37 twin / 6 × 20
4 × 2 torpedo tubes / 2 seaplanes

Algérie heavy cruiser, 1932 ①

186 m long / 20 m beam / 6.5 m draught | 10,000
31 knots | 16,112 km | 748 | 40 to 120 mm
4 × 203 twin / 6 × 100 twin / 8 × 37 / 2 × 3 torpedo tubes / 3 seaplanes

Montecuccoli-class light cruiser, 1934 ②

182 m long / 16.6 m beam / 6 m draught | 7,500 t
37 knots | 7,615 km | 580 | 30 to 100 mm
4 × 152 twin / 3 × 100 twin / 8 × 37 / 2 × 2 torpedo tubes / 2 seaplanes

Kirov-class cruiser, 1935 (based on Montecuccoli class) ②

191.3 m long / 17.6 m beam / 6.15 m draught | 7,890 t
35.9 knots | 18,500 km | 872 | 50 to 150 mm
3 × 180 triple / 6 × 100 / 6 × 45 / 4 × 12.7 / 2 × 3 torpedo tubes
96 mines / 2 seaplanes

Fubuki-class destroyer, 1927 ㉔

115 m long / 10.36 m beam 3.2 m draught
1,800 t | 38 knots
9,260 km | 211
3 × 127 twin / 2 × 12.7
3 × 3 tubes and 18 torpedoes
18 depth charges

Le Fantasque-class destroyer, 1934 ⑥

132.4 m long / 12.5 m beam 5 m draught
2,600 t | 37 knots
7,400 km | 210
5 × 140 / 2 × 37 twin
4 × 13.2 / 3 × 3 torpedo tubes / 50 mines
24 depth charges

Fletcher-class destroyer, 1941 ⑱⑴

114.8 m long / 12 m beam 5.3 m draught
2,050 t | 36.5 knots
12,000 km | 329
5 × 127 / 2 × 40
6 × 20 / 2 × 5 torpedo tubes
? depth charges

Hunt-class escort destroyer, 1939 ⑧⑥

85.34 m long / 9.6 m beam 3.8 m draught
1,050 t | 27 knots
6,500 km | 168
2 × 102 twin
4 × 40 / 2 × 20
40 depth charges

0   50 m   100 m   150 m   200 m

3 • CRUISERS AND DESTROYERS: FIGHTERS AND PROTECTORS

Generally fast and very resilient ships, designed mainly for long-distance scouting and disrupting enemy communications routes, cruisers were the mainstay of the combat fleets, supplementing, supporting and escorting the capital ships.

Cruisers varied a great deal but were primarily divided, as specified in inter-war naval treaties, into heavy cruisers (around 10,000 tonnes), designed for combat with their 155 to 203 mm guns, and light cruisers, sometimes specialized (e.g. anti-aircraft, anti-submarine, flotilla leaders), but smaller and armed with less powerful artillery (130 to 155 mm). Many were equipped with torpedoes and often one or two seaplanes.

Their chief limitation was their mid-level characteristics, making them unsuitable for direct confrontation with battleships, and vulnerable to heavy guns, torpedoes from lightweight ships and submarines, and air attacks. Varying considerably in size and power, these unarmoured ships were usually very fast. They fulfilled a number of different roles. The biggest could protect heavy warships and harass enemy ships, while the lightest hunted their opposite numbers, tracked submarines and escorted convoys. The most common cruiser guns were between 120 and 140 mm and they were generally well equipped with torpedo tubes.

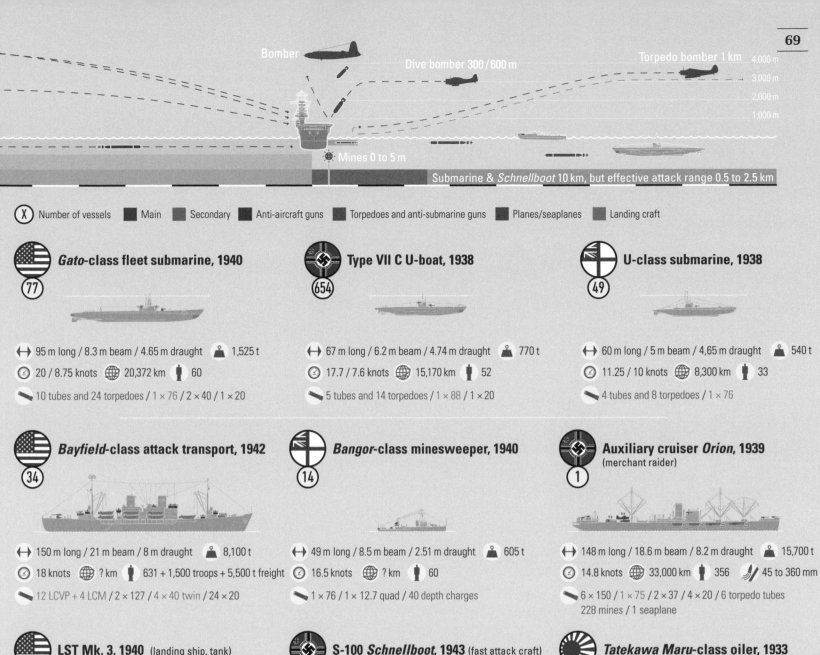

Bomber

Dive bomber 300 / 600 m

Torpedo bomber 1 km

4,000 m
3,000 m
2,000 m
1,000 m

⊕ Mines 0 to 5 m

Submarine & *Schnellboot* 10 km, but effective attack range 0.5 to 2.5 km

---

(X) Number of vessels ■ Main ■ Secondary ■ Anti-aircraft guns ■ Torpedoes and anti-submarine guns ■ Planes/seaplanes ■ Landing craft

---

Gato-class fleet submarine, 1940

(77)

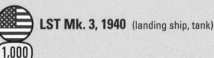

↔ 95 m long / 8.3 m beam / 4.65 m draught ⚓ 1,525 t

⏱ 20 / 8.75 knots 🌐 20,372 km 👤 60

🔫 10 tubes and 24 torpedoes / 1 × 76 / 2 × 40 / 1 × 20

Type VII C U-boat, 1938

(654)

↔ 67 m long / 6.2 m beam / 4.74 m draught ⚓ 770 t

⏱ 17.7 / 7.6 knots 🌐 15,170 km 👤 52

🔫 5 tubes and 14 torpedoes / 1 × 88 / 1 × 20

U-class submarine, 1938

(49)

↔ 60 m long / 5 m beam / 4,65 m draught ⚓ 540 t

⏱ 11.25 / 10 knots 🌐 8,300 km 👤 33

🔫 4 tubes and 8 torpedoes / 1 × 76

Bayfield-class attack transport, 1942

(34)

↔ 150 m long / 21 m beam / 8 m draught ⚓ 8,100 t

⏱ 18 knots 🌐 ? km 👤 631 + 1,500 troops + 5,500 t freight

🔫 12 LCVP + 4 LCM / 2 × 127 / 4 × 40 twin / 24 × 20

Bangor-class minesweeper, 1940

(14)

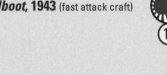

↔ 49 m long / 8.5 m beam / 2.51 m draught ⚓ 605 t

⏱ 16.5 knots 🌐 ? km 👤 60

🔫 1 × 76 / 1 × 12.7 quad / 40 depth charges

Auxiliary cruiser *Orion*, 1939
(merchant raider)

(1)

↔ 148 m long / 18.6 m beam / 8.2 m draught ⚓ 15,700 t

⏱ 14.8 knots 🌐 33,000 km 👤 356 〰 45 to 360 mm

🔫 6 × 150 / 1 × 75 / 2 × 37 / 4 × 20 / 6 torpedo tubes
228 mines / 1 seaplane

LST Mk. 3, 1940 (landing ship, tank)

(1,000)

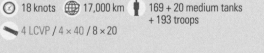

↔ 120 m long / 15 m beam / 4.42 m draught ⚓ 3,678 t

⏱ 18 knots 🌐 17,000 km 👤 169 + 20 medium tanks + 193 troops

🔫 4 LCVP / 4 × 40 / 8 × 20

S-100 *Schnellboot*, 1943 (fast attack craft)

(?)

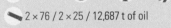

↔ 32.76 m long / 5.06 m beam / 1.47 m draught ⚓ 78.9 t

⏱ 43.8 knots 🌐 1,500 km 👤 24–30

🔫 1 × 37 / 3 × 20 twin / 2 torpedo tubes

Tatekawa Maru-class oiler, 1933

(11)

↔ 152 m long / 20 m beam / 11.4 m draught ⚓ 9,974 t

⏱ 20 knots 🌐 ? km 👤 ? 〰 0

🔫 2 × 76 / 2 × 25 / 12,687 t of oil

TORPEDOES

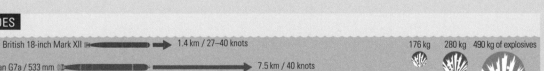

British 18-inch Mark XII → 1.4 km / 27–40 knots

German G7a / 533 mm → 7.5 km / 40 knots

Japanese Type 93 / 610 mm → 22 km / 52 knots

176 kg   280 kg   490 kg of explosives

MINES

Magnetic mine explodes in proximity to large metal objects

Acoustic mine explodes in proximity to engine

---

4 • SUBMARINES, AUXILIARY SHIPS, AMPHIBIOUS CRAFT AND MORE: ESSENTIAL BACK-UP

Traditional combat fleets needed a host of auxiliary craft of various kinds for their operations. Like large surface ships, submarines were considered primary warships, but they generally fulfilled different roles, including attacks on enemy lines of communication and coastal defence. There were several types: coastal, ocean-going and long-distance. Some nations (France, Japan) began developing cruiser submarines, heavily armed submersibles able to launch one or more seaplanes, but their performance remained disappointing.

Many other types of ships were used, of many different types and sizes, with different roles and weaponry. Their missions included protecting coasts and bases, rapid attack (e.g. light torpedoes, motor torpedo boats), troop and equipment transport, refuelling at sea (cargo ships, transport ships, oilers), care of casualties (hospital ships), repairs at sea (workshop ships, floating docks), amphibious landings (assault landing craft, ships and barges), mine-sweeping and mine-laying, escorting convoys (escort destroyers, sloops, corvettes, frigates, etc.) and more.

5 • THE BALANCE OF FORCES IN 1939

On the eve of the Second World War, the balance of the world's naval forces was still based largely on the naval disarmament and limitation treaties signed in the inter-war period (Treaty of Washington 1922, Treaties of London 1930 and 1936), which favoured British and US interests at the expense of Japan, and imposed parity in Europe between the French and Italian fleets, despite a massive revival of shipbuilding from 1936–37. In view of the timescales required for construction, the resumption of the naval arms race would only come to full fruition during the war.

Very few combat fleets could claim to have other than a purely regional role in the early 1940s. Although their fleets were old, the Royal Navy, partly reinforced by Commonwealth forces, and the US Navy favoured by the treaties were by far the most powerful and were the only navies capable of deploying fleets on multiple oceans. After them came the Imperial Japanese Navy, third in the world, with the best aircraft carrier fleet in the world (the Kidō Butai) and the potential to dominate the Pacific region. In Europe, neighbouring France and Italy were ranked next, vying for superiority in the

COMPOSITION OF MAIN COMBAT FLEETS, EARLY 1939

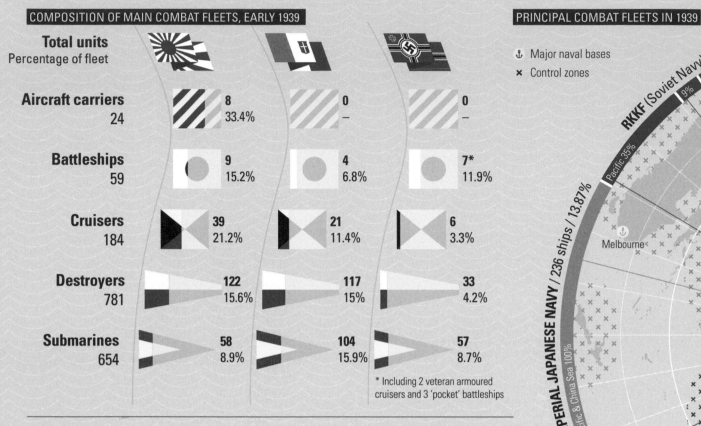

Total units
Percentage of fleet

Aircraft carriers 24	8 / 33.4%	0 / –	0 / –
Battleships 59	9 / 15.2%	4 / 6.8%	7* / 11.9%
Cruisers 184	39 / 21.2%	21 / 11.4%	6 / 3.3%
Destroyers 781	122 / 15.6%	117 / 15%	33 / 4.2%
Submarines 654	58 / 8.9%	104 / 15.9%	57 / 8.7%

* Including 2 veteran armoured cruisers and 3 'pocket' battleships

PRINCIPAL COMBAT FLEETS IN 1939

⚓ Major naval bases
✕ Control zones

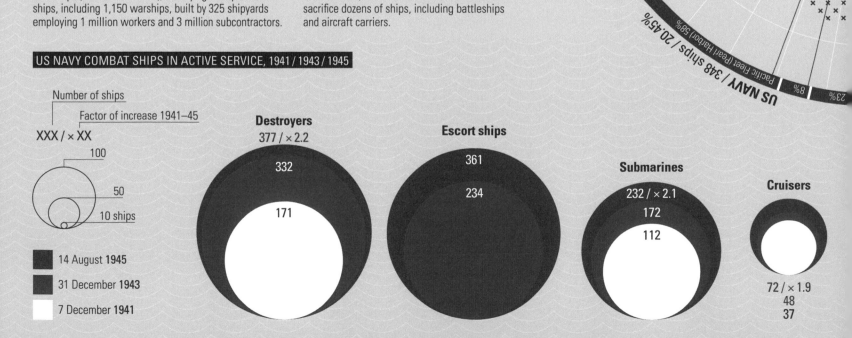

RKKF (Soviet Navy) / 286 ships / 16.8%
Black Sea — Baltic 34% — 9% — Pacific 35%

IMPERIAL JAPANESE NAVY / 236 ships / 13.87%
Singapore · Saigon · Philippines · Kure · Vladivo · Melbourne · Truk · Pearl Harbor · Pacific & China Sea 100% — 11%

US NAVY / 348 ships / 20.45%
Pacific Fleet (Pearl Harbor) 58% — 8% — 23%

6 • THE RISE OF THE US NAVY, 1941–45: BIRTH OF A NAVAL SUPERPOWER

The US fleet was in a unique position when the 1945 victory brought a sudden end to its massive shipbuilding programme. In December 1941, the US Navy had a fleet totalling 7,695 ships of all categories (2.7 million tonnes). In four years, the US Navy commissioned over 100,000 new ships (13 million tonnes), mainly light amphibious ships, including 1,150 warships, built by 325 shipyards employing 1 million workers and 3 million subcontractors.

Despite US losses during the war, this impressive growth and the destruction of the Japanese fleet automatically raised the US fleet to the status of world leader, which it never lost, outclassing all the other combat fleets. During the Bikini atomic tests in 1946, the United States could afford to sacrifice dozens of ships, including battleships and aircraft carriers.

US NAVY COMBAT SHIPS IN ACTIVE SERVICE, 1941 / 1943 / 1945

Number of ships
Factor of increase 1941–45
XXX / × XX

100
50
10 ships

■ 14 August **1945**
■ 31 December **1943**
□ 7 December **1941**

Destroyers
377 / × 2.2
332
171

Escort ships
361
234

Submarines
232 / × 2.1
172
112

Cruisers
72 / × 1.9
48
37

Mediterranean. France needed to protect its vast colonial empire, extending from the West Indies through West Africa to Indochina. The German Kriegsmarine, lagging well behind as a result of the Treaty of Versailles but strongly reinforced and modernized in the 1930s, was an outsider, unable to attack the Royal Navy directly but posing a constant threat (U-boats, camouflaged raiders, intermittent sorties by heavy ships) and with the capability for impressive combined operations (Norway). Finally came the Soviet fleet, which was both old and fragmented (Baltic, Black Sea, Arctic, Pacific),

making it a secondary force only capable of playing a regional role despite its large number of submarines.

By 1945, the Axis fleets had been almost completely neutralized or destroyed. The French fleet, tugged apart between the two sides after 1940, was severely weakened by the Mers el-Kébir attack and especially by the scuttling at Toulon (November 1942). The Royal Navy was still a powerful fleet, but was by that point heavily outnumbered by the US Navy.

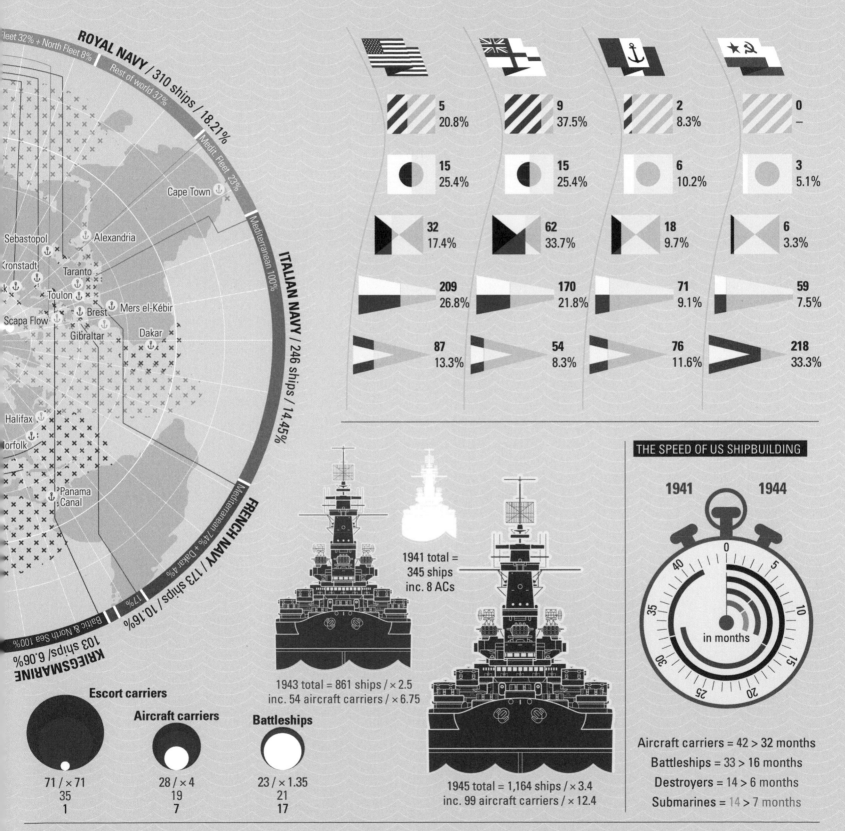

ROYAL NAVY / 310 ships / 18.21%
Fleet 32% + North Fleet 8%
Rest of world 37%
Medit. Fleet 23%

Cape Town

Sebastopol
Alexandria
Kronstadt
Taranto
Toulon
Brest
Mers el-Kébir
Scapa Flow
Gibraltar
Dakar
Halifax
Norfolk
Panama Canal

Mediterranean 100%
ITALIAN NAVY / 246 ships / 14.45%

FRENCH NAVY / 173 ships / 10.16%
Mediterranean 74% + Dakar 4%
17%
Baltic & North Sea 100%
KRIEGSMARINE / 103 ships / 6.06%

Escort carriers
71 / × 71
35
1

Aircraft carriers
28 / × 4
19
7

Battleships
23 / × 1.35
21
17

	🇺🇸	🇬🇧	⚓	☭
	5 / 20.8%	9 / 37.5%	2 / 8.3%	0 / –
	15 / 25.4%	15 / 25.4%	6 / 10.2%	3 / 5.1%
	32 / 17.4%	62 / 33.7%	18 / 9.7%	6 / 3.3%
	209 / 26.8%	170 / 21.8%	71 / 9.1%	59 / 7.5%
	87 / 13.3%	54 / 8.3%	76 / 11.6%	218 / 33.3%

1941 total = 345 ships inc. 8 ACs

1943 total = 861 ships / × 2.5 inc. 54 aircraft carriers / × 6.75

1945 total = 1,164 ships / × 3.4 inc. 99 aircraft carriers / × 12.4

THE SPEED OF US SHIPBUILDING

1941   1944

in months

Aircraft carriers = 42 > 32 months
Battleships = 33 > 16 months
Destroyers = 14 > 6 months
Submarines = 14 > 7 months

SOURCES: 1. Admiral Ernest J. King, *Official Reports, US Navy at War, 1941–1945*, Washington DC, 1959 • 2. Antony Preston (ed.), *Fighting Ships of the World*, London, 1980 • 3. Marc Benoist, *Les Marines étrangères*, Paris, 1938 • 4. *Japanese Naval and Merchant Shipping Losses During World War II by All Causes*, Joint Army-Navy Assessment Committee (Janac), 1947 • 5. *U.S. Navy Active Ship Force Levels*, Naval History and Heritage Command, US Navy • 6. Data from naval-history.net and combinedfleet.com • 7. http://www.shipbucket.com

A CARRIER BATTLE GROUP IN 1942

Considered a mere auxiliary to battleship fleets until the end of the 1930s, aircraft carriers played a leading role on the night of 11–12 November 1940 when a Royal Navy air raid on the port of Taranto sank three Italian battleships. However, the enclosed waters of Europe were not suited to large air-sea operations. The situation was different in the Pacific, where in 1941 Japan had the Kidō Butai (First Air Fleet), a group made up of six large aircraft carriers equipped with the best shipborne aircraft. Unlike the American or British forces, this single force was capable of projecting over 300 aircraft in massive raids, as the Americans discovered at Pearl Harbor on 7 December 1941. However, this surprise attack, modelled on the Taranto air raid, did the enemy an unexpected favour. By neutralizing the old battleships but missing the US aircraft carriers, which were not there, the Japanese settled the debate that was still ongoing in the navy between supporters of guns and supporters of aircraft.

In the absence of a rival, the flat-topped carrier became the nucleus of units known as task forces, which would become the basic combat unit in the Pacific. The Americans cautiously refrained from confronting the large Japanese fleet. But in the spring of 1942, the Japanese made the mistake of splitting it up. Two aircraft carriers sent to the Coral Sea were neutralized there (4–8 May 1942), cutting off the Kidō Butai off from a third of its forces. It therefore arrived at Midway (4–7 June 1942) with four aircraft carriers to face three on the US side, in addition to the aircraft actually based on the atoll. To avoid offering grouped targets, the US Navy divided its carriers into two task forces. Their raids were poorly planned but they did manage to surprise the Kidō Butai, which advanced as a group to better coordinate their waves of aircraft. Three Japanese aircraft carriers were sunk in a few minutes, and a fourth later.

This fatal blow led the Japanese to reorganize their carrier battle groups, while the Americans, having received an enormous number of new ships in 1943, planned giant task forces (nine large aircraft carriers and eight light aircraft carriers for the TF-38 in the summer of 1944), divided into smaller task forces.

1 • CONTROLLING THE AIR

In 1942 the Kidō Butai's greatest asset was the range of its aircraft, which gave it a superior reach to its opponent but meant that they were less well protected. The US forces were theoretically exposed to enemy strikes before they could counter-attack and without sufficient autonomy to give chase, it was difficult for them to use escorts effectively. However, this was compensated for by US radar, which enabled aircraft carriers to pinpoint attacks and organize a defence. Japanese radar was only at a prototype stage in 1942; inferior in quality and range, it was not fitted in aircraft carriers until the spring of 1943, when the Imperial Navy had already been defeated.

RADAR AND AIRCRAFT RANGES

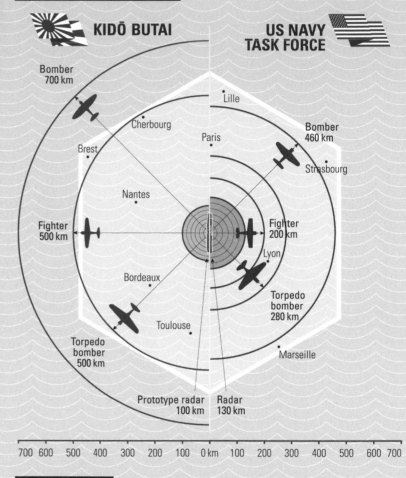

KIDŌ BUTAI — US NAVY TASK FORCE

Bomber 700 km
Lille
Cherbourg
Paris
Brest
Bomber 460 km
Strasbourg
Nantes
Fighter 500 km
Fighter 200 km
Lyon
Bordeaux
Torpedo bomber 280 km
Toulouse
Torpedo bomber 500 km
Marseille
Prototype radar 100 km
Radar 130 km

700 600 500 400 300 200 100 0 km 100 200 300 400 500 600 700

ARTILLERY RANGE

Anti-aircraft guns
C 127 mm = 14.7 km / 9.4 km
D 25 mm = 7.5 km / 5.5 km

12,5 km

Anti-aircraft guns
C 127 mm = 16 km / 11.3 km
D 40 mm = 10 km / 7 km

Main artillery
A 356 mm = 35.5 km
B 203 mm = 29 km

Main artillery
A 406 mm = 37 km
B 203 mm = 27.5 km

40 35 30 25 20 15 10 5 0 — 0 km — 0 5 10 15 20 25 30 35 40

2 • AIRCRAFT CARRIER *AKAGI*

Designed in 1920 as a battle cruiser, the *Akagi* was converted into an aircraft carrier and commissioned on 25 March 1927. It suffered from the three major defects of carriers: an inadequate air group, no radar and a closed, poorly ventilated design allowing a dangerous build-up of fuel gas. The fatal fire at Midway on 5 June 1942 was started by a single bomb falling directly between two hangars, filled with fuelled aircraft ready for combat.

■ =1 plane

D3A Val dive bombers

B5N2 Kate attack bombers

A6M2 Zeke fighters

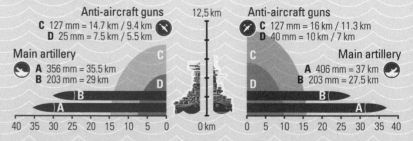

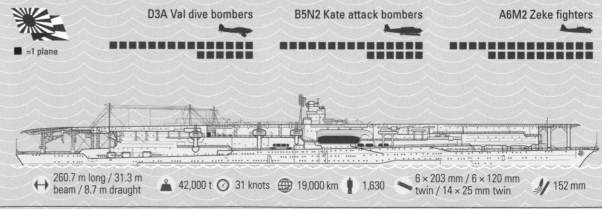

↔ 260.7 m long / 31.3 m beam / 8.7 m draught   ⚖ 42,000 t   ⏱ 31 knots   🌐 19,000 km   👤 1,630   6 × 203 mm / 6 × 120 mm twin / 14 × 25 mm twin   152 mm

SOURCES: 1. Jonathan Parshall & Anthony Tully, *Shattered Sword: The Untold Story of the Battle of Midway*, Dulles, VA, 2006 • 2. David Evans & Mark Peattie, *Kaigun: Strategy, Tactics and Technology in the Imperial Japanese*

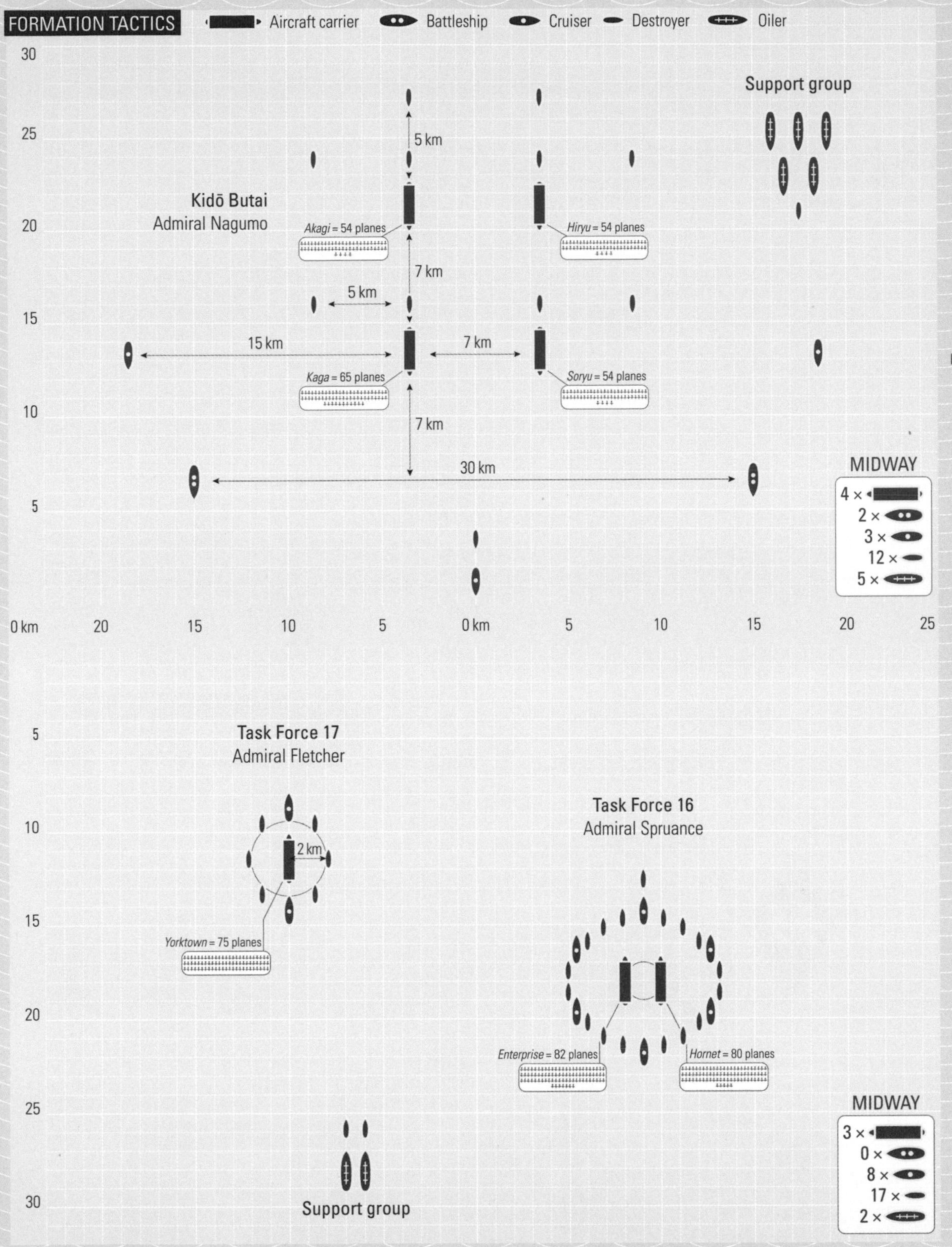
FORMATION TACTICS
Aircraft carrier
Battleship
Cruiser
Destroyer
Oiler
Kidō Butai
Admiral Nagumo
Support group
5 km
7 km
15 km
30 km
Akagi = 54 planes
Hiryu = 54 planes
Kaga = 65 planes
Soryu = 54 planes
MIDWAY
4 ×
2 ×
3 ×
12 ×
5 ×
Task Force 17
Admiral Fletcher
2 km
Yorktown = 75 planes
Task Force 16
Admiral Spruance
Enterprise = 82 planes
Hornet = 80 planes
Support group
MIDWAY
3 ×
0 ×
8 ×
17 ×
2 ×

3 • FUEL AND LOGISTICS

A task force, made up of ten or more large ships in the vast expanses of the Pacific, posed a major logistical challenge. At a speed of 20 knots, the hold capacity of a destroyer did not even allow for eight days of autonomy. But fuel consumption shot up in combat when the aircraft carriers were travelling at more than 30 knots to launch their aircraft. Ships therefore had to be followed by oilers to refuel at sea, a tricky process that the Japanese had trouble mastering.

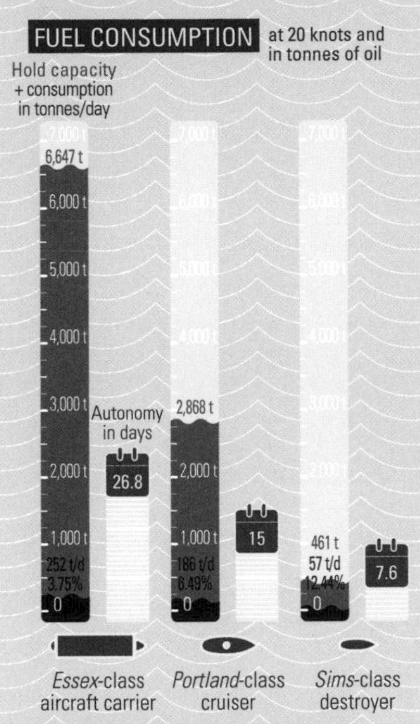
FUEL CONSUMPTION at 20 knots and in tonnes of oil
Hold capacity + consumption in tonnes/day
6,647 t
252 t/d
3.75%
Autonomy in days
26.8
2,868 t
186 t/d
6.49%
15
461 t
57 t/d
12.44%
7.6
Essex-class aircraft carrier
Portland-class cruiser
Sims-class destroyer

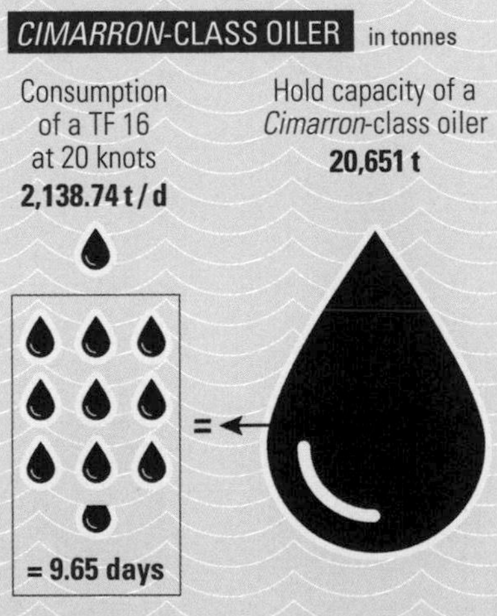
CIMARRON-CLASS OILER in tonnes
Consumption of a TF 16 at 20 knots
2,138.74 t / d
Hold capacity of a Cimarron-class oiler
20,651 t
= 9.65 days

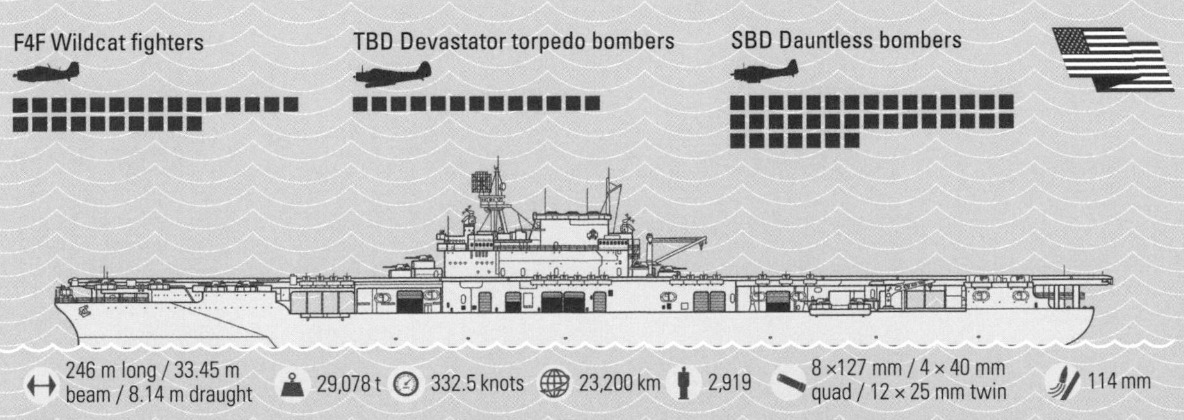
F4F Wildcat fighters
TBD Devastator torpedo bombers
SBD Dauntless bombers
246 m long / 33.45 m beam / 8.14 m draught
29,078 t
332.5 knots
23,200 km
2,919
8 × 127 mm / 4 × 40 mm quad / 12 × 25 mm twin
114 mm

4 • THE USS *ENTERPRISE*

Launched on 3 October 1936 and commissioned on 12 March 1938, the *Enterprise* was a purpose-designed aircraft carrier. Spacious and equipped with high-quality CXAM radar, at Midway it embarked 75 aircraft, increasing to 90 in 1943, a larger capability than its Japanese rivals. As far as possible, the aircraft were kept on the flight deck, with the hangars used mainly for maintenance. The *Enterprise* continued to be upgraded regularly and was not scrapped until 1958.

Navy 1887–1941, Annapolis, MD, 1997 • 3. Mark Stille, *US Navy Aircraft Carriers 1922–45: Prewar Classes*; Mark Stille, *Imperial Japanese Navy Aircraft Carriers 1921–45*, Oxford, 2005.

12. Hitlerjugend 1943–45
13. Handschar 1943–45
14. Galizien 1943–45
15. Lettische Nr. 1 1943–45
16. Reichsführer-SS 1943–45
17. Götz von Berlichingen 1943–45
18. Horst Wessel 1944–45
19. Lettische Nr. 2 1944–45
20. Estnische Nr. 1 1944–45
21. Skanderb... 1944–

THE ⚡⚡ : A STATE WITHIN A STATE

11. Nordland 1943–45

10. Frundsberg 1943–45

9. Hohenstaufen 1943–45

The initials SS are synonymous with terror and fear. The structure of this complex organization, which became a state within a state, the instrument of Himmler's obsession, is not easy to understand. However, when first forming the *Schutzstaffel* (protection squad) on 9 November 1925, Hitler had in mind a 'bodyguard, small [eight strong men], but made up of men ready to serve unconditionally, ready to march even against their brothers' in the paramilitary *Sturmabteilung* (SA). Himmler took command of it four years later. At that time it had only 280 men, well below the SA's 60,000. Whereas Hitler saw it as 'an elite troop of the Party', Himmler wanted to make it 'the elite of the Nation' and a 'vaccine capable of regenerating the German race'. Himmler was not merely a member of the Nazi Party: he formed and shaped it. So this paramilitary structure – with its leader hammering home the fact that 'the Black Order aims to turn all its members into soldiers' – diversified to make the SS 'an order that will create a race crucial to the eternal life of the German people'.

Himmler conceived the SS as a military organization, the vanguard of a racially 'pure', morally resourceful and physically fit community. He tried, without great success, to replace Christianity

1 • THE TENTACLES OF THE SS

Key:

⟶ Command

🗣 **Propaganda:** The SS had its own newspaper and gave honorary titles to high-ranking officials (*Ehrenführer*).

Military: The SS-VT were 'dispositional troops' drawn from political paramilitaries.

Police

Intelligence/police: The SS gradually took over all the other law enforcement agencies.

Cult: Wewelsburg Castle was cult centre of the SS.

Education

Legal department: Set and enforced SS laws.

Concentration/extermination: The SS-TV guarded prisons and camps and helped to secure the occupied territories; the *Einsatzgruppen* ran death squads in the USSR.

Economics: The Economic and Administrative Office was responsible for trade and management of the slave labour force.

Building a new world: Two departments (RuSHA and RKF) planned the settlement of new territories; the RKF also wanted to monitor racial purity.

Ideology/creating a 'new man': The SS opened Aryan maternity homes and took in orphans deemed 'pure' (the Lebensborn association), opened the Adolf Hitler Schools and higher education centres (*Ordensschulen*).

8. Florian Geyer 1942–45

7. Prinz Eugen 1942–45

6. Nord 1941–45

5. Wiking 1940–45

4. Polizei 1939–45

3. Totenkopf 1939–45

2. Das Reich 1939–45

1. Leibstandarte Adolf Hitler 1939–45

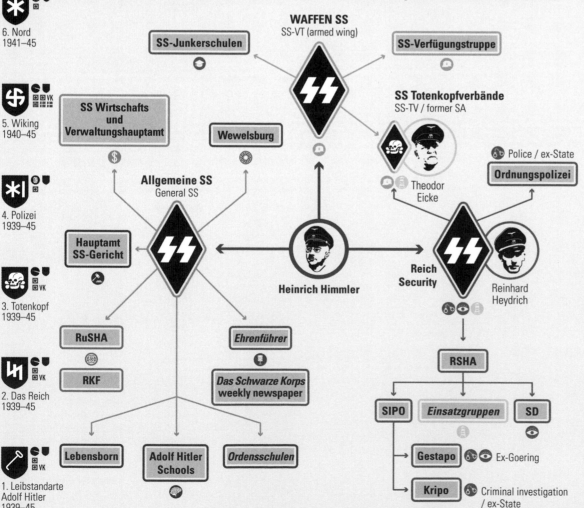

WAFFEN SS SS-VT (armed wing)

SS-Junkerschulen — SS-Verfügungstruppe

SS Totenkopfverbände SS-TV / former SA

Theodor Eicke

SS Wirtschafts und Verwaltungshauptamt

Wewelsburg

Police / ex-State — Ordnungspolizei

Allgemeine SS General SS

Heinrich Himmler

Reich Security — Reinhard Heydrich

Hauptamt SS-Gericht

RuSHA

RKF

Ehrenführer

Das Schwarze Korps weekly newspaper

RSHA

SIPO — *Einsatzgruppen* — SD

Gestapo — Ex-Goering

Kripo — Criminal investigation / ex-State

Lebensborn — Adolf Hitler Schools — *Ordensschulen*

2 • THE WAFFEN SS: A LAW IN ITSELF

The fascination of the Waffen SS overstates its influence. Although the 'historic' divisions were efficient, they only represented 10% of the Panzerwaffe and 2% of the Wehrmacht. The 10% threshold was only reached in 1944 by severely lowering standards. The Waffen SS was short of manpower, made worse by top-heavy administration. Its strict selection criteria were relaxed as early as 1940. To bring its numbers over 100,000, it admitted ethnic Germans (from German minorities outside

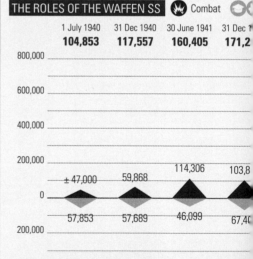

THE ROLES OF THE WAFFEN SS — 💣 Combat

	1 July 1940	31 Dec 1940	30 June 1941	31 Dec 1...
	104,853	**117,557**	**160,405**	**171,2...**

800,000

600,000

400,000

200,000

± 47,000 — 59,868 — 114,306 — 103,8...

0

57,853 — 57,689 — 46,099 — 67,4...

200,000

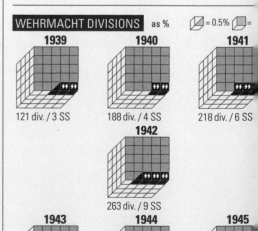

WEHRMACHT DIVISIONS — as % — = 0.5%

1939	1940	1941
121 div. / 3 SS	188 div. / 4 SS	218 div. / 6 SS

1942
263 div. / 9 SS

1943	1944	1945
276 div. / 18 SS	298 div. / 29 SS	272 div. / 36 SS

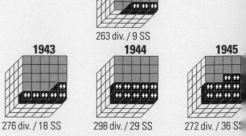

| Maria Theresia 4–45 | 23. Kama 1944–44 | 23. Nederland 1944–45 | 24. Karstjäger 1944–45 | 25. Hunyadi 1944–45 | 26. Hungaria 1944–45 | 27. Langemarck 1944–45 | 28. Wallonien 1944–45 | 29. Russische Nr. 1 1944–44 | 29. Italienische 1945 |

with a new spirituality, based on Teutonic and Nordic mythology. Even so, the SS was not backward-looking. Despite its outmoded trappings, it was meant to be a modern creation, bent on forging a new world. But its influence quickly attracted ambitious figures who were more concerned with appearances than reality. The removal of the SA leaders allowed it to expand considerably (the Allgemeine SS had 250,000 members in 1939, 100,000 of them full-time). Hitler entrusted it with the vital state functions of internal security (police and intelligence). In competition with the Party, Himmler created structures for the SS that would build the 'new man' and the Greater Reich he dreamed of. His artistic and cultural values pervaded its elites. He dreamed of turning his paramilitary units into a politically sound parallel army, but, as much to avoid alienating the Wehrmacht as

because of budgetary constraints, Hitler initially restricted the expansion of what became the Waffen SS in November 1939. The Wehrmacht only had operational control of it; the SS had its own military administration, budget and recruitment offices (there was a difference between joining the Waffen SS and joining the Allgemeine SS). It expanded more rapidly after 1943 and took advantage of the Führer's mistrust of the Wehrmacht after the assassination attempt of 20 July 1944. The Waffen SS grew by two-thirds and SS officers were given strategic posts. Himmler seized command of the replacement army (a mobilization and training organization) and two army groups. By 1944, when the SS had also gained influence over the economy through its management of the slave labour force, Himmler presided over an empire that corrupted and competed with state and partisan structures.

30. Russische Nr. 2 1944–45

31. Batschka 1944–45

32. 30 Januar 1945

the Reich), then foreigners with Nordic blood. In mid-1942, conscription was officially introduced, first for ethnic Germans and then, in late 1942, for those within the Reich (including forced recruits from Alsace-Moselle) in the form of a quota negotiated with the Wehrmacht. Racial rules were slackened and the SS began to recruit Slavs, although Himmler made a distinction between the 'German' units, associated foreigners (*Freiwilligen*) and other divisions serving under SS command. The system eventually disintegrated into small, mediocre and even phantom divisions.

3 • WHO WERE THE WAFFEN SS SOLDIERS?

The early contingents were made up mainly of police officers (because of the civil service connection), skilled workmen and young men coming to the end of their education. In the first years of the war, more low-level employees (agricultural and manual workers) joined, while professional people shunned the organization. In 1943, conscription removed these disparities before the massive influx of ethnic Germans from the East led to over-representation of rural populations, including in

the 'historic divisions', undermining their cohesion. The Wehrmacht divisions, with national recruitment, remained more representative of German society. In a Reich that was 96% Christian, Himmler hoped to create a 'purified' neo-paganist SS order ('believers in God'), a hope that was never fulfilled. The Allgemeine SS remained 80% Christian. And although joining the paramilitary involved de-Christianization, a third of camp guards considered their work compatible with their Christian faith.

33. Charlemagne 1944–45

34. Landstorm Nederland 1944–45

35. SS und Polizei 1945

36. Dirlewanger 1945

37. Lützow 1945

38. Nibelungen 1945

Training / relief / administration / camp management / other

ep 1942	31 Dec 1942	31 Dec 1943	30 June 1944	June 1945
4,025	246,717	501,049	594,443	829,400

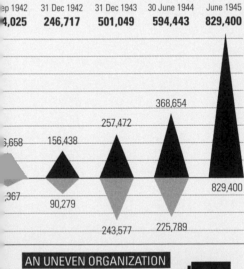

368,654
257,472
156,438
90,279
243,577   225,789
829,400
6,658
,367

THE SS: SOCIO-PROFESSIONAL ORIGINS AND DATES OF RECRUITMENT

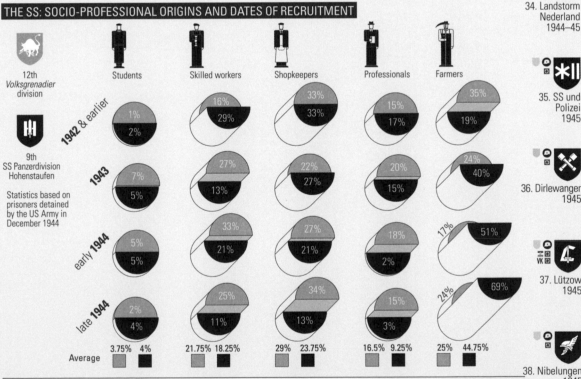

12th *Volksgrenadier* division

9th SS Panzerdivision Hohenstaufen

Statistics based on prisoners detained by the US Army in December 1944

	Students	Skilled workers	Shopkeepers	Professionals	Farmers
1942 & earlier	1% / 2%	16% / 29%	33% / 33%	15% / 17%	35% / 19%
1943	7% / 5%	27% / 13%	22% / 27%	20% / 15%	24% / 40%
early 1944	5% / 5%	33% / 21%	27% / 21%	18% / 2%	17% / 51%
late 1944	2% / 4%	25% / 11%	34% / 13%	15% / 3%	24% / 69%
Average	3.75% / 4%	21.75% / 18.25%	29% / 23.75%	16.5% / 9.25%	25% / 44.75%

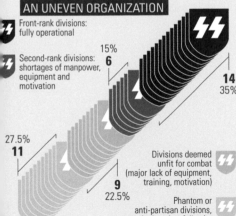

AN UNEVEN ORGANIZATION

Front-rank divisions: fully operational

Second-rank divisions: shortages of manpower, equipment and motivation

15%
6

14
35%

27.5%
11

9
22.5%

Divisions deemed unfit for combat (major lack of equipment, training, motivation)

Phantom or anti-partisan divisions, never deployed as full units

Key to divisions:

- Panzer Division
- Panzer Grenadiers
- Alpine Light Infantry
- Infantry
- Cavalry

- Front-rank division
- Second-rank division
- Unfit division
- Phantom division

Mainly 'Germanic' recruitment
- Germans
- VK Ethnic Germans
- Swedish
- Danish
- Norwegians
- Flemish
- Dutch

Mainly 'non-Germanic' recruitment
- Estonians
- Latvians
- Albanians
- Slovaks
- Hungarians
- Romanians
- Italians
- French
- Walloons

Mainly Slav recruitment
- Ukrainians
- Croats
- Bosnians
- Russians

Not including Bohemia and Moravia divisions and two Cossack divisions since membership of the SS theoretical by April 1945

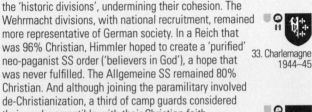

- 400,000 Germans
- 300,000 ethnic Germans
- 300,000 foreigners

SOURCES: 1. Jean-Luc Leleu, *La Waffen SS, Soldats politiques en guerre*, Paris, 2007 • 2. Heinz Höhne, *The Order of the Death's Head: The Story of Hitler's SS*, London, 1980 • 3. Robert L. Koehl, *The Black Corps: The Structure and Power Struggles of the Nazi SS*, Madison, WI, 1983 • 4. Helmut Krausnick, Hans Buchheim, Martin Broszat & Hans-Adolf Jacobsen, *Anatomy of the SS State*, London, 1968 • 5. Valdis O. Lumans, *Himmler's Auxiliaries: The Volksdeutsche Mittelstelle and the German National Minorities of Europe, 1933–1945*, Chapel Hill, NC, 1993.

3. BATTLES AND CAMPAIGNS

CHINA: THE UNRECOGNIZED ALLY

The Sino-Japanese war was a historical event of immense significance, whose ramifications are still being felt to this day. In a Western context, it is often eclipsed by a focus on the European and Pacific theatres. However, because of its size, its population, the political issues at stake and the unrest undermining it, China seemed to be both a major player and a second-rate power, faced with a Japan that was certainly dominant but unable to find a military or political solution. At first, Chiang Kai-shek's government seemed easy prey. It was weak and powerless against the Japanese attack on Manchuria in 1931, followed by the creation of the puppet state of Manchukuo in 1932.

In July 1937, the large-scale invasion following the Marco Polo bridge incident triggered the Second Sino-Japanese War (the first took place in 1894–95). Chiang Kai-shek's armies retreated, but paradoxically he was strengthened by the national alliance between his forces (the Kuomintang party), provincial warlords and the Communists (8th Route Army), although they only appeared to be rallying to his cause. In fact, the heavily manned Chinese army was nothing but a façade, very marginally modernized with help from the Germans between 1928 and 1938, then from the Americans from 1941 onwards; the China-Burma-India command (CBI) was formed in 1942 after a brief partnership with the USSR (1938–40). However, this initial modernization did somehow enable China to withstand attacks by the Japanese, whose frustration was then expressed in the terrible Nanjing massacre in the government capital. The war changed its nature in December 1941, becoming part of the global conflict. The aim of the United States was to pin down as many Japanese resources as possible far away from the Pacific, secure air bases in China and bring an Asian country into the democratic camp. For Chiang Kai-shek, the prospect of becoming the 'fourth Great Power' was a pleasant surprise. But the performance of his forces would never make him a credible player, even with American aid.

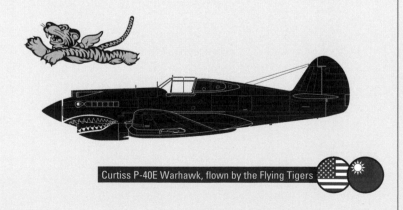

Curtiss P-40E Warhawk, flown by the Flying Tigers

SOURCES: 1. Nicolas Bernard, *La Guerre du Pacifique*, Paris, 2016 • 2. Bingyan Cai, *The Search for Allies: Chinese Alliance Behavior from 1930 to the End of WW2*, master's thesis, Hawaii Pacific University, 2009 • 3. Philip Jowett, *The Chinese Army, 1937–1949*, Oxford, 2005 • 4. Diana Lary, *The Chinese People at War: Human Suffering and Social Transformation, 1937–1945*, Cambridge, 2010 • 5. Jean-Louis Margolin, *L'Armée de l'Empereur: Violences et crimes du Japon en guerre 1937–1945*, Paris, 2007 • 6. Rana Mitter, *Forgotten Ally: China's World War II, 1937–1945*, Boston, 2013.

1 • CHINESE AND JAPANESE ARMIES IN 1938

On paper, the Chinese National Revolutionary Army had 191 divisions and 52 brigades made up of 1.7 million soldiers, plus several hundred aircraft and a small navy. In fact, apart from around ten divisions that received German training, those units had very limited manpower and were poorly armed and led. Most were merely unreliable provincial forces. X-Force, equipped and trained by the Americans and led by General Sun Li-jen (the 'Rommel of the East') proved itself an exception during the Burma campaign in 1944. The government had scarcely more than 400,000 men from the Kuomintang army and 500,000 others who were traditionally loyal.

The Japanese army was smaller yet better equipped and led. It was still capable of major offensives in 1944–45. It only started to retreat in June 1945 in the face of Chinese forces reorganized under the leadership of General Wedemeyer and receiving supplies from India and Burma.

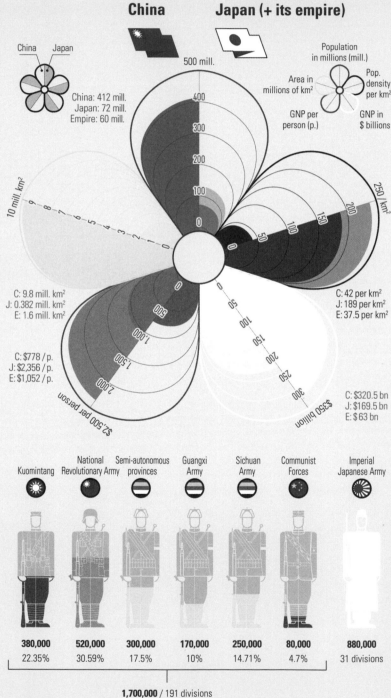

China   **Japan (+ its empire)**

China   Japan

China: 412 mill.
Japan: 72 mill.
Empire: 60 mill.

Population in millions (mill.)

Area in millions of km²

Pop. density per km²

GNP per person (p.)

GNP in $ billions

500 mill.

C: 9.8 mill. km²
J: 0.382 mill. km²
E: 1.6 mill. km²

C: 42 per km²
J: 189 per km²
E: 37.5 per km²

C: $778 / p.
J: $2,356 / p.
E: $1,052 / p.

C: $320.5 bn
J: $169.5 bn
E: $63 bn

Kuomintang	National Revolutionary Army	Semi-autonomous provinces	Guangxi Army	Sichuan Army	Communist Forces	Imperial Japanese Army
380,000	520,000	300,000	170,000	250,000	80,000	880,000
22.35%	30.59%	17.5%	10%	14.71%	4.7%	31 divisions

1,700,000 / 191 divisions

Puppet emperor Puyi 1906–67   Collaborating president Wang Jingwei 1883–1944   President Mao Zedong 1893–1976   Generalissimo Chiang Kai-shek 1887–1975   General Claire L. Chennault 1890–1958   General Joseph Stilwell 1883–1946

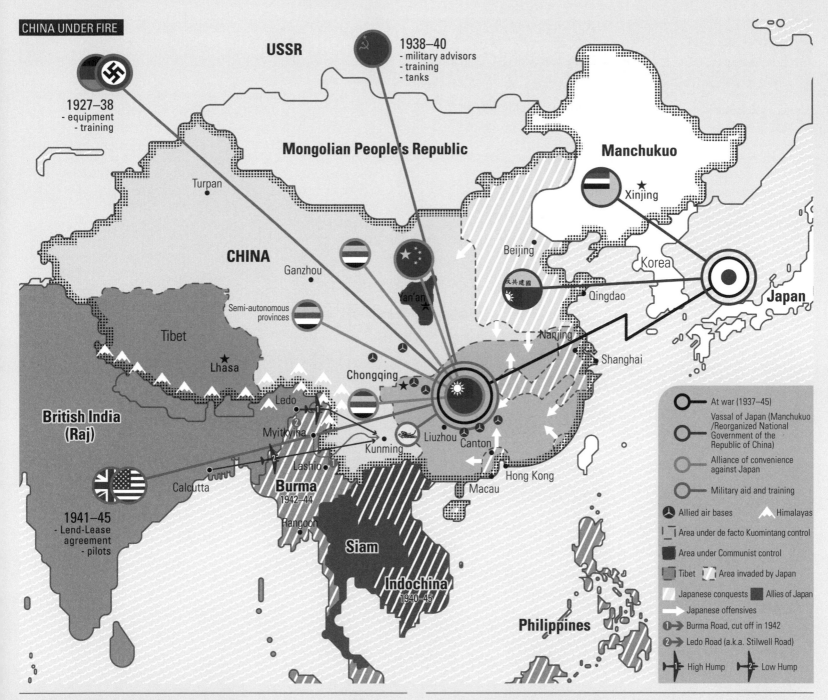

CHINA UNDER FIRE

USSR

1927–38
- equipment
- training

1938–40
- military advisors
- training
- tanks

Mongolian People's Republic

Manchukuo

Turpan

Xinjing

CHINA

Beijing

Ganzhou

Korea

Yan'an

Qingdao

Semi-autonomous
provinces

Japan

Nanjing

Tibet

Shanghai

Lhasa

Chongqing

Ledo

**British India
(Raj)**

Myitkyina

Liuzhou   Canton

Kunming

Calcutta   Lashio

Hong Kong

Burma
1942–44

Macau

Rangoon

1941–45
- Lend-Lease
agreement
- pilots

Siam

Indochina
1940–45

Philippines

◎	At war (1937–45)
◉	Vassal of Japan (Manchukuo /Reorganized National Government of the Republic of China)
◉	Alliance of convenience against Japan
○	Military aid and training

✈ Allied air bases   ▲ Himalayas

⊥ Area under de facto Kuomintang control

▨ Area under Communist control

▨ Tibet   ▨ Area invaded by Japan

▨ Japanese conquests   ▨ Allies of Japan

⇨ Japanese offensives

①⇨ Burma Road, cut off in 1942

②⇨ Ledo Road (a.k.a. Stilwell Road)

✈ High Hump   ✈ Low Hump

2 • THE HUMP: A LIFELINE TO CHINA

Supplying the Chinese forces from India and Burma was a tricky operation, especially since Chiang Kai-shek and US General Joseph Stilwell, commander of the China-Burma-India theatre (CBI) until 1944, politely detested one another. The Japanese occupation of Burma in 1942 cut off the 'Burma Road' that was used to transport 90% of supplies. The Ledo Road from India had to be opened up with great difficulty in order to compensate partially for the loss. Between April 1942 and November 1945, China was given a lifeline by 'the Hump', an enormous airbridge across the Himalayas. Flying this extremely dangerous route cost the lives of 1,200 pilots in 700 accidents. At this high cost, 650,000 tonnes of freight and 33,000 people were delivered to China, until the Burma Road was re-opened in January 1945. In 1944, the Americans tried to position strategic air forces to bomb Japan, but gave up, due to the lack of adequate logistics and the threat of the Japanese Ichigo offensive.

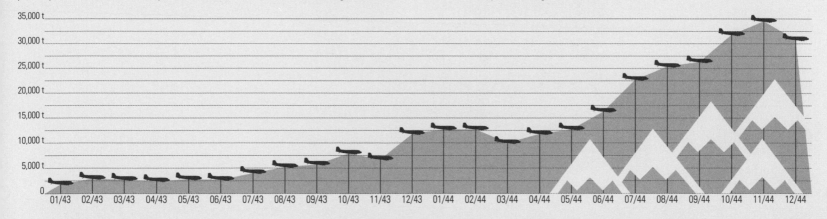

	01/43	02/43	03/43	04/43	05/43	06/43	07/43	08/43	09/43	10/43	11/43	12/43	01/44	02/44	03/44	04/44	05/44	06/44	07/44	08/44	09/44	10/44	11/44	12/44

35,000 t
30,000 t
25,000 t
20,000 t
15,000 t
10,000 t
5,000 t
0

THE INVASION OF POLAND

On 1 September 1939, the Wehrmacht, supported by Slovak troops, attacked Poland without warning over a 1,000-kilometre front. Even before a shot was fired, the Germans had two major advantages. Their army was already in combat position, while the Polish army was only just mobilizing. The Polish forces were attacked concentrically from the north, west and south, from the Reich, East Prussia, Moravia and Slovakia. The German plan was simple: two pincers from the north and south-west rushed towards Warsaw. The Polish were trying to defend their whole country. With little motorization and little protection against air attacks, and reliant on an overcentralized command system, the

army of Marshal Rydz-Śmigły was quickly overwhelmed. Helped by massive air support, the Germans broke though everywhere with six armoured divisions and nine motorized infantry divisions. Their opponents were divided and destroyed, notably at Radom and on the Bzura. By 10 September, Warsaw was already under siege.

At this point, only decisive action by the French and British, who declared war on the Third Reich on 3 September, could have improved the situation, especially since there were plans to continue the fight by guerrilla warfare in the east of the country. These slim hopes were dashed by Allied inertia and the Soviet attack on Poland on 17 September under a secret protocol to the

1 • THE BALANCE OF FORCES

On 1 September 1939, the Polish army, composed of infantry and cavalrymen, was inferior in every area. The Germans proved that grouped deployment of tanks and a modern air force were invaluable in the field. After this campaign, Panzer divisions were given greater autonomy.

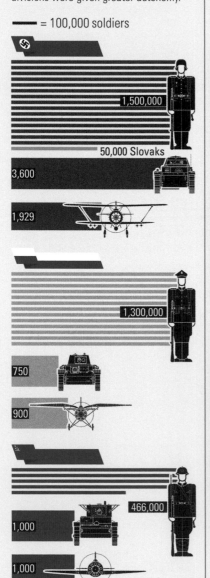

—— = 100,000 soldiers

1,500,000

50,000 Slovaks

3,600

1,929

1,300,000

750

900

466,000

1,000

1,000

2 • THE GERMAN CAMPAIGN IN POLAND, SEPTEMBER 1939

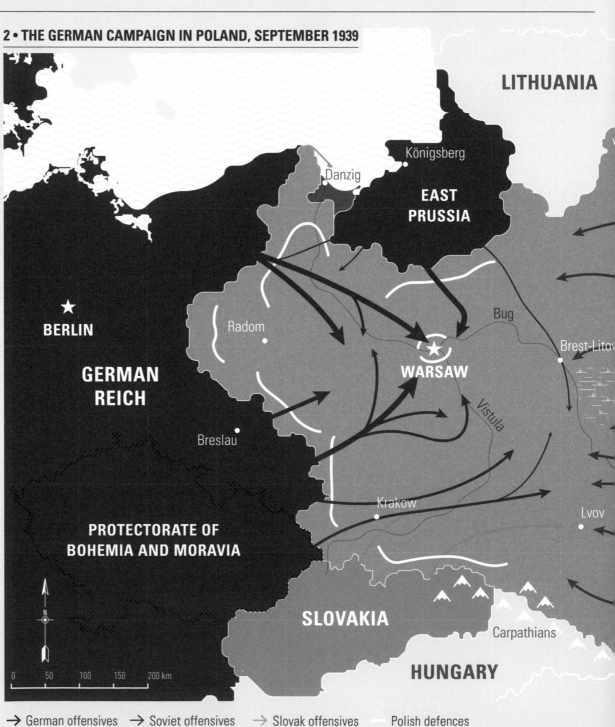

→ German offensives   → Soviet offensives   → Slovak offensives   —— Polish defences

Molotov–Ribbentrop Pact, a treaty of non-aggression between Germany and the USSR signed on 23 August 1939. In five days the Red Army linked up with the Germans on the Bug river, depriving their common opponent of any strategic space. On 28 September, Warsaw fell with its 120,000 defenders. The last troops surrendered on 6 October. The Red Army, closely observed by the Germans, performed poorly. It lacked discipline and organization and its motorized units and signals were a failure.

Although in military terms, the Polish campaign foreshadowed the French campaign, politically it was more closely akin to the attack on the Soviet Union, with its systematic elimination of national leaders.

MAJOR FIGURES

Marshal Edward Rydz-Smigły 1886–1941

Marshal Semyon Timoshenko 1895–1970

General Gerd von Rundstedt 1875–1953

General Fedor von Bock 1880–1945

Minsk

USSR

arshland

Zhytomyr

ROMANIA

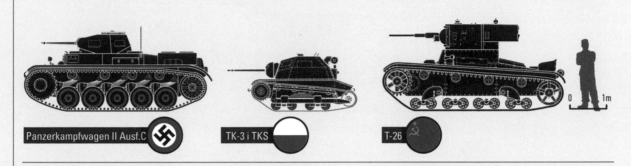

Panzerkampfwagen II Ausf.C

TK-3 i TKS

T-26

0   1m

3 • THE HUMAN COST OF THE CAMPAIGN

The Poles fought back, costing the German order of battle nearly 18,000 men, 300 tanks, 5,000 vehicles and 560 aircraft. In relative terms, they were more successful than the French, Belgians, Dutch and British eight months later. The large number of civilian casualties was due partly to the terror bombing of towns and columns of refugees and partly to the wide-scale human rights abuses. Thousands of prisoners and civilians were shot during the fighting or immediately afterwards by the Wehrmacht itself, or by the SS or the police.

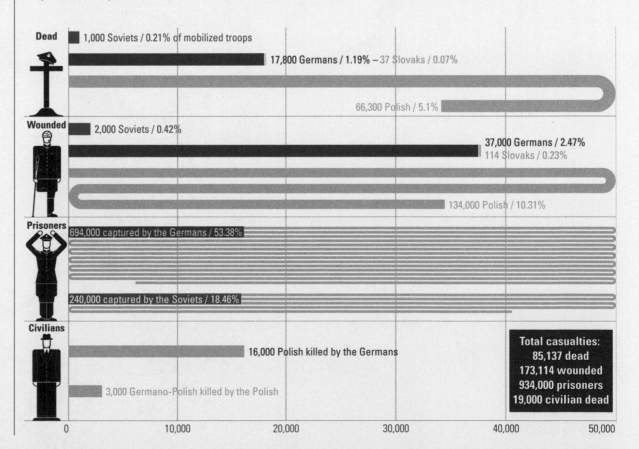

Dead
1,000 Soviets / 0.21% of mobilized troops
17,800 Germans / 1.19% — 37 Slovaks / 0.07%
66,300 Polish / 5.1%

Wounded
2,000 Soviets / 0.42%
37,000 Germans / 2.47%
114 Slovaks / 0.23%
134,000 Polish / 10.31%

Prisoners
694,000 captured by the Germans / 53.38%
240,000 captured by the Soviets / 18.46%

Civilians
16,000 Polish killed by the Germans
3,000 Germano-Polish killed by the Polish

Total casualties:
85,137 dead
173,114 wounded
934,000 prisoners
19,000 civilian dead

0   10,000   20,000   30,000   40,000   50,000

4 • CONTINUING THE WAR

In October 1939, 85,000 Polish soldiers escaped from captivity and took refuge in Romania, Hungary and Lithuania. The Germans encountered some of them back on the battlefields. The Polish government continued in exile with its allies in France and Britain. It called on all volunteers, Polish or of Polish origin, wherever they may be, to continue the war whatever the cost. It even enlisted Poles of German origin from the Wehrmacht, captured by the Allies. Its determination was a thorn in Stalin's side right up to 1945.

Stalin started with strong-arm tactics by having 22,000 officers and intelligentsia captured by his army executed in Katyń in April 1940. After the German attack on 22 June 1941, he was forced to come to an agreement and to let General Anders and his army leave the USSR. They then embarked on one of the most extraordinary odysseys of the war. The Katyń massacre came to light again in 1943 when the Germans discovered the mass graves, leading to its final severance of relations with the USSR.

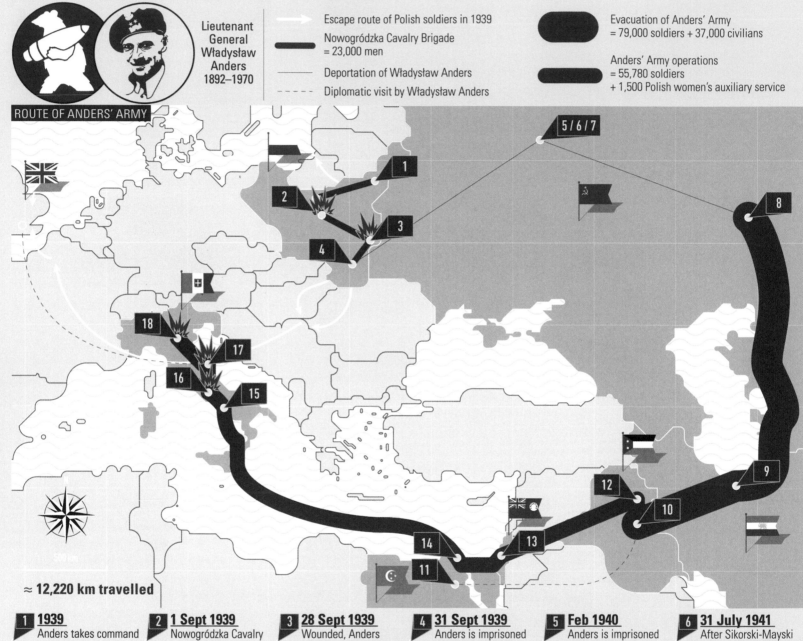

Lieutenant General Władysław Anders 1892–1970

→ Escape route of Polish soldiers in 1939

━━ Nowogródzka Cavalry Brigade = 23,000 men

── Deportation of Władysław Anders

---- Diplomatic visit by Władysław Anders

⬭ Evacuation of Anders' Army = 79,000 soldiers + 37,000 civilians

▬ Anders' Army operations = 55,780 soldiers + 1,500 Polish women's auxiliary service

ROUTE OF ANDERS' ARMY

≈ 12,220 km travelled

500 km

1 **1939**
Anders takes command of the Nowogródzka Cavalry Brigade in eastern Poland.

2 **1 Sept 1939**
Nowogródzka Cavalry Brigade deployed in Mława and Warsaw.

3 **28 Sept 1939**
Wounded, Anders retreats and is captured in Turka by the Soviets following a final battle.

4 **31 Sept 1939**
Anders is imprisoned by the NKVD in Lvov.

5 **Feb 1940**
Anders is imprisoned and tortured in the Lubyanka prison in Moscow.

6 **31 July 1941**
After Sikorski-Mayski Agreement, Anders is released and becomes commander-in-chief of Polish forces in USSR.

7 **20 March 1942**
Meeting with Joseph Stalin to negotiate the release of Polish prisoners from the gulag.

8 **Late March 1942**
Starts to reassemble his army in Buzuluk and is appointed lieutenant general.

9 **Summer 1942**
Anders' Army leaves the USSR to join British forces in Iran.

10 **Summer 1942**
Anders' Army moves to Iraq to become the Polish II Corps, integrated into the British Eighth Army.

11 **22 Aug 1942**
Anders meets Churchill in Cairo.

12 **Sept 1942**
Polish II Corps training in Khanaqin-Qizil Ribat.

13 **1943**
Regrouping of Polish II Corps in Gaza in Palestine.

14 **Jan 1944**
Landing in Egypt to take part in the Italian campaign.

15 **Jan 1944**
Landing in Naples, deployment in the British Eighth Army under command of General Leese.

16 **May 1944**
Battle of Monte Cassino: 926 dead and missing, 2,822 wounded.

17 **June/July 1944**
Capture of Ancona: 608 dead and missing, 1,789 wounded..

18 **April 1945**
Capture of Bologna: 234 dead and missing, 1,228 wounded. II Corps demobilized in Italy in early 1946.

ORIGINS OF THE POLISH VOLUNTEERS WHO FOUGHT FOR THE ALLIES

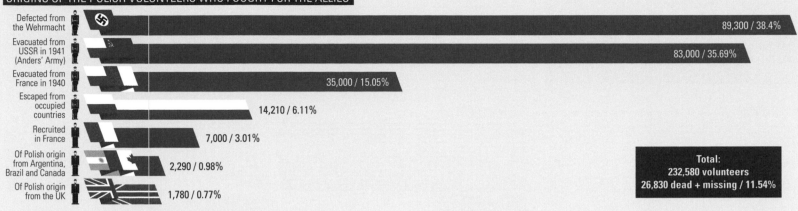

Defected from the Wehrmacht	89,300 / 38.4%
Evacuated from USSR in 1941 (Anders' Army)	83,000 / 35.69%
Evacuated from France in 1940	35,000 / 15.05%
Escaped from occupied countries	14,210 / 6.11%
Recruited in France	7,000 / 3.01%
Of Polish origin from Argentina, Brazil and Canada	2,290 / 0.98%
Of Polish origin from the UK	1,780 / 0.77%

Total:
232,580 volunteers
26,830 dead + missing / 11.54%

5 • PURGES AND DIVISION: POLAND IN DEFEAT September 1939–June 1941

Split into two, Poland was taken to pieces for the fourth time in its history, and incorporated into the Soviet and Nazi empires, which set about destroying traditional elites, politicians, intellectuals, priests, and more. The Germans germanized the territories annexed by the Reich (resulting in 400,000 deportees), before starting after June 1941 to eliminate the Polish Jews concentrated in the General Government area and in the territories annexed by the USSR in September 1939. The Soviets remodelled the socio-economic system of the territories ceded to the Soviet socialist republics of Lithuania, Bielorussia and Ukraine and eradicated any trace of Polishness by deportation to the remotest regions of the country. In addition, 50,000 Polish Jews died of hunger and illness in the ghettos before June 1941.

THE DESTRUCTION OF THE POLISH INTELLIGENTSIA September 1939 to June 1941

Killed by the Germans — 50,000

Killed by the Soviets — 25,000

Deported by the Germans — 400,000

Deported by the Soviets — 1,250,000

THE FOURTH PARTITION OF POLAND, 1940

Poland, 1938

Territory ceded to the Lithuanian Soviet Socialist Republic by the USSR

Territory annexed by the USSR

Territory annexed by the Reich

General Government of Poland

Territory ceded to Slovakia

SOURCES: 1. B. Wegner, *Das deutsche Reich und der Zweite Weltkrieg*, vol. 2 • 2. G. F. Krivosheev (ed.), *Soviet Casualties and Combat Losses in the Twentieth Century*, London, 1997 • 3. H. Kochanski, *The Eagle Unbowed: Poland and the Poles in the Second World War*, Cambridge, MA, 2012 • 4. A. B. Rossino, *Hitler Strikes Poland*, Lawrence, KT, 2003 • 5. Tomasz Szarota, in Bernd Wegner (ed.), *Zwei Wege nach Moskau*, Munich, 1991.

THE FALL OF FRANCE

On 10 May 1940, the French commander-in-chief General Gamelin responded to the invasion of the Benelux countries with the Dyle-Breda Plan. His best troops came to the rescue of the neutral nations. The thunderbolt struck three days later. Seven Panzer divisions broke through poor French defences along the Meuse, reached the Channel in eight days and surrounded 1.5 million men. Weygand, Gamelin's replacement, reported: 'Three-quarters if not four-fifths of our most up-to-date equipment has been taken.' Although it was two weeks before the pocket was captured, the invasion of France (known as *Fall Rot* or 'Case Red') started as soon as Dunkirk had fallen. Despite some fierce battles and the failure of the Italians who rushed up for the spoils on 10 June, it was all over. In six weeks, France saw the worst military disaster of its history, leading to a political crisis. On 17 June, Marshal Pétain, summoned by President Lebrun, called for an armistice. On 10 July, the parliament vested him with full powers. The Third Republic was no more.

The plans left very little doubt as to the outcome. The Germans, looking for an immediate victory, took considerable risks. They concentrated their modern resources on a mechanized front, which they deployed on difficult terrain where the French strategic reserve joined the Maginot Line. Their only two airborne divisions were released on the very first day, with 200 aircraft shot down. But it was a successful gamble because Gamelin responded by ordering a manoeuvre for which his forces were not prepared. The French strategy envisaged the war taking place on planned battlefields, punctuated with limited battles with firing breaking the movement. That concept, based on 1918, was sensible enough; when the Americans landed in 1944 they had a similar idea. But the French had not updated the strategy. They had no anti-tank guns, air defences or signals; they became lost in conjectures about tanks and forgot about role of aircraft. With the projection into Belgium, Gamelin threw himself into the lion's mouth. Germany won its only major victory in France. The encirclement, planned at operational and not tactical level, decapitated the French forces. The speed of implementation and the shallow theatre of operations then prevented a French recovery.

1 • THE BALANCE OF FORCES, 10 MAY 1940

The defeat of France was not down to demographic, industrial or technological factors, in which the Allies had a small advantage. The failure was strategic. As far as materiel was concerned, the Br-693 and the B1 bis heavy tank were impressive, but one was destroyed by Flak in hedge-hopping attacks and the other, slow and resource-intensive since it was designed for blocking or breaking through gaps on a static front, was often abandoned. By contrast, with fighter plane cover, ordinary Stukas spread terror while the basic Pz 38(t) tank, originating from Czechoslovakia, had enough weaponry, armour and mobility to suit an army that relied on speed and the paralysing effect of tanks and aircraft.

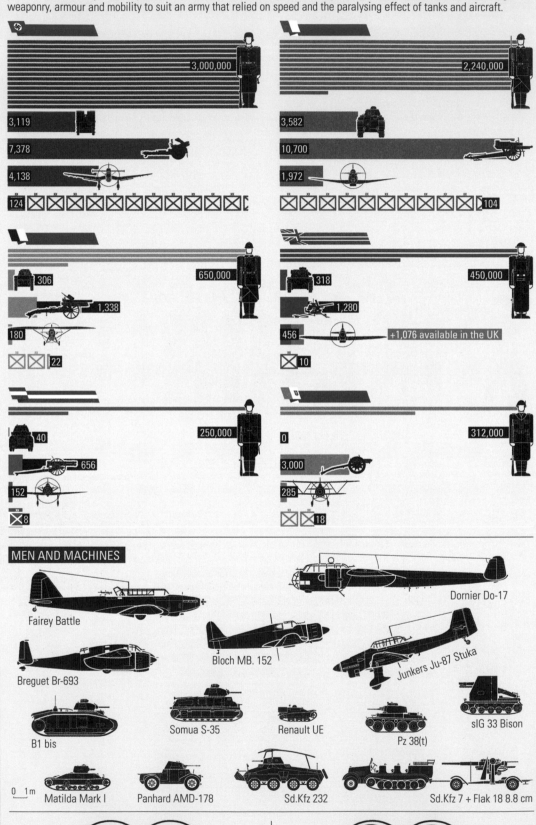

MEN AND MACHINES

Fairey Battle

Dornier Do-17

Bloch MB. 152

Breguet Br-693

Junkers Ju-87 Stuka

B1 bis

Somua S-35

Renault UE

Pz 38(t)

sIG 33 Bison

0   1m

Matilda Mark I

Panhard AMD-178

Sd.Kfz 232

Sd.Kfz 7 + Flak 18 8.8 cm

General Maurice Gamelin 1872–1958

General Maxime Weygand 1867–1965

General Heinz Guderian 1888–1954

General Erich von Manstein 1887–1973

2 • A FAILURE OF STRATEGY

1: On 10 May 1940, German paratroopers disrupt the whole Dutch army. A glider-borne troupe destroys the Belgian fort at Eben-Emael, which was blocking tanks from the plains.

2: 10 May, Army Group B sweeps into the Netherlands and Belgium.

3/3: 10 May, the Dyle-Breda Plan. Intending to capture the front, integrate the neutral armies and cover French territory, Gamelin sends in his main corps.

4: 13–21 May, the effectiveness of the strike by Army Group A, based on the Manstein Plan, is unintentionally reduced. But the Germans can afford to make mistakes (huge bottleneck in the Ardennes, the order to stop before Dunkirk), and the French command system breaks down. Gamelin has no reserves and his best divisions are stuck on the flanks.

5/5/5: After the Dutch surrender on 15 May, just under 1,500,000 men remain trapped. The disorganized Allies cannot counter-attack. The British trigger Operation Dynamo and retreat from Dunkirk. Belgium surrenders on 28 May.

6/6: On 4 June, the pocket is destroyed. Over 300,000 soldiers without equipment are evacuated and when Operation Dynamo is over, 40,000 French soldiers are forced to surrender. The final toll is horrendous, unequalled in military history.

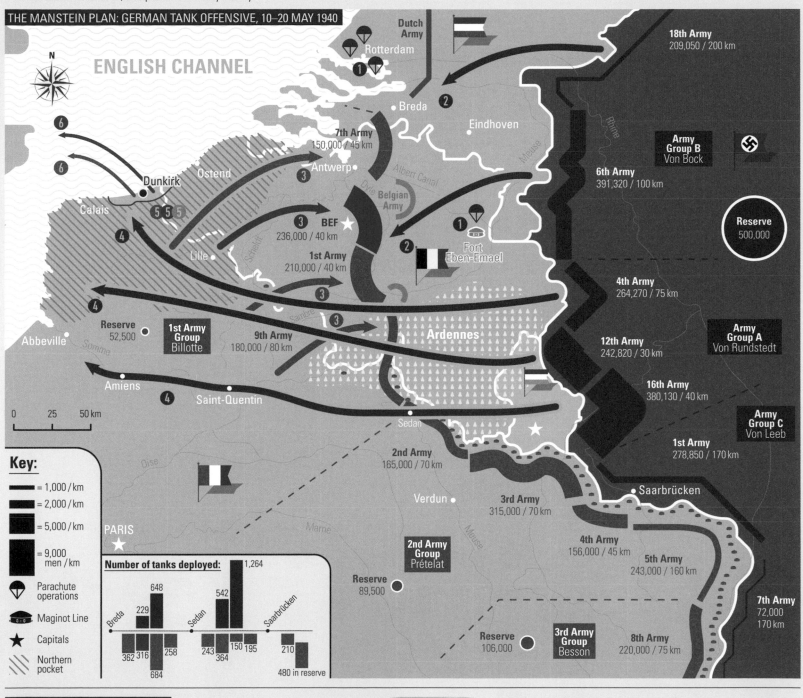

THE MANSTEIN PLAN: GERMAN TANK OFFENSIVE, 10–20 MAY 1940

ENGLISH CHANNEL

Dutch Army
Rotterdam
Breda
Eindhoven
7th Army 150,000 / 45 km
Antwerp
Belgian Army
Albert Canal
BEF 236,000 / 40 km
1st Army 210,000 / 40 km
Fort Eben-Emael
Dunkirk
Ostend
Calais
Lille
Ardennes
9th Army 180,000 / 80 km
Reserve 52,500
1st Army Group Billotte
Abbeville
Amiens
Saint-Quentin
Sedan
2nd Army 165,000 / 70 km
Verdun
2nd Army Group Prételat
Reserve 89,500
PARIS
Reserve 106,000
3rd Army Group Besson

18th Army 209,050 / 200 km
Army Group B Von Bock
6th Army 391,320 / 100 km
Reserve 500,000
4th Army 264,270 / 75 km
Army Group A Von Rundstedt
12th Army 242,820 / 30 km
16th Army 380,130 / 40 km
Army Group C Von Leeb
1st Army 278,850 / 170 km
Saarbrücken
3rd Army 315,000 / 70 km
4th Army 156,000 / 45 km
5th Army 243,000 / 160 km
7th Army 72,000 / 170 km
8th Army 220,000 / 75 km
Rhine
Meuse

0 25 50 km

Key:
= 1,000 / km
= 2,000 / km
= 5,000 / km
= 9,000 men / km

Parachute operations
Maginot Line
Capitals
Northern pocket

Number of tanks deployed:
Breda: 229, 648, 362, 316, 684, 258
Sedan: 542, 1,264, 243, 364, 150, 195
Saarbrücken: 210, 480 in reserve

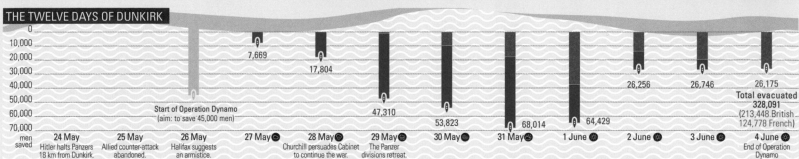

THE TWELVE DAYS OF DUNKIRK

| | men saved | 0 | 10,000 | 20,000 | 30,000 | 40,000 | 50,000 | 60,000 | 70,000 |

7,669
17,804
47,310
53,823
68,014
64,429
26,256
26,746
26,175

Total evacuated 328,091 (213,448 British 124,778 French)

24 May Hitler halts Panzers 18 km from Dunkirk.
25 May Allied counter-attack abandoned.
26 May Halifax suggests an armistice.
Start of Operation Dynamo (aim: to save 45,000 men)
27 May
28 May Churchill persuades Cabinet to continue the war.
29 May The Panzer divisions retreat.
30 May
31 May
1 June
2 June
3 June
4 June End of Operation Dynamo

3 • AIRCRAFT AND ARMOURED VEHICLES IN BATTLE

Gamelin used two ground deployment strategies: one in which tanks were divided into battalions and supported the infantry and one in which, taking the role formerly occupied by cavalry, they reconnoitred ahead of the massed infantry. This resulted in a fragmentation of resources and disastrous over-specialization (infantry tanks were robust but slow and low). The Germans, by contrast, grouped their tanks into ten divisions to exploit their advantages: shock, speed and fear. In this way, even the small Panzer I and II, deployed en masse and accompanied by heavier tanks, could take part in the manoeuvre. Furthermore, the French tanks did not usually have radios and their

single-seat turrets placed an excessive burden on the tank commander, who had to both aim and fire. Despite their better armour and weaponry, they seemed unwieldy, uncoordinated and lacking in firepower: in short, unfit for war in 1940. The situation was worse in the air, where the Germans were superior in numbers, quality (especially with bombers) and consistency. They were omnipresent, since their efficient signals allowed up to four missions per day and enabled sorties to converge on key points, while the French only organized one sortie per day. Added to this was the decision to keep back a reserve (in anticipation of a long war), which reduced the number of aircraft even more.

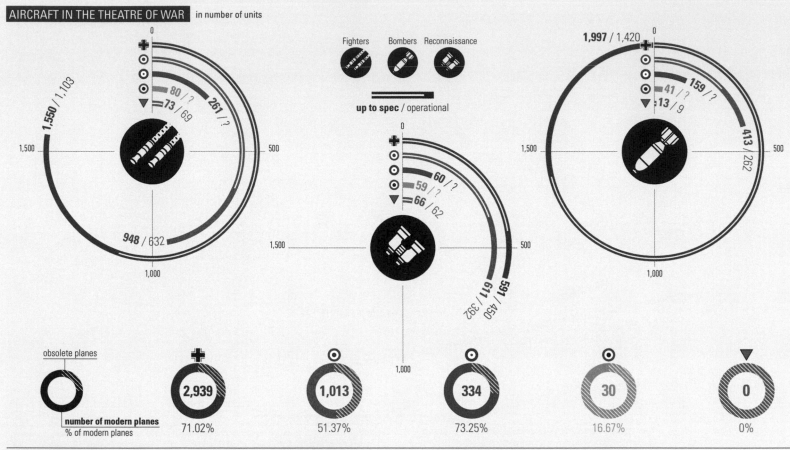

AIRCRAFT IN THE THEATRE OF WAR in number of units

Fighters   Bombers   Reconnaissance

up to spec / operational

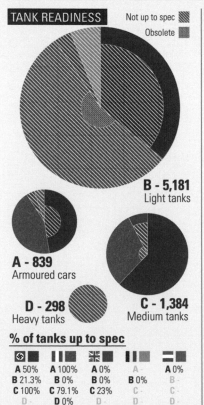

TANK READINESS

Not up to spec
Obsolete

B - 5,181
Light tanks

A - 839
Armoured cars

D - 298
Heavy tanks

C - 1,384
Medium tanks

% of tanks up to spec

	⚙	▮▮▮	✳	▮▮	▬
A	50%	100%	0%	–	0%
B	21.3%	0%	0%	0%	–
C	100%	79.1%	23%	–	–
D	–	0%	–	–	–

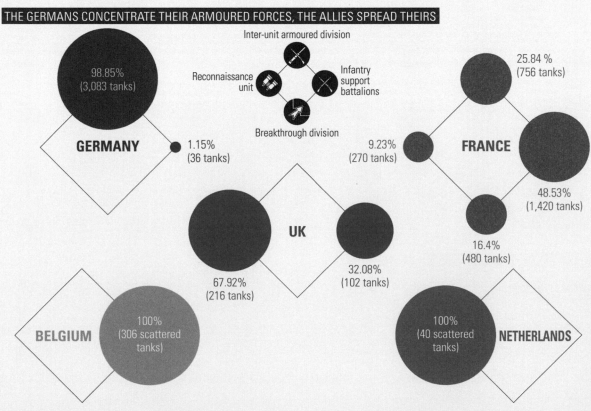

THE GERMANS CONCENTRATE THEIR ARMOURED FORCES, THE ALLIES SPREAD THEIRS

Inter-unit armoured division

Reconnaissance unit

Infantry support battalions

Breakthrough division

GERMANY
98.85% (3,083 tanks)
1.15% (36 tanks)

FRANCE
25.84 % (756 tanks)
9.23% (270 tanks)
48.53% (1,420 tanks)
16.4% (480 tanks)

UK
67.92% (216 tanks)
32.08% (102 tanks)

BELGIUM
100% (306 scattered tanks)

NETHERLANDS
100% (40 scattered tanks)

4 • *BLITZKRIEG*: THE MEUSE CROSSING AT SEDAN – A WEEK OF 'LIGHTNING WAR'

Blitzkrieg, meaning 'lightning war', is a well-known term but its significance is debated. It is often defined as a revolutionary strategy in which the combined and concentrated action of tanks and aircraft surprises the enemy and allows it to be encircled and quickly destroyed. Michael Geyer and Shimon Naveh dispute that definition. They believe that *Blitzkrieg* is a reflection of traditional German battle strategy, updated for modern technologies by pragmatists such as Guderian and Rommel. Certainly the aim of a quick decisive victory has been the German focus since the time of Frederick II. The Wehrmacht

inherited a love of surprise, concentrated resources, flexibility and retention of the initiative. Control of the front and the practice of *Auftragstaktik* (delegating the practical implementation to subordinates in the field) were already encouraged in 1918 and infiltration units (*Stosstruppen*) were used. To shock the enemy, the Germans had also invented the rolling barrage (*Feuerwalze*). These were all ways of speeding up a manoeuvre. *Blitzkrieg* merely added a few innovations that made it ten times as efficient. The Sedan breakthrough was a perfect example.

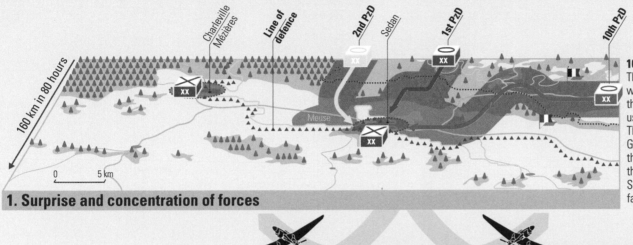

1. Surprise and concentration of forces

10–13 May (16:00)
The aim of surprising the French with a fast attack by massing on their right flank had already been used in the Schlieffen Plan in 1914. The situation was similar in 1940. The Germans surprised the enemy, passing through the Ardennes hills. Guderian's three Panzer divisions gathered at Sedan within three days. They were facing one weak French division.

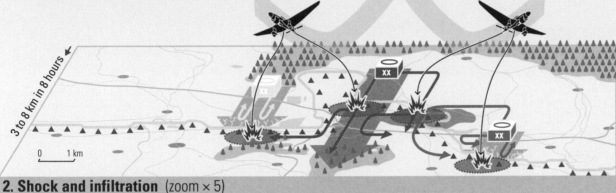

2. Shock and infiltration (zoom × 5)

13 May (16:00–24:00)
Without waiting, the Luftwaffe unleashed hell. Detachments of infantry and engineers took advantage to cross the Meuse. Many were repelled but a handful infiltrated, acting autonomously as their predecessors had in 1918 and breaking up the French front, following the line of least resistance.

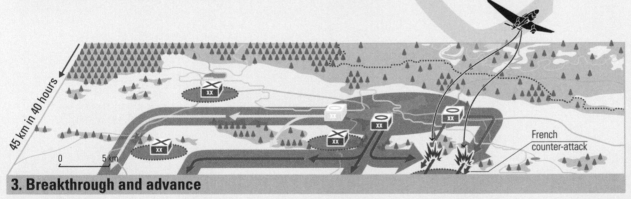

3. Breakthrough and advance

14–15 May
The tanks crossed the river. Inter-unit groups widened the breach, moving forward in giant steps. They bypassed what they could and crushed the counter-attacks in encounter battles in which the most reactive side had the advantage. Despite fatigue, Guderian continued towards the Channel. The French could not exploit the breach between the front line and the infantry outdistanced on foot.

German innovations

JERRYCANS	PERVITIN / METHAMPHETAMINE	MOTORIZATION	TELECOMMUNICATIONS	PLANES AS FLYING ARTILLERY	CREATION OF AUTONOMOUS UNIFIED COMBAT SYSTEMS
to increase autonomy (Action)	stimulant drug to aid wakefulness (Action)	of an entire corps (Action)	(Concentration / Action)	(Concentration / Action)	(Concentration / Action / Initiative)

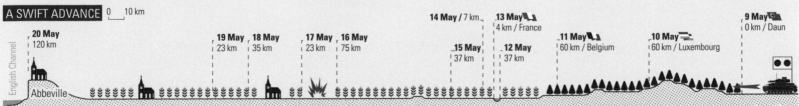

A SWIFT ADVANCE

20 May 120 km

19 May 23 km
18 May 35 km
17 May 23 km
16 May 75 km

14 May / 7 km
13 May 4 km / France

15 May 37 km
12 May 37 km

11 May 60 km / Belgium

10 May 60 km / Luxembourg

9 May 0 km / Daun

English Channel

Abbeville — Albert — Saint-Quentin — Counter-attack at Montcornet — River Meuse — Ardennes Hills

Total: 481 km in 11 days

THE BATTLE OF FRANCE: 1 GERMAN CASUALTY FOR 99 ALLIED CASUALTIES

Comparative casualties
(dead, missing, prisoners, evacuated)

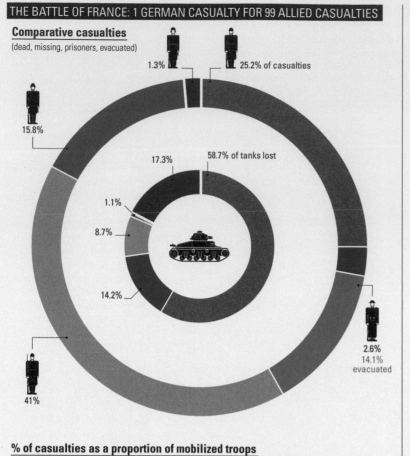

1.3%

25.2% of casualties

15.8%

17.3%

58.7% of tanks lost

1.1%

8.7%

14.2%

2.6%
14.1% evacuated

41%

% of casualties as a proportion of mobilized troops

400,000	41,000 (224,320 evacuated)	650,000	250,000	21,000
30%	15% (70%)	100%	100%	0.7%
2,070 tanks	500 tanks	306 tanks	40 tanks	612 tanks
80%	57%	100%	100%	19%

'CASE RED': THE CONQUEST OF FRANCE

BELGIUM

GERMAN REICH

Cherbourg
Le Havre
Rouen
PARIS
Metz
Brest
Rennes
Briare
Nantes
Tours
Poitiers
Vichy
15 June
Lyon
La Bourboule
Angoulème
Ussel
Pontarlier
SWITZERLAND
Bordeaux
14 June
Montauban 23 June
Toulouse
Grenoble
ITALY
Nice
Marseille
SPAIN

Key:

➡ German offensives	▬ 5 June: German offensive sets off
⇢ Panzer movements with no fighting	▬ 9 June: breakthrough on the Somme
➡ Italian offensives on 21 June	▬ 14 June: German forces enter Paris
▨ Occupied territory	▬ 16 June, evening: Pétain's government requests an armistice
▬ Maginot Line	▬ 18 June: armies of the East surrounded

▬ 25 June: armistice comes into force

Movement of GQG (French Army high command) and stopover points

Movement of French government and stopover points

6 • THE HUMAN AND MATERIAL COST

Although the death toll was not as high as the 100,000 that had been predicted, French losses of around 50,000 were recorded. Compared with the 40,000 Germans killed (31,000 confirmed, plus many missing, the prisoners not transferred to Britain having been released), the ratio of 1 to 1.5 was comparable to the ratio in 1914–18.

The German losses in June (27,000 dead and missing) were higher than those in May (21,000), demonstrating the tenacity of the French soldiers once they had overcome the initial shock, a dedication completely at odds with the mocking post-war clichés.

But in June 1940, the disparity was too wide and France did not have the resources to recover. Another myth dispelled was that the RAF was trying to save itself. It lost 900 of its 1,300 aircraft on 10 May, thereby helping to weaken the Luftwaffe, who lost 35% of their planes. But this British sacrifice was more than repaid by the 1,600 new aircraft it received, unlike its opponent.

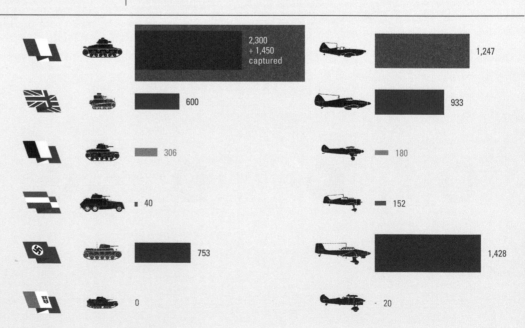

2,300 + 1,450 captured

1,247

600

933

306

180

40

152

753

1,428

0

20

SOURCES: 1. P. Facon, *L'Armée de l'air dans la tourmente*, Paris, 2005 • 2. G. Saint-Martin, *L'Arme blindée française*, vol. 1: *Mai-Juin 1940. Les blindés français dans la tourmente*, Paris, 2011 • 3. K.-H. Frieser, *The Blitzkrieg Legend*, Annapolis MD, 2005 • 4. *Germany and the Second World War*, vol. 2: *Germany's Initial Conquests in Europe*, eds. K. A. Maier *et al.*, Oxford, 2015 • 5. *GBM: Histoire de Guerre, Blindés & Matériel*,

5 • THE AFTERMATH

The German attack led to unprecedented disaster. The French army found itself isolated, having lost the best third of its divisions, 80% of its modern equipment and 800 aircraft. By comparison, the casualties were quite small. The speed spared bloodshed. The Germans, in control of the territory, were able to recover their damaged vehicles. In early June, 104 German divisions broke through the Somme front, held by just 66 brave but under-equipped divisions. By then, the French nation was collapsing. The initial preventive exodus in the autumn of 1939 was due to the trauma of the 1914–18 war, the policy of shielding the population and the fear of air raids in cities. The second exodus was on a scale never before seen in Western Europe. The German attack drove over 10 million civilians on to the roads: 90% of the population of Lille and 60% of Parisians fled. So did the government and the general headquarters of the French army (GQG). In the confusion, power disintegrated. The battle for France was lost. The French prime minister, Paul Reynaud, who supported continuing the fight overseas, felt he had been rebuffed and he resigned. France's enemies took advantage of events and insisted that an armistice was the only way out, an armistice that deprived the country of its army and one-third of its territory and put it at the mercy of the occupying forces.

A TIDE OF DISPLACED PEOPLE

= 250,000 people

People fleeing the German advance after 10 May

Belgium 2,000,000 / Luxembourg 49,000 / Netherlands 5,000 / France 7,000,000

People evacuated before 10 May

Alsace 424,000 / Moselle 277,000 / Paris 500,000

Total displaced population in June 1940
9,054,000 men, women and children

THE DIVISION OF FRANCE

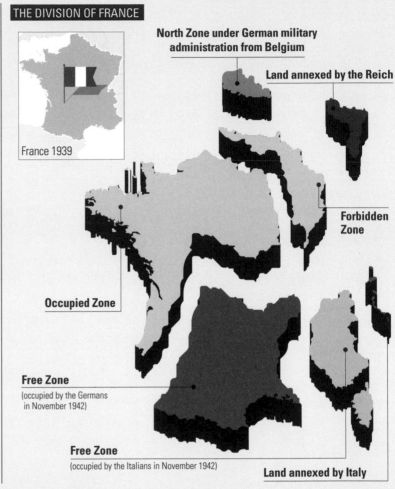

France 1939

North Zone under German military administration from Belgium

Land annexed by the Reich

Forbidden Zone

Occupied Zone

Free Zone
(occupied by the Germans in November 1942)

Free Zone
(occupied by the Italians in November 1942)

Land annexed by Italy

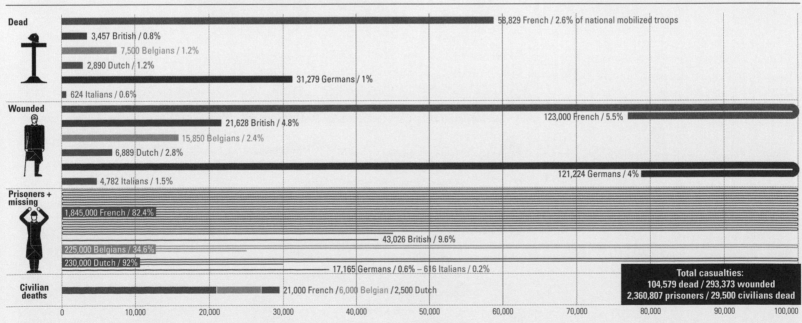

Dead
58,829 French / 2.6% of national mobilized troops
3,457 British / 0.8%
7,500 Belgians / 1.2%
2,890 Dutch / 1.2%
31,279 Germans / 1%
624 Italians / 0.6%

Wounded
21,628 British / 4.8%
15,850 Belgians / 2.4%
6,889 Dutch / 2.8%
123,000 French / 5.5%
121,224 Germans / 4%
4,782 Italians / 1.5%

Prisoners + missing
1,845,000 French / 82.4%
225,000 Belgians / 34.6%
230,000 Dutch / 92%
43,026 British / 9.6%
17,165 Germans / 0.6% – 616 Italians / 0.2%

Civilian deaths
21,000 French / 6,000 Belgian / 2,500 Dutch

Total casualties:
104,579 dead / 293,373 wounded
2,360,807 prisoners / 29,500 civilians dead

0   10,000   20,000   30,000   40,000   50,000   60,000   70,000   80,000   90,000   100,000

nos. 74 & 75 • 6. J.-L. Leleu *et al.* (eds.), *La France pendant la Seconde Guerre mondiale, Atlas historique*, Paris, 2010 • 7. M. Vaïsse (ed.), *Mai–juin 1940. Défaite française, victoire allemande, sous l'oeil des historiens étrangers*, Paris, 2000 • 8. C. Levisse-Touzé (ed.), *La Campagne de 1940*, Paris, 2001 • 9. T. L. Jentz, *Panzertruppen: The Complete Guide to the Creation & Combat Employment of Germany's Tank Force 1933–1942*, Atglen, PA, 1996.

THE BATTLE OF BRITAIN

The Battle of Britain has many facets. If we are to believe the versions of the story widely circulated after the war and portrayed in films, it refers to the period from mid-August to late October 1940, when a handful of indomitable pilots were ready to launch themselves against the Nazi winged hordes to protect their skies, save their country and so avoid invasion. Fortunately, their desperate and almost suicidal courage culminated in a miracle. Hitler, furious at a bomber raid on Berlin, abandoned his plans to invade the British Isles, leaving the RAF drained but victorious.

As the historian Richard Overy has made very clear, this story was mere propaganda. The RAF was never truly threatened with extinction. There was never a shortage of pilots or aircraft and only a handful of airfields temporarily put out of action. In fact, although RAF losses were not negligible, they were tolerable, unlike those suffered by the Luftwaffe, whose fighter planes were heavily hit.

As for the famous turning point that 'saved' Britain, it owed much less to the Führer's anger than to an error of judgment by Goering. Overestimating the losses inflicted, he thought the RAF was finished and moved on to another phase of the strategic programme: destruction of industrial sites. Since the Blitz was ongoing (the infamous raid on Coventry took place on 14 November 1940), the British, overestimating their enemy's power, had as much trouble realizing their victory as their opponents had understanding their defeat. It was not until March 1941 that the Air Ministry in London published a leaflet announcing that the Battle of Britain (Battle with a capital B for the first time) had been won. The Germans had by then regained their strength, but they were now looking towards the east.

Did Hitler really want to invade Britain? Or was the air offensive a means towards a negotiated peace? It's hard to say. Although the RAF may not have definitively saved the country, they certainly gave it a moral victory. That was no mean achievement in such times.

1 • THE BALANCE OF FORCES

The battle pitched two German *Luftflotten*, combined fighter and bomber forces, against Fighter Command, a unified British command subdivided into four groups, with No. 11 Group covering the south-east of Britain where the attacks were concentrated. The Germans had a choice of targets, with numerical superiority on their side. However, the scope of the offensive was restricted by the limited range of the Messerschmitt Bf 109 E single-seater fighter planes needed to escort the bombers. The RAF had more Spitfires and Hurricanes to deploy against it and radar optimized interception.

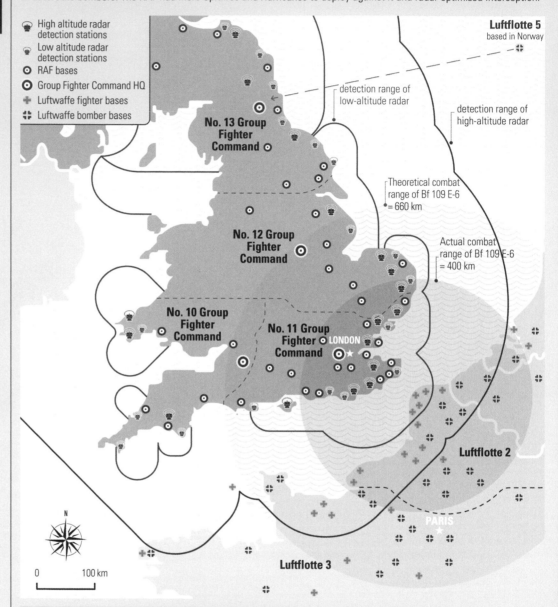

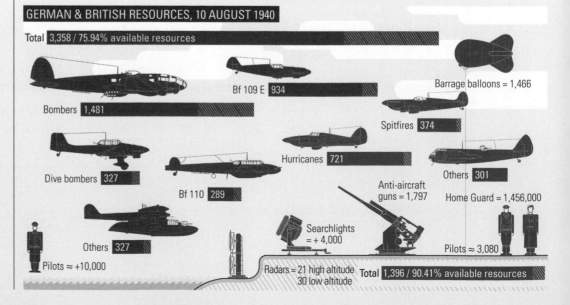

2 • PHASES OF THE BATTLE

The German offensive was divided into four phases. Until 7 August 1940, swarms of fighters harassed the RAF in the south of England and attacked the ports. The second phase, up to 6 September, targeted Fighter Command airfields in the south and around London, as well as radar installations and aeronautics factories. The third phase, starting on 7 September, consisted of raids on factories and docks in the Greater London area. Finally came the Blitz, night-time bombing raids on industrial centres, focusing mainly on London; it continued from 14 November to the summer of 1941.

PHASES OF THE BATTLE

Phase 1 18 Jun–7 Aug   **Phase 2** 8–23 Aug   24 Aug–6 Sep   **Phase 3** 7–19 Sep   20 Sep–13 Nov   **Phase 4** Night raids 14 Nov

July   August   September   October   November

NUMBER OF FIGHTER PILOTS AND PLANES

■ Britain   ■ Germany

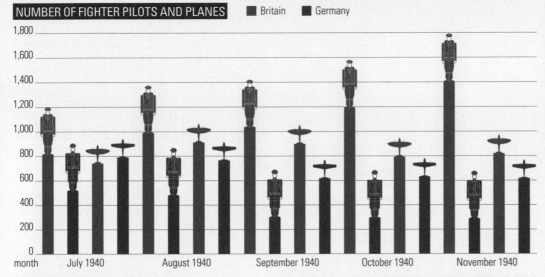

month   July 1940   August 1940   September 1940   October 1940   November 1940

FIGHTER PLANE SORTIES IN 1940   per week

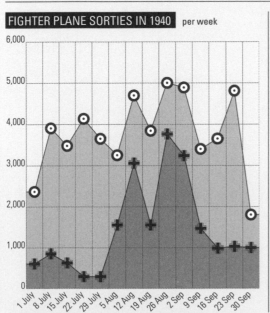

1 July, 8 July, 15 July, 22 July, 29 July, 5 Aug, 12 Aug, 19 Aug, 26 Aug, 2 Sep, 9 Sep, 16 Sep, 23 Sep, 30 Sep

BOMBING OF BRITISH CITIES IN THE BLITZ

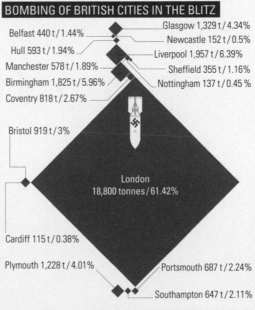

Belfast 440 t / 1.44%
Hull 593 t / 1.94%
Manchester 578 t / 1.89%
Birmingham 1,825 t / 5.96%
Coventry 818 t / 2.67%
Glasgow 1,329 t / 4.34%
Newcastle 152 t / 0.5%
Liverpool 1,957 t / 6.39%
Sheffield 355 t / 1.16%
Nottingham 137 t / 0.45%
Bristol 919 t / 3%
London 18,800 tonnes / 61.42%
Cardiff 115 t / 0.38%
Plymouth 1,228 t / 4.01%
Portsmouth 687 t / 2.24%
Southampton 647 t / 2.11%

FIGHTER COMMAND WARNING SYSTEM

Radar = 20 mins. warning of an attack
Barrage balloons
Sector Control
Command Centre observers   Observers
Fighter Command HQ   Group HQ
Anti-air guns on alert
Air base   Spitfire = 13 mins. to take off

3 • THE CASUALTIES

Although Fighter Command undeniably suffered, it inflicted seven and a half times as many permanent losses, counting the Germans shot down over Britain and immediately captured, while the British often returned to combat the same day. Moreover, the RAF had a more efficient and sustainable pilot management system (rotation, training, replacement) and the aircraft it lost were quickly replaced. On the other hand, although the Blitz was primarily aimed at factories, the civilian population suffered from the night bombing raids.

PILOTS LOST

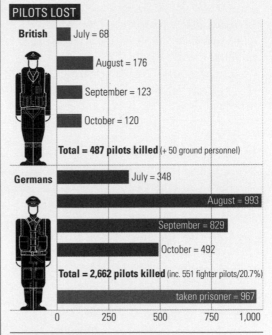

British
July = 68
August = 176
September = 123
October = 120
Total = 487 pilots killed (+ 50 ground personnel)

Germans
July = 348
August = 993
September = 829
October = 492
Total = 2,662 pilots killed (inc. 551 fighter pilots/20.7%)
taken prisoner = 967

0   250   500   750   1,000

PLANES LOST

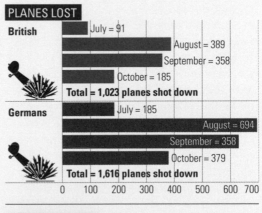

British
July = 91
August = 389
September = 358
October = 185
Total = 1,023 planes shot down

Germans
July = 185
August = 694
September = 358
October = 379
Total = 1,616 planes shot down

0   100   200   300   400   500   600   700

CIVILIAN LOSSES

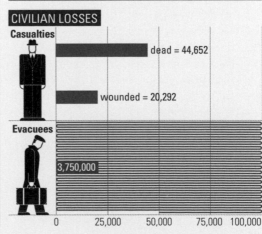

Casualties
dead = 44,652
wounded = 20,292

Evacuees
3,750,000

0   25,000   50,000   75,000   100,000

SOURCES: 1. Richard Overy, *The Battle of Britain: Myth and Reality*, London, 2010; Richard Overy, *The Bombers and the Bombed: Allied Air War over Europe, 1940–1945*, New York, 2014 • 2. Peter Dye, 'Logistics and the Battle of Britain', *Air Force Journal of Logistics*, 22 December 2000 • 3. *After the Battle of Britain (Mark II)*, Old Harlow, Essex, 1982, p. 259.

A TIDAL WAVE FROM JAPAN

Commonly known as the 'War in the Pacific', the war between imperial Japan and the Western Allies lasted from 7 December 1941 to 2 September 1945, according to the standard chronology; this, however, reflects a narrow and US-centric view of the conflict. In fact, its roots and its impact were far broader, going back to the 1930s. They involved the whole of East and South-East Asia, starting with China but also including the Indian and Indo-Chinese peninsulas, Mongolia, Korea and the USSR.

From a Japanese point of view, this was in fact a 'war of Greater East Asia' which started with the invasion of China in 1937, or even earlier with the Fifteen-Year War, a conflict that began with the annexation of Manchuria in 1931, and continued until Japan's surrender in 1945, encompassing the Nomonhan Incident (or Battle of Khalkhyn Gol) against the Red Army, and the gradual takeover of French Indochina from 1940 to 1945.

Even confined to its traditional framework, the Asian-Pacific War extended to the Indian Ocean, Burma, India and China. Through its alliance with Nazi Germany and Fascist Italy under the 1940 Tripartite Pact, its ultra-nationalist policy and its military, particularly naval, might, Japan put itself on a collision course with the USA, a fact that became clear after Roosevelt decided in July 1941 to impose an economic embargo on Japan. Tokyo then had the choice of abandoning its brutally won Chinese conquests to normalize relations with the West or taking advantage of Allied and Soviet weakness in Europe to carve out by force a 'Greater East Asia Co-Prosperity Sphere' for its own exclusive benefit, including the strategic resources of the South-East Asian islands and in particular the oil in the Dutch East Indies. Although well aware of the disproportionate balance of forces and long-term economic implications, Emperor Hirohito, absolute ruler of Japan, agreed to this reckless plan. He believed the explanation by his military leaders that it was possible to achieve victory by making the Japanese positions unassailable and forcing the Allies, especially the United States, to negotiate a 'new order' for Asia.

On 7 December 1941, while limited (around ten divisions) but well-prepared Japanese forces were getting ready to sweep into the Philippines, Malaysia, Singapore and the Dutch East Indies, the aircraft carrier fleet, the Kidō Butai, at that time the best in the world, carried out a surprise attack on the US fleet in the Pacific at Pearl Harbor, its main base in Hawaii.

1 • PEARL HARBOR: A DECEPTIVE VICTORY

Remembered by history as 'a day of infamy' and a tragic defeat inflicted on the US fleet, the military effects of the attack on Pearl Harbor were in fact relatively limited, since the primary outcome was the temporary neutralization of a fleet of old battleships, largely obsolete because they were too slow; all except two were later recommissioned. In particular, the attack failed to hit the US aircraft carriers. The raid and the destruction of the Royal Navy's Z Force on 10 December 1941 only gave Japan a few months to consolidate its victories, but did not change the fundamental balance of power.

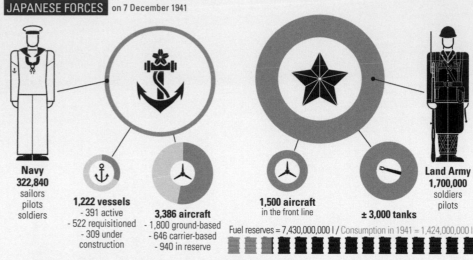

JAPANESE FORCES on 7 December 1941

Navy 322,840 sailors pilots soldiers

1,222 vessels
- 391 active
- 522 requisitioned
- 309 under construction

3,386 aircraft
- 1,800 ground-based
- 646 carrier-based
- 940 in reserve

1,500 aircraft in the front line

± 3,000 tanks

Land Army 1,700,000 soldiers pilots

Fuel reserves = 7,430,000,000 l / Consumption in 1941 = 1,424,000,000 l

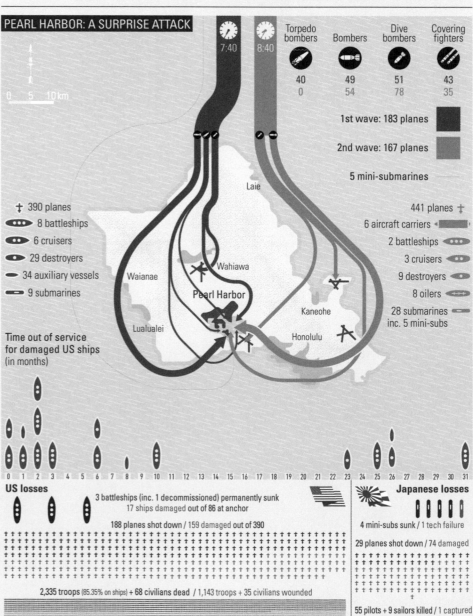

PEARL HARBOR: A SURPRISE ATTACK

	Torpedo bombers	Bombers	Dive bombers	Covering fighters
7:40	40	49	51	43
8:40	0	54	78	35

1st wave: 183 planes
2nd wave: 167 planes
5 mini-submarines

0   5   10 km

Laie

† 390 planes
8 battleships
6 cruisers
29 destroyers
34 auxiliary vessels
9 submarines

Waianae   Wahiawa
Pearl Harbor
Lualualei   Kaneohe
Honolulu

441 planes †
6 aircraft carriers
2 battleships
3 cruisers
9 destroyers
8 oilers
28 submarines inc. 5 mini-subs

Time out of service for damaged US ships (in months)

0 1 2 3 4 5 6 7 8 9 10 11 12 13 14 15 16 17 18 19 20 21 22 23 24 25 26 27 28 29 30 31

US losses

3 battleships (inc. 1 decommissioned) permanently sunk
17 ships damaged out of 86 at anchor

188 planes shot down / 159 damaged out of 390

Japanese losses

4 mini-subs sunk / 1 tech failure

29 planes shot down / 74 damaged

2,335 troops (85.35% on ships) + 68 civilians dead / 1,143 troops + 35 civilians wounded

55 pilots + 9 sailors killed / 1 captured

2 • JAPAN'S CONQUESTS: DECEMBER 1941–JUNE 1942

Realizing it could not defeat the USA, the Japanese command, starting with Admiral Yamamoto, planned to gain time with a rapid and brutal offensive, the first stage in which was the immediate neutralization of the US Pacific fleet in Pearl Harbor, Hawaii, without a declaration of war. In six months, during which the Japanese were able to keep the strategic initiative in the Pacific as planned, the initial mission for the fleet, backed by the army, was to take the US-controlled Philippines, British Malaysia and strategically important Singapore, while securing resources in the West's colonies (Java, Sumatra, Borneo, New Guinea, etc.), isolating China by taking over Burma and creating a vast defensive perimeter based on the Central and South Pacific archipelagos as far as the Gilbert and Solomon Islands, a direct threat to the coasts of Australia. In the second phase, Yamamoto toyed with the idea of finishing off the US fleet by encouraging it to fight a major decisive battle around the island of Midway.

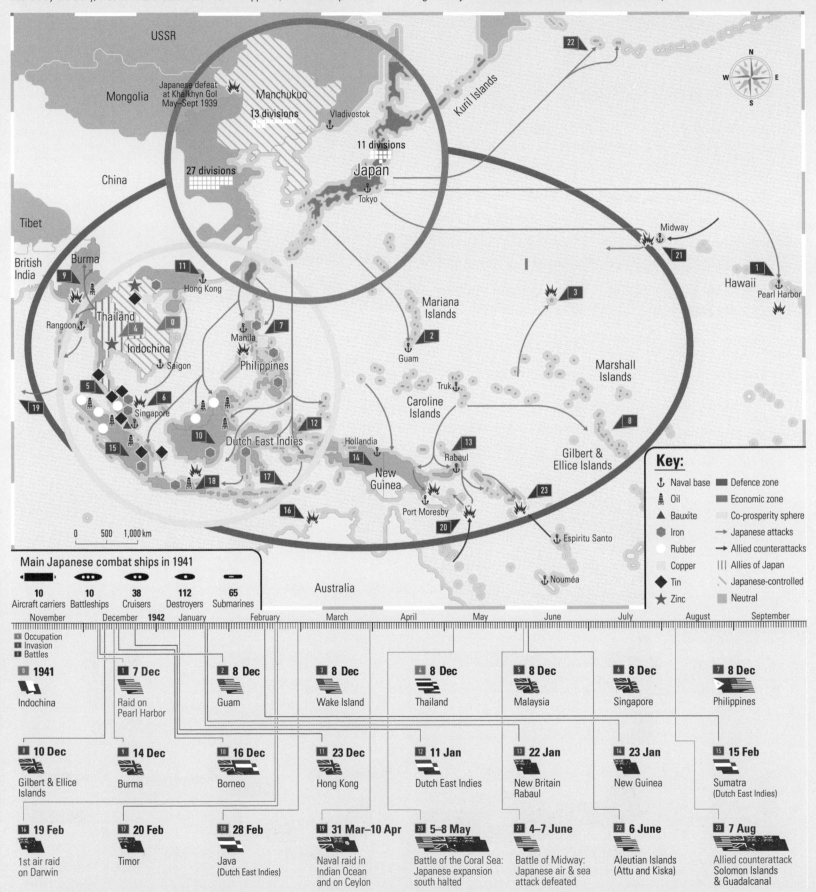

Key:
⚓ Naval base   ■ Defence zone
⛽ Oil   ■ Economic zone
▲ Bauxite   □ Co-prosperity sphere
⬡ Iron   → Japanese attacks
○ Rubber   → Allied counterattacks
□ Copper ||| Allies of Japan
◆ Tin   ╲ Japanese-controlled
★ Zinc   ▨ Neutral

Main Japanese combat ships in 1941

10	10	38	112	65
Aircraft carriers	Battleships	Cruisers	Destroyers	Submarines

■ Occupation
■ Invasion
■ Battles

0 1941	1 7 Dec	2 8 Dec	3 8 Dec	4 8 Dec	5 8 Dec	6 8 Dec	7 8 Dec
Indochina	Raid on Pearl Harbor	Guam	Wake Island	Thailand	Malaysia	Singapore	Philippines

8 10 Dec	9 14 Dec	10 16 Dec	11 23 Dec	12 11 Jan	13 22 Jan	14 23 Jan	15 15 Feb
Gilbert & Ellice Islands	Burma	Borneo	Hong Kong	Dutch East Indies	New Britain Rabaul	New Guinea	Sumatra (Dutch East Indies)

16 19 Feb	17 20 Feb	18 28 Feb	19 31 Mar–10 Apr	20 5–8 May	21 4–7 June	22 6 June	23 7 Aug
1st air raid on Darwin	Timor	Java (Dutch East Indies)	Naval raid in Indian Ocean and on Ceylon	Battle of the Coral Sea: Japanese expansion south halted	Battle of Midway: Japanese air & sea attack defeated	Aleutian Islands (Attu and Kiska)	Allied counterattack Solomon Islands & Guadalcanal

3 • A WAR OF ATTRITION: RETAKING THE SOUTH PACIFIC

After an uninterrupted run of victories lasting several months, the spectacular Japanese conquests were brought to a halt in the spring of 1942, in the Coral Sea in May then in Midway in June. Admiral Yamamoto's battle plan to finish off the US Pacific Fleet ended in disaster when his main weapon, the Kidō Butai, lost four out of six large aircraft carriers. From August 1942, the Americans regained the initiative, embarking on a war of attrition to retake the Solomon Islands in the South Pacific, starting with the island of Guadalcanal. This costly major battle, fought for several months at sea, on the ground and in the air, enabled them to eat away at the Japanese forces, whose commanders made the mistake of clinging on to secondary positions while waiting for Admiral Nimitz's fleet to be strengthened in 1943.

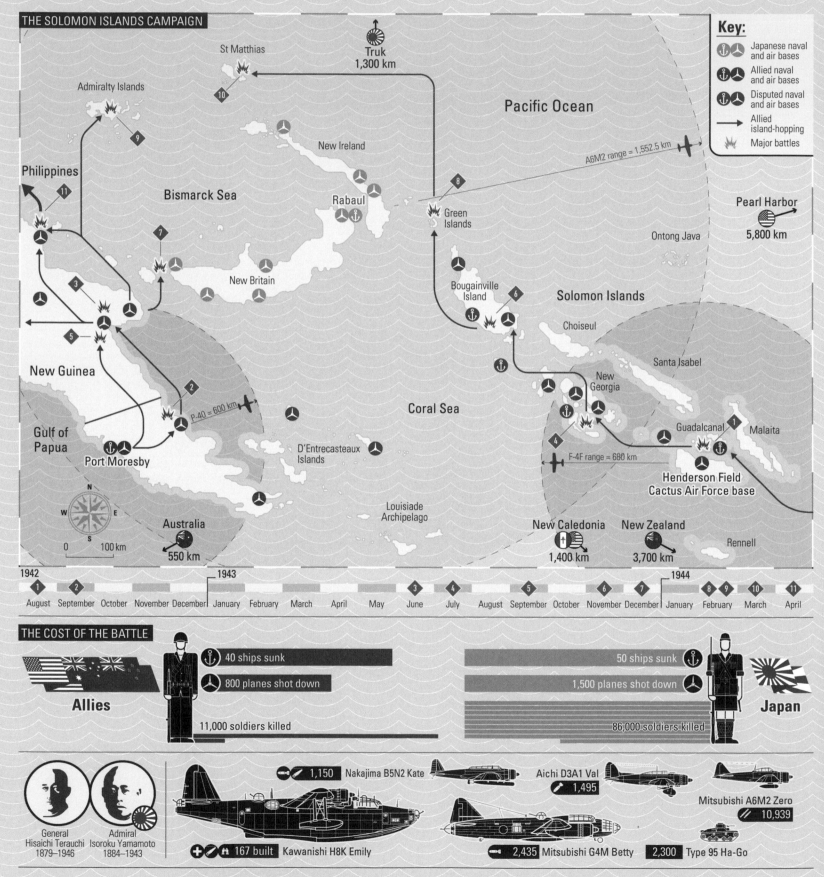

THE SOLOMON ISLANDS CAMPAIGN

Key:
- Japanese naval and air bases
- Allied naval and air bases
- Disputed naval and air bases
- Allied island-hopping
- Major battles

St Matthias
Truk 1,300 km
Admiralty Islands
Pacific Ocean
New Ireland
Philippines
Bismarck Sea
A6M2 range = 1,552.5 km
Rabaul
Green Islands
Pearl Harbor 5,800 km
Ontong Java
New Britain
Bougainville Island
Solomon Islands
Choiseul
New Guinea
Santa Isabel
New Georgia
P-40 = 600 km
Coral Sea
Guadalcanal
Malaita
Gulf of Papua
Port Moresby
D'Entrecasteaux Islands
F-4F range = 680 km
Henderson Field Cactus Air Force base
Louisiade Archipelago
Australia 550 km
New Caledonia 1,400 km
New Zealand 3,700 km
Rennell

0 100 km

1942
1 August
2 September
October
November
December
1943
January
February
March
April
May
3 June
4 July
August
5 September
October
6 November
7 December
1944
8 January
9 February
10 March
11 April

THE COST OF THE BATTLE

Allies
- 40 ships sunk
- 800 planes shot down
- 11,000 soldiers killed

Japan
- 50 ships sunk
- 1,500 planes shot down
- 86,000 soldiers killed

General Hisaichi Terauchi 1879–1946
Admiral Isoroku Yamamoto 1884–1943

167 built Kawanishi H8K Emily
1,150 Nakajima B5N2 Kate
Aichi D3A1 Val 1,495
Mitsubishi A6M2 Zero 10,939
2,435 Mitsubishi G4M Betty
2,300 Type 95 Ha-Go

SOURCES: 1. Nicolas Bernard, *La Guerre du Pacifique*, Paris, 2016 • 2. John Costello, *The Pacific War*, New York, 1981 • 3. S. E. Morison, *History of US Naval Operations in World War II*, New York, 2001 (reprint) •

4 • THE SILENT SERVICE: A VITAL WEAPON IN THE PACIFIC

Lesser known than their German counterparts, the famous U-boats, the US Navy's submarines, known as the 'Silent Service', played a vital role in the war in the Pacific, particularly the large *Gato*-class submarines. Admiral Halsey himself called them the most decisive weapon in the war. At the cost of proportionally the heaviest losses in the whole US Navy (nearly 20% of ships lost), they crippled the Japanese economy between 1943 and 1945 by cutting the country's industries off from their raw materials in the East Indies, starting with oil. By 1944, the remainder of the Japanese fleet had to be stationed as close as possible to oilfields and refineries to secure its supplies. One of the most serious strategic errors the Japanese made may well have been neglecting the security of their tankers by not providing them with adequate escorts.

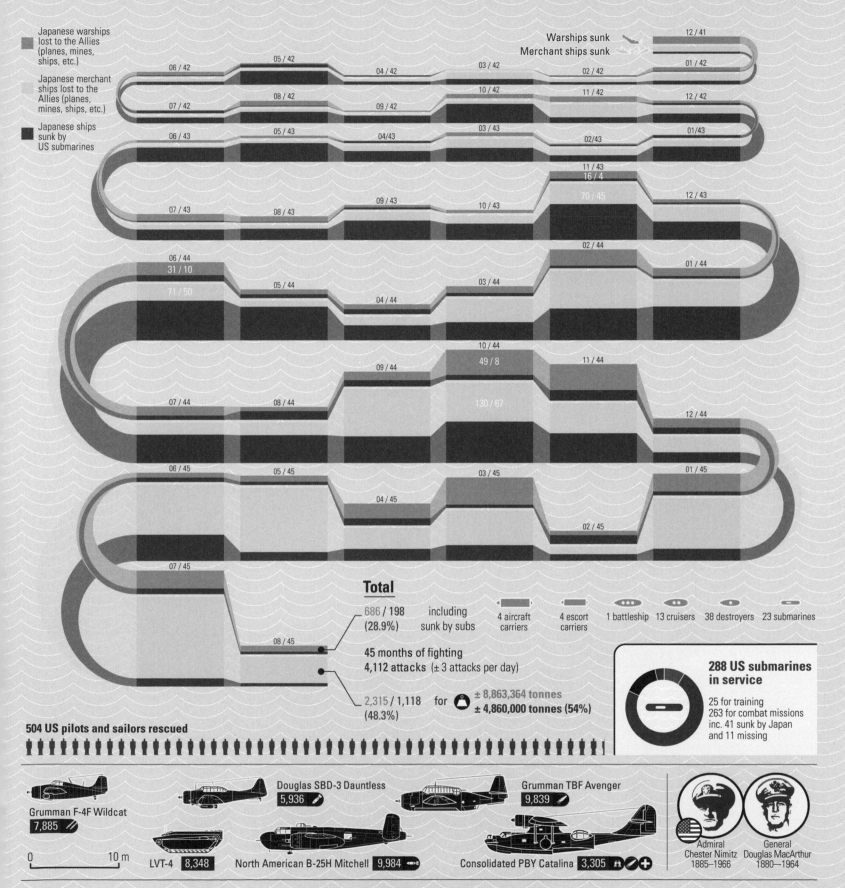

Japanese warships lost to the Allies (planes, mines, ships, etc.)

Japanese merchant ships lost to the Allies (planes, mines, ships, etc.)

Japanese ships sunk by US submarines

Warships sunk
Merchant ships sunk

Total

686 / 198 (28.9%) including sunk by subs

45 months of fighting
4,112 attacks (± 3 attacks per day)

2,315 / 1,118 (48.3%) for ± 8,863,364 tonnes
± 4,860,000 tonnes (54%)

4 aircraft carriers   4 escort carriers   1 battleship   13 cruisers   38 destroyers   23 submarines

288 US submarines in service

25 for training
263 for combat missions inc. 41 sunk by Japan and 11 missing

504 US pilots and sailors rescued

Grumman F-4F Wildcat 7,885

Douglas SBD-3 Dauntless 5,936

Grumman TBF Avenger 9,839

LVT-4 8,348

North American B-25H Mitchell 9,984

Consolidated PBY Catalina 3,305

0   10 m

Admiral Chester Nimitz 1885–1966

General Douglas MacArthur 1880–1964

4. Carl Smith, *Pearl Harbor 1941: The Day of Infamy*, Oxford, 2001 • 5. *History of Imperial General Headquarters*, JM no. 45, US Army, 1959.

OPERATION BARBAROSSA:

When it attacked the Soviet Union on 22 June 1941, the Wehrmacht was by far the best army in the world, on the ground and in the air. No observer thought the Red Army had the slightest chance. Its command, tactics, inter-unit combat, training and cohesion, factors more important than the element of surprise, were clearly inferior. The first months of the campaign followed similar lines to the Wehrmacht's invasion of Poland and France, but to the power of three: five massive encirclements resulted in over two million prisoners, 10,000 aircraft and 12,000 tanks were destroyed or captured, the advance took them to the gates of Leningrad, Moscow and Rostov. However, apparently blinded by their intrinsic superiority

and by ideological assumptions, the Germans made several mistakes which led to their eventual failure. They had underestimated the enemy's human and material resources to an unbelievable degree. They were expecting to find 200 divisions and in fact there were 500. The assumptions on which they had based their logistics were much too optimistic. By September 1941, the troops started to face shortages, which accelerated their attrition. In particular, German military and political leaders had taken it for granted that the Bolshevik regime would collapse after the defeats. The number of prisoners, deserters and renegades of all kinds encouraged them to expect a political implosion – but it did not come.

1 • THE BALANCE OF FORCES

The apparent Soviet superiority in aircraft and tanks was deceptive. Poorly led, without adequate logistics or communications, incapable of inter-unit combat, the Soviet units were no match for the Panzers or the Luftwaffe, despite their sometimes high-quality equipment. Although its infantry was partly horse-drawn, the Wehrmacht was much more

motorized than its adversary, which was heavily reliant on railways. With the exception of the Finns, the million Romanian, Finnish, Hungarian, Italian and Slovak soldiers engaged did not have the same fighting attitude as the Germans. But they were important, since they freed up the Wehrmacht for secondary operations and the tasks of occupation.

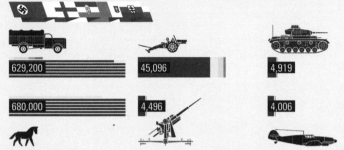

629,200 / 680,000 / 45,096 / 4,496 / 4,919 / 4,006

2 • SURPRISE AIR ATTACKS

In the first four days, the Luftwaffe focused all its efforts on destroying Russian aircraft on the ground and in the air. Lack of preparation and stubbornness were more vital than the element of surprise. The aircraft, a mixture of old and new, were packed into far too few airfields, many of them without control towers, hangars, anti-aircraft defences or radios. After the initial attacks, the Soviets could have spread out their aircraft along the chain of airfields behind the old Stalin Line, 300 kilometres east

of the border. But they did not do so, preferring to respond to calls from ground units and send young pilots without radios or specific targets to be massacred.

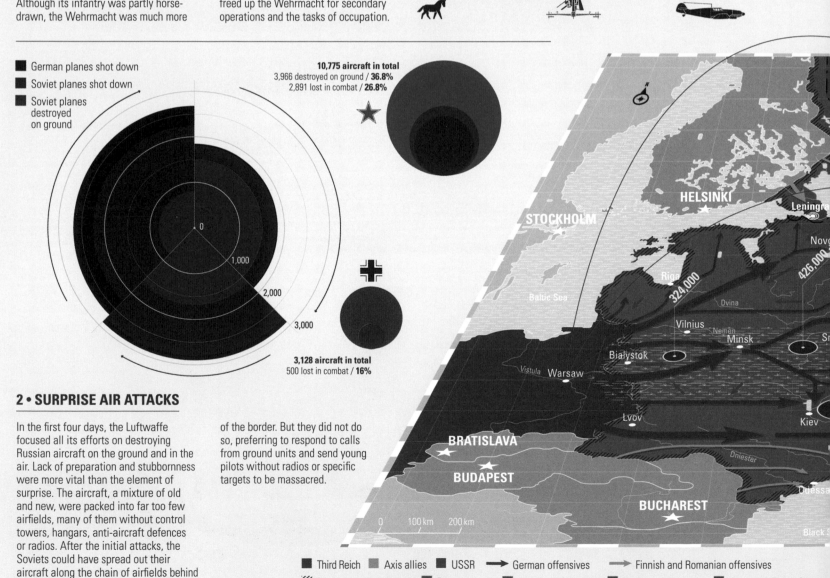

■ German planes shot down
■ Soviet planes shot down
■ Soviet planes destroyed on ground

10,775 aircraft in total
3,966 destroyed on ground / **36.8%**
2,891 lost in combat / **26.8%**

3,128 aircraft in total
500 lost in combat / **16%**

0 / 1,000 / 2,000 / 3,000

■ Third Reich   ■ Axis allies   ■ USSR   → German offensives   → Finnish and Romanian offensives
▨ Borders on 22 June 1941   ■ Front on 9 July   ■ Front on 1 September   ■ Front on 9 September   ■ Front on 5 December

HELSINKI   STOCKHOLM   Leningrad   Novg   426,000   Riga   324,000   Baltic Sea   Dvina   Vilnius   Nemen   Minsk   Białystok   Sm   Vistula   Warsaw   Łvov   Dniester   Kiev   BRATISLAVA   BUDAPEST   Odessa   BUCHAREST   Black S

0   100 km   200 km

A BATTLE OF EXTREMES

Stalin's government held out, with its leader at the forefront. There was merciless repression of the military and various dissidents, real or assumed; brutal mobilization of the entire population and all material resources; an appeal to Russian patriotism ensuring, amid the chaos of defeat, that the Red Army would continue its counter-attacks, that the railways would be used to evacuate 1,000 strategic factories to the east, and that time would be gained to gather reserves, learn from the enemy, reorganize units and tactics.

Operation Barbarossa was no ordinary military campaign. It was a colonial project of monstrous brutality, a campaign to destroy an ideology (Bolshevism) and its supposed agents, government officials and Jews. Millions were killed at the front, but millions also died behind the lines, in towns and villages where the *Einsatzgruppen* stirred up pogroms, shot Jewish men, women and children, people believed to be partisans and political officials, and where two million prisoners of war were left to die in the open air. The five million deaths made the second half of 1941 probably the most lethal in history. Operation Barbarossa was a breach of every rule of civilized society, committed in Europe by Europeans themselves.

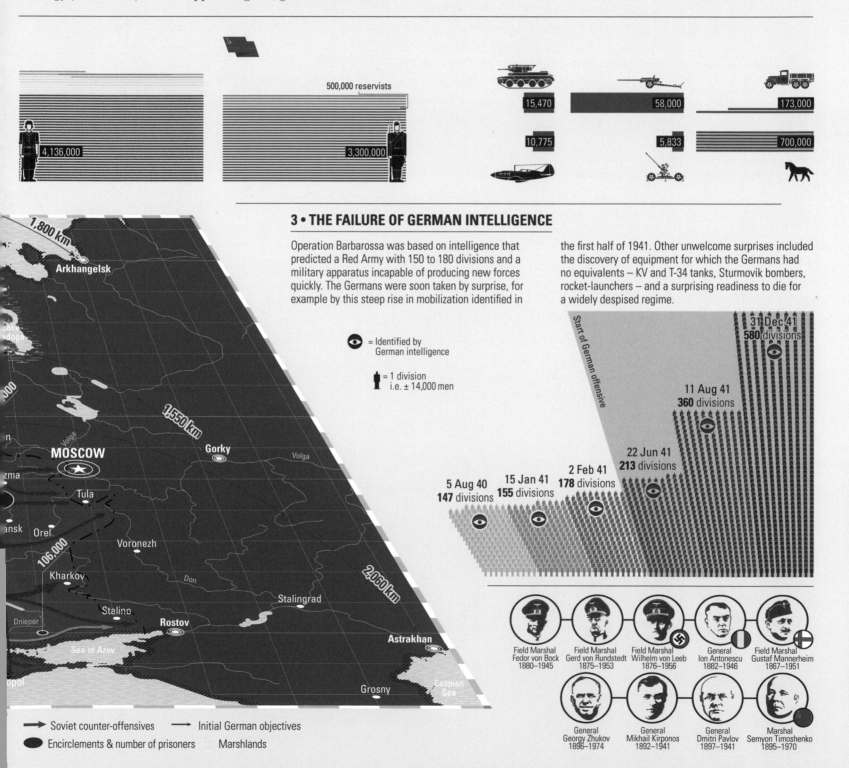

500,000 reservists

4,136,000

3,300,000

15,470   58,000   173,000

10,775   5,833   700,000

3 • THE FAILURE OF GERMAN INTELLIGENCE

Operation Barbarossa was based on intelligence that predicted a Red Army with 150 to 180 divisions and a military apparatus incapable of producing new forces quickly. The Germans were soon taken by surprise, for example by this steep rise in mobilization identified in the first half of 1941. Other unwelcome surprises included the discovery of equipment for which the Germans had no equivalents – KV and T-34 tanks, Sturmovik bombers, rocket-launchers – and a surprising readiness to die for a widely despised regime.

👁 = Identified by German intelligence

👤 = 1 division i.e. ± 14,000 men

Start of German offensive

31 Dec 41
580 divisions

11 Aug 41
360 divisions

22 Jun 41
213 divisions

2 Feb 41
178 divisions

5 Aug 40
147 divisions

15 Jan 41
155 divisions

1,800 km

Arkhangelsk

1,550 km

Volga

MOSCOW

Gorky

Volga

Tula

Orel

Voronezh

Don

Kharkov

Stalingrad

2,060 km

Stalino

106,000

Dnieper

Rostov

Sea of Azov

Astrakhan

Grosny

Caspian Sea

→ Soviet counter-offensives   → Initial German objectives

⬮ Encirclements & number of prisoners   Marshlands

Field Marshal Fedor von Bock 1880–1945

Field Marshal Gerd von Rundstedt 1875–1953

Field Marshal Wilhelm von Leeb 1876–1956

General Ion Antonescu 1882–1946

Field Marshal Gustaf Mannerheim 1867–1951

General Georgy Zhukov 1896–1974

General Mikhail Kirponos 1892–1941

General Dmitri Pavlov 1897–1941

Marshal Semyon Timoshenko 1895–1970

4 • COLLAPSE OF THE 7TH PANZER DIVISION

The map opposite shows the route taken by the 17 armoured divisions (accompanied by 12 motorized divisions) that took part in Operation Barbarossa. The 7th Panzer Division literally wore itself out travelling nearly 1,700 kilometres on roads that were appallingly bad, especially during summer storms and autumn rains. In six months it was involved in 8 violent battles and countless skirmishes. The August engagement against Konev's 19th Army in Dukhovchina alone cost it 500 men and 70 tanks.

Its combat capability also depended on the transport of fuel, ammunition and spare parts. The number of trains reaching the rear depots of the three German Army Groups started to decline severely from September due to a shortage of trains and manpower, to bad weather and to destruction by the Red Army. The columns of trucks were unable to transport everything that was needed from the depots to the forward units. The 500,000 trucks that had been available on 22 June 1941

were reduced to 135,000 by 15 November. Ammunition and fuel supplies were prioritized over food and winter clothing, so troops had to loot these from the local population.

Losses were much higher than expected. Contrary to widespread belief, they were higher in summer, particularly July, than in the winter counter-offensive. In August, German leaders were starting to see signs of exhaustion in the troops. Soldiers wrote in their letters: 'Three campaigns in France are better than one in Russia.' The temperature graph shows an early cold winter, but it was not exceptional; there was one like that every three or four years, so it could have been predicted.

The winter alone was not responsible for the German defeat outside Moscow. The Wehrmacht was already falling apart on 15 November before the temperature dropped, pushed well beyond its limits by leaders out of their depth and without strategic plans, pursuing the wild hope that the Stalinist government would fall.

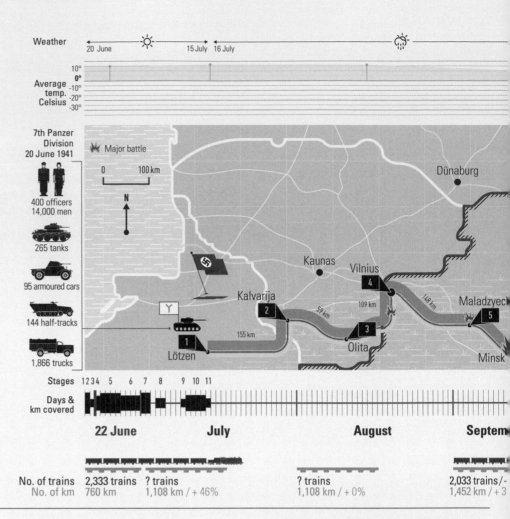

5 • WINTER COUNTER-OFFENSIVES

One reason for the high German and even higher Soviet losses was the high number of Soviet attacks. There were nineteen counter-offensives before the Moscow counter-offensive: six on the Leningrad axis, three of which – Soltsy-Dno (14–18 July), Staraya Russa 12–23 August) and Tikhvin (12 November–31 December) – are notable for the operational difficulties they caused the Germans; eight on the central axis, including Senno-Lepel (5–9 July), Babruysk (13 July–7 August), Smolensk (21 July–9 August), Dukhovchina (17 August–8 September), Ynelya (30 August–8 September); and five in Ukraine, including Lutsk-Rovno-Brody (26 June–3 July), Novograd-

Volynskyi (10–14 July), Rostov (22–30 November) and Crimea (26 December–10 January).

The counter-offensive launched by Zhukov outside Moscow on 5 December 1941 was decisive. It drove the Wehrmacht back 100 to 200 km to the west and destroyed much of its materiel. It signalled the failure of Operation Barbarossa and left 80% of the Wehrmacht trapped in a war of attrition.

- ■ Third Reich ■ Axis allies
- ▨ Borders on 22 June 1941
- ▨ Retaken land ■ USSR
- → Soviet counter-offensives
- ⬭ Cities under siege

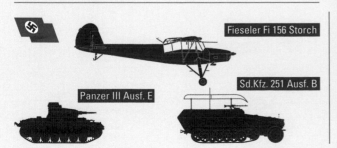

Fieseler Fi 156 Storch

Sd.Kfz. 251 Ausf. B

Panzer III Ausf. E

SOURCES: 1. *Das deutsche Reich und der Zweite Weltkrieg*, vol. 4 • 2. Rüdiger Overmans, *Deutsche militärische Verluste im Zweiten Weltkrieg*, Munich, 2004 • 3. G. F. Krivosheev (ed.), *Soviet Casualties and Combat Losses in the*

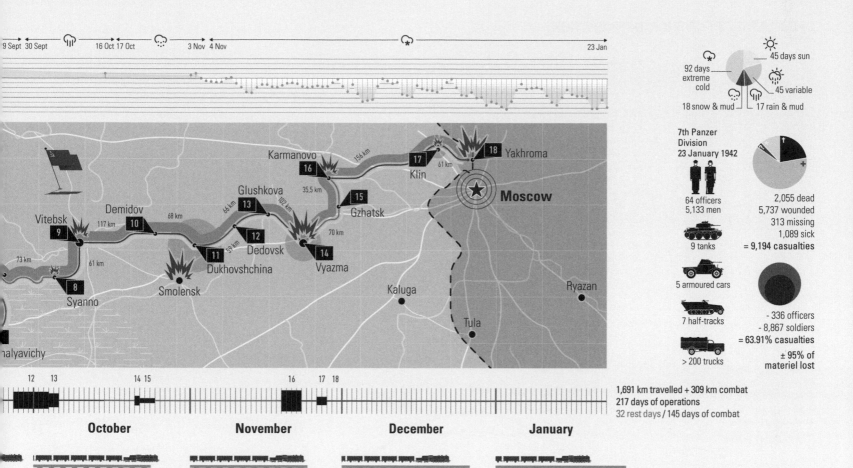

9 Sept   30 Sept   16 Oct   17 Oct   3 Nov   4 Nov   23 Jan

45 days sun

92 days extreme cold

45 variable

18 snow & mud   17 rain & mud

7th Panzer Division 23 January 1942

64 officers
5,133 men

9 tanks

5 armoured cars

7 half-tracks

> 200 trucks

2,055 dead
5,737 wounded
313 missing
1,089 sick
= 9,194 casualties

- 336 officers
- 8,867 soldiers
= 63.91% casualties

± 95% of materiel lost

Map labels:

Vitebsk 9 · Demidov 10 · Glushkova 13 · Karmanovo 16 · Klin 17 · Yakhroma 18 · Gzhatst 15 · Vyazma 14 · Dedovsk 12 · Dukhovshchina 11 · Smolensk · Syanno 8 · Malyavichy · Kaluga · Tula · Ryazan · Moscow

117 km · 68 km · 64 km · 107 km · 35,5 km · 156 km · 61 km · 70 km · 57 km · 61 km · 73 km

1,691 km travelled + 309 km combat
217 days of operations
32 rest days / 145 days of combat

October	November	December	January
1,860 trains / - 8.06%	1,701 trains / - 8.55%	1,643 trains / - 3.41%	1,420 trains / - 13.57%
1,587 km / + 9%	1,587 km / + 0%	1,768 km / + 11%	1,768 km / -

Soldiers dead
1,500,000 Soviets
350,660 Germans
80,000 Axis

Civilian deaths
1,000,000 Soviets
500,000 Jews executed by the Germans

Soldiers wounded
1,500,000 Soviets
800,000 Germans

Soldiers missing
43,000 Germans

Total casualties:
3,930,660 soldiers dead
2,300,000 soldiers wounded
3,300,000 taken prisoner
1,500,000 civilians dead

Prisoners
3,300,000 Soviets
of which 2,000,000 starved to death by end of February 1942

Planes
10,600 Soviet / 2,505 German

Tanks
2,939 German / 20,500 Soviet

6 • THE FINAL TOLL

For every German soldier killed, 5 Soviet soldiers fell, 10 counting the prisoners left to die of cold, disease and hunger between September 1941 and February 1942. The Red Army's material losses were enormous. Over the entire war, four Soviet tanks were lost for every Panzer, but in 1941 the ratio rose to 10 to 1 and for aircraft, 4 to 1.

This mass slaughter was partly due to the mediocrity of the Soviet command at every level. All too often, the infantry was sent to attack in repeated waves without reconnaissance or protection from heavy weapons. The number of prisoners was attributable to 5 large encirclements, but also to soldiers surrendering or sometimes going over to the enemy en masse, at least some of them for political reasons.

The number of summary executions of Soviet prisoners (including many wounded) on the battlefield is not known, but all indications are that the total was extremely high.

There were many reasons for the deaths of a million civilians in 1941: bombing, combat, executions and deprivation of every kind, as well as the 500,000 Jews wiped out by the German police and SS with the aid of Baltic and Ukrainian nationalists and the full support of the Wehrmacht. And this was just the beginning.

Polikarpov I-16

KV-1

T-34/76

0   1m

Twentieth Century, London, 1997 • 4. Nigel Askey, *Operation Barbarossa: The Complete Organization and Statistical Analysis, and Military Simulation*, lulu.com, 2016.

THE BATTLE OF THE ATLANTIC

'The only thing that ever really frightened me during the war was the U-boat peril,' Winston Churchill wrote in his memoirs. The Battle of the Atlantic was in fact the crux of a huge maritime battle between the Axis and the Allies which, between 1939 and 1946, had ramifications in every sea in the world and used a range of different methods (including aircraft, mines, surface ships, camouflaged raiders, commando operations and decryption). In the narrower and more traditional sense, it was an attempt by German U-boats (and a few Italian submarines stationed in Bordeaux) to disrupt Allied naval communications in the North Atlantic. By attacking its enemy's cargo ships and oil tankers, the Reich aimed both to cripple the British economy, which was highly dependent on imports, and prevent an Allied landing on mainland Europe.

1 • STRATEGIC ISSUES

The main challenge in the Battle of the Atlantic was to protect sea routes between North America and Europe, allowing equipment, troops and supplies to be transported to the various theatres of war. This was of particular concern to Britain but also to the USSR from the summer of 1941, since it received lend-lease supplies via the Murmansk-Archangel Arctic route. From a US point of view, the challenge was also to preserve the sea barrier that protected it against a potential hostile naval coalition.

PHASES OF THE BATTLE

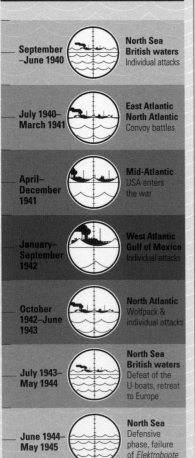

September–June 1940		North Sea British waters Individual attacks
July 1940–March 1941		East Atlantic North Atlantic Convoy battles
April–December 1941		Mid-Atlantic USA enters the war
January–September 1942		West Atlantic Gulf of Mexico Individual attacks
October 1942–June 1943		North Atlantic Wolfpack & individual attacks
July 1943–May 1944		North Sea British waters Defeat of the U-boats, retreat to Europe
June 1944–May 1945		North Sea Defensive phase, failure of Elektroboote

2 • ADMIRAL DÖNITZ'S 'WOLFPACKS' AGAINST THE ALLIES

The German navy's primary weapons were the Type VII U-boat, which could operate in the North Atlantic, and to a lesser extent the Type IX, capable of reaching America's shores. U-boats were few in number at the start of the war due to the diplomatic restrictions of the 1930s and they also suffered from structural defects such as faulty torpedoes. Despite frequent losses, they became more numerous and effective when 'wolfpack' tactics were introduced in 1941 and new technical innovations were incorporated, including the Dutch-developed submarine snorkel in 1943, which allowed subs to stay underwater for longer periods. However, nothing could compensate for Allied escalation. The *Elektroboot*, allowing fast travel under water, was certainly innovative but it came too late in the war.

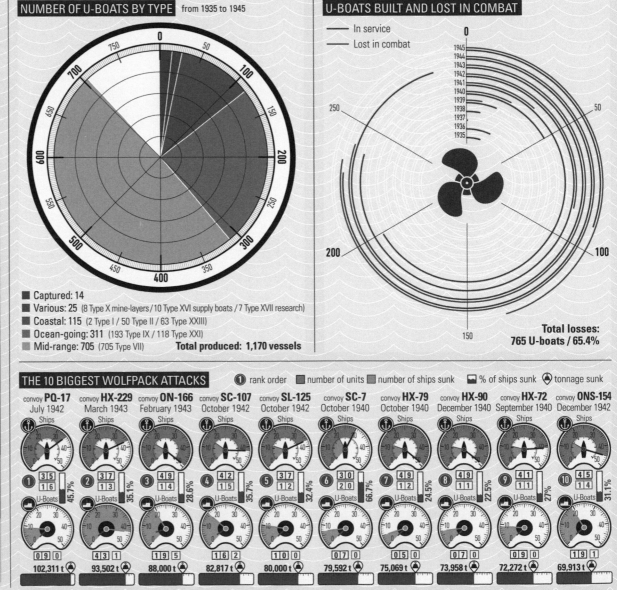

NUMBER OF U-BOATS BY TYPE from 1935 to 1945

- Captured: 14
- Various: 25 (8 Type X mine-layers / 10 Type XVI supply boats / 7 Type XVII research)
- Coastal: 115 (2 Type I / 50 Type II / 63 Type XXIII)
- Ocean-going: 311 (193 Type IX / 118 Type XXI)
- Mid-range: 705 (705 Type VII)   **Total produced: 1,170 vessels**

U-BOATS BUILT AND LOST IN COMBAT

- In service
- Lost in combat

Total losses: 765 U-boats / 65.4%

THE 10 BIGGEST WOLFPACK ATTACKS

① rank order ■ number of units ■ number of ships sunk ■ % of ships sunk ⚓ tonnage sunk

	convoy PQ-17 July 1942	convoy HX-229 March 1943	convoy ON-166 February 1943	convoy SC-107 October 1942	convoy SL-125 October 1942	convoy SC-7 October 1940	convoy HX-79 October 1940	convoy HX-90 December 1940	convoy HX-72 September 1940	convoy ONS-154 December 1942
rank	①	②	③	④	⑤	⑥	⑦	⑧	⑨	⑩
Ships	35	37	49	42	37	30	49	49	41	45
U-Boats	13	13	14	15	12	20	12	11	11	14
% ships sunk	45.7%	35.1%	28.6%	35.7%	32.4%	66.7%	24.5%	22.5%	27%	31.1%
	0 9 0	4 3 1	1 9 5	1 6 2	1 0 0	0 7 0	0 5 0	0 7 0	0 9 0	1 9 1
tonnage	102,311 t	93,502 t	88,000 t	82,817 t	80,000 t	79,592 t	75,069 t	73,958 t	72,272 t	69,913 t

SOURCES: 1. *History of Convoy and Routing*, Washington, DC, 1945 • 2. *ASW in World War II*, OEG report no. 51, Washington, DC, 1946 • 3. *German Submarine Losses*, Washington, DC, 1963 • 4. Nathan Miller, *War at Sea: A Naval History of World War II*, Oxford, 1997; Gordon Williamson, *Kriegsmarine U-Boats*, Oxford, 2002 • 5. Guy Malbosc, *La Bataille de l'Atlantique*, Paris, 2010 • 6. Axel Niestlé, *German U-Boat*

The battle began in 1939 with the earliest attacks on convoys, a legacy from the previous war. It peaked in 1941–42 with the rise of the *Rudeltaktik* or 'wolfpack' tactics developed by Admiral Dönitz, working out of submarine bases in coastal locations (France and Norway). It gradually started to die down in 1943 with an irretrievable breakdown of the industrial and technological balance and the code war (Ultra decryption). Although more numerous than before (up to 160 at sea simultaneously in April 1943, compared with 40 in September 1939), U-boats lost their upper hand and suffered very heavy losses without any hope of offsetting the massive production of Allied ships.

These confrontations in the Atlantic were undeniably fierce, costing the Allies 2,200 ships and tens of thousands of men, including 30,000 merchant seamen, while the Reich lost over 25,000 submariners on board around 700 vessels. All the same, the scale of the battle must not be exaggerated in the light of the most spectacular U-boat attacks on convoys. For instance, figures show that the vast majority of convoys crossed the Atlantic without being attacked, or with only minor losses. Overall, the Battle of the Atlantic that gripped the public was really more of a low-level irritation. It was important and worrying during the period of British isolation in 1941 and up to the spring of 1943, but it would never pose a serious threat to Anglo-American control of the seas.

ALLIED MERCHANT FLEET TONNAGE SUNK BY U-BOATS

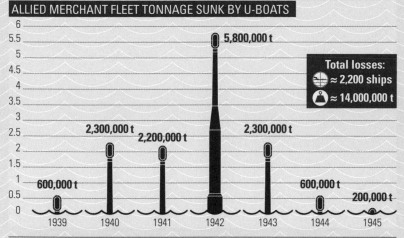

Total losses:
⊘ ≈ 2,200 ships
⚱ ≈ 14,000,000 t

NUMBER OF CONVOY CROSSINGS AND LOSSES

❚ = 500 ships

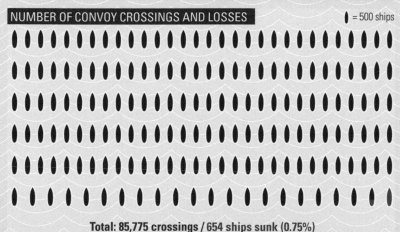

Total: 85,775 crossings / 654 ships sunk (0.75%)

ALLIED BOMBARDMENTS OF NAVAL BASES IN FRANCE   from 1940 to 1944

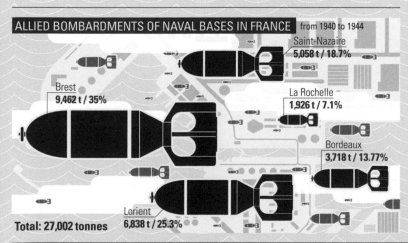

Saint-Nazaire
5,058 t / 18.7%

Brest
9,462 t / 35%

La Rochelle
1,926 t / 7.1%

Bordeaux
3,718 t / 13.77%

Lorient
6,838 t / 25.3%

Total: 27,002 tonnes

3 • BALANCE SHEET: A BATTLE LOST IN ADVANCE?

By the middle of 1943, the battle was reversed, with a dramatic rise in U-boats destroyed and at the same time a fall in ships sunk. Dönitz thought that a net reduction in Allied shipping of seven million tonnes a year should ensure success. In fact, due to requisitions, shipbuilding and America's entry into the war, these results were only achieved after three years of effort, even as Allied production soared. Between 1943 and 1945, shipyards in the USA and elsewhere built ships with a tonnage of over 30 million.

ALLIED SHIPS: CONSTRUCTION AND DESTRUCTION

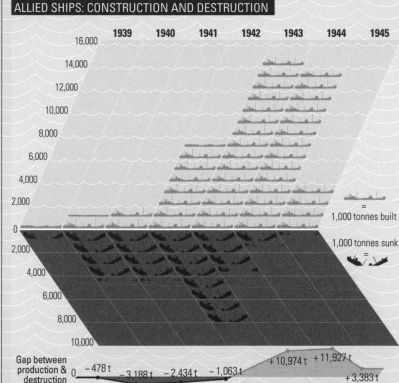

= 1,000 tonnes built

= 1,000 tonnes sunk

Gap between production & destruction: 0   − 478 t   − 3,188 t   − 2,434 t   − 1,063 t   + 10,974 t   + 11,927 t   + 3,383 t

🇬🇧 *Flower*-class corvette
Allied convoy escort

Losses During World War II, Annapolis, MD, 1998 • 7. *The Defeat of the Enemy Attack upon Shipping, 1939–1945*, London, 1997 • 8. Yves Durand, *Histoire de la Deuxième Guerre mondiale*, Brussels, 1999

• 9. S. W. Roskill, *The War at Sea, 1939–1945*, London, 1954–61 • 10. http://www.u-boote.fr/u-158.htm • 11. http://uboat.net/ops/convoys/convoys.php

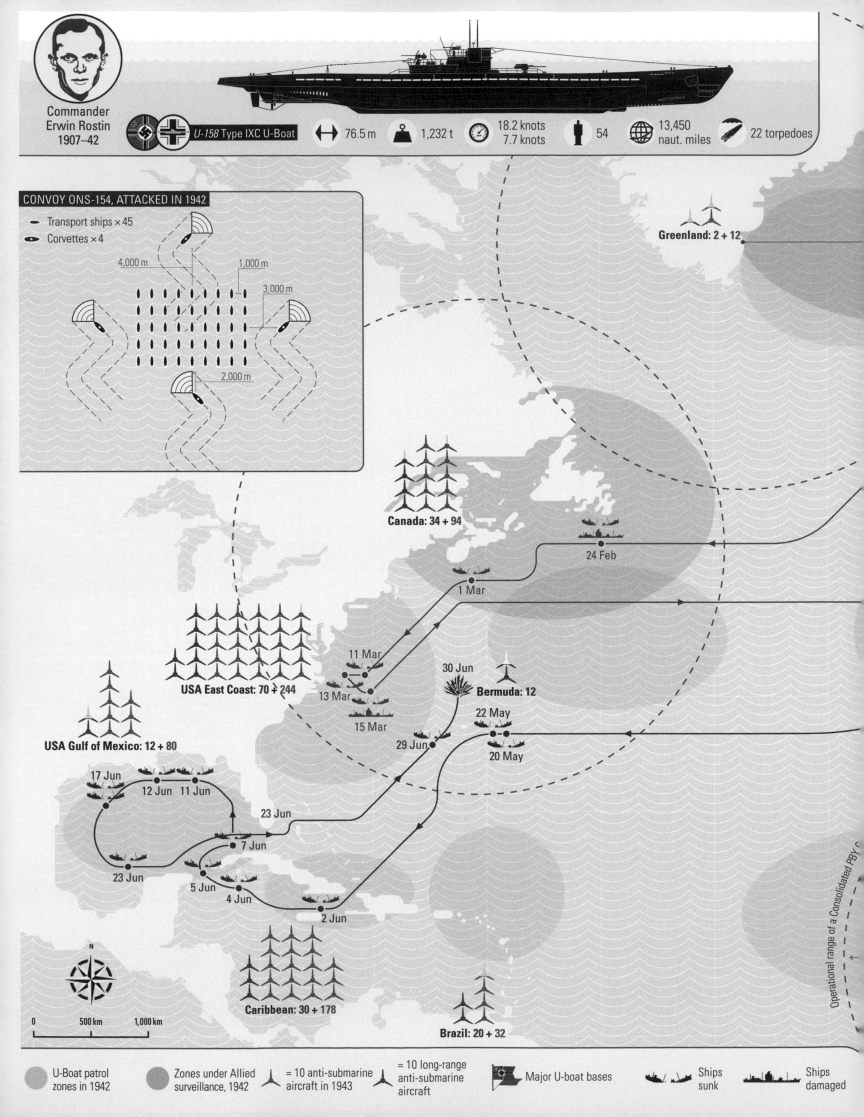

Commander
Erwin Rostin
1907–42

U-158 Type IXC U-Boat   76.5 m   1,232 t   18.2 knots / 7.7 knots   54   13,450 naut. miles   22 torpedoes

CONVOY ONS-154, ATTACKED IN 1942

— Transport ships ×45
— Corvettes ×4

4,000 m
1,000 m
3,000 m
2,000 m

Greenland: 2 + 12

Canada: 34 + 94

24 Feb

1 Mar

11 Mar

13 Mar

15 Mar

USA East Coast: 70 + 244

30 Jun
Bermuda: 12

22 May

29 Jun
20 May

USA Gulf of Mexico: 12 + 80

17 Jun
12 Jun 11 Jun

23 Jun

7 Jun

23 Jun

5 Jun
4 Jun

2 Jun

N

0   500 km   1,000 km

Caribbean: 30 + 178

Brazil: 20 + 32

Operational range of a Consolidated PBY

● U-Boat patrol zones in 1942
● Zones under Allied surveillance, 1942
= 10 anti-submarine aircraft in 1943
= 10 long-range anti-submarine aircraft
Major U-boat bases
Ships sunk
Ships damaged

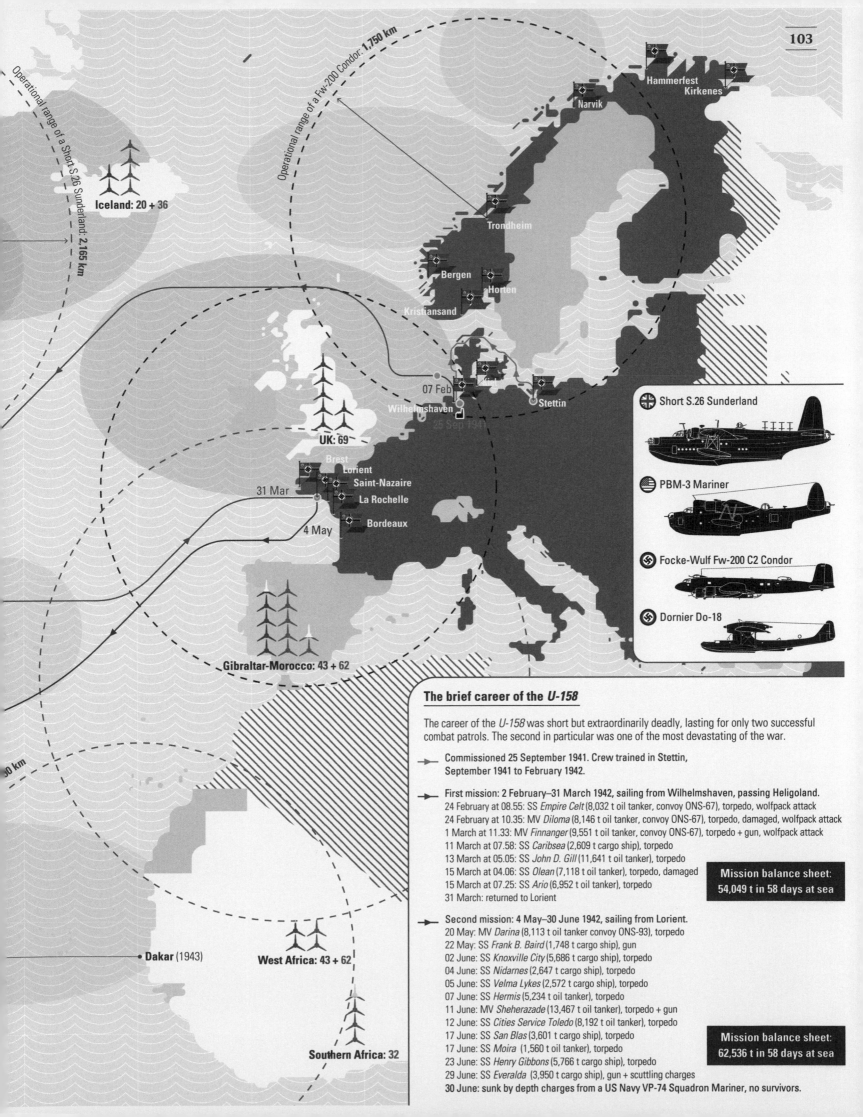

103

Operational range of a Short S.26 Sunderland: 2,165 km

Operational range of a Fw-200 Condor: 1,750 km

Iceland: 20 + 36

Hammerfest
Kirkenes
Narvik

Trondheim

Bergen
Horten
Kristiansand

Kiel
Stettin

07 Feb
Wilhelmshaven
25 Sep 1941

UK: 69

Brest
Lorient
Saint-Nazaire
La Rochelle
Bordeaux

31 Mar

4 May

Gibraltar-Morocco: 43 + 62

Dakar (1943)

West Africa: 43 + 62

Southern Africa: 32

Short S.26 Sunderland
PBM-3 Mariner
Focke-Wulf Fw-200 C2 Condor
Dornier Do-18

The brief career of the *U-158*

The career of the *U-158* was short but extraordinarily deadly, lasting for only two successful combat patrols. The second in particular was one of the most devastating of the war.

Commissioned 25 September 1941. Crew trained in Stettin, September 1941 to February 1942.

First mission: 2 February–31 March 1942, sailing from Wilhelmshaven, passing Heligoland.
24 February at 08.55: SS *Empire Celt* (8,032 t oil tanker, convoy ONS-67), torpedo, wolfpack attack
24 February at 10.35: MV *Diloma* (8,146 t oil tanker, convoy ONS-67), torpedo, damaged, wolfpack attack
1 March at 11.33: MV *Finnanger* (9,551 t oil tanker, convoy ONS-67), torpedo + gun, wolfpack attack
11 March at 07.58: SS *Caribsea* (2,609 t cargo ship), torpedo
13 March at 05.05: SS *John D. Gill* (11,641 t oil tanker), torpedo
15 March at 04.06: SS *Olean* (7,118 t oil tanker), torpedo, damaged
15 March at 07.25: SS *Ario* (6,952 t oil tanker), torpedo
31 March: returned to Lorient

Mission balance sheet: 54,049 t in 58 days at sea

Second mission: 4 May–30 June 1942, sailing from Lorient.
20 May: MV *Darina* (8,113 t oil tanker convoy ONS-93), torpedo
22 May: SS *Frank B. Baird* (1,748 t cargo ship), gun
02 June: SS *Knoxville City* (5,686 t cargo ship), torpedo
04 June: SS *Nidarnes* (2,647 t cargo ship), torpedo
05 June: SS *Velma Lykes* (2,572 t cargo ship), torpedo
07 June: SS *Hermis* (5,234 t oil tanker), torpedo
11 June: MV *Sheherazade* (13,467 t oil tanker), torpedo + gun
12 June: SS *Cities Service Toledo* (8,192 t oil tanker), torpedo
17 June: SS *San Blas* (3,601 t cargo ship), torpedo
17 June: SS *Moira* (1,560 t oil tanker), torpedo
23 June: SS *Henry Gibbons* (5,766 t cargo ship), torpedo
29 June: SS *Everalda* (3,950 t cargo ship), gun + scuttling charges
30 June: sunk by depth charges from a US Navy VP-74 Squadron Mariner, no survivors.

Mission balance sheet: 62,536 t in 58 days at sea

WAR IN THE MEDITERRANEAN

The spread of war to the Mediterranean basin was due as much to a spontaneous decision as to inherent inevitability.

The impromptu element was that on 10 June 1940, Mussolini declared war on the Allies, in the belief that the war would soon be over. It did not matter to him that his army was not operational, or that a third of his merchant fleet scattered around the world was immediately seized. Convinced that France was on its knees and the war was therefore over, he opportunistically imagined inviting himself to the victors' table. The inevitability came because the Fascists were fascinated by war. It was not just a way of realizing the imperialist

dream of *Mare Nostrum* – 'our sea'; it was a rite of passage designed to lead to the birth of the 'new man', a virile, tough hero who would be dedicated to the Fascist state and Il Duce. There had not been a single year since 1934 when the Italian army was not fighting.

This fascination so blinded Mussolini that he failed to see the gap between his limited economic resources and his extravagant ambitions (Corsica, Tunisia, Egypt, the Balkans). The Mediterranean was a theatre where both sea and air needed to be controlled to protect the convoys. Italy did not have the industry, the equipment, the integrated command or the logistical expertise needed for these

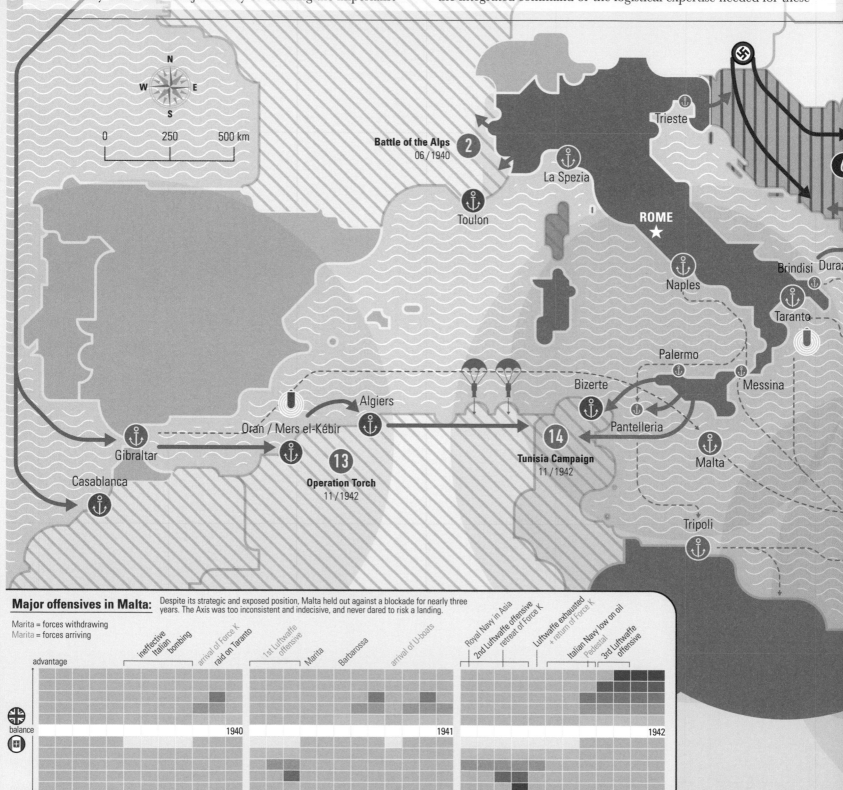

Major offensives in Malta: Despite its strategic and exposed position, Malta held out against a blockade for nearly three years. The Axis was too inconsistent and indecisive, and never dared to risk a landing.

operations. On land, the desert expanses required mechanized units. These were rare commodities, as were modern aircraft. In spite of this weakness, Mussolini took advantage of France's neutralization and waged a 'parallel war', independent of Germany. His colonies were springboards towards British Somalia, Egypt and Greece, and he deployed his best troops (100,000 in East Africa, 188,000 in Libya and 165,000 in Albania). Everywhere he attacked, but everywhere he was pushed back: 130,000 men were captured in Libya in December 1940, 90,000 in East Africa in April 1941. After a counter-attack, the Greeks entered Albania. The British raid on Taranto, prefiguring Pearl Harbor, struck at the Italian navy.

By destabilizing the region, Mussolini threatened Germany's interests. Hitler had to intervene to secure Romanian oil and safeguard the neutrality of Turkey, which supplied Germany with minerals. In January 1941, the Luftwaffe appeared suddenly in the skies above Malta. In February, the Afrika Korps landed. In April, Panzers swept into the Balkans. Yugoslavia, which had refused to join the Axis, fell in two weeks. Greece held out for a week longer.

The parallel war was over. The Germans were in charge and the Mediterranean front became a peripheral theatre of war. Although Churchill dreamed of using it as a springboard to strike at the soft underbelly of the Axis, it was over for the British too, as shown by their withdrawal of resources to fight in the Far East. For two years, each side went into the lead alternately, depending on the resources it was prepared to put in. Opportunities were wasted due to a lack of decisiveness. In the autumn of 1942, the balance of forces shifted permanently. The Mediterranean became Allied territory.

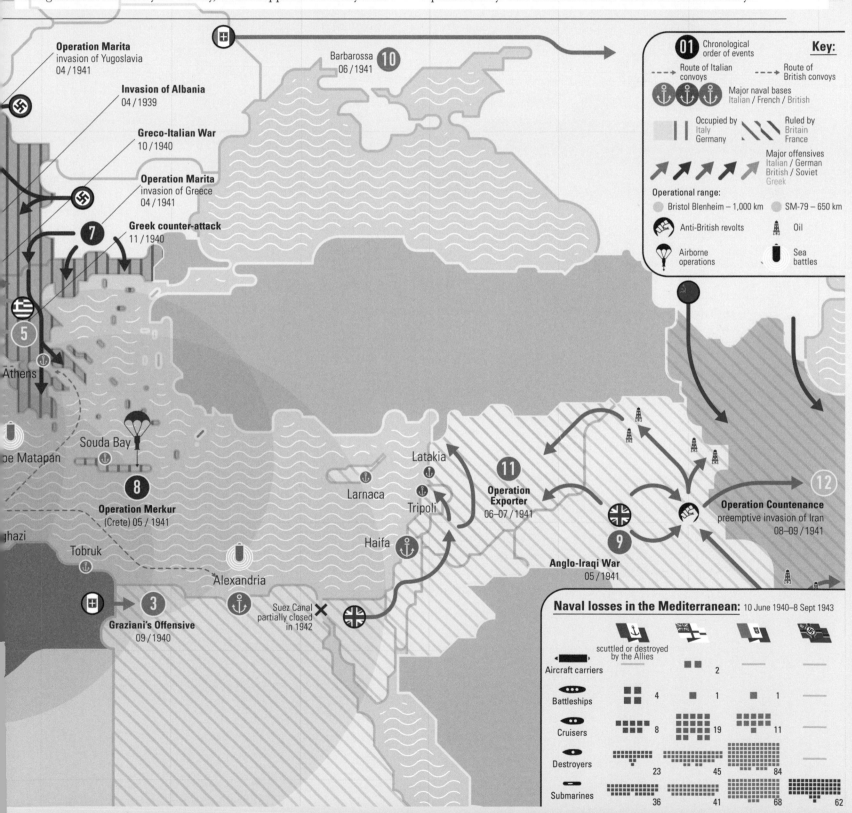

Operation Marita
invasion of Yugoslavia
04 / 1941

Invasion of Albania
04 / 1939

Greco-Italian War
10 / 1940

Operation Marita
invasion of Greece
04 / 1941

Greek counter-attack
11 / 1940

Barbarossa
06 / 1941 **10**

7

5

Athens

Souda Bay

Cape Matapan

8

Operation Merkur
(Crete) 05 / 1941

Benghazi

Tobruk

Alexandria

3

Graziani's Offensive
09 / 1940

Suez Canal
partially closed
in 1942

Latakia

Larnaca

Tripoli

Haifa

11

Operation
Exporter
06–07 / 1941

9

Anglo-Iraqi War
05 / 1941

12

Operation Countenance
preemptive invasion of Iran
08–09 / 1941

Key:

01 Chronological order of events

- - → Route of Italian convoys
- - → Route of British convoys

⚓⚓⚓ Major naval bases
Italian / French / British

Occupied by Italy / Germany

Ruled by Britain / France

Major offensives
Italian / German / British / Soviet / Greek

Operational range:
● Bristol Blenheim – 1,000 km
● SM-79 – 650 km

✊ Anti-British revolts
🛢 Oil
🪂 Airborne operations
⬤ Sea battles

Naval losses in the Mediterranean: 10 June 1940–8 Sept 1943

scuttled or destroyed by the Allies

Aircraft carriers		2		
Battleships	4	1	1	
Cruisers	8	19	11	
Destroyers	23	45	84	
Submarines	36	41	68	62

2 • THE OTHER CONVOY WAR: 1940–42

To avoid exposing their Mediterranean convoys, the British bypassed Africa when supplying Egypt. Axis convoys came within range of the submarines, destroyers and planes based in Malta, but that island, which Italy failed to conquer in 1940, also needed supplies itself. Operations were therefore confined to escorting or harassing the convoys of both sides. Given the size of the area, concealment was impossible and battles were short and fierce. Danger was everywhere: above and beneath the waves and in the air.

Covering a convoy required extensive resources, from escort vessels to aircraft carriers. The Italians ran out of fuel. The advantage swung back and forth like a pendulum. The first six months of every year were German-Italian, the second six months British, but neither side managed to cut off enemy supplies. Malta was not crippled until summer 1942, but was saved partly by Operation Pedestal and also by the wearing down of the Luftwaffe. Rommel received 80% of his supplies from the Italian navy (Regia Marina).

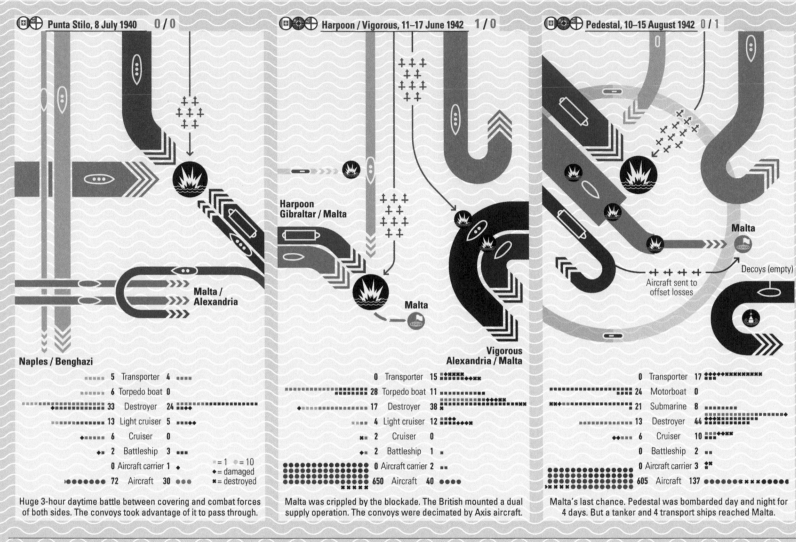

Punta Stilo, 8 July 1940 0 / 0

Harpoon / Vigorous, 11–17 June 1942 1 / 0

Pedestal, 10–15 August 1942 0 / 1

Harpoon
Gibraltar / Malta

Malta

Malta

Decoys (empty)

Aircraft sent to
offset losses

Malta /
Alexandria

Vigorous
Alexandria / Malta

Naples / Benghazi

	Punta Stilo		
5	Transporter	4	
6	Torpedo boat	0	
33	Destroyer	24	
13	Light cruiser	5	
6	Cruiser	0	
2	Battleship	3	
0	Aircraft carrier	1	
72	Aircraft	30	

= 1 = 10
♦ = damaged
✖ = destroyed

	Harpoon / Vigorous		
0	Transporter	15	
28	Torpedo boat	11	
17	Destroyer	38	
4	Light cruiser	12	
2	Cruiser	0	
2	Battleship	1	
0	Aircraft carrier	2	
650	Aircraft	40	

	Pedestal		
0	Transporter	17	
24	Motorboat	0	
21	Submarine	8	
13	Destroyer	44	
6	Cruiser	10	
0	Battleship	2	
0	Aircraft carrier	3	
605	Aircraft	137	

Huge 3-hour daytime battle between covering and combat forces of both sides. The convoys took advantage of it to pass through.

Malta was crippled by the blockade. The British mounted a dual supply operation. The convoys were decimated by Axis aircraft.

Malta's last chance. Pedestal was bombarded day and night for 4 days. But a tanker and 4 transport ships reached Malta.

THE OTHER CONVOY WAR

Impact on Axis supplies in French North Africa

Lives on board / Lives lost

Freight on board / Freight lost (in tonnes)

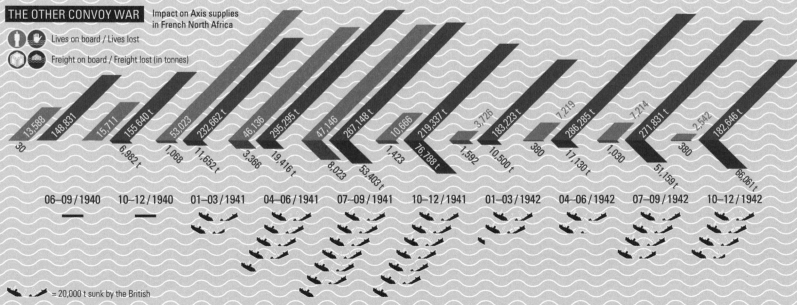

13,558	15,711	53,023	46,136	47,146	10,666	3,726	7,219	7,214	2,542
148,831	155,640 t	232,662 t	295,295 t	267,148 t	219,337 t	183,223 t	286,285 t	271,831 t	182,646 t
30	6,982 t	11,652 t	19,416 t	53,403 t	76,788 t	10,500 t	17,130 t	51,159 t	66,061 t
	1,068	3,366	8,023	1,423	1,592	380	1,030	380	

06–09 / 1940   10–12 / 1940   01–03 / 1941   04–06 / 1941   07–09 / 1941   10–12 / 1941   01–03 / 1942   04–06 / 1942   07–09 / 1942   10–12 / 1942

= 20,000 t sunk by the British

SOURCES: 1. T. Spooner, *Supreme Gallantry: Malta's Role in the Allied Victory, 1939–1945*, London, 1996 • 2. K. Gundelach, *Die Luftwaffe im Mittelmeer, 1940–1945*, Frankfurt, 1981 • 3. *Das Deutsche Reich und der Zweite Weltkrieg*, vols. III & VI, Munich, 1994 & 2001 • 4. A. Cocchia, *La difesa del traffico con l'Africa settentrionale, la marina italiana*, vols. 6 & 7, 1958 & 1962 • 5. J. J. Sadkovich, *The Italian Navy in World War II*, Westport,

3 • MUSSOLINI OVERREACHES HIMSELF

Fascist Italy was the first country in Europe to go to war. By 1935 it had conquered Ethiopia, a victory that was both barbaric (300,000 to 500,000 civilian victims) and deceptive. The enemy had no heavy weapons and only 50,000 rifles. Mussolini then lent backing to Franco in 1939 before invading Albania in 1939. These operations drained the defence budget. Consequently, the Italian air force only had a thousand modern aircraft in 1940 and its assembly lines were working at only a tenth of the rate of the British lines. The Italian army, far from the '8 million bayonets' Mussolini boasted of, only had a million and a half men and 19 full divisions. 200 of its tanks were true tanks (M11/39 and M13/40); the others were merely 'tankettes': tracked vehicles with a machine gun.

The Italian navy was balanced and modern and had 500,000 tonnes of shipping, but the British had advantages in the form of aircraft carriers, radar and Ultra decryption. The Italian complement of officers was 40% short and it only had fuel for one year.

The life of Italian soldiers was miserable. They were poorly armed, short of supplies, often poorly commanded (by 'political' generals), and badly led at the top by Mussolini, who was waging a parallel war that fragmented his forces. By the end of 1941, Italy had already lost 22% of its manpower and the East African territories. But this did not stop Il Duce from sending more than 100,000 men to the USSR (from where very few would return) and deploying 450,000 to secure the Balkans.

ITALY'S WAR ON ALL FRONTS

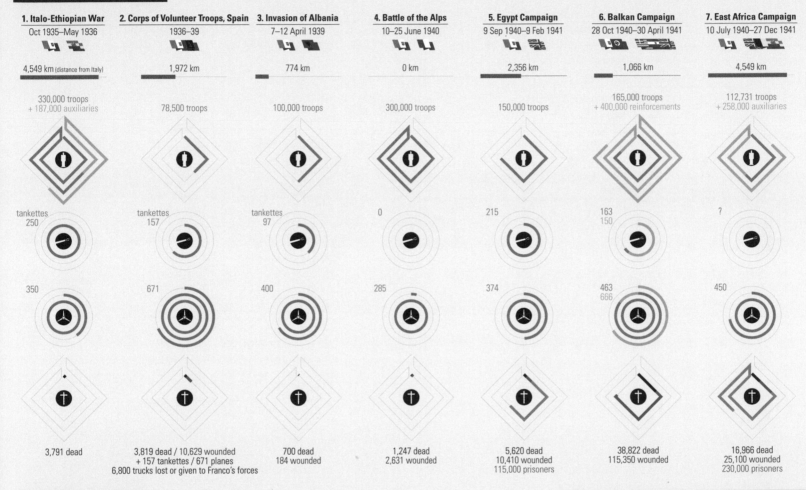

1. Italo-Ethiopian War	2. Corps of Volunteer Troops, Spain	3. Invasion of Albania	4. Battle of the Alps	5. Egypt Campaign	6. Balkan Campaign	7. East Africa Campaign
Oct 1935–May 1936	1936–39	7–12 April 1939	10–25 June 1940	9 Sep 1940–9 Feb 1941	28 Oct 1940–30 April 1941	10 July 1940–27 Dec 1941
4,549 km (distance from Italy)	1,972 km	774 km	0 km	2,356 km	1,066 km	4,549 km
330,000 troops + 187,000 auxiliaries	78,500 troops	100,000 troops	300,000 troops	150,000 troops	165,000 troops + 400,000 reinforcements	112,731 troops + 258,000 auxiliaries
tankettes 250	tankettes 157	tankettes 97	0	215	163 / 150	?
350	671	400	285	374	463 / 666	450
3,791 dead	3,819 dead / 10,629 wounded + 157 tankettes / 671 planes 6,800 trucks lost or given to Franco's forces	700 dead 184 wounded	1,247 dead 2,631 wounded	5,620 dead 10,410 wounded 115,000 prisoners	38,822 dead 115,350 wounded	16,966 dead 25,100 wounded 230,000 prisoners

ITALIAN FORCES IN 1940   ● = 1 ■ = 10 ✖ = 100

Soldiers / Blackshirts: 1,347,000 troops / ± 340,000 Blackshirts

Tanks: 200

Aircraft:
✖✖✖✖: 527 reconnaissance planes (108)
✖✖✖✖✖✖✖: 759 fighters (165)
✖✖✖✖✖✖✖✖✖✖: 1,064 bombers (281)
Aircraft: 2,675 inc. 554 non-operational and 325 in Ethiopia

Trucks: 38,000

Ships:
●●●● 4 battleships ●●●●●●●●●●●●●● 7 cruisers / 12 light
■■■■■■■■■■■■■ 125 destroyers ■■■■■■■■■■■ 113 submarines
Ships: 261

THE ITALIAN ARMY IN 1940: POORLY PREPARED

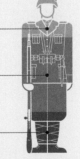

20 divisions
60% manned, incomplete or obsolete equipment, 50% of horses and vehicles needed

34 divisions
75% manned, fully armed, lacking vehicles

19 divisions
fully equipped

Admiral James Somerville 1882–1949
 Fairey Swordfish Mk I

 Savoia Marchetti SM.79

Admiral Angelo Iachino 1889–1976

CT, 1994 • 6. *History of the Second World War, The Mediterranean & the Middle East*, 6 vols., 1954–88 •
7. M. Knox, *Mussolini Unleashed, 1939–1941: Politics and Strategy in Fascist Italy's Last War*, Cambridge, 1986.

THE DESERT WAR

The desert war was a matter of geography. Firstly, the front was very narrow, a few dozen kilometres squeezed between the sea and the Sahara. Only light units such as the Long Range Desert Group could venture further into the interior for commando operations against the enemy's rear. With no roads, the troops could not receive supplies, so they were forced to follow the coast road (via Balbia) and it became possible to block them off from it. The desert war was therefore punctuated with frontal assaults on heavily mined entrenched positions (Tobruk, Gazala, El-Alamein, Mareth). Artillery and engineers were key players. But once a breakthrough had been

achieved and movement started, all operations were led by motorized and mechanized units. In those sandy expanses, speed, boldness and a willingness to seize the initiative were key advantages. This was even more the case for German officers in general – and Rommel in particular – who were trained in tactical autonomy. In a few hours, the battlefield expanded, forcing units to advance on foot.

At that point, the defeated side could only go back, relying on the second geographical factor: the huge distances involved. The war was happening at the end of a massive supply chain. For the British it was 23,000 km via Cape Town, a two-month voyage.

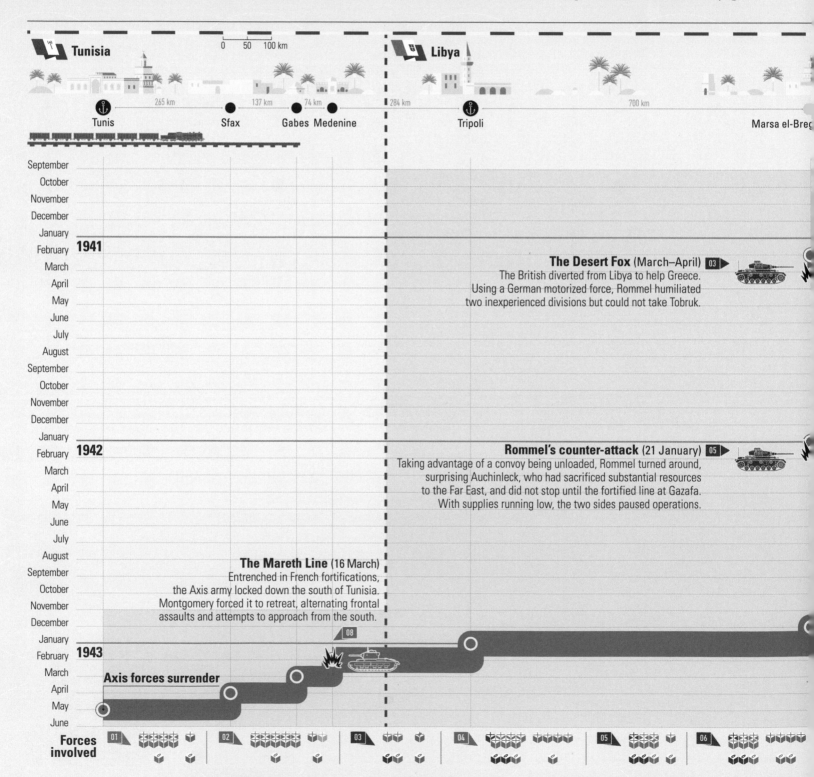

Tunisia   **Libya**

0   50   100 km

265 km   137 km   74 km   284 km   700 km

Tunis   Sfax   Gabes Medenine   Tripoli   Marsa el-Breg

September
October
November
December
January
February **1941**
March
April
May
June
July
August
September
October
November
December
January
February **1942**
March
April
May
June
July
August
September
October
November
December
January
February **1943**
March
April
May
June

The Desert Fox (March–April) 03
The British diverted from Libya to help Greece.
Using a German motorized force, Rommel humiliated
two inexperienced divisions but could not take Tobruk.

Rommel's counter-attack (21 January) 05
Taking advantage of a convoy being unloaded, Rommel turned around,
surprising Auchinleck, who had sacrificed substantial resources
to the Far East, and did not stop until the fortified line at Gazafa.
With supplies running low, the two sides paused operations.

The Mareth Line (16 March)
Entrenched in French fortifications,
the Axis army locked down the south of Tunisia.
Montgomery forced it to retreat, alternating frontal
assaults and attempts to approach from the south.

08

Axis forces surrender

Forces involved   01   02   03   04   05   06

For Germany it was 1,800 km, but it was necessary to cross the dangerous Mediterranean. Once unloaded, supplies had to be carried hundreds of kilometres on poor roads. Without motorized logistics it was impossible to fight. Every victory caused problems for the victor, especially since the climate, the sand and the dust wore out equipment in a few days. Repair workshops played a vital role. So the war became like a pendulum. The British moved 1,000 km further into Libya and were blocked by the Germans and Italians who ended up coming to a halt in Egypt after a one-week lightning raid. The necessary break in fighting then worked to the advantage of the British, who were fighting on 'home turf', and the cycle started all over again. Only the Allied landing in Morocco and Algeria on 8 November 1942 transformed the situation by catching the Axis forces in a pincer movement. The distances also shaped the structure of

the forces. The further from their port they were fighting, the smaller they needed to be. It was not because the theatre was considered of secondary importance that troop strength was limited; it was mainly because it was impossible to provide supplies for more. A financial assessment showed that there were already too many. Yet Rommel had one-twelfth of the Wehrmacht's motorized resources for one seventy-eighth of its manpower. The solution for the Reich would have been to take Alexandria, expelling the Royal Navy from the eastern Mediterranean. The Haifa refinery, which supplied the British Eighth Army, would have been within range of the Luftwaffe and Rommel would have had a major port at the gateway to the Middle East. So he was not entirely wrong when he started a desperate rush in the summer of 1942. It was the only way he could achieve a strategic victory. But he fell around a hundred kilometres short.

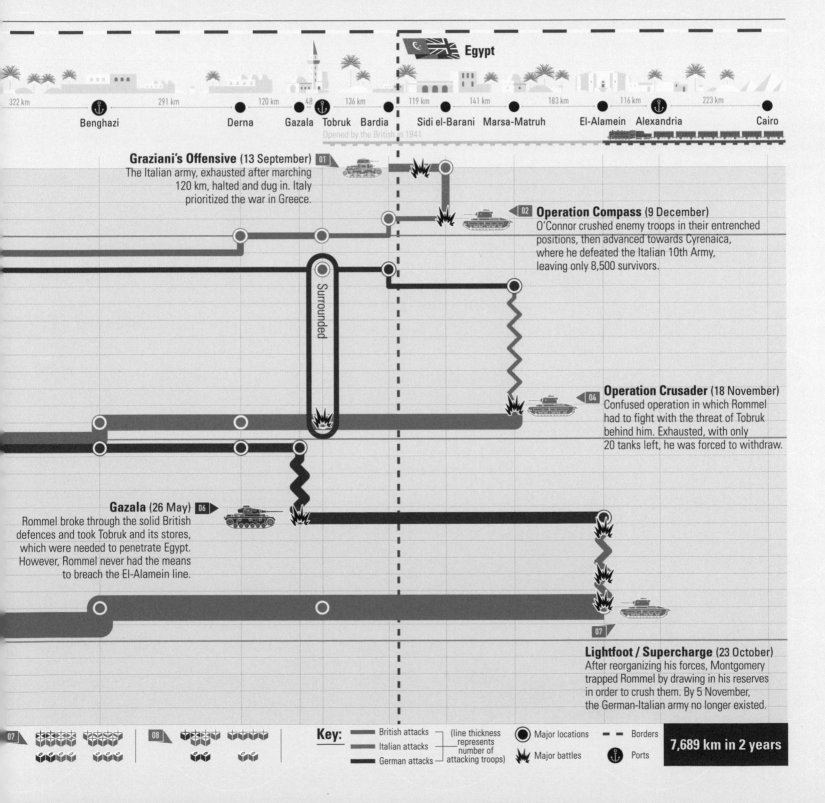

Egypt

322 km · 291 km · 120 km · 48 · 136 km · 119 km · 141 km · 183 km · 116 km · 223 km

Benghazi · Derna · Gazala · Tobruk · Bardia · Sidi el-Barani · Marsa-Matruh · El-Alamein · Alexandria · Cairo

Opened by the British in 1941

Graziani's Offensive (13 September) 01
The Italian army, exhausted after marching 120 km, halted and dug in. Italy prioritized the war in Greece.

Operation Compass (9 December) 02
O'Connor crushed enemy troops in their entrenched positions, then advanced towards Cyrenaica, where he defeated the Italian 10th Army, leaving only 8,500 survivors.

Surrounded

Operation Crusader (18 November) 04
Confused operation in which Rommel had to fight with the threat of Tobruk behind him. Exhausted, with only 20 tanks left, he was forced to withdraw.

Gazala (26 May) 06
Rommel broke through the solid British defences and took Tobruk and its stores, which were needed to penetrate Egypt. However, Rommel never had the means to breach the El-Alamein line.

07

Lightfoot / Supercharge (23 October)
After reorganizing his forces, Montgomery trapped Rommel by drawing in his reserves in order to crush them. By 5 November, the German-Italian army no longer existed.

07 · 08

Key:
— British attacks
— Italian attacks (line thickness represents number of attacking troops)
— German attacks

⬤ Major locations
💥 Major battles
- - - Borders
⚓ Ports

7,689 km in 2 years

2 • A BATTLE IN DETAIL: GAZALA, 26 MAY–14 JUNE 1942

The two armies, re-equipped after a four-month break, faced each other a few kilometres from Tobruk in May 1942. The British were entrenched in a network of fortified points covered by 70 km of minefields. Each 'box' housed an infantry bridge reinforced with artillery, as at Bir Hakeim. At the rear, armoured brigades and inter-unit flying columns stood ready to close the gap. But Rommel bypassed the obstacle to the south and suddenly appeared behind the stunned British forces. However, although the mechanized columns of the Axis had crossed the sand dunes, the supply columns could not do so. They had to go via Bir Hakeim, which resisted. The British rallied. The Afrika Korps

(DAK) was isolated and forced to entrench in a 'hedgehog'. Its survival depended on a new supply corridor being opened up, which was done on 1 June. The British missed their opportunity. Although they had many more tanks, they had been duped. Firstly, the Germans manoeuvred to draw them within range of the anti-tank guns or take them on the flank and, secondly, the British attack was disorganized. On 14 June, after losing three-quarters of their armoured vehicles and seeing most of the infantry surrounded in their boxes, Ritchie ordered a retreat. The infantry, including the French at Bir Hakeim, escaped. But Tobruk and its depots were lost and the road to Alexandria was open.

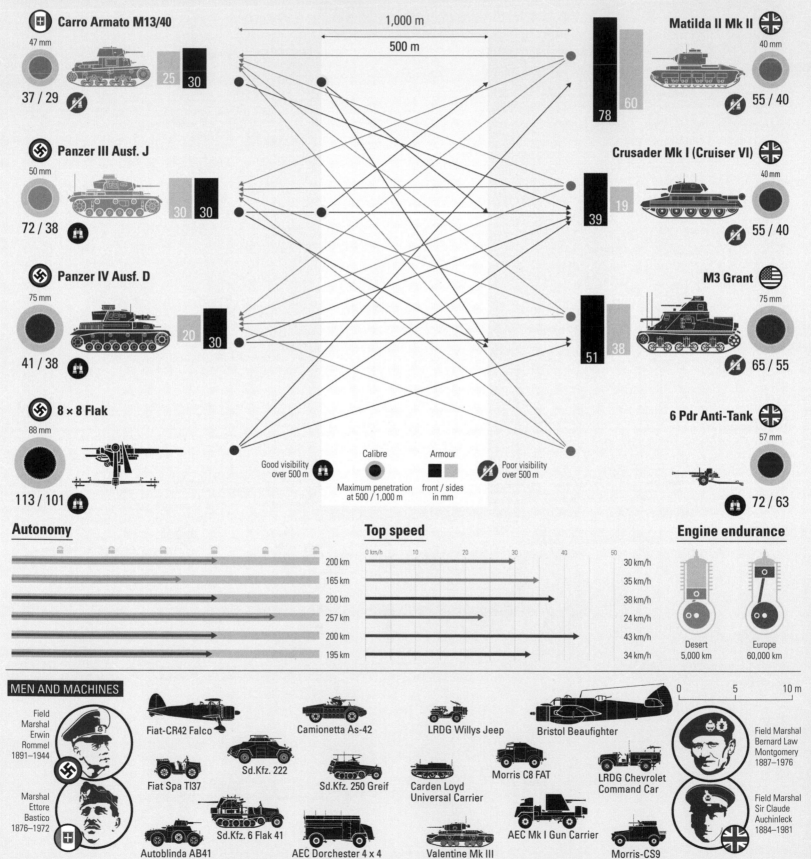

Carro Armato M13/40
47 mm
37 / 29
25 | 30

Panzer III Ausf. J
50 mm
72 / 38
30 | 30

Panzer IV Ausf. D
75 mm
41 / 38
20 | 30

8 × 8 Flak
88 mm
113 / 101

1,000 m
500 m

Matilda II Mk II
40 mm
55 / 40
78 | 60

Crusader Mk I (Cruiser VI)
40 mm
55 / 40
39 | 19

M3 Grant
75 mm
65 / 55
51 | 38

6 Pdr Anti-Tank
57 mm
72 / 63

Good visibility over 500 m
Calibre — Maximum penetration at 500 / 1,000 m
Armour — front / sides in mm
Poor visibility over 500 m

Autonomy
200 km
165 km
200 km
257 km
200 km
195 km

Top speed
0 km/h   10   20   30   40   50
30 km/h
35 km/h
38 km/h
24 km/h
43 km/h
34 km/h

Engine endurance
Desert 5,000 km
Europe 60,000 km

MEN AND MACHINES

Field Marshal Erwin Rommel 1891–1944

Marshal Ettore Bastico 1876–1972

Fiat-CR42 Falco
Fiat Spa Tl37
Autoblinda AB41
Sd.Kfz. 222
Sd.Kfz. 6 Flak 41
AEC Dorchester 4 x 4
Camionetta As-42
Sd.Kfz. 250 Greif

LRDG Willys Jeep
Carden Loyd Universal Carrier
Morris C8 FAT
Valentine Mk III
AEC Mk I Gun Carrier

Bristol Beaufighter
LRDG Chevrolet Command Car
Morris-CS9

0   5   10 m

Field Marshal Bernard Law Montgomery 1887–1976

Field Marshal Sir Claude Auchinleck 1884–1981

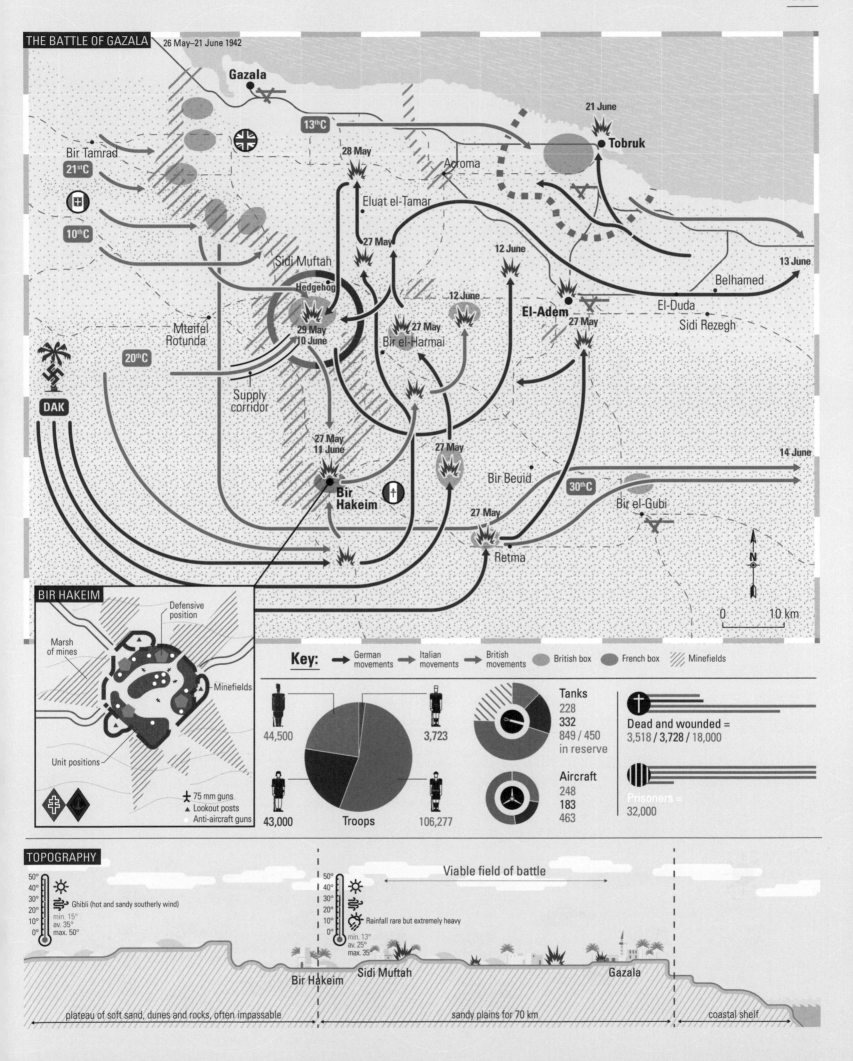

THE BATTLE OF GAZALA
26 May–21 June 1942

Gazala

21st C Bir Tamrad

10th C

13th C

28 May

Eluat el-Tamar

27 May

Sidi Muftah

Hedgehog

20th C

Mteifel Rotunda

29 May
10 June

Supply corridor

DAK

27 May
11 June

Bir el-Harmai
27 May

27 May

Bir Hakeim

27 May

27 May
Retma

12 June

12 June

El-Adem

27 May

Acroma

21 June
Tobruk

Belhamed

13 June

El-Duda

Sidi Rezegh

Bir Beuid

30th C

Bir el-Gubi

14 June

N

0   10 km

BIR HAKEIM

Defensive position

Marsh of mines

Minefields

Unit positions

✦ 75 mm guns
▲ Lookout posts
• Anti-aircraft guns

Key:
→ German movements   → Italian movements   → British movements   ● British box   ● French box   ⧄ Minefields

44,500   3,723

43,000   Troops   106,277

Tanks
228
332
849 / 450
in reserve

Aircraft
248
183
463

Dead and wounded =
3,518 / **3,728** / 18,000

Prisoners =
32,000

TOPOGRAPHY

50° 40° 30° 20° 10° 0°
☼ Ghibli (hot and sandy southerly wind)
min. 15°
av. 35°
max. 50°

50° 40° 30° 20° 10° 0°
☼ Rainfall rare but extremely heavy
min. 13°
av. 25°
max. 35°

Viable field of battle

Bir Hakeim   Sidi Muftah   Gazala

plateau of soft sand, dunes and rocks, often impassable   sandy plains for 70 km   coastal shelf

3 • LOGISTICS: ROMMEL'S ACHILLES HEEL

Rommel had supply problems throughout the campaign. Three explanations have been suggested. First, there were not enough convoys. Mussolini's negligence from 1940 had deprived the merchant fleet of a third of its tonnage (including the biggest cargo ships). Malta sunk another third. In 1942, there was insufficient manpower to transport the 4,480 tonnes per day needed for the campaign in French North Africa. A second issue was that the ports of Tripoli and Benghazi were too small and too shallow and the quays were too short. But their structure was improved, making it possible to unload adequate supplies of 5,000 tonnes per day in April. The worst bottleneck was caused by a shortage of trucks. The German-Italian forces only had between 6,000 and 10,000, scarcely enough to move actual supplies and two-thirds fewer than needed if the navy had satisfied Rommel's demands, and capacity on the Tobruk to El-Alamein railway (332 tonnes per day) was tiny. So bigger deliveries would have been stranded at the ports.

THE SHRINKING ITALIAN MERCHANT FLEET

1938 / 3,318,000 t

1940 / 2,102,000 t

- 1,216,000 t seized en route

1942 / 1,661,000 t
inc. 818,000 t seized in France

- 1,259,000 t sunk

1943 / 1,219,904 t

- 441,096 t sunk

THE FAILURE OF THE LOGISTICS CHAIN

2,118 tonnes/day shipped
1,827 t/d to the front
292 t/d to the rear
207 t/d to civilians
85 t/d to the Navy

58% to Tripoli
15 days en route

1,349 t/d delivered to the front

7 days en route
42% to Benghazi

El-Alamein

The 1,349 t/d received at the front required a fleet of 8,941 trucks

4,480 t/d required
3,200 t/d for the front (inc. 33.5% Italian and 38% DAK), 480 t/d petrol for transport trucks, 560 t/d for the rear

Number of trucks
▶ required to meet demand: 21,173   ▶ maximum: 10,000   ▶ minimum: 6,000

10,000   15,000
5,000   20,000
0

average:
2,118 t/d unloaded

maximum:
5,322 t/d unloaded
in April 1942

required: 4,480 t/d

Unloaded at ports
(in tonnes/day)

COMPARATIVE DISTANCES TO THE NORTH AFRICAN FRONT AND THE RUSSIAN FRONT

Moscow

1,069 km   1,742 km

Brest
Litovsk   Stalingrad

Tripoli   El-Alamein

Poor railway links

1,481 km   Tobruk   2,060 km

5 • THE HUMAN AND STRATEGIC COST

The desert war was less bloody than other campaigns (70 deaths per day, all sides combined). This was due to the limited forces deployed and long breaks between operations (10 months out of 32). Even so, the active periods were relentless. The other striking fact was the number of prisoners, inflated by the 130,000 Italians captured in December 1940 and the final surrender in Tunisia (between 200,000 and 250,000). However secondary it might have been in terms of the resources dedicated to it, the African theatre undoubtedly contributed to the eventual Allied victory, firstly by protecting the Middle East, secondly by bringing about the end of the Italian army (438,000 losses including East Africa) and finally by exposing the southern flank of Hitler's Europe.

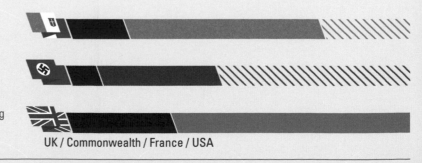

UK / Commonwealth / France / USA

SOURCES: 1. *Das Deutsche Reich und der Zweite Weltkrieg*, vols. III & VI, Munich, 1994 & 2001 • 2. Piero Crociani & Pier Paolo Battistelli, *Italian Soldier in North Africa 1941–43*, Oxford, 2013 • 3. *History of the Second World War, The Mediterranean & the Middle East*, 6 vols., 1954–88 • 4. Jack Greene & Alessandro Massignani, *Rommel's North Africa Campaign*, Boston, 1994 • 5. *BA/MA RW4/479, RW*

4 • THE END OF THE AFRICAN CAMPAIGN

Rommel failed to take El-Alamein twice. Montgomery, in command of the British Eighth Army since August 1942, attacked in his turn. Conscious of its inferiority in the war of movement, Britain opted for a methodical strategy to draw in the enemy and use up their reserves. The fierce fighting, costing many Commonwealth lives in particular, heavily drained the Afrika Korps. The Axis might have rallied in Libya if the Allies had not landed in French North Africa at the same time, diverting the reinforcements.

The Axis withdrawal that followed may seem surprising. In fact, keeping a bridgehead protected Southern Europe and in particular Italy. Hitler beat the Allies to Tunisia and was planning to set up a base there, which would be easy to supply since Tunisia had modern ports close to Italy, and easy to defend due to the mountains in the west and fortifications closing off the border to the south. So it was a sensible move, but insufficient since the Axis was defeated in May 1943 after a hard campaign.

3rd BATTLE OF EL-ALAMEIN 23 October–3 November 1942

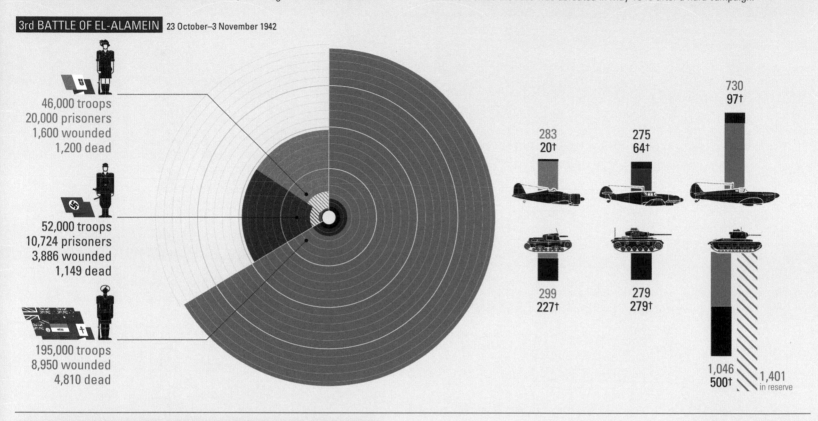

46,000 troops
20,000 prisoners
1,600 wounded
1,200 dead

52,000 troops
10,724 prisoners
3,886 wounded
1,149 dead

195,000 troops
8,950 wounded
4,810 dead

283
20†

275
64†

730
97†

299
227†

279
279†

1,046
500†

1,401
in reserve

COMPARATIVE MONTHLY AXIS DEPLOYMENTS IN LIBYA AND TUNISIA

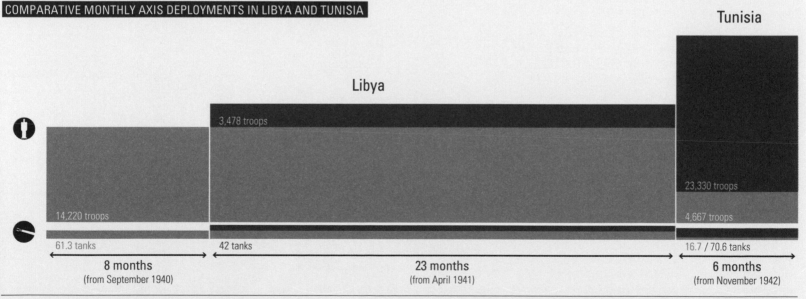

Libya

Tunisia

3,478 troops

23,330 troops

14,220 troops

4,667 troops

61.3 tanks

42 tanks

16.7 / 70.6 tanks

8 months
(from September 1940)

23 months
(from April 1941)

6 months
(from November 1942)

22,341 dead
70,000 wounded / 250,000 prisoners

12,602 dead
43,212 wounded / 121,344 prisoners

40,378 dead
143,158 wounded / 66,500 prisoners

6/556 and *6/558, RW 6/543*, Istituto Centrale di Statistica, *Morti e dispersi per cause belliche negli anni 1940–45*, Rome, 1957 • 6. Colin F. Baxter, *The War in North Africa, 1940–1943*, Westport, CT, 1996.

STALINGRAD

The battle for Stalingrad was a huge mêlée centring on the city itself, which lasted from 11 July 1942 to 2 February 1943. It can be divided into four phases. In the first phase, from 11 July to 23 August 1942, the German 6th Army, commanded by General Paulus, advanced 200 kilometres east, from the river Chir to the Volga, via the enormous loop of the Don. Stalingrad was isolated on three sides. The second phase was the urban battle that took place from 23 August to 18 November. For the first time in history, the scene of the confrontation was a large industrial city 20 kilometres across, where combat was shrunk by a factor by 10, and battlefields were reduced to a single street, house or factory. Despite intensive fire, the German 6th Army, supported by parts of the 4th Panzer Army, did not manage to drive the 62nd Army, commanded by General Chuikov since 12 September, from the west bank of the Volga. The third phase was the Soviet counter-attack, Operation Uranus, prepared far ahead and part of a complex strategic plan. Uranus succeeded in forty-eight hours, leading, on 23 November, to encirclement of the German 6th Army and sections of the 4th Panzer Army: 330,000 men. In the fourth phase, up to 2 February, the 6th Army was completely destroyed in and around Stalingrad, after the Luftwaffe airlift and Manstein's disengagement raid had failed.

Although it cannot be said to have marked a turning point in the conflict in itself or to have been in any way decisive, the Battle of Stalingrad had enormous repercussions. This is obvious from the casualty toll: German losses were heavy but they were much less severe than those suffered by the Red Army, and the Wehrmacht eventually managed to stabilize the front by the end of February 1943. The importance of the victory on the Volga was more strategic and psychological. Never again would Hitler be able to mount an operation with a strategic aim and he also gave up the idea of an easy victory in the east. Stalin would not lose the Caucasus and his oil wells, or the new supply route opened up by the Americans through Iraq. Psychologically, the myth of the Wehrmacht's superiority and invincibility was shattered. For the first time, the Germans realized that they could lose the war and their relationship with their charismatic Führer deteriorated. The Red Army overcame the grave crisis in the summer of 1942 and Stalin, more confident in its capabilities, slightly relaxed his political control over it.

1 • AN URBAN BATTLEGROUND

A series of four offensives enabled the Germans to take control of 90% of the city. But few in number and unable to exploit their superior firepower and mobility in an urban environment, their divisions were quickly worn out, as evidenced by their increasingly slow rate of progress and their mounting losses. Soviet batteries harassed them from the other bank of the Volga, while at Spartakovka in the north, a quarter of them were almost constantly pinned down by offensives. The 6th Army was also physically exhausted. Facing a 62nd Army that struck at night and brought out 500 snipers, its men were unable to rest.

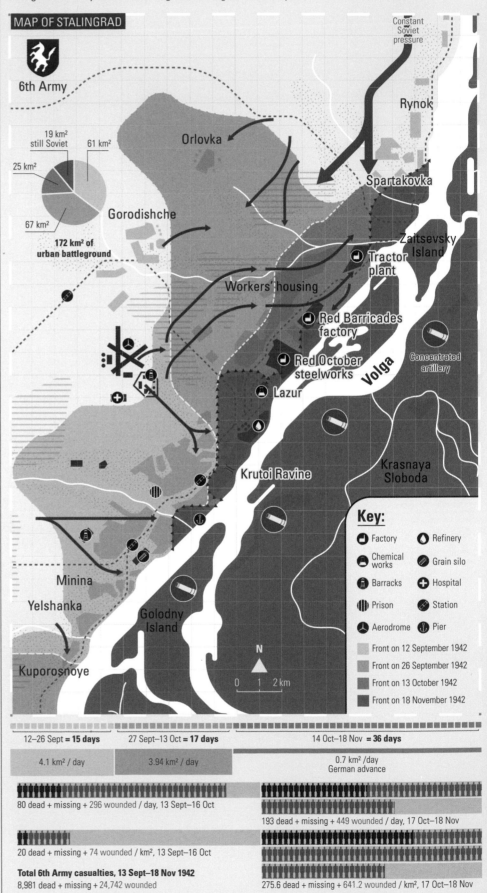

MAP OF STALINGRAD

6th Army

Constant Soviet pressure

Rynok

19 km² still Soviet
61 km²
25 km²
67 km²
172 km² of urban battleground

Orlovka

Spartakovka

Gorodishche

Zaitsevsky Island

Tractor plant

Workers' housing

Red Barricades factory

Concentrated artillery

Red October steelworks

Volga

Lazur

Krutoi Ravine

Krasnaya Sloboda

Minina

Yelshanka

Golodny Island

Kuporosnoye

Key:

- Factory
- Chemical works
- Barracks
- Prison
- Aerodrome
- Refinery
- Grain silo
- Hospital
- Station
- Pier

- Front on 12 September 1942
- Front on 26 September 1942
- Front on 13 October 1942
- Front on 18 November 1942

N

0 1 2 km

12–26 Sept = **15 days**	27 Sept–13 Oct = **17 days**	14 Oct–18 Nov = **36 days**
4.1 km² / day	3.94 km² / day	0.7 km² /day German advance

80 dead + missing + 296 wounded / day, 13 Sept–16 Oct

193 dead + missing + 449 wounded / day, 17 Oct–18 Nov

20 dead + missing + 74 wounded / km², 13 Sept–16 Oct

Total 6th Army casualties, 13 Sept–18 Nov 1942
8,981 dead + missing + 24,742 wounded

275.6 dead + missing + 641.2 wounded / km², 17 Oct–18 Nov

2 • A DRAIN ON HUMAN LIVES

After the end of September, the Soviets realized that they had to pin down and wear out the 6th Army in urban combat, while the counter-offensive was being planned outside the city. To do that, the battle needed just-in-time supplies, in small quantities for immediate use. In an unprecedented feat of logistics, the equivalent of 15 divisions crossed the Volga and arrived, sometimes by the skin of their teeth, to prevent the collapse of the 62nd Army. The new arrivals suffered terrible losses, but each time the enemy was stopped a few hundred metres from the river. It says a great deal about the short-sightedness of Hitler, the Wehrmacht High Command and Paulus that the Germans allowed 10 of their best divisions to be trapped in pointless combat for over two months, leaving the under-equipped Romanians to guard their flanks. The fact that the intelligence service did not locate the Soviet concentrations in the north-west and south of the city was one of its biggest failures of the war.

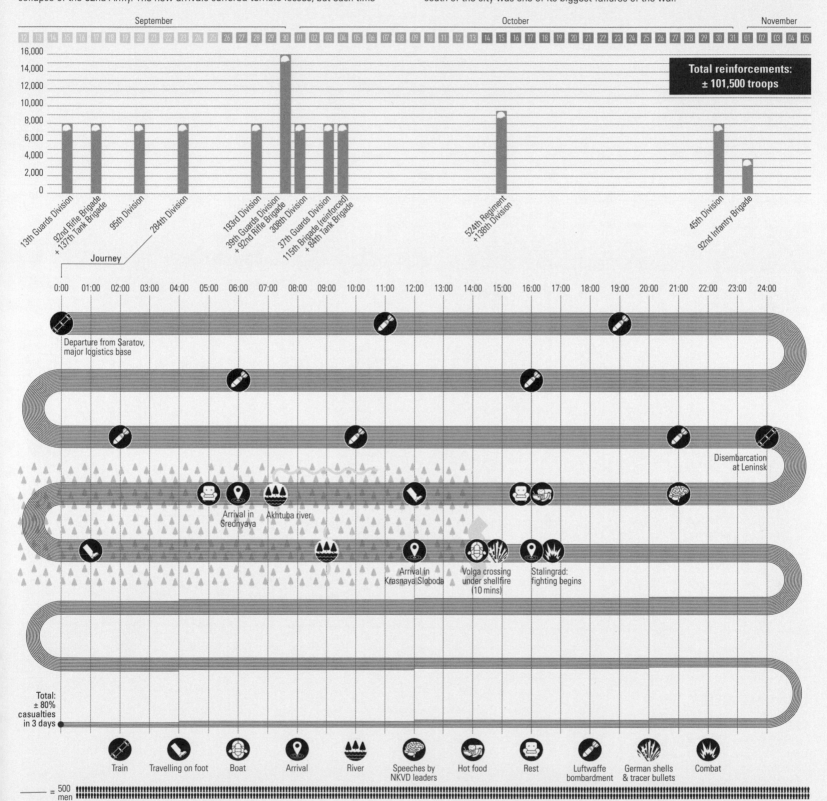

Total reinforcements:
± 101,500 troops

13th Guards Division
92nd Rifle Brigade + 137th Tank Brigade
95th Division
284th Division
193rd Division
39th Guards Division + 92nd Rifle Brigade
308th Division
37th Guards Division
115th Brigade (reinforced) + 84th Tank Brigade
524th Regiment + 138th Division
45th Division
92nd Infantry Brigade

Journey

Departure from Saratov, major logistics base

Arrival in Srednyaya

Akhtuba river

Disembarcation at Leninsk

Arrival in Krasnaya Sloboda

Volga crossing under shellfire (10 mins)

Stalingrad: fighting begins

Total: ± 80% casualties in 3 days

Train · Travelling on foot · Boat · Arrival · River · Speeches by NKVD leaders · Hot food · Rest · Luftwaffe bombardment · German shells & tracer bullets · Combat

= 500 men

The nightmare journey of a Soviet reinforcement division:
The unit embarked at Saratov and travelled for three days, coming under Luftwaffe attack several times. They left the trains at Leninsk, 50 km east of Stalingrad. The troops were harangued by propagandists who explained the importance of the fight and reminded them of Stalin's order: 'Not one step back!' The last hot meal was distributed, together with a handout on how to act in street combat. They set out on foot at night along the river Aktuba, crossing at Srednyaya. Then they passed through the forests of the wide Volga delta, arriving at Krasnaya Sloboda on the east bank of the river. At night, the men boarded a large number of small boats. The crossing took 10 minutes, under a hail of tracer bullets and shells. The unit landed on the west bank in the shadow of Krutoi Ravine, 200 metres from the fighting. It was immediately thrown into the fray. Three days later, only 20% of the men were left. A new unit then arrived via the same route.

3 • SOVIET COUNTER-OFFENSIVES

Operation Uranus, the encirclement of the 6th Army around Stalingrad, was not the only or even the most important operation endorsed by the Stavka in October 1942. In the north, 1,000 km from Stalingrad, Zhukov had to destroy the 9th Army (Operation Mars) before taking on most of the Army Group Centre (Jupiter). It was a bloody fiasco with only one advantage: it stopped the Panzer divisions being moved south. Although Uranus was a complete success, its logical sequel, Saturn, the destruction of Army Groups B

and A in the taking of Rostov, had to be downgraded to 'Little Saturn'. Two unexpected factors forced the Stavka to change its plans. First, the encircled troops were much more numerous and combative than expected and, secondly, Manstein managed to get within 48 kilometres of the 6th Army (Operation Winter Storm). To stop their prey escaping, the Stavka had to use the two armies intended for Saturn to block Manstein and occupy the airfields supplying Paulus (Little Saturn).

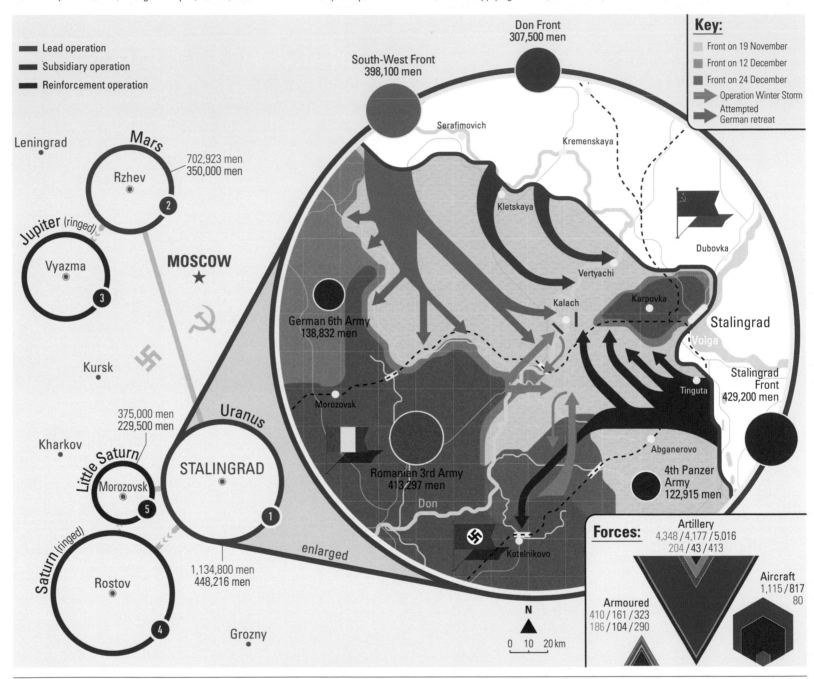

Key:

- Lead operation
- Subsidiary operation
- Reinforcement operation

Front on 19 November
Front on 12 December
Front on 24 December
Operation Winter Storm
Attempted German retreat

Forces:

Artillery
4,348 / 4,177 / 5,016
204 / 43 / 413

Armoured
410 / 161 / 323
186 / 104 / 290

Aircraft
1,115 / 817
80

4 • A FAILED AIRLIFT

Although the Luftwaffe had pioneered airlifts, their attempt at Stalingrad failed completely. It would never manage to supply the besieged troops with what they needed, despite massive losses of JU-52 transport planes. Bad weather, anti-aircraft defences and enemy fighters, heavy wear on equipment and surprise Soviet attacks on two airfields made the mission impossible. It was also a vain hope that Paulus's men, starving and frozen, with no artillery support or fuel, would be able to leave in force.

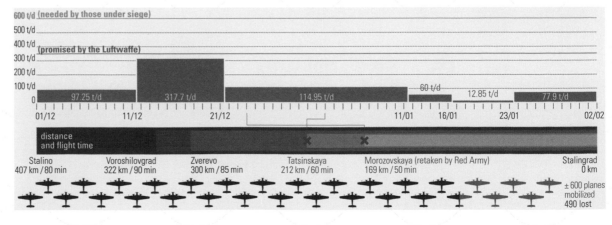

600 t/d (needed by those under siege)

400 t/d (promised by the Luftwaffe)

| | 97.25 t/d | 317.7 t/d | 114.95 t/d | 60 t/d | 12.85 t/d | 77.9 t/d |

01/12 — 11/12 — 21/12 — 11/01 — 16/01 — 23/01 — 02/02

distance and flight time

| Stalino | Voroshilovgrad | Zverevo | Tatsinskaya | Morozovskaya (retaken by Red Army) | Stalingrad |
| 407 km / 80 min | 322 km / 90 min | 300 km / 85 min | 212 km / 60 min | 169 km / 50 min | 0 km |

± 600 planes mobilized
490 lost

5 • PRISONERS OF WAR

It took the Soviets over two months to capture the whole of the Stalingrad pocket. Ironically the final battles would be fought once more in the rubble of the city. No surrender agreement was signed. It is not overstating the case to say that the incredible resistance by the German infantry saved Army Groups A and B by immobilizing six Soviet armies and an enormous artillery. They equalled Chuikov's 62nd Army in courage. For 70% of the 110,000 prisoners, short of food for two months, the long marches to the departure stations and temporary holding camps would be fatal, with nights in the open in temperatures of -20°C, coupled with mental exhaustion and a rampant typhus epidemic. In 1955, Chancellor Adenauer went to collect the survivors in Moscow.

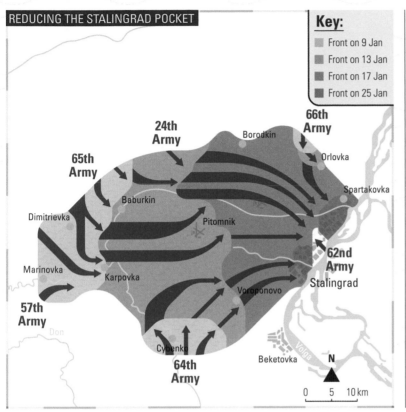

REDUCING THE STALINGRAD POCKET

Key:
- Front on 9 Jan
- Front on 13 Jan
- Front on 17 Jan
- Front on 25 Jan

24th Army
65th Army
66th Army
Borodkin
Orlovka
Spartakovka
Baburkin
Dimitrievka
Pitomnik
62nd Army
Stalingrad
Marinovka
Karpovka
Voroponovo
57th Army
Cybenko
Beketovka
64th Army
Don
Volga
N
0 5 10 km

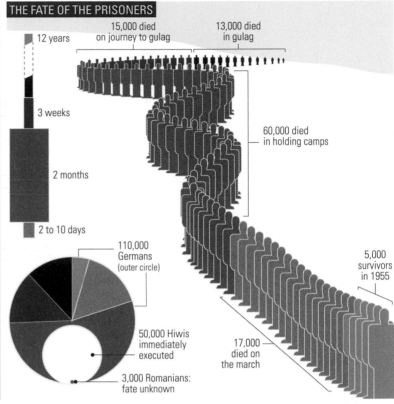

THE FATE OF THE PRISONERS

12 years
15,000 died on journey to gulag
13,000 died in gulag
3 weeks
60,000 died in holding camps
2 months
2 to 10 days
110,000 Germans (outer circle)
50,000 Hiwis immediately executed
3,000 Romanians: fate unknown
17,000 died on the march
5,000 survivors in 1955

6 • CASUALTIES

The Battle of Stalingrad in its broadest sense, including the operations against the Hungarians and Italians in the middle Don basin, resulted in nearly 2 million people being killed or wounded, not forgetting 100,000 inhabitants of the city. Although German losses were heavy, they were not as catastrophic as claimed. On the other hand, this campaign in the winter of 1942 to 1943 sounded the death knell for military engagement by Germany's allies. Italy, Hungary and Romania lost most of their forces and virtually all their equipment. The first two would withdraw from the USSR shortly afterwards. The Germans' hostile attitude to their allies destroyed any feeling of brotherhood in arms. The Soviet losses were, as usual, very high but they were considered acceptable given the damage suffered by the enemy forces and the huge operational and strategic gains for the Red Army. The Red Army knew that the Germans could no longer win, but it still had to show that it could be victorious.

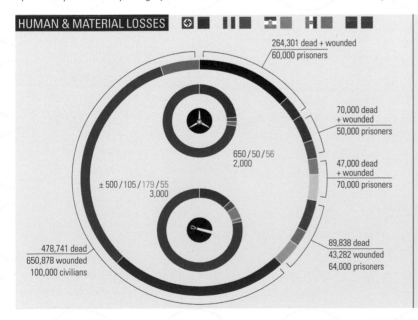

HUMAN & MATERIAL LOSSES

264,301 dead + wounded
60,000 prisoners
70,000 dead + wounded
50,000 prisoners
650 / 50 / 56
2,000
± 500 / 105 / 179 / 55
3,000
47,000 dead + wounded
70,000 prisoners
478,741 dead
650,878 wounded
100,000 civilians
89,838 dead
43,282 wounded
64,000 prisoners

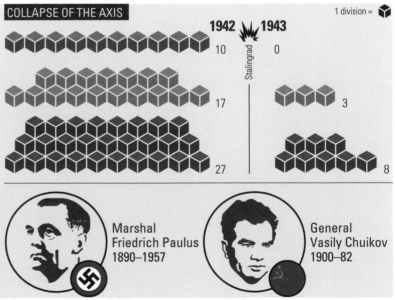

COLLAPSE OF THE AXIS

1 division =

1942   1943
10   0
Stalingrad
17   3
27   8

Marshal Friedrich Paulus 1890–1957

General Vasily Chuikov 1900–82

SOURCES: 1. Manfred Kehrig, *Stalingrad, Analyse und Dokumentation einer Schlacht*, Stuttgart, 1974 • 2. David M. Glantz, *The Stalingrad Trilogy*, Lawrence, KS, 2010 • 3. *Das deutsche Reich und der Zweite Weltkrieg*, vol. 6 • 4. G. F. Krivosheev (ed.), *Soviet Casualties and Combat Losses in the Twentieth Century*, London, 1997.

THE ALLIED RECONQUEST OF THE PACIFIC

Once they had recovered from the shock of the first few months of conflict and contained the Japanese expansion around Australia, Melanesia and India, the Allies began to fight a war of attrition concentrated mainly in the Solomon Islands for much of 1942. The island of Guadalcanal was the scene of a fierce six-month land, sea and air battle, aimed chiefly at gaining control of the small airfield known as Henderson Field in the north of the island. Furious fighting also took place in New Guinea for control of the Kokoda Trail and the Australian base of Port Moresby. From 1943 onwards, the Allies moved on to a second

phase of operations, gradually retaking the initiative everywhere with the support of US arsenals, which were the spectacular fruits of the massive building programmes of 1940–41.

However, the US offensive aimed at breaking the hold of Japanese power started quietly without waiting for the build-up of ground and naval air forces. In 1942, submarines began a systematic campaign against Japan's supply networks, achieving decisive results after a difficult start. Allied networks, by contrast, were never truly threatened by the Japanese submarine fleet, despite its size. It was primarily deployed against warships and

1 • A SLOW ALLIED RECOVERY

From 1943 onwards, the Americans advanced along two different axes in order to penetrate Japanese defences in the Pacific. MacArthur led the theatre of operations in the South Pacific, aiming to retake the Philippines via the north coast of New Guinea after breaking through the 'Bismarck barrier' and cutting off the major Japanese base at Rabaul. In the central Pacific, Admiral Nimitz's Big Blue Fleet first started moving in short stages, ignoring and isolating most of the Japanese island garrisons to focus on

a few key targets: Tarawa, Entwetok, Saipan, Tinian and, in the interests of US morale, the reconquest of Guam, an American territory lost at the beginning of the war. In the second phase, once the Japanese fleet had been destroyed, the two pincers converged on Japan itself, first with the very difficult capture of Iwo Jima by the US Marine Corps in February–March 1945, the first island to be conquered that was actually Japanese, and then in April with Operation Iceberg, a US landing on the island of Okinawa.

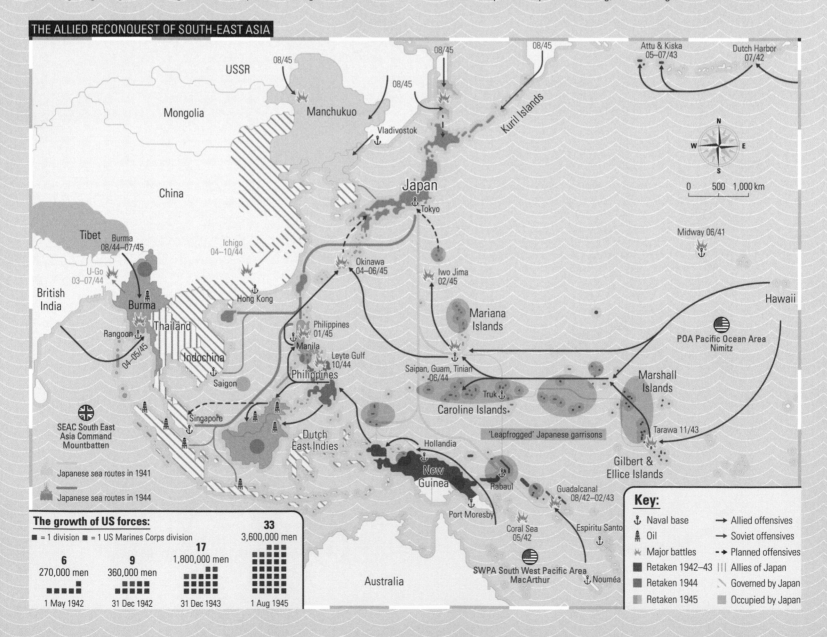

THE ALLIED RECONQUEST OF SOUTH-EAST ASIA

The growth of US forces:

■ = 1 division ■ = 1 US Marines Corps division

6 270,000 men	**9** 360,000 men	**17** 1,800,000 men	**33** 3,600,000 men
1 May 1942	31 Dec 1942	31 Dec 1943	1 Aug 1945

Key:
- ⚓ Naval base
- 🛢 Oil
- ✸ Major battles
- ■ Retaken 1942–43
- ■ Retaken 1944
- ■ Retaken 1945
- → Allied offensives
- → Soviet offensives
- ‑‑➤ Planned offensives
- ||| Allies of Japan
- \\ Governed by Japan
- Occupied by Japan

Japanese sea routes in 1941

Japanese sea routes in 1944

'Leapfrogged' Japanese garrisons

the amphibious fleet, with a limited impact. In all, only 58 Allied merchant ships were lost between December 1941 and 1945.

In the final two years of the war, Japan's defensive perimeter was constantly under attack and its war economy was slowly crippled by an intensive submarine campaign. Unable to offer any resistance at sea, seeing its fleet destroyed in 1944 (the Battle of the Philippine Sea followed by the Battle of Leyte Gulf) and its island positions falling one by one to American amphibious offensives, the Japanese command tried to retake the initiative in China, where the Imperial Army had its last significant successes

(Ichigo offensive), and in India, where an attempted invasion (Operation U-Go) failed when faced with the British defences at Imphal and Kohima. At the end of 1944, the only strategic option left to Japan was to fight a desperate defensive battle resulting in maximum losses, particularly amongst kamikaze pilots, who were volunteers to varying degrees. The battles of Iwo Jima, Manila, Okinawa and Rangoon (Burma) in 1945 were the last major stages in the reconquest by the Allies, who began preparations at the start of the summer to fight the final battle in Japan itself.

2 • THE JAPANESE FLEET'S LAST STAND

After failures at Midway and the Solomon Islands (1942–43) and in the Philippine Sea (June 1944), the Kidō Butai made its last stand in the biggest naval battle in the war in Leyte Gulf in October 1944. The audacious Sho-Go (Victory) Plan was a trap for the US fleet protecting an American landing attempt in the Philippines (**0**). The aim was to lure the aircraft carriers of the Third Fleet far away with a decoy (Admiral Ozawa's aircraft carriers) so that Japanese battleships could edge between the islands, taking the US

landing troops by surprise. Unaware of any danger (**1**), Halsey rose to the bait, chasing and destroying the Japanese northern fleet (**3**). In the south, US battleships intervened victoriously in the Surigao Strait (**2**). But at Cape Samar on 25 October, Japanese battleships came close to striking a fatal blow (**4**) before being forced to withdraw with heavy losses, after the sacrifice of US escort carriers. After three days (24–26 October), the Japanese fleet had played its last card and no longer existed as a fighting force.

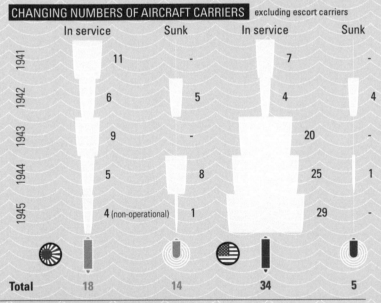

CHANGING NUMBERS OF AIRCRAFT CARRIERS — excluding escort carriers

	In service	Sunk	In service	Sunk
1941	11	-	7	-
1942	6	5	4	4
1943	9	-	20	-
1944	5	8	25	1
1945	4 (non-operational)	1	29	-
Total	18	14	34	5

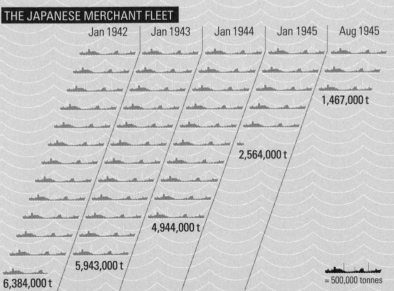

THE JAPANESE MERCHANT FLEET

Jan 1942	Jan 1943	Jan 1944	Jan 1945	Aug 1945
				1,467,000 t
			2,564,000 t	
		4,944,000 t		
	5,943,000 t			
6,384,000 t				

= 500,000 tonnes

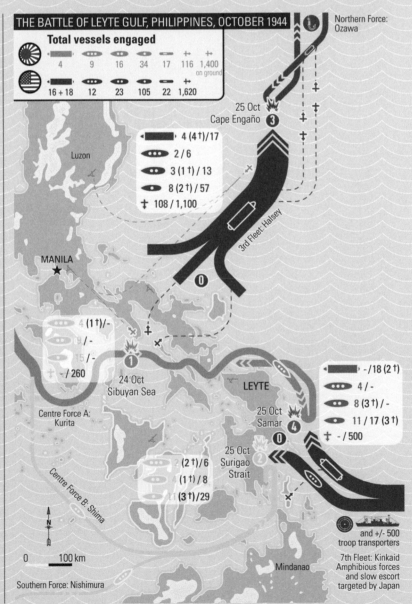

THE BATTLE OF LEYTE GULF, PHILIPPINES, OCTOBER 1944

Total vessels engaged

Japan	4	9	16	34	17	116	1,400 on ground
USA	16 + 18	12	23	105	22	1,620

Northern Force: Ozawa

25 Oct Cape Engaño — **3**

- 4 (4†)/17
- 2/6
- 3 (1†)/13
- 8 (2†)/57
- † 108 / 1,100

Luzon

3rd Fleet: Halsey

MANILA ★

0

- 4 (1†)/-
- 9/-
- 15/-
- † -/260

24 Oct Sibuyan Sea — **1**

Centre Force A: Kurita

LEYTE

- -/18 (2†)
- 4/-
- 8 (3†)/-
- 11/17 (3†)
- † -/500

25 Oct Samar — **4** — **0**

25 Oct Surigao Strait — **2**

Centre Force B: Shima

- 2 (2†)/6
- (1†)/8
- (3†)/29

0   100 km

N

Mindanao

Southern Force: Nishimura

and +/- 500 troop transporters

7th Fleet: Kinkaid Amphibious forces and slow escort targeted by Japan

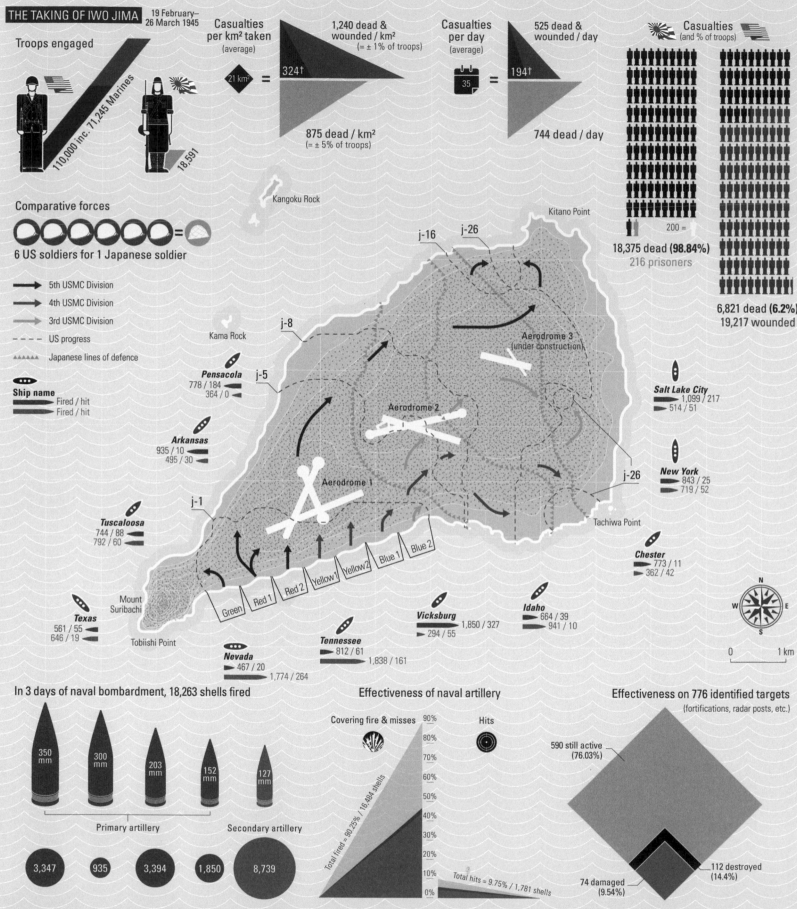

THE TAKING OF IWO JIMA
19 February–26 March 1945

Troops engaged

110,000 inc. 71,245 Marines

18,591

Comparative forces

6 US soldiers for 1 Japanese soldier

- 5th USMC Division
- 4th USMC Division
- 3rd USMC Division
- US progress
- Japanese lines of defence

Ship name
- Fired / hit
- Fired / hit

Casualties per km² taken (average)

21 km^2 = 324†

1,240 dead & wounded / km² (= ± 1% of troops)

875 dead / km² (= ± 5% of troops)

Casualties per day (average)

35 = 194†

525 dead & wounded / day

744 dead / day

Casualties (and % of troops)

200 =

18,375 dead (98.84%)
216 prisoners

6,821 dead (6.2%)
19,217 wounded

Map labels

Kangoku Rock

Kama Rock

Kitano Point

j-16 j-26

j-8

j-5

Aerodrome 3 (under construction)

Aerodrome 2

Pensacola
778 / 184
364 / 0

Arkansas
935 / 10
495 / 30

Salt Lake City
1,099 / 217
514 / 51

New York
843 / 25
719 / 52

j-26

Tuscaloosa
744 / 88
792 / 60

j-1

Aerodrome 1

Green | Red 1 | Red 2 | Yellow 1 | Yellow 2 | Blue 1 | Blue 2

Tachiwa Point

Chester
773 / 11
362 / 42

Mount Suribachi

Texas
561 / 55
646 / 19

Tobiishi Point

Nevada
467 / 20
1,774 / 264

Tennessee
812 / 61
1,838 / 161

Vicksburg
1,850 / 327
294 / 55

Idaho
664 / 39
941 / 10

N / S / E / W compass

0 1 km

In 3 days of naval bombardment, 18,263 shells fired

350 mm | 300 mm | 203 mm | 152 mm | 127 mm

Primary artillery | Secondary artillery

3,347 | 935 | 3,394 | 1,850 | 8,739

Effectiveness of naval artillery

Covering fire & misses

Hits

90% 80% 70% 60% 50% 40% 30% 20% 10% 0%

Total fired = 90.25% / 16,482 shells

Total hits ≈ 9.75% / 1,781 shells

Effectiveness on 776 identified targets
(fortifications, radar posts, etc.)

590 still active (76.03%)

112 destroyed (14.4%)

74 damaged (9.54%)

Iwo Jima was one of the toughest and bloodiest battles of the war in the Pacific, the only one in which total American losses exceeded those of the Japanese. The US Marine Corps was tasked with the landing. The capture of the island was planned to take five days, after several weeks of airborne preparation and three days of systematic naval bombardment intended to destroy the Japanese defences. In the end, however, it took more than a month of fierce fighting to overcome the Japanese garrison, who were protected by extremely durable underground fortifications, left largely intact by the mostly ineffective preliminary bombing.

SOURCES: 1. Nicolas Bernard, *La Guerre du Pacifique*, Paris, 2016 • 2. John Costello, *The Pacific War*, New York, 1981 • 3. S. E. Morison, *History of US Naval Operations in World War II*, New York, 2001 (reprint) • 4. *The Japanese Monographs*, US Army, 1959 • 5. William P. Gruner, *US Pacific Submarines In World War II*, HNSA, 2010 • 6. http://www.allworldwars.com/Iwo-Jima-Naval-Gunfire-Support.html

THE *YAMATO*: THE WAR CAREER OF AN IMPOTENT GIANT

The career of the heavy battleship *Yamato*, the former flagship mockingly nicknamed 'Hotel *Yamato*' by sailors, began on 8 August 1940 (0,1) and until 1943 was confined to liaison and escort duties between Truk and the mainland (2, 4), and a few unsuccessful war sorties (3, 5). It shot few shells until 1944 (6) and was sunk by US Navy aircraft in April 1945 (7).

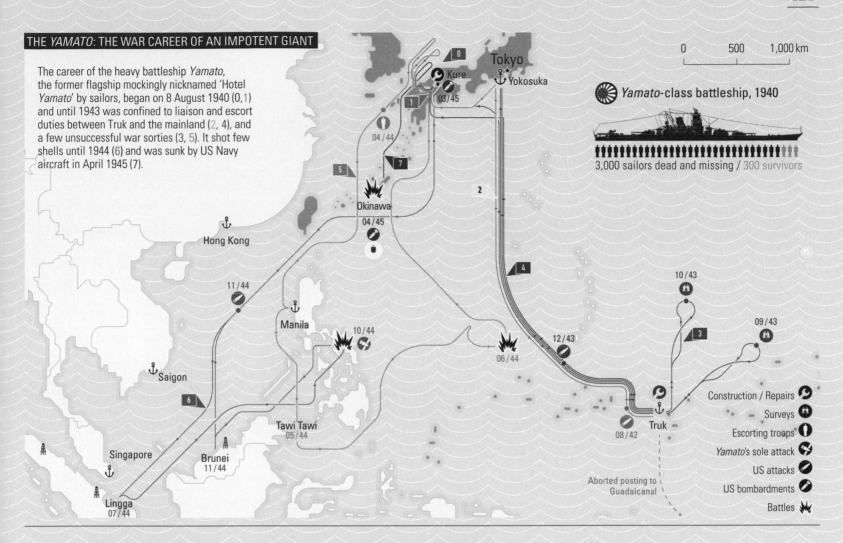

Yamato-class battleship, 1940

3,000 sailors dead and missing / 300 survivors

Construction / Repairs
Surveys
Escorting troops
Yamato's sole attack
US attacks
US bombardments
Battles

Aborted posting to Guadalcanal

3 • THE PACIFIC: THE DEADLIEST THEATRE OF OPERATIONS FOR THE AMERICANS

Although fewer troops were deployed than in Europe, and across geographically broader and more fragmented theatres of operations, most of the fighting in the Pacific was extremely intensive and bloody, in limited areas and for limited periods. Firstly, Japanese losses were usually excessive, since retreat or surrender were forbidden in Japan's military culture. Until the battle of Okinawa, in which for the first time several Japanese soldiers laid down their weapons, very few Japanese prisoners were taken and these were often casualties unable to defend themselves or demotivated Korean auxiliaries. What is more, US losses were proportionally higher than elsewhere. Over a similar period and at a similar strength, an average of three times more Americans fell in battle in the Pacific than in Africa or Europe.

AVERAGE COMBAT LOSSES OF US GROUND FORCES 1942–45

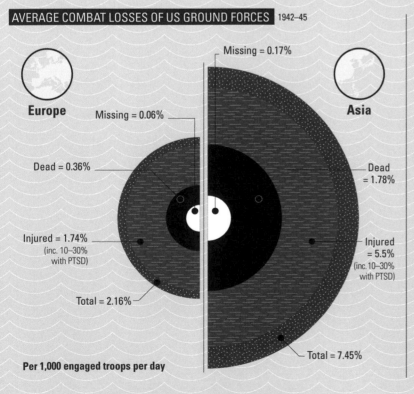

Missing = 0.17%

Europe

Missing = 0.06%

Dead = 0.36%

Injured = 1.74%
(inc. 10–30% with PTSD)

Total = 2.16%

Asia

Dead = 1.78%

Injured = 5.5%
(inc. 10–30% with PTSD)

Total = 7.45%

Per 1,000 engaged troops per day

THE COST OF OKINAWA Apr–June 1945

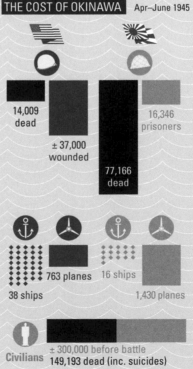

14,009 dead

± 37,000 wounded

16,346 prisoners

77,166 dead

38 ships — 763 planes — 16 ships — 1,430 planes

Civilians — ± 300,000 before battle
149,193 dead (inc. suicides)

'GLORIOUS DEATHS'

Survival rates of Japanese soldiers in battle

= 10%

1942 Guadalcanal = 2.8%

1943 Tarawa = 0.6%

1944 Saipan = 3%

1944 Guam = 1.7%

1945 Iwo Jima = 1.2%

Okinawa = 12%

KURSK: THE TIDE TURNS

In the spring of 1943, Hitler decided that the Eastern Front was still the main front and that the Wehrmacht should launch a further attack to prevent an anticipated Soviet offensive, retain the operational initiative and build up reserves by shortening the front. After a month of procrastination, Hitler finally agreed reluctantly to the Kursk salient as the location for a limited offensive, to be launched on 1 May. The basic plan was to cut off the salient. The Army Group Centre's 9th Army, under the command of General Model, would attack towards Kursk from the north. The 4th Panzer Army and the Kempf army detachment from Field Marshal von Manstein's Army Group South would also move towards Kursk but from the south. Once Kursk was taken, the Germans planned to capture most of the Central Front forces of General Rokossovsky and the Voronezh Front forces of General Vatutin, hoping to take thousands of prisoners, who would be put to work for German industries. The date of the attack was postponed several times and eventually set for 5 July. Hitler was awaiting delivery of new armoured equipment (Ferdinand self-propelled heavy guns and Panzer tanks), but the main reason for the postponement was the capitulation of the Axis forces in Tunis on 13 May 1943. Hitler no longer wanted to engage in the east until a reserve army had been built up in Germany to make up for the defection of his Italian ally, which he rightly considered inevitable. It was not until the end of June that he was confident on that score.

The Soviets also decided to await the German attack and use the two months' respite to strengthen their defences in the Kursk salient, which they turned into a virtual fortress. They prepared three linked counter-offensives, towards Orel and Kharkov and in the Donbass basin, which would be triggered once the enemy was drained outside Kursk. Aware of the USSR's preparations, the Germans needed to reach Kursk as quickly as possible. They therefore concentrated the cream of the armoured units and the Luftwaffe on two very narrow fronts. Their failure after a week meant that the Wehrmacht permanently lost the initiative on the Eastern Front. After that, it merely retreated until its final defeat. Although it lost far fewer men and less materiel than the enemy, it nevertheless had to relinquish an even more important asset: its dominant position. For the first time, the German army was unable to win a summer battle, despite deploying 20 armoured divisions and the latest technology.

1 • ONE GERMAN OPERATION, THREE SOVIET COUNTER-ATTACKS

The Kursk Strategic Offensive refers to four overlapping operations spread over 250 km and a period of 50 days. **(1)** The German pincer attack, Operation Citadel, a north-to-south attack from Orel (9th Army) and a second from south to north (Army Group South) from Kharkov. The first succeeded in penetrating 30 km into the Soviet defences before becoming exhausted by 11 July. The second advanced over 50 km before being suspended on 16 July. The double failure was due to the triggering of two Soviet counter-offensives. **(2)** The first of these, Operation Kutuzov, struck towards Orel on 12 July, forcing Model to turn around. **(3)** The second, Operation Donbass, began on 17 July on the Mius and Donets and forced Hitler to halt Manstein's tanks since he wanted to preserve the 'Soviet Ruhr' at all costs. Although the Donbass offensive was a Soviet failure, it led to **(4)** the third Red Army counter-offensive, Operation Rumyantsev, on 3 August. The liberation of Kharkov on 23 August ended the conflict inaccurately named the 'Battle of Kursk'.

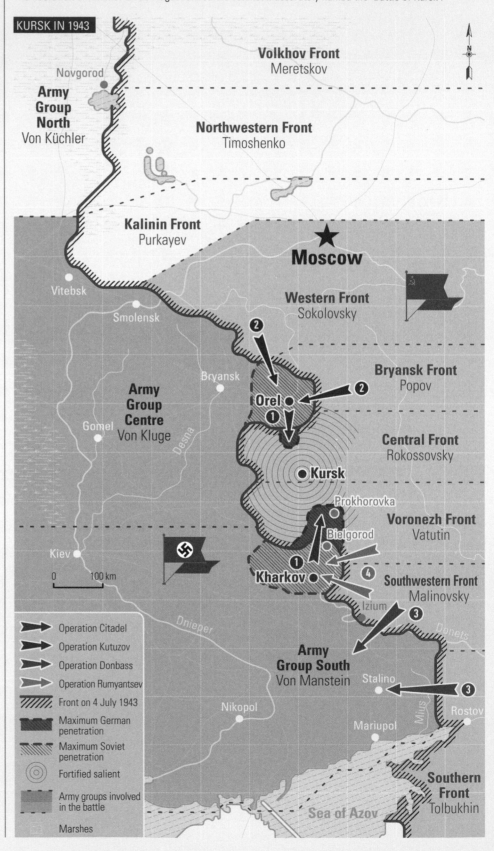

KURSK IN 1943

Volkhov Front
Meretskov

Novgorod

Army Group North
Von Küchler

Northwestern Front
Timoshenko

Kalinin Front
Purkayev

★ **Moscow**

Vitebsk

Western Front
Sokolovsky

Smolensk

Bryansk Front
Popov

Bryansk

Army Group Centre
Von Kluge

Orel

Gomel

Central Front
Rokossovsky

Desna

● Kursk

Prokhorovka

Voronezh Front
Vatutin

Bielgorod

Kiev

Kharkov

Southwestern Front
Malinovsky

Izium

Dnieper

Army Group South
Von Manstein

Stalino

Donets

Nikopol

Mius

Rostov

Mariupol

Southern Front
Tolbukhin

Sea of Azov

0   100 km

➤ Operation Citadel
➤ Operation Kutuzov
➤ Operation Donbass
➤ Operation Rumyantsev
░ Front on 4 July 1943
▬ Maximum German penetration
▨ Maximum Soviet penetration
◉ Fortified salient
Army groups involved in the battle
Marshes

2 • GERMAN TANK SUPERIORITY

It is clear from an overview of the Kursk offensive that the Soviets were numerically superior. But in the case of armoured vehicles, this has to be strictly qualified. The quality of the German equipment was vastly superior. The T-34/76, not to mention the light T-70, were far outclassed by the Ferdinand, Tiger, Panther and even the Panzer IV with its long gun. Head-on, the Tiger was invulnerable at any distance to any Soviet tank, anti-tank gun or self-propelled gun used at Kursk. The only exceptions were the SU-122 self-propelled howitzer and the 57 mm anti-tank gun, both of which were rare in 1943. Nevertheless, it was as much due to the Soviet command's tactical shortcomings as to their technological inferiority that the Soviets lost six times as many armoured vehicles as the Germans.

TANK AGAINST TANK: WHO WINS?

weather · sunny
Engagement distance 1,500 m
terrain · clear and flat

Pz VI Tiger **147**
Pz V Panther **198**
Pz IV Ausf G & H **685**
Pz IV Ausf F **50**
Pz II & Pz III **859**
Sturmgeschütz IV **436**
Sturmpanzer IV Brummbär **55**
Pz 38 (t) Grille **42**
Panzerjäger Ferdinand **98**
Panzerjager Hornisse ± **100**
Marder II **350**
Wespe + Hummel **260**

3,800 T-34/76
22 KV-1
178 Allied tanks
1,340 T-60 / T-70
37 SU-152
128 SU-122
96 SU-76

■ Tanks
■ Reconnaissance tanks
■ Assault guns
■ Tank destroyers
■ Self-propelled guns
→ Pierces front armour
● Number of units deployed

3 • DEEP DEFENCE: A COMPLEX SYSTEM

The Soviet defensive preparations in the Kursk salient were the most extensive made in the Second World War. The city of Kursk and the area behind it were protected over a depth of 110 kilometres by three defensive belts and three defensive front lines. These contained 9,000 kilometres of trenches, barbed wire, one million mines and explosive charges, 1,000 kilometres of anti-tank ditches and several hundred anti-tank support points.

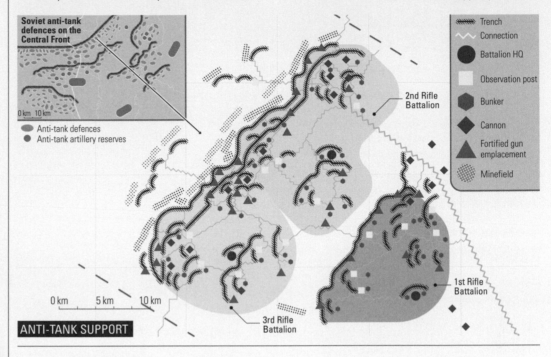

Soviet anti-tank defences on the Central Front
0 km 10 km
⬭ Anti-tank defences
● Anti-tank artillery reserves

~ Trench
⌇ Connection
● Battalion HQ
□ Observation post
⬡ Bunker
◆ Cannon
▲ Fortified gun emplacement
▦ Minefield

2nd Rifle Battalion
1st Rifle Battalion
3rd Rifle Battalion
0 km 5 km 10 km

ANTI-TANK SUPPORT

4 • BALANCE OF FORCES AND LOSSES
Balance of forces on 4 July 1943, losses on 4 August 1943

The Soviets won a Pyrrhic victory at Kursk, suffering massive losses of men and materiel. The carnage was caused not so much by their poor-quality equipment as by inadequate command of the armoured and airborne units. In the field, the Germans were still superior to their enemies in inter-unit cooperation, radio communications, concentration of resources and the general standard of training. The Soviet high command continued to sacrifice masses of men in frontal attacks instead of manoeuvring. That was probably partly for cultural reasons and also because the Red Army, unlike the Wehrmacht, was able to replace its lost troops fairly easily.

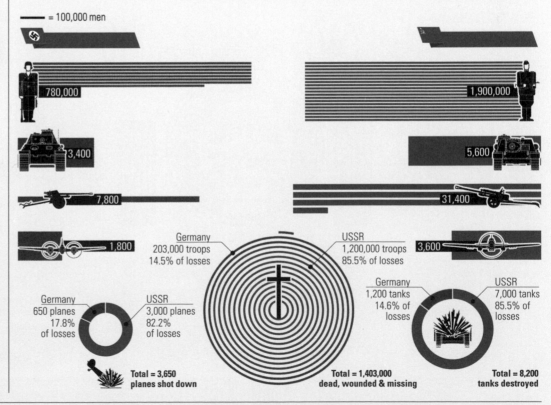

━ = 100,000 men

780,000 — 1,900,000
3,400 — 5,600
7,800 — 31,400
1,800 — 3,600

Germany 203,000 troops 14.5% of losses
USSR 1,200,000 troops 85.5% of losses
Germany 650 planes 17.8% of losses
USSR 3,000 planes 82.2% of losses
Germany 1,200 tanks 14.6% of losses
USSR 7,000 tanks 85.5% of losses

Total = 3,650 planes shot down
Total = 1,403,000 dead, wounded & missing
Total = 8,200 tanks destroyed

SOURCES: 1. Jean Lopez, *Koursk*, Paris, 2011 • 2. Roman Töppel, *Kursk 1943: The Greatest Battle of the Second World War*, Solihull, 2018 • 3. A. Frankson & N. Zetterling, *Kursk 1943: A Statistical Analysis*, London, 2000.

AIRBORNE CAMPAIGNS AGAINST THE REICH

What is strategic bombing? According to historian Serge Gadal, it means attacking the enemy's centres of power in order to destroy its military potential or demoralize its population. The principles of strategic bombing, established in the First World War, were developed in the inter-war period by the Italian Giulio Douhet, and by others such as US General Billy Mitchell. They believed that air power was key and capable of achieving victory on its own through a campaign

1 • BRITISH BOMBING RAIDS AND COMBINED ALLIED OPERATIONS

The British already had a small long-range bomber force in 1939. Along with military objectives, London was soon planning attacks on specifically civilian targets, notably working-class neighbourhoods in large German towns, especially in the Ruhr, for psychological and propaganda reasons. After the Area Bombing Directive of February 1942 and with the mass introduction of large four-engined planes, the costly day-time attacks of 1939–41 were succeeded by night raids with incendiary bombs. The raids were inaccurate and not very effective and the losses high. However, America's entry into the war made it possible to organize a coordinated offensive of systematic strategic bombing raids on Germany and occupied Europe by 1943, known as Combined Bombing

Operations (CBO). Divided into several phases and with day and night shared between the British and the Americans, the operations were intended to destroy the Reich's production capabilities (154 defined targets) and undermine the morale of the population, as well as preparing for (and supporting) an Allied landing in Europe. The raids started properly in the autumn with a huge offensive to destroy the Luftwaffe's fighter strength (Operation Pointblank). The 'thousand-bomber' raids, unusual in 1942, became regular occurrences in 1944. Of the 968 American bombing missions in Europe, 68 involved more than 1,000 bombers and hundreds of escort fighters, sometimes distributed between several targets.

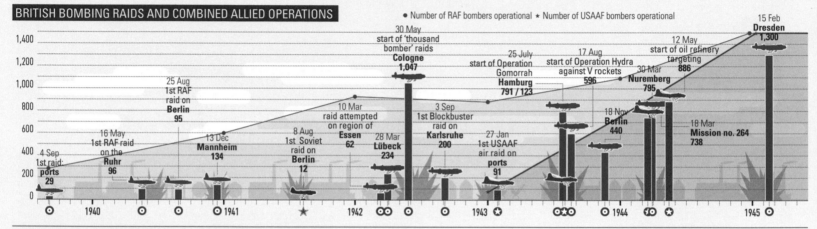

BRITISH BOMBING RAIDS AND COMBINED ALLIED OPERATIONS

● Number of RAF bombers operational ✴ Number of USAAF bombers operational

DIVISION OF WORK BETWEEN THE RAF AND USAAF IN EUROPE

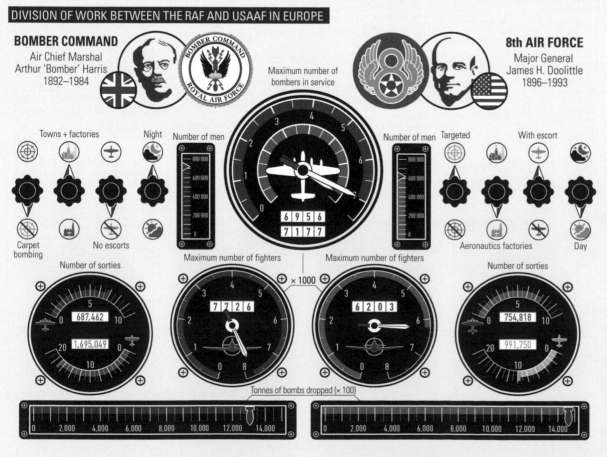

BOMBER COMMAND
Air Chief Marshal
Arthur 'Bomber' Harris
1892–1984

8th AIR FORCE
Major General
James H. Doolittle
1896–1993

BOMB TYPES USED

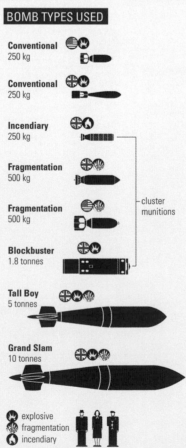

Conventional 250 kg

Conventional 250 kg

Incendiary 250 kg

Fragmentation 500 kg

Fragmentation 500 kg

– cluster munitions

Blockbuster 1.8 tonnes

Tall Boy 5 tonnes

Grand Slam 10 tonnes

explosive
fragmentation
incendiary

of strategic strikes on targets that were both economic (industrial centres) and psychological (civilian populations).

In 1939, it was almost universally considered morally wrong to bomb towns, particularly after the bombing of Guernica in 1937. But the initial determination not to do so, notably expressed in a famous appeal by Roosevelt to the warring parties in September 1939, did not outlast the early phases of the war. One by one, the last 'moral' qualms were broken down, especially after the Luftwaffe bombed Warsaw, Rotterdam, London and Belgrade. Although not all of Douhet's ideas were necessarily adopted, the fact is that the waging of a strategic war in the air became a priority for Britain from 1940 and the Americans from 1942, as the only real way to fight the Reich until the conditions could be created for a landing in Europe.

2 • THE GERMAN RESPONSE

From 1940, the Luftwaffe developed various systems for defending the skies of the Reich by day and night and countering the threat of Allied bombers. These included the Kammhuber Line, a radar defence network on the North Sea coasts, tactical changes (*Wilde Sau*, the use of day fighters to counter raids by night bombers over towns), development of heavy night fighters (twin-engined Bf 110, Ju-88, Do-217, etc.) and later in the war, interceptor jets (Me 163 Komet). Although severely tested by Operation Pointblank, the Luftflotte Reich, which defended Germany's air space, continued its coordinated fightback, relying on a powerful network of 55,000 anti-aircraft guns. However, Germany had to draw on considerable resources to provide these defences, including hundreds of pilots, thousands of aircraft and heavy Flak guns and hundreds of thousands of workers dedicated exclusively to rebuilding. Even so, these resources were not sufficient, given the growing superiority of the Allied air forces. Although it fought courageously until the end, the Luftwaffe was outclassed from 1943 onwards.

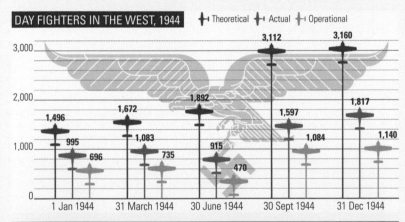

DAY FIGHTERS IN THE WEST, 1944 — Theoretical — Actual — Operational

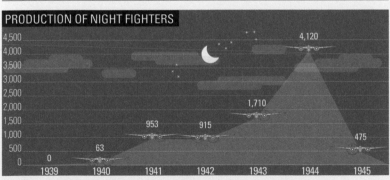

PRODUCTION OF NIGHT FIGHTERS

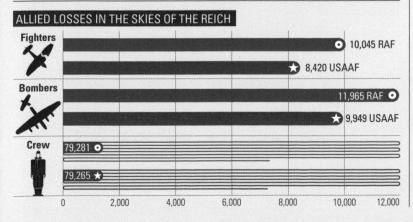

ALLIED LOSSES IN THE SKIES OF THE REICH

3 • CASUALTIES AND DAMAGE

Of the nearly 3 million tonnes of Allied bombs dropped on Europe, around half fell on German territory (the rest were on occupied Europe or allies of the Axis). There were 350 raids on Berlin alone, in which tens of thousands were killed. Although it fell below Allied forecasts, the final casualty toll in Germany was very high, at around 600,000 dead with widespread destruction in cities. This was particularly true in the case of firestorms like those in Hamburg, Dresden and Pforzheim. Was the strategic bombing campaign a success? That is debatable, but if the resources deployed, the casualties and the damage rate are compared with the results, it is generally reckoned to have been a failure. Its two major strategic aims, destroying the Germans' will to resist and their production capabilities, were not achieved. The role of Allied aircraft continued to be primarily tactical, enabling the landing and offensive in Europe.

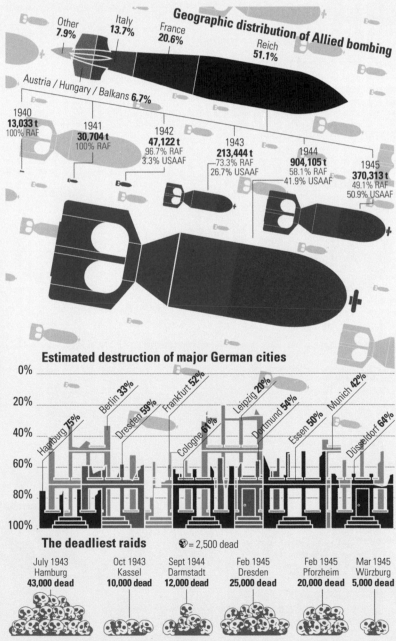

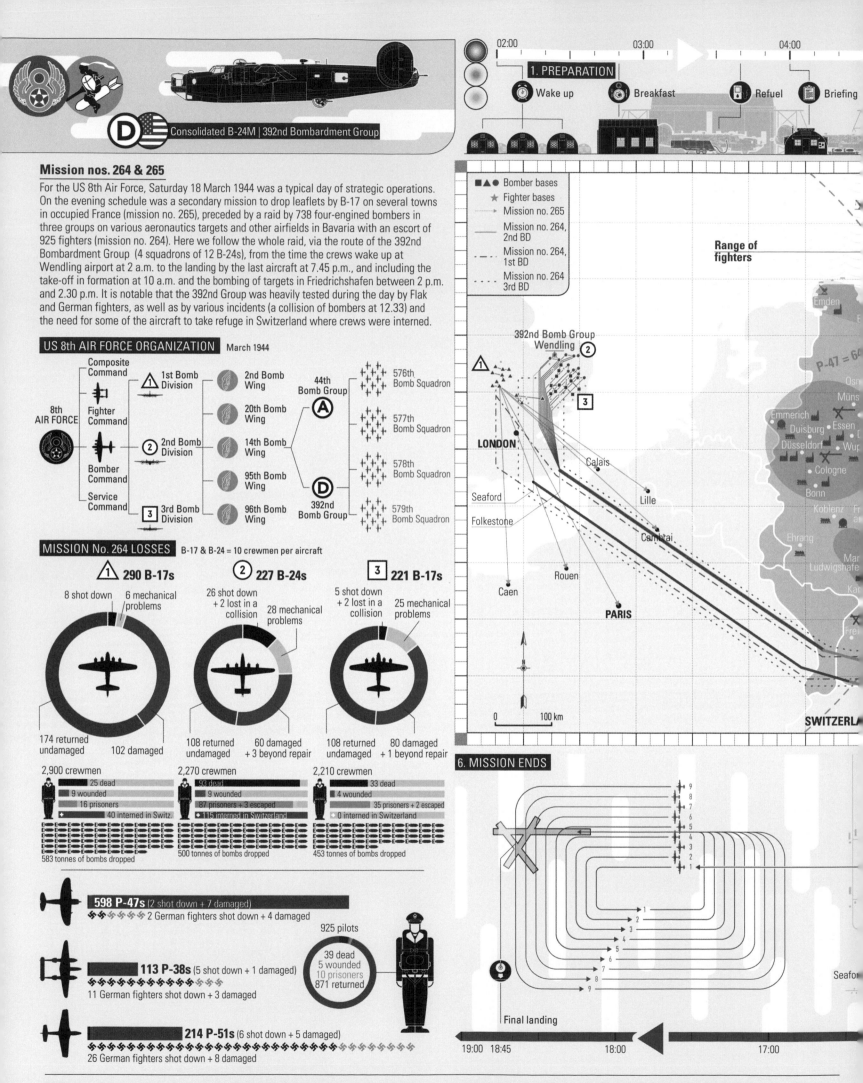

D · Consolidated B-24M | 392nd Bombardment Group

Mission nos. 264 & 265

For the US 8th Air Force, Saturday 18 March 1944 was a typical day of strategic operations. On the evening schedule was a secondary mission to drop leaflets by B-17 on several towns in occupied France (mission no. 265), preceded by a raid by 738 four-engined bombers in three groups on various aeronautics targets and other airfields in Bavaria with an escort of 925 fighters (mission no. 264). Here we follow the whole raid, via the route of the 392nd Bombardment Group (4 squadrons of 12 B-24s), from the time the crews wake up at Wendling airport at 2 a.m. to the landing by the last aircraft at 7.45 p.m., and including the take-off in formation at 10 a.m. and the bombing of targets in Friedrichshafen between 2 p.m. and 2.30 p.m. It is notable that the 392nd Group was heavily tested during the day by Flak and German fighters, as well as by various incidents (a collision of bombers at 12.33) and the need for some of the aircraft to take refuge in Switzerland where crews were interned.

US 8th AIR FORCE ORGANIZATION   March 1944

8th AIR FORCE
- Composite Command
- Fighter Command
- Bomber Command
- Service Command

1st Bomb Division
2nd Bomb Division
3rd Bomb Division

- 2nd Bomb Wing
- 20th Bomb Wing
- 14th Bomb Wing
- 95th Bomb Wing
- 96th Bomb Wing

A · 44th Bomb Group
D · 392nd Bomb Group

- 576th Bomb Squadron
- 577th Bomb Squadron
- 578th Bomb Squadron
- 579th Bomb Squadron

MISSION No. 264 LOSSES   B-17 & B-24 = 10 crewmen per aircraft

1 · 290 B-17s
- 8 shot down
- 6 mechanical problems
- 174 returned undamaged
- 102 damaged

2,900 crewmen
- 25 dead
- 9 wounded
- 16 prisoners
- 40 interned in Switz.
583 tonnes of bombs dropped

2 · 227 B-24s
- 26 shot down + 2 lost in a collision
- 28 mechanical problems
- 108 returned undamaged
- 60 damaged + 3 beyond repair

2,270 crewmen
- 93 dead
- 9 wounded
- 87 prisoners + 3 escaped
- 115 interned in Switzerland
500 tonnes of bombs dropped

3 · 221 B-17s
- 5 shot down + 2 lost in a collision
- 25 mechanical problems
- 108 returned undamaged
- 80 damaged + 1 beyond repair

2,210 crewmen
- 33 dead
- 4 wounded
- 35 prisoners + 2 escaped
- 0 interned in Switzerland
453 tonnes of bombs dropped

598 P-47s (2 shot down + 7 damaged)
2 German fighters shot down + 4 damaged

113 P-38s (5 shot down + 1 damaged)
11 German fighters shot down + 3 damaged

214 P-51s (6 shot down + 5 damaged)
26 German fighters shot down + 8 damaged

925 pilots
- 39 dead
- 5 wounded
- 10 prisoners
- 871 returned

1. PREPARATION
02:00 — Wake up
Breakfast
03:00
Refuel — 04:00
Briefing

Bomber bases ■ ▲ ●
Fighter bases ★
Mission no. 265
Mission no. 264, 2nd BD
Mission no. 264, 1st BD
Mission no. 264, 3rd BD

Range of fighters

392nd Bomb Group Wendling

Emden
P-47 = 64...
Osn...
Münster
Emmerich
Duisburg · Essen
Düsseldorf · Wup...
Cologne
Bonn
Koblenz
Ehrang
Ludwigshafe...
Frei...

LONDON
Seaford
Folkestone
Caen

Calais
Lille
Cambrai
Rouen
PARIS

0   100 km

SWITZERLA...

6. MISSION ENDS

Final landing

19:00 18:45   18:00   17:00

Seafor...

SOURCES: 1. D. Richards & H. Saunders, *Royal Air Force, 1939–1945*, 1954 • 2. M. Hastings, *Bomber Command*, London, 2012 • 3. W. Murray, *Strategy for Defeat*, Montgomery, AL, 1983 • 4. W. Craven & J. Cate (eds.), *The Army Air Forces in World War II*, Washington, DC, 1949 • 5. *Strategic Bombing Survey, Europe* • 6. D. Caldwell & R. Muller, *The Luftwaffe Over Germany*, London, 2007 • 7. F. Vajda & P. Dancey,

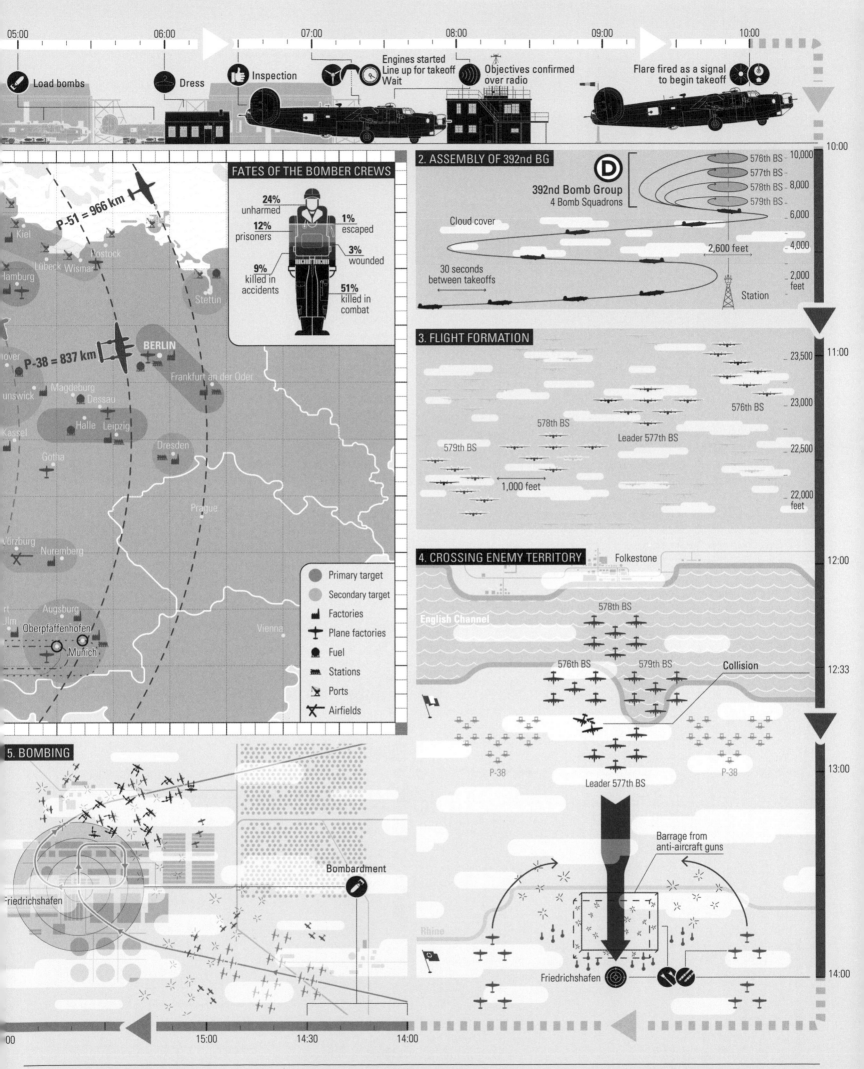

Timeline (top):

05:00 — 06:00 — 07:00 — 08:00 — 09:00 — 10:00

- Load bombs
- Dress
- Inspection
- Engines started / Line up for takeoff / Wait
- Objectives confirmed over radio
- Flare fired as a signal to begin takeoff

10:00

Map (left):

P-51 = 966 km
P-38 = 837 km

Kiel
Rostock
Lübeck · Wismar
Hamburg
Stettin
BERLIN
Frankfurt an der Oder
hover
Magdeburg
unswick · Dessau
Halle · Leipzig
Kassel
Dresden
Gotha
Prague
Würzburg
Nuremberg
Augsburg
Ulm · Oberpfaffenhofen
Munich
Vienna

FATES OF THE BOMBER CREWS

- 24% unharmed
- 1% escaped
- 12% prisoners
- 3% wounded
- 9% killed in accidents
- 51% killed in combat

Legend:
- Primary target
- Secondary target
- ⚒ Factories
- ✈ Plane factories
- ⛽ Fuel
- 🚂 Stations
- Ports
- Airfields

2. ASSEMBLY OF 392nd BG

D
392nd Bomb Group
4 Bomb Squadrons

- 576th BS
- 577th BS
- 578th BS
- 579th BS

10,000
8,000
6,000
4,000
2,000 feet

Cloud cover
2,600 feet
30 seconds between takeoffs
Station

10:00

3. FLIGHT FORMATION

23,500
23,000
22,500
22,000 feet

576th BS
578th BS
Leader 577th BS
579th BS
1,000 feet

11:00

4. CROSSING ENEMY TERRITORY

Folkestone
English Channel
578th BS
576th BS
579th BS
Collision
P-38
Leader 577th BS
P-38

12:00
12:33

5. BOMBING

Friedrichshafen
Bombardment

Rhine

Barrage from anti-aircraft guns
Friedrichshafen

13:00
14:00

Bottom timeline:
00 — 15:00 — 14:30 — 14:00

German Aircraft Industry and Production, 1933–1945, Shrewsbury, 1998 • 8. C. Webster & N. Frankland, *The Strategic Air Offensive against Germany*, London, 1961 • 9. *The Bombing of Germany 1940–1945*, Exeter, 2016 • 10. John W. Archer, 'Y avait-il une vie avant une mission de bombardement', *Aero Journal*, no. 39, 2014 • 11. http://www.8thafhs.org/combat1944a.htm • 12. http://www.americanairmuseum.com/

THE ITALIAN IMPASSE

In May 1943, Churchill persuaded the Americans to use Tunisia as a springboard. It was a good opportunity to eliminate Italy from the conflict and potentially, by the domino effect, other German allies. It was also the best way to support Stalin in the run-up to Operation Overlord, which had been postponed to the spring of 1944. In this way, the Allies would stockpile a wealth of experience. But the Americans were reluctant to engage. As a result, the campaign was run with no clear strategic objectives and was characterized by improvisation, compromise and frustration. It dragged on for 600 days and the few benefits would not make up for the heavy losses, equal to 40% of those suffered in key offensives in north-west Europe.

The first phase, in which Sicily was taken in two months, illustrated the difficulties of a landing by force (inadequate planning, inept execution, underestimating the enemy) and of persuading Montgomery and Patton to cooperate when they despised each other to the point of allowing large numbers of Axis troops to escape. However, it had the political merit of bringing about the overthrow of Mussolini, who was imprisoned by King Victor Emmanuel III. Marshal Badoglio opened negotiations. The Allies were planning to arrive at the gates of Rome on the day of the surrender, but, erring on the side of caution, they thought it safer to remain shielded by aircraft. They struck in the south. The Germans, having anticipated Italy's defection, fought back and blocked the Allies north of Naples. They captured hundreds of thousands of Italians, especially in the Balkans, encouraged them to continue fighting on the German side and slaughtered any who resisted.

The Allied attack became bogged down and drew the local population into the war, although the idea had been to allow Italy to withdraw. The country was torn apart. The official government joined the Allied camp, while Mussolini, having been released by the Germans, took over the leadership of the Italian Social Republic, a puppet government.

Churchill, however, believed in Italy's strategic importance. This was consistent with the British military culture of peripheral action, and Italy was the only theatre in which the British were still on an equal footing with the Americans in terms of manpower and authority. They had to meet with success there. The Allies came to a standstill in front of the Gustav Line. In January 1944, Alexander unsuccessfully attempted an encirclement by landing at Anzio. In the end, it was the North African mountain troops from Juin's French corps who broke through the line in the spring. Kesselring, caught off balance, conceded 400 kilometres and only recovered in Tuscany. Faced with the Gothic Line, the Allies had to start all over again.

Deprived of their best troops, who had departed for Provence, the British had to abandon their plans to land in the Balkans or at Trieste to open up the way to Central Europe. The campaign dragged on. The civil war also led to a series of atrocities, including the execution of Mussolini and his mistress, Clara Petacci.

SOURCES: 1. *The Mediterranean Theater of Operations*, US Army Center of Military History, 4 vols., 1957–77 • 2. Carlo D'Este, *World War II in the Mediterranean 1942–1945*, Chapel Hill, NC, 1990 • 3. Douglas Porch, *Hitler's Mediterranean Gamble: The North African and the Mediterranean Campaigns in World War II*, London, 2004 • 4. Carlo D'Este, *Fatal Decision: Anzio & the Battle for Rome*, London, 1991.

1 • THE FALL OF FASCISM

The Italian Fascist regime was incapable of mobilizing men, energy or the economy. Mussolini was indolent and failed to stand up to industry. As a result, production fell 11 points between 1938 and 1942. A series of disasters cost more than 700,000 men in three years, which would have been tolerable if it were not for the added half-million garrisoned in the Balkans and the 100,000 in France. Consequently, Italy had only 10 operational divisions and fewer than 200 tanks left to defend itself. The fact that so few survivors returned was also traumatic (4% from Russia and none from East Africa). 17% of soldiers deserted in Sicily. Strikes broke out. On 24 July, the Fascist Grand Council held a vote of no confidence in Mussolini. The next day, the king had him arrested.

THE ITALIAN ARMY: DISASTER ON THE EASTERN FRONT

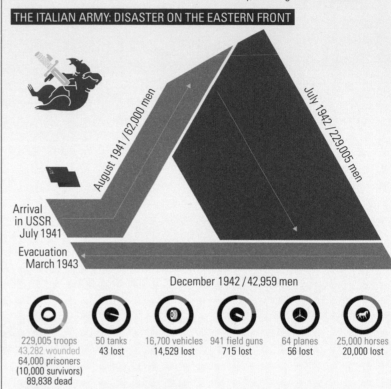

August 1941 / 62,000 men

July 1942 / 229,005 men

Arrival in USSR July 1941

Evacuation March 1943

December 1942 / 42,959 men

229,005 troops
43,282 wounded
64,000 prisoners
(10,000 survivors)
89,838 dead

50 tanks
43 lost

16,700 vehicles
14,529 lost

941 field guns
715 lost

64 planes
56 lost

25,000 horses
20,000 lost

FORCES AND CASUALTIES IN SICILY   from 10 July 1943 to 17 August 1943

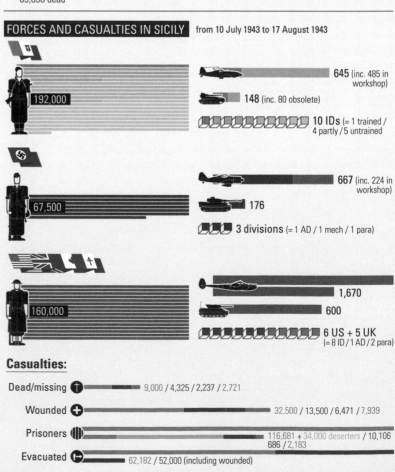

192,000

645 (inc. 485 in workshop)

148 (inc. 80 obsolete)

10 IDs (= 1 trained / 4 partly / 5 untrained)

67,500

667 (inc. 224 in workshop)

176

3 divisions (= 1 AD / 1 mech / 1 para)

160,000

1,670

600

6 US + 5 UK (= 8 ID / 1 AD / 2 para)

Casualties:

Dead/missing 9,000 / 4,325 / 2,237 / 2,721

Wounded 32,500 / 13,500 / 6,471 / 7,939

Prisoners 116,681 + 34,000 deserters / 10,106
686 / 2,183

Evacuated 62,182 / 52,000 (including wounded)

2 • THE ITALIAN CAMPAIGN

Italy's geography – mountainous terrain, rivers with steep banks, harsh winters – heavily favoured the defence forces. The front was so narrow that it was impossible to deploy large forces, fortunately for the Germans who were therefore equal in numbers of divisions. Nor did Hitler skimp on quality, striking a balance between solid infantry such as paratroopers and mechanized mobile groups. Kesselring fought intelligently. He abandoned the idea of pushing the Allies back to the sea, instead clinging more closely to the land. The slow advance was also due to the Allies. General Alexander was a poor coalition leader, a flaw for someone in command of dozens of nationalities including Brazilians, Indians, Poles and Italians. He also suffered from the withdrawal of officers (Bradley, Patton, Montgomery and his supporters), units (in July 1944, two Franco-American corps were pulled back for the landing in Provence) and materiel (by spring 1944, there were no longer enough barges to land behind the Germans).

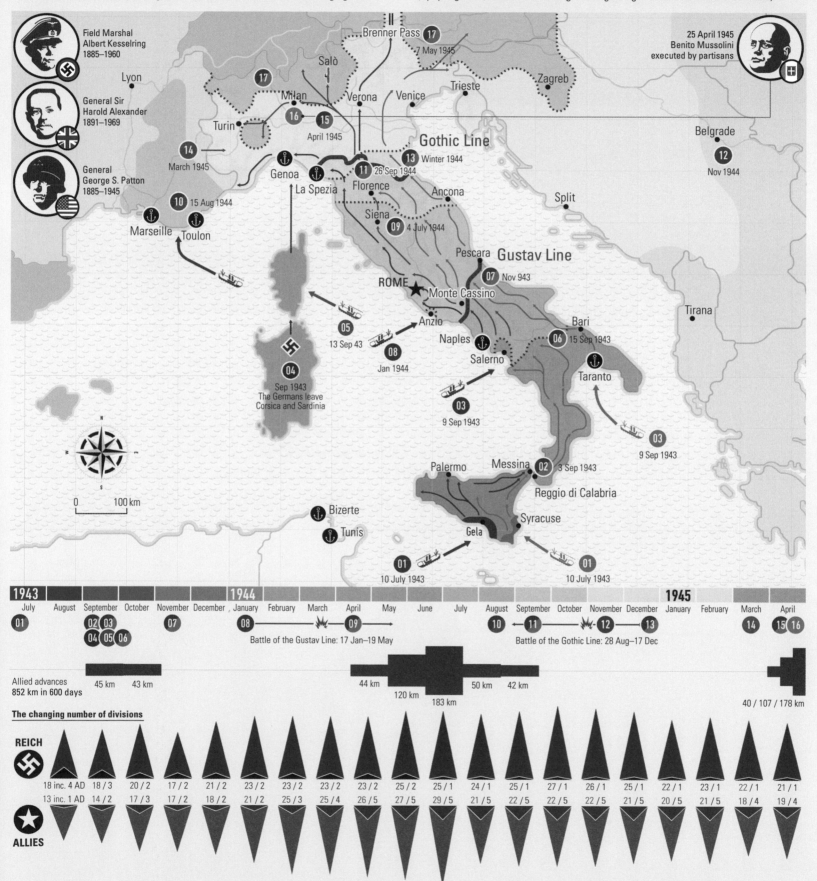

Field Marshal Albert Kesselring 1885–1960

General Sir Harold Alexander 1891–1969

General George S. Patton 1885–1945

25 April 1945 Benito Mussolini executed by partisans

Brenner Pass **17** 7 May 1945

Salò

Lyon

17 Milan Verona Venice Trieste Zagreb

16 **15** April 1945 Turin

Gothic Line

Belgrade **12** Nov 1944

14 March 1945 Genoa **11** 26 Sep 1944 **13** Winter 1944

La Spezia Florence Ancona

Split

10 15 Aug 1944 Siena **09** 4 July 1944

Marseille Toulon

Pescara Gustav Line

07 Nov 943 ROME Monte Cassino

05 13 Sep 43 Anzio Bari

04 Sep 1943 The Germans leave Corsica and Sardinia **08** Jan 1944 Naples **06** 15 Sep 1943

Salerno Taranto

03 9 Sep 1943 **03** 9 Sep 1943

Palermo Messina **02** 3 Sep 1943

Reggio di Calabria

Bizerte Syracuse

Tunis Gela

01 10 July 1943 **01** 10 July 1943

Tirana

0 100 km

1943						1944												1945			
July	August	September	October	November	December	January	February	March	April	May	June	July	August	September	October	November	December	January	February	March	April
01		02 03 04 05 06		07		08			09					10	11		12	13		14	15 16	

Battle of the Gustav Line: 17 Jan–19 May
Battle of the Gothic Line: 28 Aug–17 Dec

Allied advances 852 km in 600 days

45 km 43 km 44 km 120 km 183 km 50 km 42 km 40 / 107 / 178 km

The changing number of divisions

REICH

18 inc. 4 AD	18 / 3	20 / 2	17 / 2	21 / 2	23 / 2	23 / 2	23 / 2	23 / 2	25 / 2	25 / 1	24 / 1	25 / 1	27 / 1	26 / 1	25 / 1	22 / 1	23 / 1	22 / 1	21 / 1
13 inc. 1 AD	14 / 2	17 / 3	17 / 2	18 / 2	21 / 2	25 / 3	25 / 4	26 / 5	27 / 5	29 / 5	21 / 5	22 / 5	22 / 5	22 / 5	21 / 5	20 / 5	21 / 5	18 / 4	19 / 4

ALLIES

D-DAY AND THE BATTLE OF NORMANDY

The hopes invested in it, its huge scale and the impression it made on the collective imagination all made D-Day one of the great military operations. A cornerstone of the campaign to liberate Western Europe, 6 June 1944 was in fact the culmination of an offensive planned eighteen months earlier and continued for eighty-five days over a period known as 'Hell on the Seine'. Although the landing itself was a huge success, in the desperate advance of the following weeks it was feared that troops would be trapped for a long time at the bridgehead, a repeat of the Dardanelles campaign of 1915. While the Americans became stuck in the hedge-covered terrain, the British and Canadians came to a standstill outside Caen. Criticism was levelled at Montgomery, appointed temporary commander of the ground forces with the task of pushing the

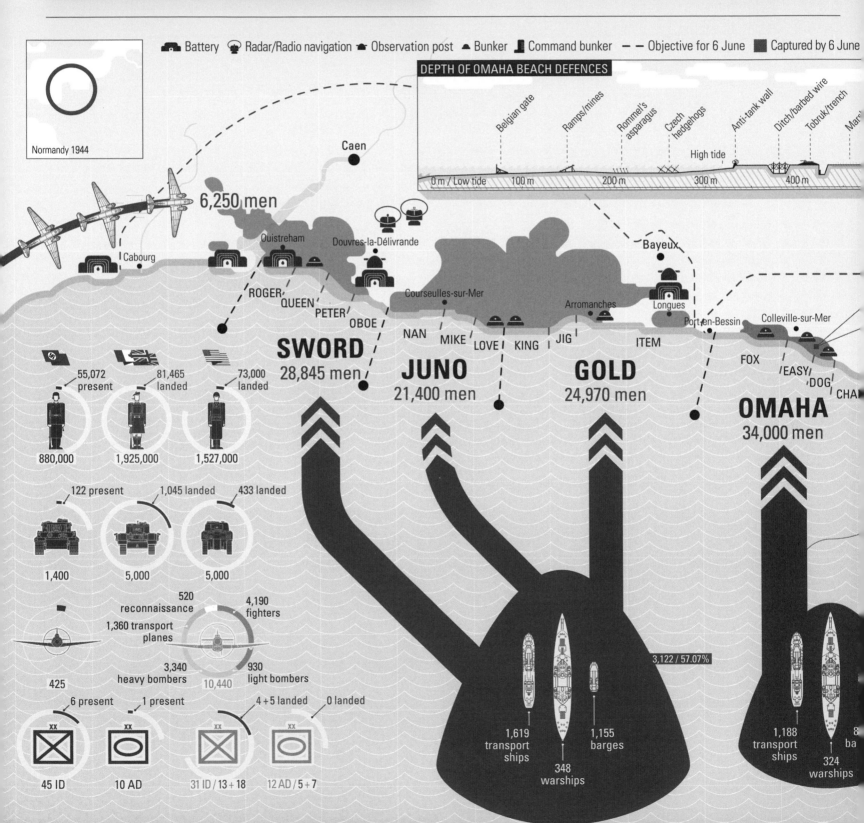

Battery · Radar/Radio navigation · Observation post · Bunker · Command bunker · – – Objective for 6 June · Captured by 6 June

Normandy 1944

DEPTH OF OMAHA BEACH DEFENCES

Belgian gate · Ramps/mines · Rommel's asparagus · Czech hedgehogs · Anti-tank wall · Ditch/barbed wire · Tobruk/trench · Mar[...]

High tide

0 m / Low tide · 100 m · 200 m · 300 m · 400 m

Caen

6,250 men

Cabourg
Ouistreham
Douvres-la-Délivrande
Bayeux
Courseulles-sur-Mer
Arromanches
Longues
Port-en-Bessin
Colleville-sur-Mer

ROGER
QUEEN
PETER
OBOE
NAN
MIKE
LOVE
KING
JIG
ITEM
FOX
EASY
DOG
CHA[...]

SWORD 28,845 men

JUNO 21,400 men

GOLD 24,970 men

OMAHA 34,000 men

55,072 present
880,000

81,465 landed
1,925,000

73,000 landed
1,527,000

122 present
1,400

1,045 landed
5,000

433 landed
5,000

520 reconnaissance
1,360 transport planes
3,340 heavy bombers
425

4,190 fighters
930 light bombers
10,440

6 present
1 present
4 + 5 landed
0 landed

45 ID
10 AD
31 ID / 13 + 18
12 AD / 5 + 7

3,122 / 57.07%

1,619 transport ships
348 warships
1,155 barges

1,188 transport ships
324 warships
8[...] ba[...]

Germans back beyond the Seine in three months (Operation Overlord). But crippled by the collapse of its logistics chain and weakened by the immobilization of an army in the Pas-de-Calais while waiting for another landing, with the Soviet offensive (Operation Bagration) draining available reserves away from France, the German army was becoming exhausted by this war of attrition.

The decisive moment came on 25 July to the south of Saint-Lô. A fierce American attack broke through the front and the Germans hesitated. They did not have enough fuel or ammunition. The success was also due to a unique combination: Montgomery's plan (attack on a narrow front, a large number of reserves) was carried out to perfection by responsive American forces. In a week, Patton entered Brittany.

Hitler ordered a counter-offensive at Mortain to cut off the American forces, but his predictable failure hastened the end. The Germans were trapped. It was only the tactical inconsistency of the Allied generals that allowed three-quarters of the German forces to escape at two points (Falaise and the Seine). Normandy was no Stalingrad, but the casualties were huge. The Germans abandoned most of their materiel and lost their best troops.

The battle ended in an Allied victory on an unexpectedly large scale, combining skilful planning, careful preparation and operational implementation that, although sometimes clumsy, was sound. When Montgomery handed over command to Eisenhower on 1 September, with the Seine crossed and the enemy broken, he had truly earned his promotion to field marshal.

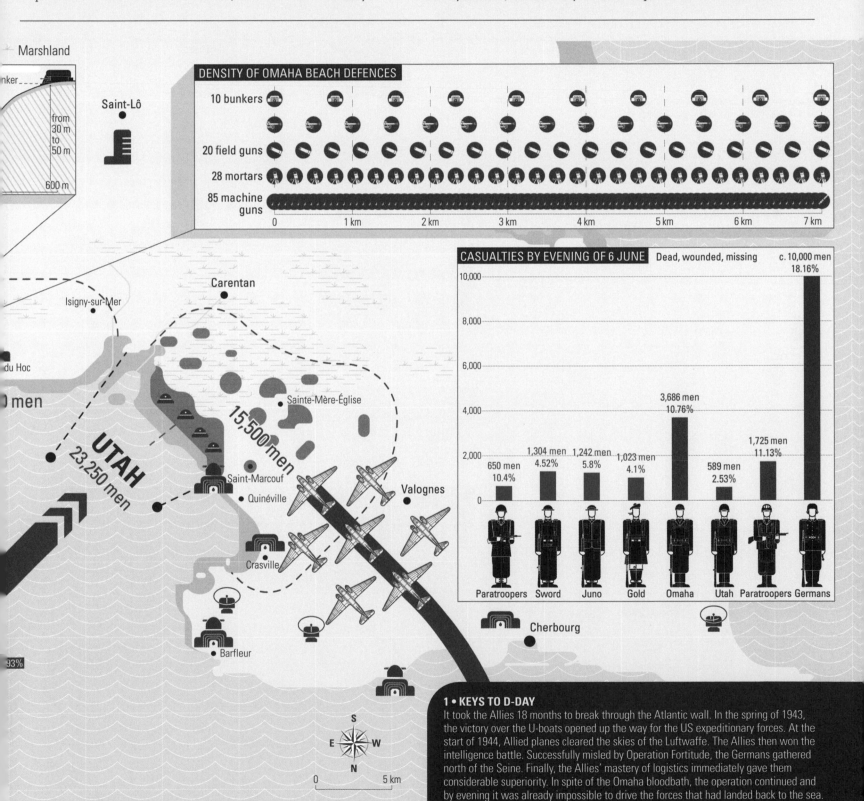

DENSITY OF OMAHA BEACH DEFENCES

- 10 bunkers
- 20 field guns
- 28 mortars
- 85 machine guns

0   1 km   2 km   3 km   4 km   5 km   6 km   7 km

CASUALTIES BY EVENING OF 6 JUNE

Dead, wounded, missing

Unit	Casualties	Percentage
Paratroopers	650 men	10.4%
Sword	1,304 men	4.52%
Juno	1,242 men	5.8%
Gold	1,023 men	4.1%
Omaha	3,686 men	10.76%
Utah	589 men	2.53%
Paratroopers	1,725 men	11.13%
Germans	c. 10,000 men	18.16%

Marshland

Saint-Lô

from 30 m to 50 m

600 m

Carentan

Isigny-sur-Mer

du Hoc

Sainte-Mère-Église

UTAH 23,250 men

15,500 men

Saint-Marcouf

Quinéville

Valognes

Crasville

Barfleur

Cherbourg

93%

S E W N

0   5 km

1 • KEYS TO D-DAY

It took the Allies 18 months to break through the Atlantic wall. In the spring of 1943, the victory over the U-boats opened up the way for the US expeditionary forces. At the start of 1944, Allied planes cleared the skies of the Luftwaffe. The Allies then won the intelligence battle. Successfully misled by Operation Fortitude, the Germans gathered north of the Seine. Finally, the Allies' mastery of logistics immediately gave them considerable superiority. In spite of the Omaha bloodbath, the operation continued and by evening it was already impossible to drive the forces that had landed back to the sea.

2 • THE BATTLE OF NORMANDY

The priority for Monty was to take Cherbourg and Brittany, which were vital for further operations. The British wanted to pin down the German tanks to help the American advance. The German Westheer (Western Army), realizing that the plains of Caen were the only point from which the Allies could be driven back, joined the battle. With a shortage of infantry and inter-unit problems, the British became bogged down. In the west, the Americans were at a standstill on the hedge-covered ground, partly paying for the inexperience of their leaders. By mid-July, the battle seemed to have ground to a halt.

The apparent equality of forces (38 Allied divisions against 39 German) and similar losses were cancelled out by a breakdown in supplies. But the expertise of the beach crews, the success of the artificial harbour and the reopening of the port of Cherbourg enabled the Allies to make up their losses and retain the initiative. The slow arrival of reinforcements and supplies was disastrous for Rommel. In April, the railway network had been dismantled by Allied raids and the Resistance. Non-mechanized units went up to the front on foot in disorganized groups and then vanished, with no replacements. On the defensive and compelled to plug the gaps, the Germans were unable to build up reserves. Eventually they could hold out no longer.

THE RACE FOR REINFORCEMENTS

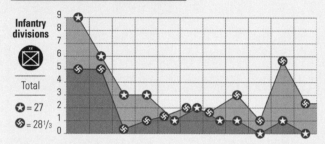

Infantry divisions
Total
★ = 27
卐 = 28 1/3

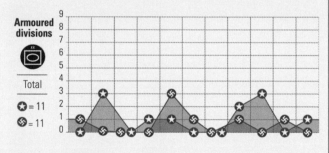

Armoured divisions
Total
★ = 11
卐 = 11

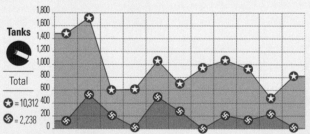

Tanks
Total
★ = 10,312
卐 = 2,238

6 Jun 13 Jun 20 Jun 27 Jun 4 Jul 11 Jul 18 Jul 25 Jul 1 Aug 8 Aug 15 Aug

MAJOR FIGURES

General of the Army Omar Bradley 1893–1981

General of the Army Dwight D. Eisenhower 1890–1969

Field Marshal Bernard Law Montgomery 1887–1976

FIVE KEY BATTLES

Armoured division   Infantry division   Airborne division   Armoured brigade   Combat group

3 • 25–31 July (7 days)
Operation Cobra: the breakthrough

×4   ×4   ×5   3,600 †/day

×10   ×4   1,800 †/day

A magnificent victory. Patton's tanks swept through a gap in German defences, reaching Brittany in five days and then Lorraine in five weeks.

4 • 10
The Falaise P

×12   ×10   6,0

The counter-attack at Mortain left tactical negligence and inter-unit

2 • 3–19 July (17 days)
Battle of the Hedgerows

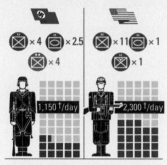

×4   ×2.5   ×4   1,150 †/day

×11   ×1   ×1   2,300 †/day

The US tactic of attacking on a wide front failed over hedge-covered terrain with poor fire support (tanks, artillery, aircraft).

1 • 7–30 June (24 days)
Cherbourg: a vital port

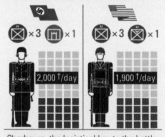

×3   ×1   2,000 †/day

×3   ×1   1,900 †/day

Cherbourg, the logistical key to the battle, was taken after an impressive operation.

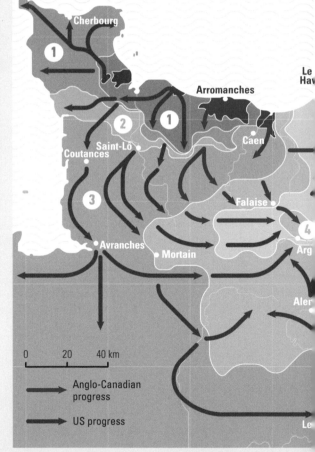

Cherbourg
Arromanches
Le Hav
Caen
Saint-Lô
Coutances
Falaise
Avranches
Mortain
Arg
Aler
Le

0   20   40 km

→ Anglo-Canadian progress
→ US progress

THE FAILURE OF GERMAN LOGISTICS

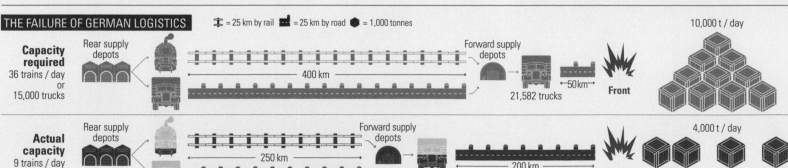

= 25 km by rail   = 25 km by road   = 1,000 tonnes

Capacity required
36 trains / day or 15,000 trucks

Rear supply depots   400 km   Forward supply depots   21,582 trucks   ←50km→   Front   10,000 t / day

Actual capacity
9 trains / day 2,000 trucks

Rear supply depots   250 km   Forward supply depots   10,883 trucks   200 km   Front   4,000 t / day

2,000 t road   1,000 t rail   1,000 t river

Field Marshal Erwin Rommel 1891–1944

Field Marshal Günther von Kluge 1882–1944

 Garrisoned company   ■ = 100 casualties (wounded/missing/dead)

3 • A COSTLY BATTLE

Although Allied losses were heavy (2,500 deaths per day), they could still be replaced fairly easily with the exception of the Anglo-Canadian infantry. It was undoubtedly the Germans who suffered the greatest losses. The Westheer abandoned most of its equipment and lost its best men. Meanwhile in the air, the Luftwaffe, irretrievably outclassed, made desperate efforts but to no effect.

THE HUMAN AND MATERIAL COST

Civilians

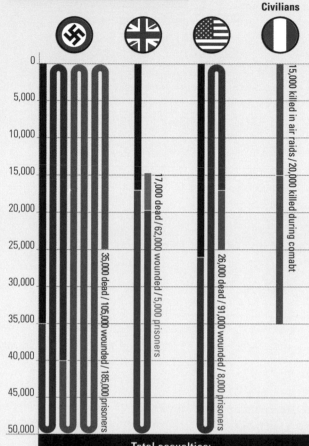

15,000 killed in air raids / 20,000 killed during combat

35,000 dead / 105,000 wounded / 185,000 prisoners

17,000 dead / 62,000 wounded / 5,000 prisoners

26,000 dead / 91,000 wounded / 8,000 prisoners

Total casualties:
78,000 dead / 258,000 wounded
198,000 prisoners & missing / 35,000 civilians dead

1,187 / 661

1,211 / 620

1,500 / 2,100

(12 days)
...sed opportunity

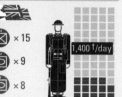

× 15
× 9
× 8

1,400 †/day

...rap, which the Allies closed. Due to ...e 7th Army was allowed to escape.

5 • 20–31 August (12 days)
A failed encirclement on the Seine

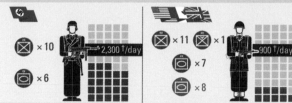

× 10
× 6

2,300 †/day

× 11   × 1
× 7
× 8

900 †/day

The Americans moved slowly down the Seine while the British halted manoeuvres in order to cross the Seine more easily east of Rouen. 205,000 Germans escaped.

Rouen

⑤

PARIS ★

Chartres

Orléans

N

INFANTRY FORCES, JULY 1944

● = 1 soldier out of combat   ● = 1 fresh soldier

●●●●●●●●●●●●●●●●●●●●
●●●●●●●●●●●●●●●●●●●●
●●●●●●●●●●●●●●●●●●●●
●●●●●●●●●●●●●●●●●●●●
●●●●●●●●●●●●●●●●●●●●
●

USA =
101% replacement of losses

●●●●●●●●●●●●●●●●●●●●
●●●●●●●●●●●●●●●●●●●●
●●●●●●●●●●●●●●●●●●●●
●●●●●●●●●●●●●●●●●●●●

UK =
80% replacement of losses

●●●●●●●●●●●●●●●●●●●●
●●●●●●●●●●●●●●●●●●●●
●●●●●●●●●●●●●●●●●●●●
●●●●●●●●●●●●●●●●●●●●

Germany =
6% replacement of losses

COMPARISON OF DAILY SUPPLIES FOR A GERMAN AND A US DIVISION

10th SS Panzer Division

Supplies required

73 t munitions
140 t fuel
100 t parts
40 t food

Total = 353 tonnes

Supplies available

55 t munitions
35 t fuel
15 t parts
10 t food

Total = 115 t
32.6%

Supplies required

375 t munitions
103 t fuel
137 t parts
40 t food

Total = 655 tonnes

Supplies available

150 t munitions
103 t fuel
100 t parts
40 t food

Total = 393 t
60%

2nd US Armored Division

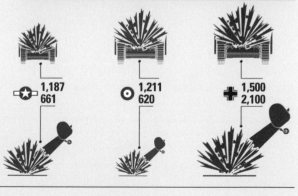

SOURCES: 1. Russell A. Hart, *Clash of Arms: How the Allies Won in Normandy*, Norman OK, 2001 • 2. Niklas Zetterling, *Normandy 1944: German Military Organization, Combat Power and Organizational Effectiveness*, Winnipeg, 2000 • 3. Olivier Wieviorka, *Normandy: The Landings to the Liberation of Paris*, Cambridge, MA, 2008.

US LOGISTICS IN EUROPE

The Americans had to project forces across the oceans to seven different theatres of operations. They understood the challenge, taking size constraints into account and designing weaponry from the start so that spare parts could be standardized. To overcome these problems, the US Army had a flexible management system, gigantic port infrastructures that avoided bottlenecks and thousand of Liberty Ships, cargo ships that created a link between well-stocked industries and the armed forces. Each theatre was generously supplied with standardized equipment. This was not wasteful; with delivery periods between 90 and 120 days, it was essential to anticipate every requirement. For example, nearly 2,000 Sherman tanks needed to be in the process of delivery just to make up the losses in the fleet of 4,000 tanks deployed in Europe. This transoceanic chain was a remarkable achievement and when occasional shortages did occur, it was either because the item had not been manufactured in time, or it was still in a cargo ship waiting to be unloaded, or it was impossible to transport it along the land part of its route.

It was this latter obstacle that caused the US Army the most problems. All the armies depended on the railways because the roads did not have the capacity to carry the quantities involved and they all found that road transport was not flexible enough to keep pace with mechanized units. The Germans and the Soviets circumvented this problem by the 'backpack method', with soldiers carrying as much as possible so that they could be autonomous for as long as possible, but in a few days they would run out of fuel. Nevertheless, the Americans had not anticipated the breakthrough in Normandy and they were forced to improvise a supply chain via a route that gave them a lifeline for six weeks before it stalled. Their system was inadequate, but they quickly learned a lesson and from the spring of 1945 they had reorganized their chain, introducing a fairly flexible operational stage in order to stretch out over several hundred kilometres. The US Army was then the only army capable of engaging in global warfare, the only one with the equipment and know-how to operate deep inside enemy positions over long periods.

1 • AN UNPRECEDENTED DISTRIBUTION OF FORCES

THE US SEA TRANSPORT NETWORK

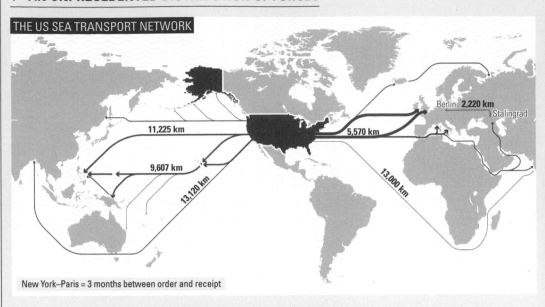

New York–Paris = 3 months between order and receipt

OPERATION BOLERO: THE MOVEMENT OF US FORCES TO THE UK

1942

241,839 troops

1,923,228 tonnes of equipment

1943

676,508

5,461,761 t

Jan–May 1944

6,046,659 t

752,653

DEPLOYMENT AND SUPPLY OF US FORCES ACROSS EUROPE   in millions

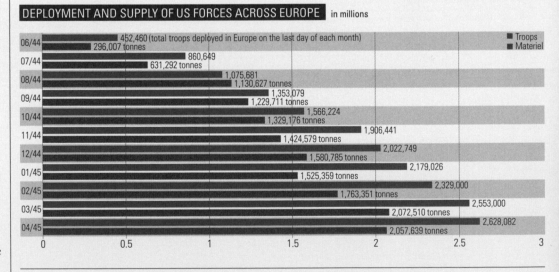

Month	Troops	Materiel
06/44	452,460 (total troops deployed in Europe on the last day of each month)	296,007 tonnes
07/44	860,649	631,292 tonnes
08/44	1,075,681	1,130,627 tonnes
09/44	1,353,079	1,229,711 tonnes
10/44	1,566,224	1,329,176 tonnes
11/44	1,906,441	1,424,579 tonnes
12/44	2,022,749	1,580,785 tonnes
01/45	2,179,026	1,525,359 tonnes
02/45	2,329,000	1,763,351 tonnes
03/45	2,553,000	2,072,510 tonnes
04/45	2,628,082	2,057,639 tonnes

Liberty Ships

These were cargo ships that were basic (11 knots) but efficient (payload 10,800 tonnes), and designed to be assembled from prefabricated sections in just 42 days. A total of 2,709 were built.

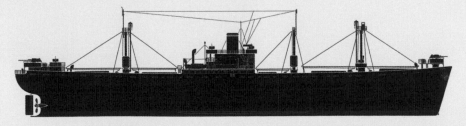

The GMC CCKW and the Federal 4 × 4 tractor truck

The GMC CCKW, a six-wheeler with great versatility and simplicity, was well suited to the front but a poor choice for the Red Ball Express convoys as it could carry only 7 tonnes. By 1944 it was replaced by tractor trucks that could pull semi-trailers, each carrying 15 to 18 tonnes and with one trailer easily being switched for another.

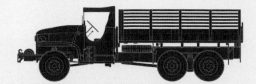 

2 • THE AMERICAN LOGISTICS REVOLUTION, JUNE 1944–APRIL 1945

A. The theory:

A logistics chain on the 1918 model in two stages: rail for long distances and road for short distances. It was suitable for large quantities and slow movement. The trucks were all-terrain vehicles with high fuel consumption and limited payloads.

B. Improvisation in August 1944

The rapid advance after Operation Cobra (600 km in four weeks) did not allow enough time to rebuild the rail network and move the depots. The Americans improvised a one-way route (the Red Ball Express) for long-distance supplies, but it was just a stop-gap measure (small GMC trucks, huge wear and tear, poor following of procedures, inter-unit disputes). The use of working sections of railway involved time-consuming offloading and reloading. As a result, the chain broke down, holding up operations.

C. Revolution in spring 1945: a three-stage chain

In 1945, in order to extend the logistics chain, the Americans introduced an intermediate stage: the operational stage. Each army had a one-way route used by large semi-trailers, pending the reopening of the rail routes. Procedures were improved. Army depots were broken down into sub-units, some operational, some redeployed to the front.

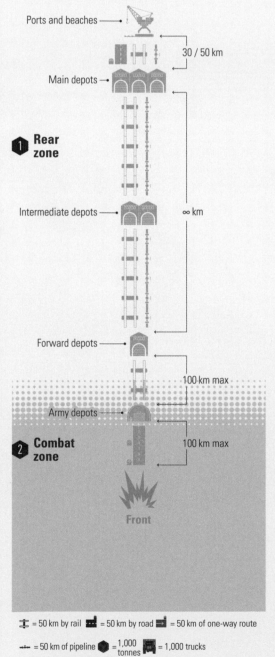 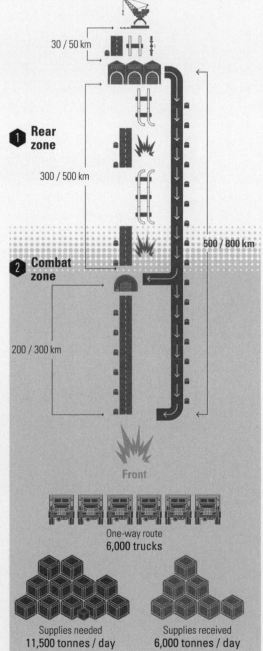 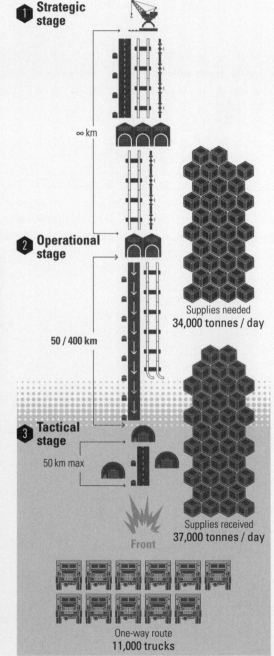

SOURCES: 1. Nicolas Aubin, *Les Routes de la liberté*, Paris, 2014 • 2. Roland G. Ruppenthal, *Logistical Support of the Armies*, 2 vols, Washington, DC, 1952.

OPERATION BAGRATION

The Soviet offensive known as Operation Bagration began on 22 June 1944, on the anniversary of the German Operation Barbarossa, and lasted for over two months. It ended with the destruction of the Army Group Centre and resulted in the heaviest German losses since the beginning of the war. It unbalanced the whole front so much that, as an indirect result, the Wehrmacht also lost its Army Group North, hemmed in and reduced to powerlessness in the Baltic states, and its Army Group South Ukraine, destroyed in Romania. The Red Army advanced an extraordinary 600 km to the west, as far as the borders of East Prussia, the edge of Warsaw, Hungary and Yugoslavia. The political impact of these military successes was remarkable. Finland, Romania and Bulgaria changed sides and the latter two started the process of Sovietization, while the subjection of Poland grew faster. It is impossible to understand Bagration without being aware of three crucial factors.

1) The Red Army was now vastly superior to the Wehrmacht in both manpower and equipment, including in the air. It no longer lagged as far behind in matters of command and control and, with the American trucks that had been supplied, it had the mobility that its opponent now lacked.

2) This superiority enabled it to launch a series of six offensives from Finland to the Black Sea, creating a system that was both military and political. Bagration was just one of these, although it was the most spectacular.

3) The Germans were also unable to move forces from west to east as they had in previous years, since Stalin was now in possession of vital information: the Western countries were going to land in France in May or June 1944. He had heard this from Roosevelt at the Tehran Conference in November 1943. The US President had asked him to launch a simultaneous offensive. This became the first real East–West co-operative operation. Encouraged, the Soviet strategists began to consider penetrating two or three times as deep as they had ventured so far. Stalin also agreed to this bold move because in the wake of the Anglo-American landings, he feared what Hitler was hoping for: a change of alliances. It was in this spirit that he viewed one of the consequences of Operation Bagration: the plot to assassinate Hitler on 20 July. Far from weakening the Reich, the failure of the plot temporarily strengthened it, yet condemned it to fight on until the point of its own destruction.

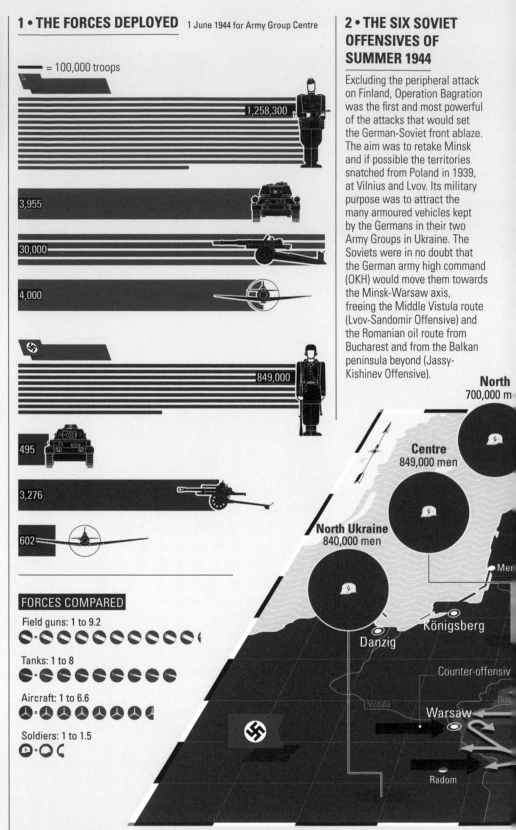

1 • THE FORCES DEPLOYED 1 June 1944 for Army Group Centre

= 100,000 troops

1,258,300

3,955

30,000

4,000

849,000

495

3,276

602

FORCES COMPARED

Field guns: 1 to 9.2

Tanks: 1 to 8

Aircraft: 1 to 6.6

Soldiers: 1 to 1.5

2 • THE SIX SOVIET OFFENSIVES OF SUMMER 1944

Excluding the peripheral attack on Finland, Operation Bagration was the first and most powerful of the attacks that would set the German-Soviet front ablaze. The aim was to retake Minsk and if possible the territories snatched from Poland in 1939, at Vilnius and Lvov. Its military purpose was to attract the many armoured vehicles kept by the Germans in their two Army Groups in Ukraine. The Soviets were in no doubt that the German army high command (OKH) would move them towards the Minsk-Warsaw axis, freeing the Middle Vistula route (Lvov-Sandomir Offensive) and the Romanian oil route from Bucharest and from the Balkan peninsula beyond (Jassy-Kishinev Offensive).

North
700,000 m

Centre
849,000 men

North Ukraine
840,000 men

Danzig

Königsberg

Mer

Counter-offensiv

Vistula

Bug

Warsaw

Radom

3 • CASUALTIES

In the summer of 1944, the Wehrmacht suffered its worst bloodshed of the war. The 400,000 men lost in Bielorussia, the leaders of the 28 divisions and 8 corps were the nucleus of the German army in the east. The men who succeeded them had neither their nerve nor their experience nor their knowledge of the Soviets. Like the Kaiser's army after the spring and summer battles of 1918, after Bagration the German Ostheer (Eastern Army) used up its human resources chaotically, with diminishing effectiveness. It had also irretrievably lost its upper hand over the enemy, replaced by an intense fear. In its military, psychological and geopolitical repercussions, this was a more serious catastrophe for the Reich than Stalingrad.

SOURCES: 1. Jean Lopez, *Opération Bagration. La revanche de Staline (été 1944)*, Paris, 2014.

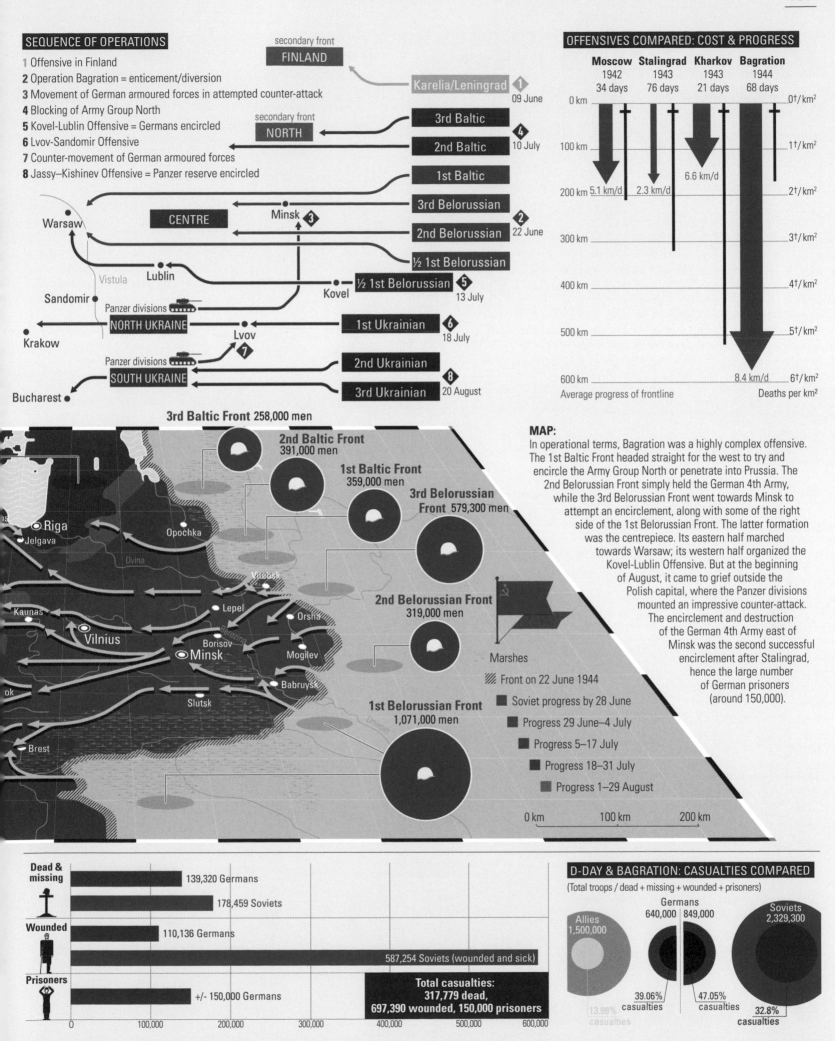

SEQUENCE OF OPERATIONS

1 Offensive in Finland
2 Operation Bagration = enticement/diversion
3 Movement of German armoured forces in attempted counter-attack
4 Blocking of Army Group North
5 Kovel-Lublin Offensive = Germans encircled
6 Lvov-Sandomir Offensive
7 Counter-movement of German armoured forces
8 Jassy–Kishinev Offensive = Panzer reserve encircled

secondary front
FINLAND

Karelia/Leningrad **1**
09 June

secondary front
NORTH

3rd Baltic **4**
10 July

2nd Baltic

1st Baltic

3rd Belorussian **2**
22 June

2nd Belorussian

½ 1st Belorussian

½ 1st Belorussian **5**
13 July

CENTRE
Minsk **3**

Warsaw

Vistula
Lublin
Sandomir
Kovel
Panzer divisions
NORTH UKRAINE
Lvov **7**

1st Ukrainian **6**
18 July

Krakow

Panzer divisions
SOUTH UKRAINE

2nd Ukrainian **8**

3rd Ukrainian
20 August

Bucharest

OFFENSIVES COMPARED: COST & PROGRESS

	Moscow 1942 34 days	Stalingrad 1943 76 days	Kharkov 1943 21 days	Bagration 1944 68 days

0 km — 0†/km²
100 km — 1†/km²
200 km — 2†/km²
300 km — 3†/km²
400 km — 4†/km²
500 km — 5†/km²
600 km — 6†/km²

5.1 km/d   2.3 km/d   6.6 km/d

8.4 km/d

Average progress of frontline   Deaths per km²

3rd Baltic Front 258,000 men

2nd Baltic Front 391,000 men

1st Baltic Front 359,000 men

3rd Belorussian Front 579,300 men

2nd Belorussian Front 319,000 men

1st Belorussian Front 1,071,000 men

Riga
Jelgava
Opochka
Dvina
Vitebsk
Kaunas
Lepel
Orsha
Berezina
Vilnius
Borisov
Mogilev
Minsk
Babruysk
Slutsk
Dnieper
Brest

Marshes

Front on 22 June 1944

Soviet progress by 28 June

Progress 29 June–4 July

Progress 5–17 July

Progress 18–31 July

Progress 1–29 August

0 km   100 km   200 km

MAP:

In operational terms, Bagration was a highly complex offensive. The 1st Baltic Front headed straight for the west to try and encircle the Army Group North or penetrate into Prussia. The 2nd Belorussian Front simply held the German 4th Army, while the 3rd Belorussian Front went towards Minsk to attempt an encirclement, along with some of the right side of the 1st Belorussian Front. The latter formation was the centrepiece. Its eastern half marched towards Warsaw; its western half organized the Kovel-Lublin Offensive. But at the beginning of August, it came to grief outside the Polish capital, where the Panzer divisions mounted an impressive counter-attack. The encirclement and destruction of the German 4th Army east of Minsk was the second successful encirclement after Stalingrad, hence the large number of German prisoners (around 150,000).

Dead & missing
139,320 Germans
178,459 Soviets

Wounded
110,136 Germans
587,254 Soviets (wounded and sick)

Prisoners
+/- 150,000 Germans

**Total casualties:
317,779 dead,
697,390 wounded, 150,000 prisoners**

0   100,000   200,000   300,000   400,000   500,000   600,000

D-DAY & BAGRATION: CASUALTIES COMPARED

(Total troops / dead + missing + wounded + prisoners)

Germans

Allies
1,500,000

Germans
640,000   849,000

Soviets
2,329,300

13.98% casualties

39.06% casualties

47.05% casualties

32.8% casualties

THE BATTLE FOR GERMANY

The failure of the Ardennes counter-offensive put an end to the Nazis' wild ambitions. However it still took another hundred days or so to kill the many-headed Hydra that clung to power. Every extra day gave Hitler time to murder more Jews. Then in the final weeks, his hatred was redirected at the German people. They were unworthy to survive him and must die with him. No negotiations, no armistice, only fighting. Laid low by illness, hunted down, reduced to living in a damp bunker, Hitler continued to add fuel to the fire until, cornered and besieged, he committed suicide on 30 April 1945. But this relentlessness was not Hitler's will alone. It was only possible with the complicity of a bureaucracy and an

army indulged by the Nazi regime, united by the same vision of the world and willing to stand together to the point of destruction.

Consequently, these four months were the bloodiest of the war. 30,000 people died every day. It was a horrific frenzy, first for the regime's slave workers and 'parasites', massacred on every imaginable pretext, then for civilians and lastly for the combatants on both sides. From a military point of view, the German campaign was much more than simply killing. The fighting was ferocious. The Reich raised new units right to the end and it was only the shortage of fuel in April that eventually made any cohesive resistance impossible. Allied military expertise was at its height. Around Budapest, the

1 • THE ALLIES

In 1945, US strategy prevailed over British strategy. Ulysses S. Grant believed that the secret of victory was to destroy the enemy's army by using crushing force supported by concentrated fire in a particular place and at a particular time. In addition, the goal was to attack the enemy wherever the balance of forces was favourable. Destruction would result from the fighting, not the manoeuvre. This is the doctrine that ultimately led to Eisenhower's 'broad front' strategy. It called for tactical and material superiority, which was certainly the case in 1945 when the balance of forces was particularly favourable.

STRATEGIC OBJECTIVES
Destroy the German army.

CONCEPT OF OPERATIONS

Destroy German armies west of the Rhine.

Cross the Rhine on a broad front to saturate German defences.

Take the economic heartland of the Ruhr to choke the enemy.

Occupy Germany.

CONCRETE REALIZATION

1
8 Feb–10 Mar
Operations Veritable and Grenade, which broke the Westheer's hold.

2
18 Feb–23 Mar
The US Army marches on the Rhine against a weakened enemy.

3
22 Mar–3 Apr
Encirclement of the Ruhr.

4
4 April–8 May
The continuation.

WESTERN FORCES COMPARED
Troops: 1 to 5.7 (420,000 against 2,420,000)

Tanks: 1 to 6.5 (1,832 against 12,000)

Planes: 1 to 9.7 (1,900 against 18,500, inc. 6,400 heavy bombers)

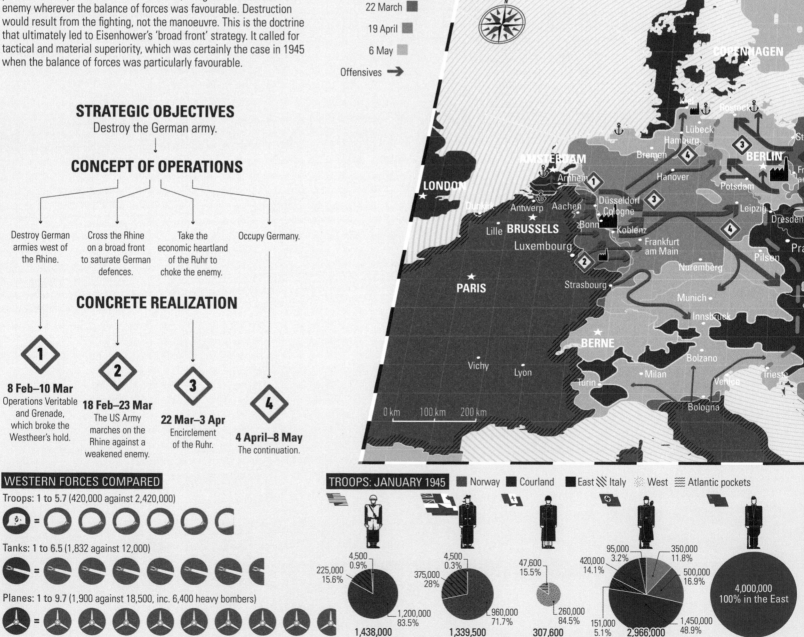

Front on 17 Jan 1945
22 March
19 April
6 May
Offensives →

Remains of Reich on 7 May 1945 · Neutral states

COPENHAGEN · BERLIN · Stettin · Lübeck · Hamburg · Bremen · Hanover · Potsdam · Leipzig · Dresden · AMSTERDAM · Arnhem · Düsseldorf · Cologne · LONDON · Dunkirk · Antwerp · Aachen · Bonn · Koblenz · Prague · Pilsen · BRUSSELS · Lille · Luxembourg · Frankfurt am Main · Nuremberg · PARIS · Strasbourg · Munich · Innsbruck · BERNE · Vichy · Lyon · Bolzano · Milan · Trieste · Turin · Venice · Bologna

0 km · 100 km · 200 km

TROOPS: JANUARY 1945
Norway · Courland · East · Italy · West · Atlantic pockets

1,438,000
- 225,000 — 15.6%
- 4,500 — 0.9%
- 1,200,000 — 83.5%

1,339,500
- 375,000 — 28%
- 4,500 — 0.3%
- 960,000 — 71.7%

307,600
- 47,600 — 15.5%
- 260,000 — 84.5%

2,966,000
- 95,000 — 3.2%
- 350,000 — 11.8%
- 420,000 — 14.1%
- 500,000 — 16.9%
- 151,000 — 5.1%
- 1,450,000 — 48.9%

4,000,000
100% in the East

Red Army brilliantly countered the final German armoured offensives and showed that it had the upper hand over its enemy both defensively and offensively. The Soviets mounted massive offensives in the east, coordinated millions of soldiers, thousands of tanks and destroyed the Ostheer (Eastern Army) over a depth of 500 kilometres before taking Berlin, Europe's doggedly defended third city, in only eleven days. The Soviet victory was above all a victory for military thinking, the art of operations.

In the west, victory was more of a tactical achievement. The methodical British and the flexible Americans destroyed the Westheer west of the Rhine in a series of sophisticated operations, making use of a cutting-edge arsenal and benefitting from inter-service cooperation. The Rhine crossings improvised by the Americans and planned by the British were successful, the encirclement of the Ruhr exemplary. The continuation would have taken them to Berlin first, if Eisenhower had not decided otherwise (mainly, according to historians Daniel Feldmann and Cédric Mas, because the diplomatic American did not want to offend Stalin by honouring the insufferable Montgomery, whose better-placed forces would necessarily have been at the forefront of the advance). The German campaign, the last battle against Nazism, was fought by the rules that a third world war might have followed in the 1950s.

Adolf Hitler
Chancellor of the Reich
1889–30 April 1945
(death by suicide)

2 • THE SOVIETS

The Soviet strategy was highly innovative. It did not reduce the enemy to an army that must be destroyed but saw it as a system to be paralysed and broken down. That aim was achieved via a combination of major operations spread over different locations at different times. Appropriate sequencing and acquiring depth were more reliable ways of destroying the system than intermittent encirclements or a war of attrition. This approach is known as the art of operations. The Soviet victory owed much more to their conceptual superiority than to their numerical and material superiority.

STRATEGIC OBJECTIVES
Destroy the Nazi system by depriving it of its strategic power, economic resources, access to the Baltic and political centres. Secure guarantees in Eastern Europe.

CONCEPT OF OPERATIONS

Stretch the enemy with operations on the flanks (Hungary and East Prussia). | Strike at the centre. | Final offensive on Berlin

CONCRETE REALIZATION

1 **1 Oct 1944–15 Mar 1945** The Soviets immobilized most of the Panzerwaffe near Budapest. The Germans launched three counter-offensives in early January to break the siege of the capital, then two more in March to halt the Soviet advance on the last Axis oilfield.

2 **12 Jan–3 Feb** The Vistula–Oder Offensive broke the German army from the Baltic to Silesia.

3 **16 April–9 May** The Berlin Offensive reached the Elbe and took the capital.

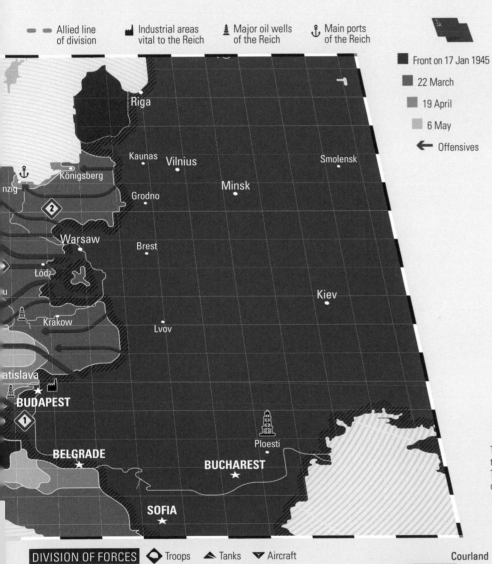

Allied line of division — Industrial areas vital to the Reich — Major oil wells of the Reich — Main ports of the Reich — Front on 17 Jan 1945 — 22 March — 19 April — 6 May — ← Offensives

Riga, Königsberg, Danzig, Kaunas, Vilnius, Smolensk, Grodno, Minsk, Warsaw, Brest, Łódź, Kiev, Kraków, Lvov, Bratislava, BUDAPEST, BELGRADE, BUCHAREST, Ploesti, SOFIA

DIVISION OF FORCES ◇ Troops ▲ Tanks ▼ Aircraft

Courland, Norway, Atlantic pockets, West, East, Italy

EASTERN FORCES COMPARED including Courland
Troops: 1 to 2 (1,950,000 against 4,000,000)
Tanks: 1 to 2.4 (4,091 against 10,000)
Planes: 1 to 4.3 (1,875 against 8,000)

3 • THE SOVIETS: MASTERS IN THE ART OF DEEP STRIKES

In order to crush the Reich, the Soviets launched massive offensives (3.4 million men and 8,500 tanks for the Vistula-Oder Offensive), unequalled on the Allied side. To organize such a huge operation on four fronts called for remarkable skill. The offensive was 500 km long and reached a similar depth. But a broad front did not prevent them from focusing on a few points, each around 30 km wide, and spreading their forces in order to sequence the attack in three phases: 1) penetration, 2) breakthrough and 3) exploitation.

Each phase was carried out by a different type of unit. The deployment of the reserves was particularly crucial. If they were deployed too soon, it would inevitably cause a bottleneck. If they were deployed too late, the enemy would have time to block the breach. All the Soviets lacked was an efficient logistics system. The offensive was forced to a halt once the combatants had used up the supplies they were carrying. Otherwise, the Soviets would have reached Berlin by February.

SOVIET BREAKTHROUGH TACTICS IN ACTION
with the 1st Belorussian Front (January 1945)

1. Phase 1: 5 km penetration of enemy front by infantry corps concentrated in the centre, supported by escort tanks and a large amount of artillery.

2. Phase 2: 15 km penetration by two tank corps until enemy front opens.

3. Phase 3: Introduction of the exploitation echelon, which quickly springs forward some 300 to 500 km. Its size, speed and the scattering of the enemy maintain its momentum. Destruction results not from encirclement but from fragmentation of German forces.

4. Meanwhile, the flanks are held with as few resources as possible. Attacks then take advantage of the collapse of the front in order to crush the remains of the enemy army.

5. The Wehrmacht tries to block the breach at source with its tactical reserve, then mounts a counter-offensive whose only chance of success is to surprise the exploitation echelon when it runs out of fuel, which no longer happens by 1945.

6. Phase 4: Once the objective is reached, a strategic pause of several weeks is allowed to reset the mechanism (regrouping, re-equipment and establishment of a new rear base).

1st echelon   2nd echelon   3rd echelon

Infantry army   Tank army
Armoured corps   Artillery corps
Armoured division   Artillery division

5 km
10 km

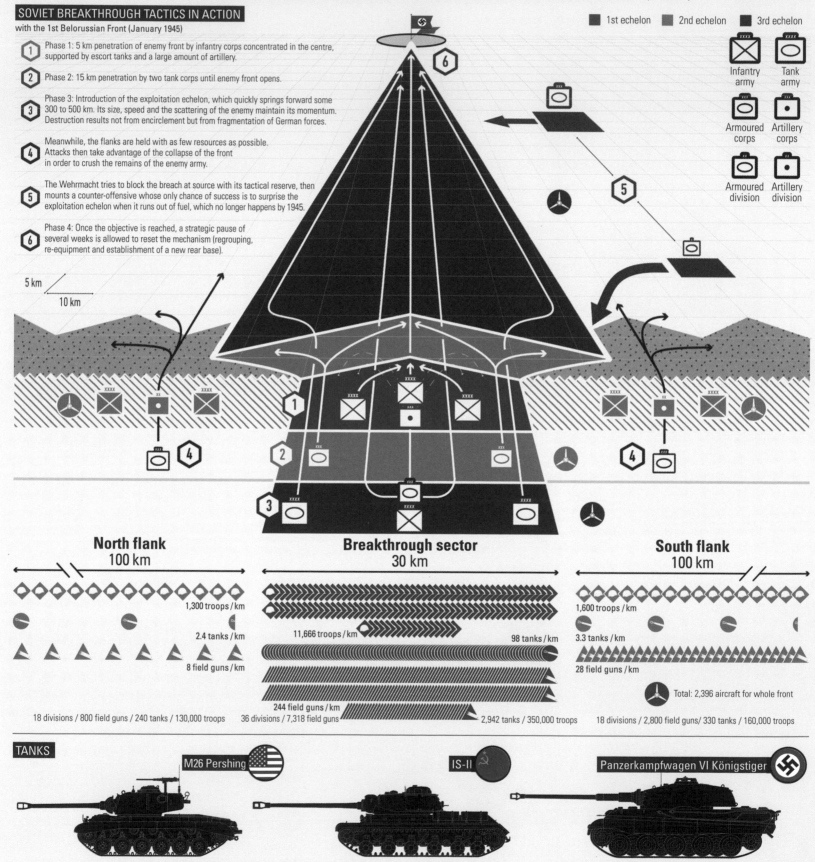

North flank
100 km
1,300 troops / km
2.4 tanks / km
8 field guns / km
18 divisions / 800 field guns / 240 tanks / 130,000 troops

Breakthrough sector
30 km
11,666 troops / km
98 tanks / km
244 field guns / km
36 divisions / 7,318 field guns   2,942 tanks / 350,000 troops

South flank
100 km
1,600 troops / km
3.3 tanks / km
28 field guns / km
Total: 2,396 aircraft for whole front
18 divisions / 2,800 field guns/ 330 tanks / 160,000 troops

TANKS

M26 Pershing

IS-II

Panzerkampfwagen VI Königstiger

SOURCES: 1. Jean Lopez, *Berlin. Les Offensives géantes de l'Armée rouge Vistule-Oder-Elbe (12 janvier–9 mai 1945)*, Paris, 2010 • 2. Daniel Feldmann & Cédric Mas, *La Campagne du Rhin. Les Alliés entrent en Allemagne*

MAJOR FIGURES

General
Jean de Lattre de Tassigny
1889–1952

General
Henry Duncan Crerar
1888–1965

General
William Hood Simpson
1888–1980

Field Marshal
Walter Model
1891–1945

General
Gotthard Heinrici
1886–1971

General
Helmuth Weidling
1891–1955

Marshal
Georgy Zhukov
1896–1974

Marshal
Ivan Konev
1897–1973

Marshal
Konstantin Rokossovsky
1896–1968

4 • BERLIN AND OTHER SIEGES

Except for the numbers involved, Berlin was no different from other urban sieges, labyrinths in which confused hordes of people slaughtered each other. The Soviets did not experience a higher rate of losses there despite their swift attack. Surprisingly, the attackers often suffered less than the defenders: perhaps the initiative was an advantage. The contrast between the siege of Brest and much fiercer sieges in the East is striking: 10% of defenders were killed in Brest, compared with 25 to 50% in the east.

FIVE SIEGES pop/km² measured using pre-war figures and urban density

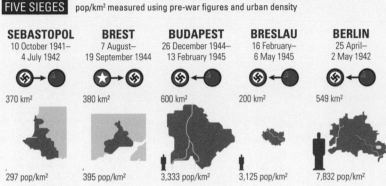

	SEBASTOPOL	BREST	BUDAPEST	BRESLAU	BERLIN
	10 October 1941–4 July 1942	7 August–19 September 1944	26 December 1944–13 February 1945	16 February–6 May 1945	25 April–2 May 1942
Area	370 km²	380 km²	600 km²	200 km²	549 km²
Density	297 pop/km²	395 pop/km²	3,333 pop/km²	3,125 pop/km²	7,832 pop/km²

Duration (days of siege / days of attack)

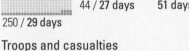

250 / 29 days   44 / 27 days   51 days   80 / 65 days   8 days

Troops and casualties

92,000	40,000	79,000	50,000	92,000
18,000 dead 65,000 prisoners	4,000 dead 23,000 prisoners	39,000 dead 40,000 prisoners	6,000 dead 44,000 prisoners	22,000 dead 70,000 prisoners

204,000	52,000	177,000	70,000	400,000
7,660 dead 28,197 wounded	2,000 dead 7,000 wounded	44,000 dead 100,000 wounded	7,000 dead 15,000 wounded	13,000 dead 65,000 wounded

Pace (km² taken per day of attack)

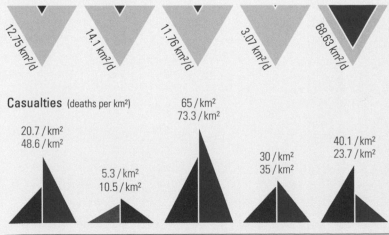

12.75 km²/d   14.1 km²/d   11.76 km²/d   3.07 km²/d   68.63 km²/d

Casualties (deaths per km²)

20.7 / km²
48.6 / km²

5.3 / km²
10.5 / km²

65 / km²
73.3 / km²

30 / km²
35 / km²

40.1 / km²
23.7 / km²

5 • CASUALTIES

The fierce fighting was not the only explanation for the high toll at the war's end. It was also due to the lethality of the new weapons, their dense deployment, and, in the East, living conditions and mistreatment that were often fatal for prisoners. Germany was drained by two battles of attrition that exhausted the Wehrmacht (Budapest and the Allied operations west of the Rhine), a terrible blow that shattered the Westheer (Vistula-Oder) culminating in encirclement of a moribund Westheer in the Ruhr.

FOUR DEFEATS THAT WIPED OUT THE WEHRMACHT

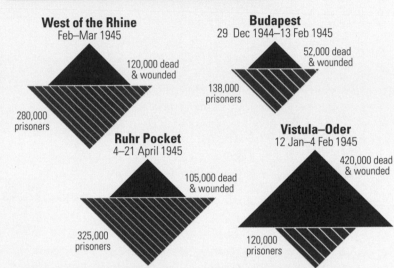

West of the Rhine
Feb–Mar 1945
120,000 dead & wounded
280,000 prisoners

Budapest
29 Dec 1944–13 Feb 1945
52,000 dead & wounded
138,000 prisoners

Ruhr Pocket
4–21 April 1945
105,000 dead & wounded
325,000 prisoners

Vistula–Oder
12 Jan–4 Feb 1945
420,000 dead & wounded
120,000 prisoners

Total troops by front and casualties after the 4 battles

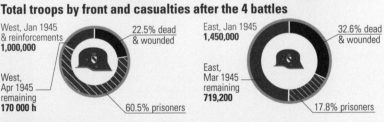

West, Jan 1945 & reinforcements
1,000,000

West, Apr 1945 remaining
170 000 h

22.5% dead & wounded

60.5% prisoners

East, Jan 1945
1,450,000

East, Mar 1945 remaining
719,200

32.6% dead & wounded

17.8% prisoners

CASUALTIES Dead and wounded in 1945

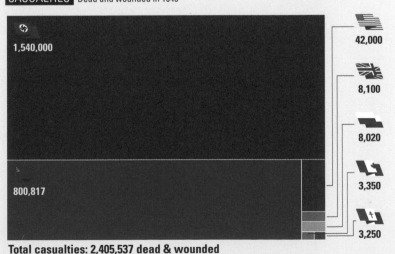

1,540,000

800,817

42,000

8,100

8,020

3,350

3,250

Total casualties: 2,405,537 dead & wounded

(janvier–mai 1945), Paris, 2016 • 3. Krisztián Ungváry, *Battle for Budapest: 100 Days in World War II*, London, 2003 • 4. G. F. Krivosheev (ed.), *Soviet Casualties and Combat Losses in the Twentieth Century*, London, 1997.

JAPAN: THE FINAL DAYS

Japan's surrender is usually ascribed to the atomic bombing of Hiroshima and Nagasaki, but it also had a number of much more complex causes.

In the summer of 1945, Japan's major cities and industrial centres had been systematically pounded for months by strategic US bombing raids and the Japanese economy was on its knees. In July, the Allied demand for unconditional surrender strengthened the positions of hardliners on the Japanese high command. Well aware that they had irretrievably lost the war, they nevertheless took advantage of an Allied amphibious invasion of Japan (then in its planning stages under the name Operation Downfall) to play their last card. They would inflict such heavy losses on the Americans, particularly by sacrificing thousands of kamikaze pilots, that public opinion would be swayed and it would become possible, with Soviet mediation, to secure more favourable peace terms, notably the preservation of the imperial throne. But the atomic bombing of Hiroshima and Nagasaki by the Americans on 6 and 9 August and the rapid success of the Soviet offensives in Manchuria, Korea and Sakhalin, which even threatened Hokkaido, the northernmost of Japan's main islands, hastened the Japanese surrender. It was feared that Japan would be invaded and the empire broken up. Emperor Hirohito had to speak personally on the radio for the first time and his entourage had to put down an attempted coup by young officers of the guard. US forces immediately occupied the country and on 2 September 1945, Japan officially surrendered on board the battleship *Missouri*. In its survey of the effects of strategic bombing shortly after the end of the war, the US special committee wrote: 'Based on a detailed investigation of all the facts, and supported by the testimony of the surviving Japanese leaders involved, it is the Survey's opinion that certainly prior to 31 December 1945, and in all probability prior to 1 November 1945, Japan would have surrendered even if the atomic bombs had not been dropped, even if Russia had not entered the war, and even if no invasion had been planned or contemplated.'

SOURCES: 1. *US Strategic Bombing Survey, Pacific*, US Army, 1946 • 2. Nicolas Bernard, *La Guerre du Pacifique*, Paris, 2016 • 3. John Costello, *The Pacific War*, New York, 1981 • 4. Richard Overy, *The Air War 1939–1945*, Washington, DC, 2005 • 5. *The Japanese Monographs*, US Army, 1959.

1 • COLLAPSE OF THE JAPANESE ECONOMY

In the late 1930s, despite huge progress, the Japanese economy was still fragile, heavily dependent on imports of raw materials and oil, and lagging far behind the potential of Britain and the USA. Nevertheless, with military forces (especially air and sea) that were remarkably efficient compared with those of the ill-prepared West, the Japanese command hoped to gain the space it needed within a few months to make its positions in the Pacific unassailable and negotiate from a position of strength. This miscalculation proved disastrous and the Japanese economy gradually collapsed between 1943 and 1945 under US pressure.

COMPARATIVE GROWTH OF GDP Base 100 in 1938

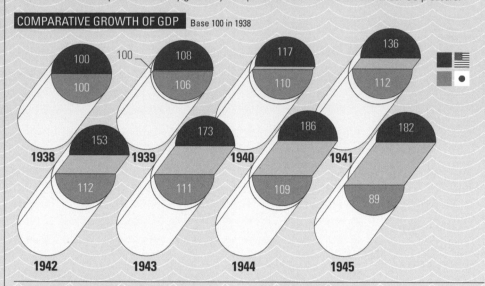

	1938	1939	1940	1941
USA	100	108	117	136
Japan	100	106	110	112

	1942	1943	1944	1945
USA	153	173	186	182
Japan	112	111	109	89

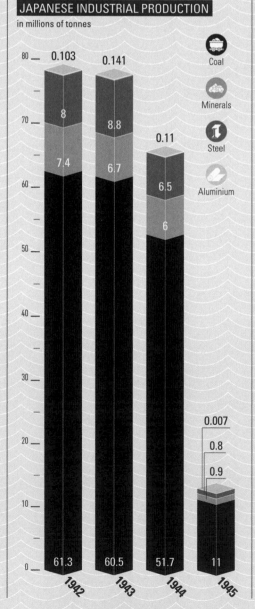

JAPANESE INDUSTRIAL PRODUCTION
in millions of tonnes

- Coal
- Minerals
- Steel
- Aluminium

	1942	1943	1944	1945
	0.103	0.141	0.11	0.007
	8	8.8	6.5	0.8
	7.4	6.7	6	0.9
	61.3	60.5	51.7	11

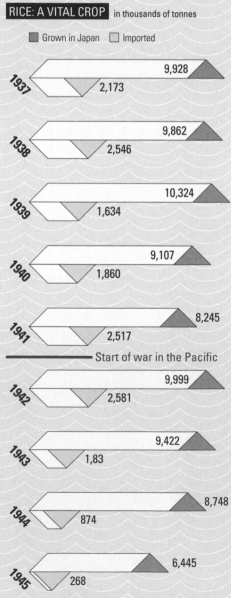

RICE: A VITAL CROP in thousands of tonnes

■ Grown in Japan □ Imported

Year	Grown in Japan	Imported
1937	9,928	2,173
1938	9,862	2,546
1939	10,324	1,634
1940	9,107	1,860
1941	8,245	2,517

———— Start of war in the Pacific ————

Year	Grown in Japan	Imported
1942	9,999	2,581
1943	9,422	1,83
1944	8,748	874
1945	6,445	268

2 • JAPAN IN FLAMES

Before the atomic bombs were dropped, dozens of Japanese industrial cities were ravaged by the B-29 Superfortress planes of the US 21st Air Force. Strategic bombing was considered at an early stage but due to logistic and geographical constraints, the first, apart from the symbolic Doolittle raid in 1942, was not launched from China until the second half of 1944. These precision raids were decided to be too costly and ineffective and from February 1945, General LeMay began night-time incendiary carpet-bombing raids, from bases captured in the Mariana Islands. This devastated many towns and Japanese fighter planes and anti-aircraft defences were powerless at high altitudes. The most deadly raid of the war killed over 100,000 people in Tokyo on 9 March 1945. Over 90% of Toyama, an industrial city with a population of 150,000 on the north coast, was razed to the ground on the night of 1 August 1945. At least 330,000 people were killed in that raid and 414 B-29s and 2,600 crew members were lost.

OUTCOME OF THE US STRATEGIC BOMBING OF JAPAN

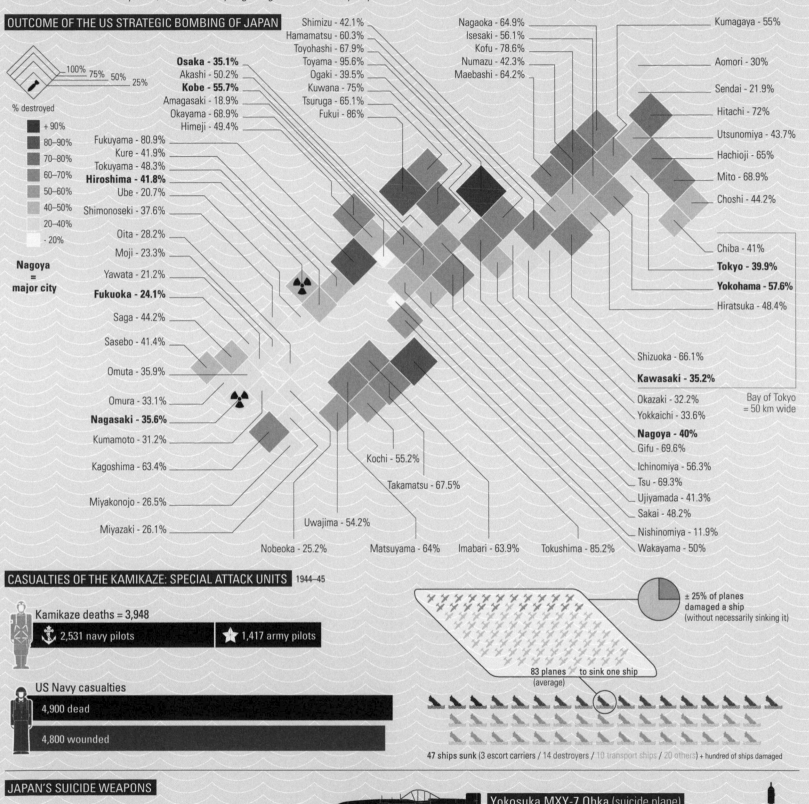

100% 75% 50% 25%

% destroyed

- +90%
- 80–90%
- 70–80%
- 60–70%
- 50–60%
- 40–50%
- 20–40%
- -20%

Nagoya = major city

Shimizu - 42.1%
Hamamatsu - 60.3%
Toyohashi - 67.9%
Toyama - 95.6%
Ogaki - 39.5%
Kuwana - 75%
Tsuruga - 65.1%
Fukui - 86%

Osaka - 35.1%
Akashi - 50.2%
Kobe - 55.7%
Amagasaki - 18.9%
Okayama - 68.9%
Himeji - 49.4%

Fukuyama - 80.9%
Kure - 41.9%
Tokuyama - 48.3%
Hiroshima - 41.8%
Ube - 20.7%
Shimonoseki - 37.6%

Oita - 28.2%
Moji - 23.3%
Yawata - 21.2%
Fukuoka - 24.1%
Saga - 44.2%
Sasebo - 41.4%
Omuta - 35.9%
Omura - 33.1%
Nagasaki - 35.6%
Kumamoto - 31.2%
Kagoshima - 63.4%
Miyakonojo - 26.5%
Miyazaki - 26.1%

Nagaoka - 64.9%
Isesaki - 56.1%
Kofu - 78.6%
Numazu - 42.3%
Maebashi - 64.2%

Kumagaya - 55%
Aomori - 30%
Sendai - 21.9%
Hitachi - 72%
Utsunomiya - 43.7%
Hachioji - 65%
Mito - 68.9%
Choshi - 44.2%

Chiba - 41%
Tokyo - 39.9%
Yokohama - 57.6%
Hiratsuka - 48.4%

Shizuoka - 66.1%
Kawasaki - 35.2%
Okazaki - 32.2%
Yokkaichi - 33.6%
Nagoya - 40%
Gifu - 69.6%
Ichinomiya - 56.3%
Tsu - 69.3%
Ujiyamada - 41.3%
Sakai - 48.2%
Nishinomiya - 11.9%
Wakayama - 50%

Bay of Tokyo = 50 km wide

Kochi - 55.2%
Takamatsu - 67.5%
Uwajima - 54.2%
Nobeoka - 25.2%
Matsuyama - 64%
Imabari - 63.9%
Tokushima - 85.2%

CASUALTIES OF THE KAMIKAZE: SPECIAL ATTACK UNITS 1944–45

Kamikaze deaths = 3,948

⚓ 2,531 navy pilots   ★ 1,417 army pilots

US Navy casualties

4,900 dead

4,800 wounded

± 25% of planes damaged a ship (without necessarily sinking it)

83 planes to sink one ship (average)

47 ships sunk (3 escort carriers / 14 destroyers / 10 transport ships / 20 others) + hundred of ships damaged

JAPAN'S SUICIDE WEAPONS

Kaiten type 1 (suicide manned torpedo)

Yokosuka MXY-7 Ohka (suicide plane)

Shin'yo class (suicide motorboat)

Fukuryu (suicide diver)

4. AFTERMATH AND CONSEQUENCES

CIVILIAN AND MILITARY LOSSES

Establishing truly accurate figures for the terrible death toll of the Second World War has proved to be an impossible task for the last seven decades. At best, it is possible to draw up and compare estimates of varying degrees of accuracy for each country. Military losses (in combat, in prison or from disease) are often the easiest to determine, although there are often enormous regional disparities and numerous problems with methodology, depending on whether calculations are based on nationality, region of origin or branch of the armed forces, whether or not they include 'paramilitary' categories (such as the resistance) or non-combatants.

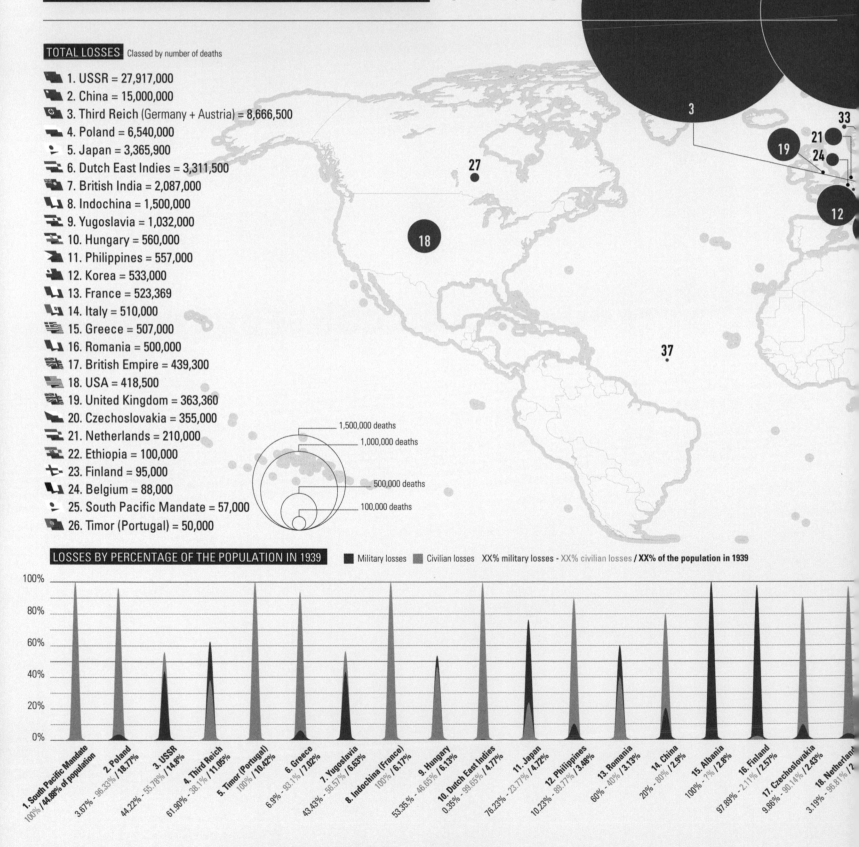

TOTAL LOSSES Classed by number of deaths

1. USSR = 27,917,000
2. China = 15,000,000
3. Third Reich (Germany + Austria) = 8,666,500
4. Poland = 6,540,000
5. Japan = 3,365,900
6. Dutch East Indies = 3,311,500
7. British India = 2,087,000
8. Indochina = 1,500,000
9. Yugoslavia = 1,032,000
10. Hungary = 560,000
11. Philippines = 557,000
12. Korea = 533,000
13. France = 523,369
14. Italy = 510,000
15. Greece = 507,000
16. Romania = 500,000
17. British Empire = 439,300
18. USA = 418,500
19. United Kingdom = 363,360
20. Czechoslovakia = 355,000
21. Netherlands = 210,000
22. Ethiopia = 100,000
23. Finland = 95,000
24. Belgium = 88,000
25. South Pacific Mandate = 57,000
26. Timor (Portugal) = 50,000

1,500,000 deaths
1,000,000 deaths
500,000 deaths
100,000 deaths

LOSSES BY PERCENTAGE OF THE POPULATION IN 1939 ■ Military losses ■ Civilian losses **XX%** military losses - XX% civilian losses / **XX% of the population in 1939**

1. South Pacific Mandate 100% / **44.88% of population**
2. Poland 3.67% - 96.33% / **18.77%**
3. USSR 44.22% - 55.78% / **14.8%**
4. Third Reich 61.90% - 38.1% / **11.05%**
5. Timor (Portugal) 100% / **10.42%**
6. Greece 6.9% - 93.1% / **7.02%**
7. Yugoslavia 43.43% - 56.57% / **6.63%**
8. Indochina (France) 100% / **6.17%**
9. Hungary 53.35% - 46.65% / **6.13%**
10. Dutch East Indies 0.35% - 99.65% / **4.77%**
11. Japan 76.23% - 23.77% / **4.72%**
12. Philippines 10.23% - 88.77% / **3.48%**
13. Romania 60% - 40% / **3.13%**
14. China 20% - 80% / **2.9%**
15. Albania 100% / **2.8%**
16. Finland 97.89% - 2.11% / **2.57%**
17. Czechoslovakia 9.86% - 90.14% / **2.43%**
18. Netherlands 3.19% - 96.81% / **2**

directly exposed to combat (such as the merchant navy or the US Coast Guard), and whether they are based on an aggregation of previously established figures or on broad demographic research. For this reason, estimates can vary significantly, even widely as time passes by and further research is carried out.

Finally, apart from deaths directly attributable to combat, forced labour and related crimes, indirect excess mortality due to deprivation, famine and disease caused by the war is even more difficult to determine and quantify for each country and can be recorded in different ways. Although the 'conventional' toll of the Second World War has long been estimated at around 40 to 50 million deaths, we now know that if it is extended, especially in Asia and Africa, to include indirect victims of wartime conditions, the total is actually over 75 million. In any event, that figure represents around 3.5% of the world's population in 1940. If this percentage were applied to the current global population, a war on that scale would claim over 200 million victims.

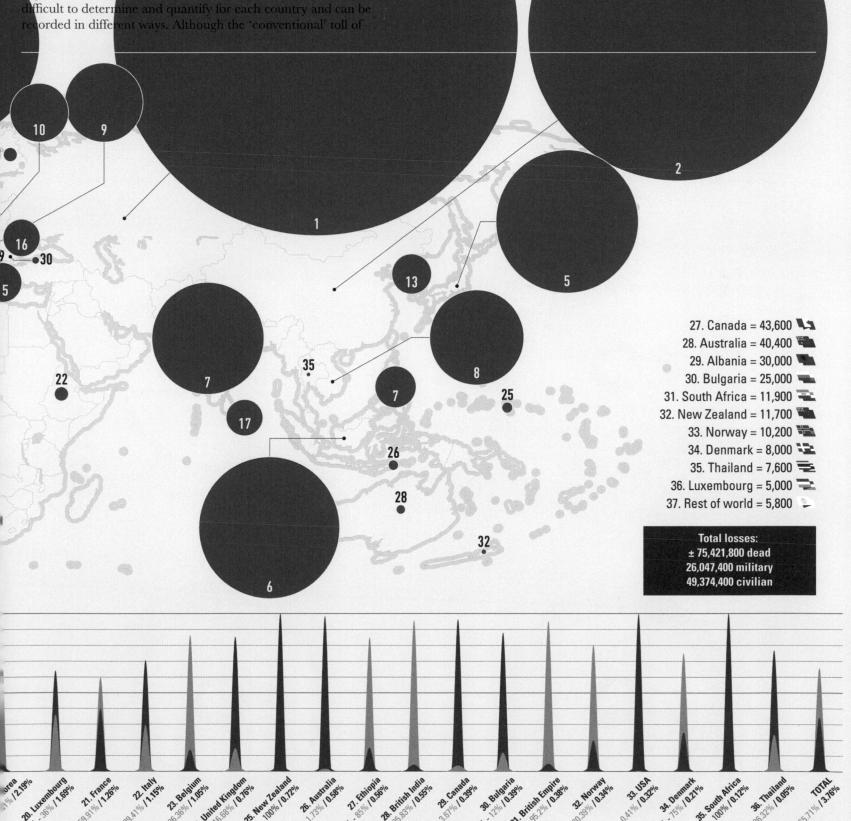

27. Canada = 43,600
28. Australia = 40,400
29. Albania = 30,000
30. Bulgaria = 25,000
31. South Africa = 11,900
32. New Zealand = 11,700
33. Norway = 10,200
34. Denmark = 8,000
35. Thailand = 7,600
36. Luxembourg = 5,000
37. Rest of world = 5,800

Total losses:
± 75,421,800 dead
26,047,400 military
49,374,400 civilian

1 • MILITARY LOSSES

The definition of 'military losses' calls for a certain amount of explanation, because the term can sometimes create confusion and lead to serious errors in assessment and comparison. In fact, it covers all serving troops placed temporarily or permanently out of action: killed, seriously or slightly wounded, suffering from disease or trauma, or captured by the enemy (if their fate is unknown, they are counted as 'missing'). Permanent losses are soldiers who cannot be returned to service even after a period of treatment or rest: in addition to those killed, this includes the permanently disabled and other categories invalided out under schemes that vary considerably at different times and in different armed forces. In 1945, the German army, in its final days, lined up battalions of convalescents for the desperate defence of the Reich, a concept that would have been unthinkable in the US army, for instance. A distinction is also made between losses in combat and in the combat zone and losses through accident, disease and suicide outside of those zones.

The casualty figures for D-Day in Normandy, which have been further adjusted in recent years, reflect these distortions. Over 10,000 Allied soldiers fell on 6 June 1944, but only some of those (fewer than 3,000) could be counted among the dead. Most of the others were rescued, treated or in some cases taken prisoner. To take the overall US figures as an example, losses for the whole of the war totalled over a million with all categories included, but the number of deaths was a little over 400,000 and the number actually killed in combat 292,000. All of these factors, as well as differences in recording methods between nations and territorial changes, result in sizeable and frequent distortions in the figures, even those produced by the most reliable research.

Taking into account these clarifications and reservations, with over 25 million killed, the military toll of the Second World War is undoubtedly greater than that of the First World War (with a total of 10 million dead), but breaks down very differently. France, which had lost nearly 1.5 million of its men of fighting age in the First World War, suffered comparatively less in demographic terms (about 200,000 dead), while the figures for Germany and the USSR were much higher than those for 1914–18. More than 5 million Germans and around 11 million Soviets serving the military were lost, compared with around 2 million in the Second Reich and the same number in the Russian Empire in the previous war. China and Japan, which had been absent or virtually so from the balance sheets for the Great War, lost perhaps 3 and 2.5 million soldiers respectively. In view of the disparate and incomplete sources and the chaos of the civil war that followed, it is in fact impossible to determine Chinese casualty figures with any accuracy. In any event, between the four of them, the USSR, Germany, China and Japan suffered the greatest military losses in the Second World War, many more than the other combatants in scale if not as a proportion of the population. Britain and its colonies, despite their sacrifices, suffered relatively few military losses and the United States, at least, hardly any within the civilian population.

1. Japan: 2,565,878

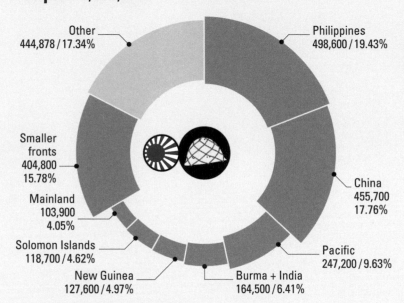

Other
444,878 / 17.34%

Philippines
498,600 / 19.43%

Smaller fronts
404,800
15.78%

Mainland
103,900
4.05%

Solomon Islands
118,700 / 4.62%

New Guinea
127,600 / 4.97%

Burma + India
164,500 / 6.41%

Pacific
247,200 / 9.63%

China
455,700
17.76%

2. UK & Commonwealth: 516,179   — UK   Dominions   ■ Empire

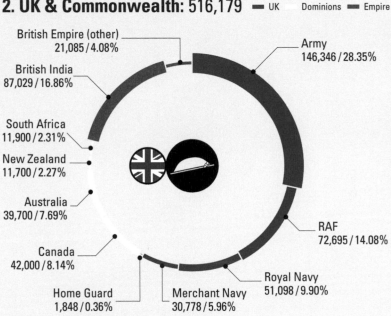

British Empire (other)
21,085 / 4.08%

Army
146,346 / 28.35%

British India
87,029 / 16.86%

South Africa
11,900 / 2.31%

New Zealand
11,700 / 2.27%

Australia
39,700 / 7.69%

Canada
42,000 / 8.14%

Home Guard
1,848 / 0.36%

Merchant Navy
30,778 / 5.96%

Royal Navy
51,098 / 9.90%

RAF
72,695 / 14.08%

3. Yugoslavia: 451,000

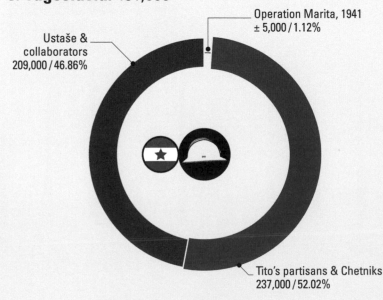

Ustaše & collaborators
209,000 / 46.86%

Operation Marita, 1941
± 5,000 / 1.12%

Tito's partisans & Chetniks
237,000 / 52.02%

4. USA: 416,837

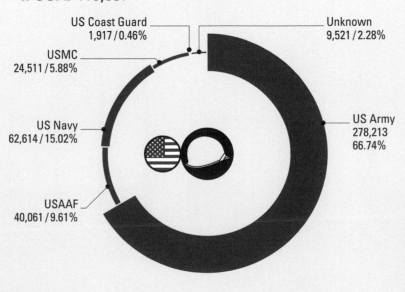

US Coast Guard
1,917 / 0.46%

Unknown
9,521 / 2.28%

USMC
24,511 / 5.88%

US Navy
62,614 / 15.02%

US Army
278,213
66.74%

USAAF
40,061 / 9.61%

5. Italy: 360,000

SS / RSI
13,021 / 3.62%

Blackshirts
10,006 / 2.78%

Partisans
15,197 / 4.22%

Unknown
10,787 / 3%

Army
246,432
68.45%

Askaris + colonies
20,000 / 5.56%

Air Force
13,210 / 3.67%

Navy
31,347 / 8.78%

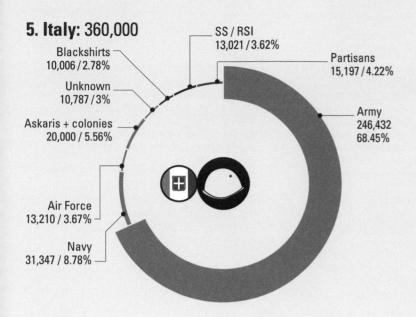

6. Romania: 296,648

Allies (44–45)
21,035 / 7.09%

Axis (41–44)
72,291 / 24.37%

Prisoners in USSR
203,322 / 68.54%

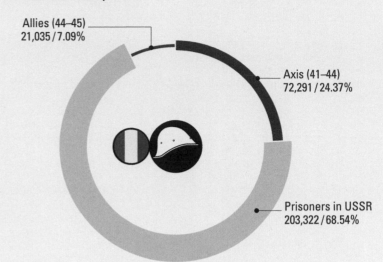

7. Poland: 239,000

Allies
42,000 / 17.57%

1939
66,000 / 27.62%

Resistance
100,000 / 41.84%

Katyn
massacre
19,000 / 7.95%

Prisoners
12,000 / 5.02%

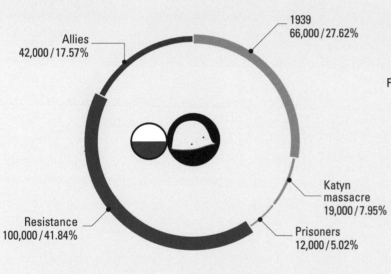

8. France: 218,103

Militia
4,333 / 1.9%

SS + LVF
8,000 / 3.7%

1939–40
65,000 / 29.7%

Forced conscripts
32,000 / 14.6%

Liberation Army
27,570 / 12.6%

Prisoners
45,000 / 20.6%

Resistance
33,000 / 15.4%

Free French
3,200 / 1.5%

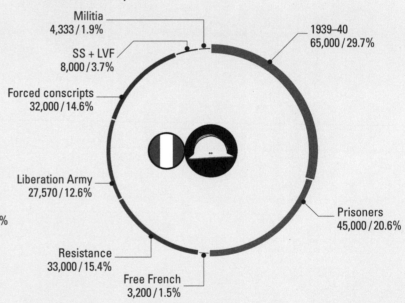

9. Finland: 93,000

Unknown
9,760 / 10.49%

Prisoners
403 / 0.43%

SS
256 / 0.28%

1944–45
1,036 / 1.11%

1939–40
22,830 / 24.55%

1941–44
58,715 / 63.13%

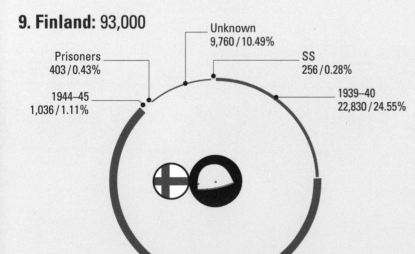

10. Greece: 35,000

1940–41
13,327 / 38.08%

Resistance
20,573 / 58.78%

Allies (1941–45)
1,100 / 3.14%

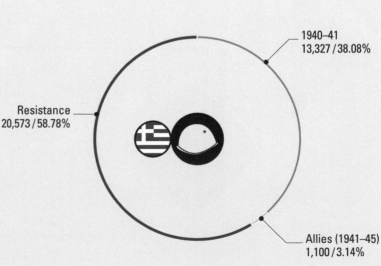

2 • THE YEARS OF CARNAGE: CIVILIAN CASUALTIES

It is a notable and tragic fact of the Second World War that for the first time, civilian losses far exceeded military losses. The most obvious example is of course the Holocaust, the systematic extermination by the Nazis of five to six million European Jews. But it was not only in the Third Reich and Central Europe that mass civilian deaths were directly attributable to the war. The Nazis alone were directly responsible for the slaughter of at least 10 million victims whose deaths were 'racially' motivated, not to mention political deportees and resistance fighters. Apart from the Jewish populations of occupied Europe, several million Eastern and Central European Slavs and Roma (gypsies) were killed and at least 200,000 mentally and physically disabled people put to death. It is estimated that 5 million civilians in Asia, including 3 million Chinese, were direct victims of the brutal Japanese occupation, whose atrocities culminated in the chemical and biological warfare programme of the notorious Unit 731. In the USSR, alongside the millions of victims of the Nazi occupation, at least a million deportees died in the Siberian gulags and 6 million from starvation and chaos in the unoccupied zones.

In addition to the toll of the war itself and internal repression, the war caused high levels of excess mortality, even in regions where there was no fighting. Geographically, civilian losses probably added up to over 15 million victims in the USSR (including excess mortality), at least 12 million in China, including 7 to 8 million direct victims, nearly 6 million in Poland (3.3 million Jews and about 2 million non-Jewish Poles), 3 million in the Dutch East Indies, 2 million in India and 1.5 million in Indochina.

The civilian populations of the defeated countries also paid the price of the war. Three million Germans died as a result of the war or its immediate aftermath (e.g. displaced populations) and nearly one million Japanese also died, mainly as victims of American bombing.

These are illustrative figures based on the most recent studies, although they are open to debate and cannot be considered complete or definitive. They must be viewed (the highest figures in particular) as horrifying orders of magnitude, given the present stage of knowledge and research.

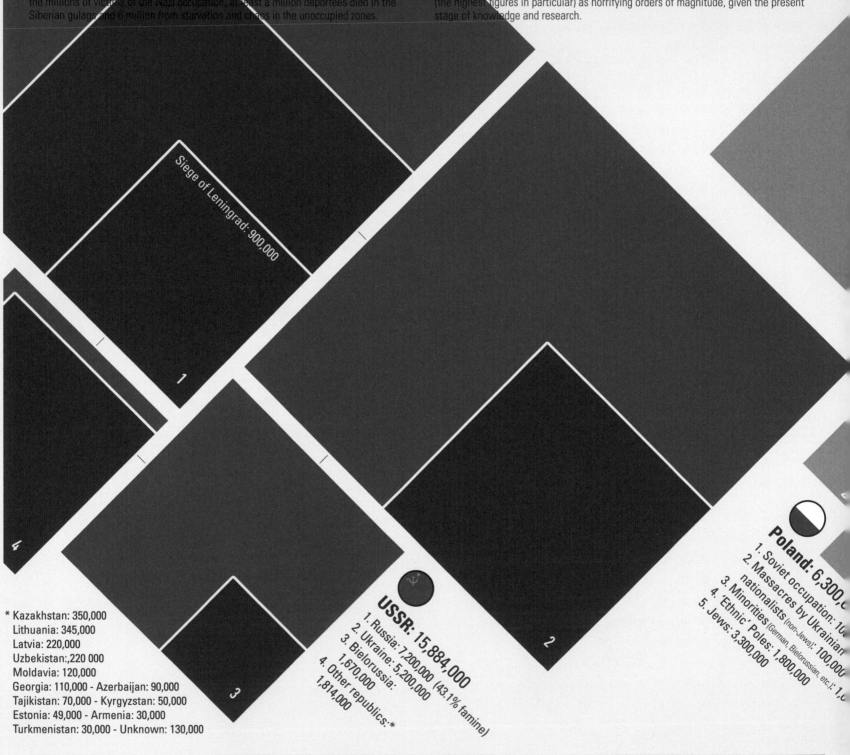

Siege of Leningrad: 900,000

* Kazakhstan: 350,000
Lithuania: 345,000
Latvia: 220,000
Uzbekistan:,220 000
Moldavia: 120,000
Georgia: 110,000 - Azerbaijan: 90,000
Tajikistan: 70,000 - Kyrgyzstan: 50,000
Estonia: 49,000 - Armenia: 30,000
Turkmenistan: 30,000 - Unknown: 130,000

USSR: 15,884,000
1. Russia: 7,200,000
2. Ukraine: 5,200,000
3. Bielorussia: 1,670,000 (43.1% famine)
4. Other republics:* 1,814,000

Poland: 6,300,0
1. Soviet occupation: 10
2. Massacres by Ukrainian nationalists: 100,00
3. Minorities (German, Bielorussian, etc.): 1,0
4. Minorities (German, Bielorussian, etc.): 1,0
5. Jews: 3,300,000

SOURCES: 1. Offices of national statistics (e.g. US Census Bureau) • 2. Government history archives (e.g. Service Historique de la Défense, France) • 3. National specialist commission reports (e.g. *Blackbook of the Occupation*, Athens, 2006, for Greece) • 4. Tamás Stark, *Hungary's Human Losses in World War II*, Uppsala, 1995 • 5. Michael Clodfelter, *Warfare and Armed Conflicts: A Statistical Reference to Casualty and Other Figures*, Jefferson, NC, 1992 • 6. G. F. Krivosheev (ed.), *Soviet Casualties and Combat Losses in the Twentieth Century*, London, 1997 • 7. John Keegan, *The Second World War*, London, 2011 • 8. Rüdiger

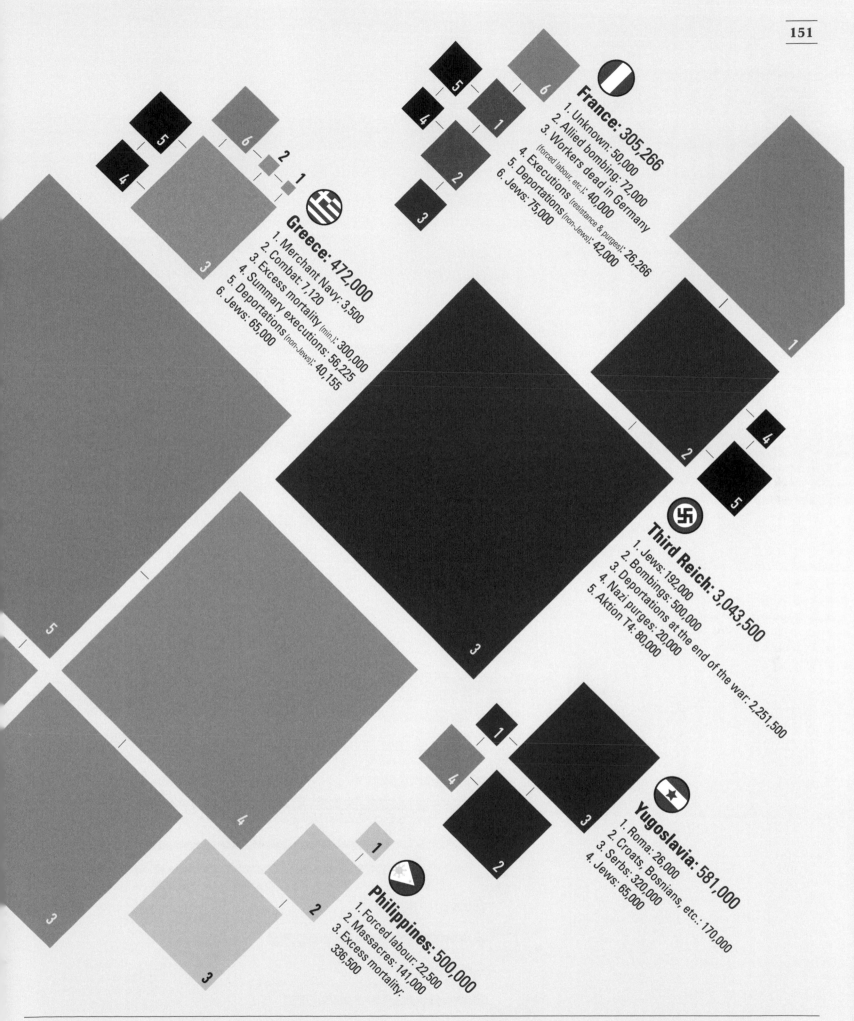

France: 305,266
1. Unknown: 50,000
2. Allied bombing: 72,000
3. Workers dead in Germany (forced labour, etc.): 40,000
4. Executions (resistance & purges): 26,266
5. Deportations (non-Jews): 42,000
6. Jews: 75,000

Greece: 472,000
1. Merchant Navy: 3,500
2. Combat: 7,120
3. Excess mortality (min.): 300,000
4. Summary executions: 56,225
5. Deportations (non-Jews): 40,155
6. Jews: 65,000

Third Reich: 3,043,500
1. Jews: 192,000
2. Bombings: 500,000
3. Deportations at the end of the war: 2,251,500
4. Nazi purges: 20,000
5. Aktion T4: 80,000

Yugoslavia: 581,000
1. Roma: 26,000
2. Croats, Bosnians, etc.: 170,000
3. Serbs: 320,000
4. Jews: 65,000

Philippines: 500,000
1. Forced labour: 22,500
2. Massacres: 141,000
3. Excess mortality: 336,500

Overmans, *Deutsche militärische Verluste im Zweiten Weltkrieg*, Munich, 2004 • 9. Martin Gilbert (ed.), *The Routledge Atlas of the Second World War*, London, 2009 • 10. Jean-François Muracciole & Guillaume Piketty (eds.), *Encyclopédie de la Seconde Guerre mondiale*, Paris, 2015 • 11. Jean-Luc Leleu, Françoise

Passera, Jean Quellien & Michel Daeffler (eds.), *La France pendant la Seconde Guerre mondiale, Atlas historique*, Paris, 2010.

THE REICH'S MILITARY LOSSES

German military losses totalled 5.3 million deaths, compared with the 2 million soldiers killed between 1914 and 1918. This total does not include around 30,000 foreign volunteers who died fighting for the Germans. Two facts stand out. Two-thirds of those killed were fighting the Red Army and half died in the last twelve months of the conflict, with the highest figures between January and April 1945 (10,000 every day). The total of Afrika Korps deaths over a 27-month period were less than those suffered by the Army Group Centre during the first three days of Operation Bagration, the Soviet offensive in the summer of 1944. Unsurprisingly the army accounted for four-fifths of total losses, due to its massive deployment in the East and its dominant role in the Wehrmacht. The percentage of losses among flight and U-boat crews was also very high, rising from 1943 onwards.

The age groups most affected, over 40% of deaths, were those born in 1919 and 1920, i.e. young men between the ages of 20 and 25. In all, 16.8% of Germans of fighting age, i.e. those born between 1900 and 1928, died in the conflict.

The massive number of prisoners taken by the Allies, 11 million, was purely due to the fact that the whole territory of the Reich was occupied and 100% of its military apparatus destroyed. Here again, the figures were overwhelming in the final year, when over two-thirds of the prisoners were taken. It might seem surprising that the Soviets only took 28% of the prisoners when they consistently faced 60% of the German forces. Everything was played out over the final three months, with many surrendering in the West while troops in the East were killed or escaped to give themselves up to the Americans. Over 12% of German prisoners in Soviet gulags never returned. This high figure was mainly due to forced labour and appalling living conditions, although these were no worse than those of most of the Soviet population.

1 • GERMAN MILITARY CASUALTIES

Annual losses followed a simple pattern. The number of deaths rose as the war progressed. More people were killed in the last four months of the war than in its first four years. Comparing branches of the armed forces, the death toll was highest in the SS, at 34.86% of troops, although the figure for the army was close (30.9%). The Russian front was by far the most deadly. The most lethal periods were, in order, January to March 1945 (the Red Army's winter offensive), June to August 1944 (the summer offensive) and December 1942 to February 1943 (Stalingrad). Half of all those killed in the East died in those nine months.

COMPARATIVE LOSSES = 5,318,731 dead

By year:

1939–40 -1.92% | 1941 6.7% | 1942 10.75% | 1943 15.27% | 1944 33.88% | 1945 (4 months) 28.95% | 1946 - 2.53%

By branch: Navy 2.6%   Volkssturm 1.47%   Police 1.18%   Flak / Hitler Youth / SA etc. 1.71%

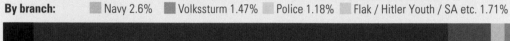

SS 5.9%   Army 79.01%   Luftwaffe 8.14%

By troops deployed (exc. Volkssturm/police/paramilitary groups): 18,200,000 total

Waffen SS: 900,000 total / 313,749 dead   Navy: 1,200,000 total / 138,429 dead

Army: 13,600,000 total 4,202,230 dead   Luftwaffe: 2,500,000 432,706 dead

2 • GERMANY'S PRISONERS OF WAR 1939–45

Fewer than 0.7% of the Germans held prisoner by the British and Americans died in captivity. The number rose to 3.62% for those held by the French, a number of whom were assigned to perform dangerous labour.

PRISONERS OF WAR

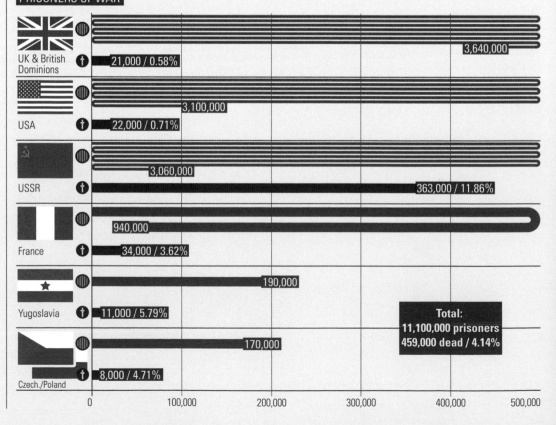

UK & British Dominions — 3,640,000 — 21,000 / 0.58%

USA — 3,100,000 — 22,000 / 0.71%

USSR — 3,060,000 — 363,000 / 11.86%

France — 940,000 — 34,000 / 3.62%

Yugoslavia — 190,000 — 11,000 / 5.79%

Czech./Poland — 170,000 — 8,000 / 4.71%

Total: 11,100,000 prisoners 459,000 dead / 4.14%

0   100,000   200,000   300,000   400,000   500,000

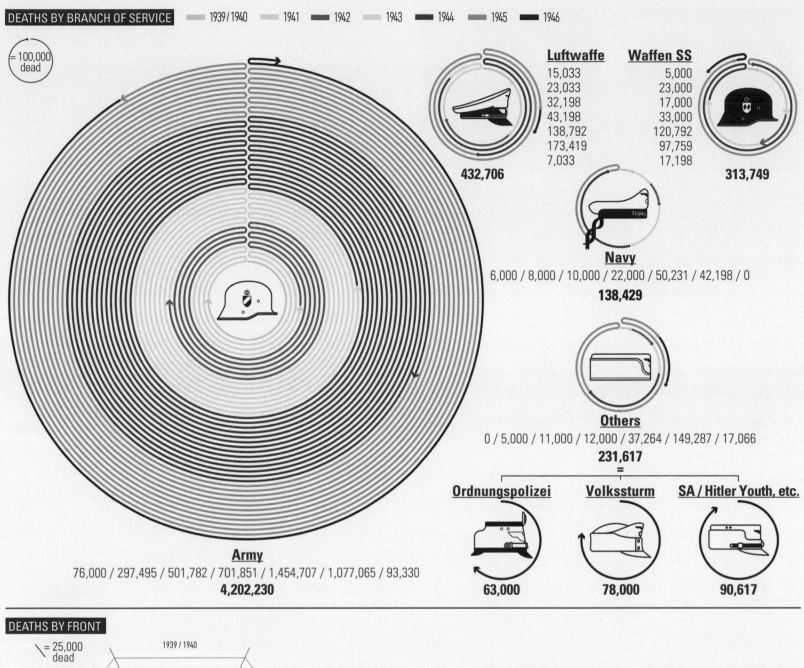

DEATHS BY BRANCH OF SERVICE

■ 1939/1940 ■ 1941 ■ 1942 ■ 1943 ■ 1944 ■ 1945 ■ 1946

= 100,000 dead

Luftwaffe
15,033
23,033
32,198
43,198
138,792
173,419
7,033
432,706

Waffen SS
5,000
23,000
17,000
33,000
120,792
97,759
17,198
313,749

Navy
6,000 / 8,000 / 10,000 / 22,000 / 50,231 / 42,198 / 0
138,429

Others
0 / 5,000 / 11,000 / 12,000 / 37,264 / 149,287 / 17,066
231,617
=

Ordnungspolizei
63,000

Volkssturm
78,000

SA / Hitler Youth, etc.
90,617

Army
76,000 / 297,495 / 501,782 / 701,851 / 1,454,707 / 1,077,065 / 93,330
4,202,230

DEATHS BY FRONT

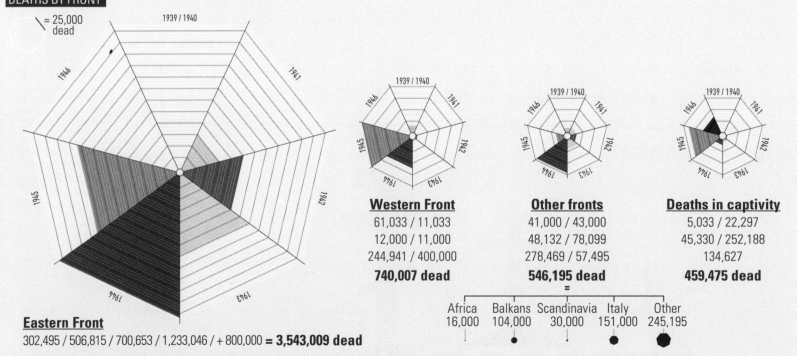

\ = 25,000 dead

Eastern Front
302,495 / 506,815 / 700,653 / 1,233,046 / + 800,000 = **3,543,009 dead**

Western Front
61,033 / 11,033
12,000 / 11,000
244,941 / 400,000
740,007 dead

Other fronts
41,000 / 43,000
48,132 / 78,099
278,469 / 57,495
546,195 dead
=

Deaths in captivity
5,033 / 22,297
45,330 / 252,188
134,627
459,475 dead

Africa 16,000
Balkans 104,000
Scandinavia 30,000
Italy 151,000
Other 245,195

SOURCES: 1. Rüdiger Overmans, *Deutsche militärische Verluste im Zweiten Weltkrieg*, Munich, 2004.

SOVIET MILITARY LOSSES

How many of those who served in the Red Army and Navy died in what the Russians termed the 'Great Patriotic War'? It was not until the end of its lifespan that the Soviet government agreed to open up the archives on this explosive issue. The most comprehensive survey was published by General Grigori F. Krivosheev in 1993 when Boris Yeltsin was president. Although often criticized, this work has not so far been superseded and it is still the most reliable data set. The archives themselves are incomplete. In the chaos of the initial defeats, losses were not recorded and the fate of hundreds of thousands of deserters remains unknown.

Whatever the true figures, assuming they can be determined one day, the Red Army suffered a dramatic drain on manpower, as can be seen from its total definitive losses, which were at least twice those of the Axis forces they were fighting. Soviet losses also remained high up to the very last day. There were many reasons for this, but the major one was the contempt for human life expressed by every aspect of the Stalinist system. The end was always seen to justify the means. Officers, themselves ruled by fear, launched many pointless frontal attacks, and not just by penal battalions from which very few of their 422,000 convicts returned. Like their Tsarist predecessors, they often preferred to send in waves of troops, rather than moving and coordinating fire. The lack of training, a major scourge of the Red Army, meant that the infantry had very little chance of survival in the hell of the mechanized battlefield.

Several million prisoners in Nazi camps also died from hunger, cold and disease or were shot, and this is not counting Jews, political officials and wounded troops who died or were killed as soon as they were captured. Inadequate investment in the health system, constant hunger and lack of hygiene also accounted for the high death rate in hospitals from disease or the effects of an injury. Alcoholism and violent behaviour accounted for a rate of lethal accidents higher than in any other army. Finally, the NKVD shot ten times more people than the Wehrmacht. No other army, even in Asia, suffered as much.

1 • SOVIET MILITARY CASUALTIES

The first eighteen months of the war were the bloodiest for the Red Army. It also lost a huge number of prisoners in Operation Barbarossa in 1941, the Kharkov and Crimea disasters in 1942 and the Battle of Stalingrad. Even with their numerical and material superiority in 1944 and 1945, the Soviets still suffered losses on a par with those of their enemy. The very short Manchurian campaign against the Japanese seemed like a military parade by comparison.

Unsurprisingly, the peasant infantry paid the highest price. But the tank crews also suffered. Of the 403,772 armoured troops trained by the Red Army, 310,487 were killed along with 96,500 tanks and field guns lost in the fighting.

LOSSES BY BRANCH OF SERVICE AND UNIT

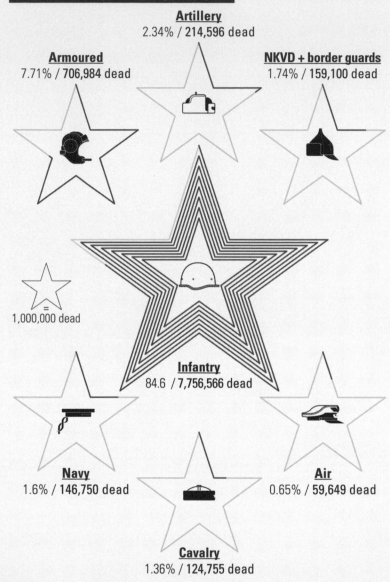

Artillery
2.34% / 214,596 dead

Armoured
7.71% / 706,984 dead

NKVD + border guards
1.74% / 159,100 dead

=
1,000,000 dead

Infantry
84.6 / 7,756,566 dead

Navy
1.6% / 146,750 dead

Air
0.65% / 59,649 dead

Cavalry
1.36% / 124,755 dead

SOVIET MILITARY LOSSES, 1941–45

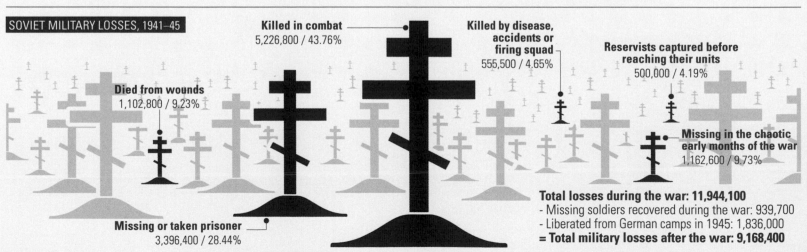

Killed in combat
5,226,800 / 43.76%

Killed by disease, accidents or firing squad
555,500 / 4.65%

Reservists captured before reaching their units
500,000 / 4.19%

Died from wounds
1,102,800 / 9.23%

Missing in the chaotic early months of the war
1,162,600 / 9.73%

Missing or taken prisoner
3,396,400 / 28.44%

Total losses during the war: 11,944,100
- Missing soldiers recovered during the war: 939,700
- Liberated from German camps in 1945: 1,836,000
= **Total military losses after the war: 9,168,400**

MILITARY LOSSES PER QUARTER (DEAD, MISSING, PRISONERS)

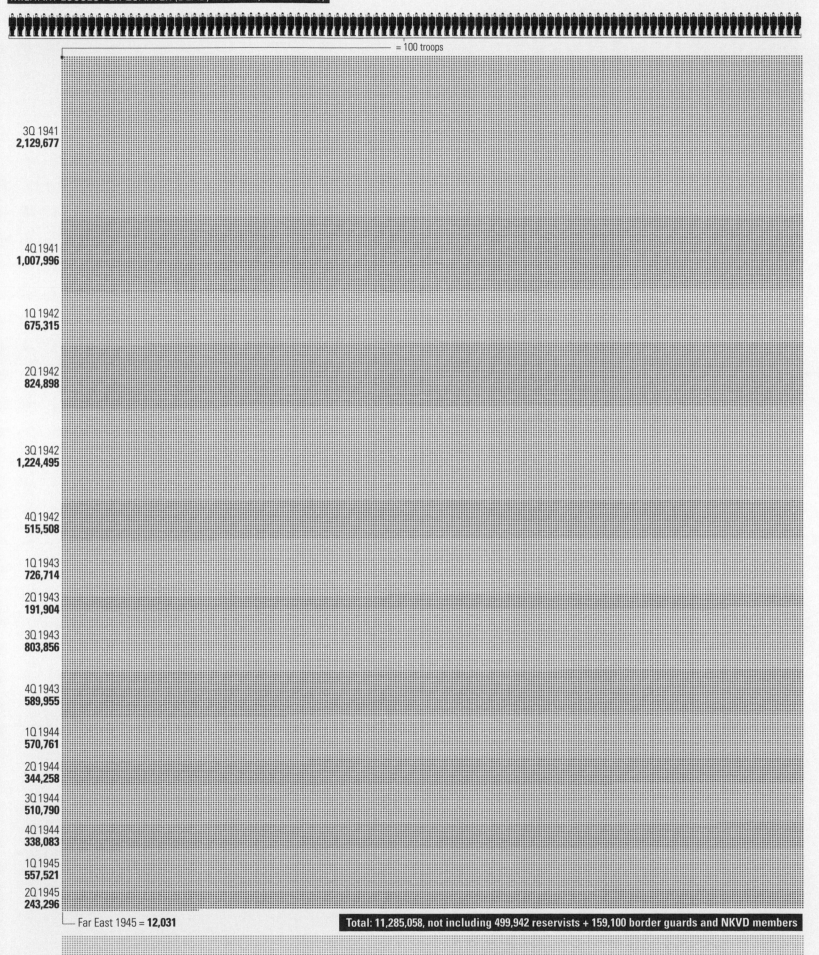

= 100 troops

3Q 1941
2,129,677

4Q 1941
1,007,996

1Q 1942
675,315

2Q 1942
824,898

3Q 1942
1,224,495

4Q 1942
515,508

1Q 1943
726,714

2Q 1943
191,904

3Q 1943
803,856

4Q 1943
589,955

1Q 1944
570,761

2Q 1944
344,258

3Q 1944
510,790

4Q 1944
338,083

1Q 1945
557,521

2Q 1945
243,296

Far East 1945 = **12,031**

Total: 11,285,058, not including 499,942 reservists + 159,100 border guards and NKVD members

Total US losses for entire conflict = **416,837 dead** / 3.61%

2 • FEMALE CASUALTIES

88% of Soviet servicewomen were recruited in 1942 and 1943 when the manpower crisis was at its most acute, but few were involved in combat. Casualties were mostly telephonists, nurses, drivers, secretaries and traffic controllers assigned to units at the front.

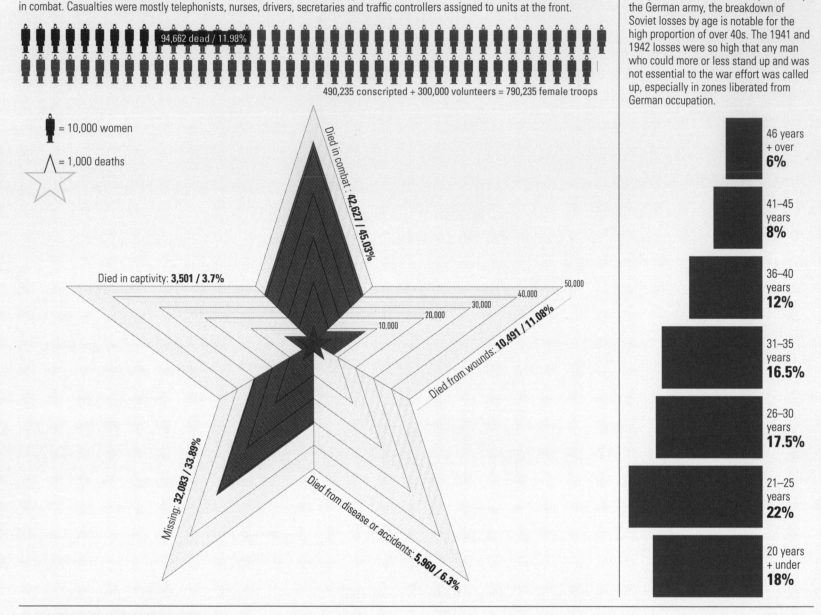

94,662 dead / 11.98%

490,235 conscripted + 300,000 volunteers = 790,235 female troops

♦ = 10,000 women

△ = 1,000 deaths

Died in combat: **42,627 / 45.03%**

Died in captivity: **3,501 / 3.7%**

10,000 · 20,000 · 30,000 · 40,000 · 50,000

Died from wounds: **10,491 / 11.08%**

Missing: **32,083 / 33.89%**

Died from disease or accidents: **5,960 / 6.3%**

3 • LOSSES BY AGE GROUP

Compared with other armies, particularly the German army, the breakdown of Soviet losses by age is notable for the high proportion of over 40s. The 1941 and 1942 losses were so high that any man who could more or less stand up and was not essential to the war effort was called up, especially in zones liberated from German occupation.

46 years + over **6%**

41–45 years **8%**

36–40 years **12%**

31–35 years **16.5%**

26–30 years **17.5%**

21–25 years **22%**

20 years + under **18%**

4 • LOSSES BY NATIONALITY

It is difficult to compare the percentage of military losses by nationality and the proportion that each nationality represented of the Soviet population as a whole. The 1939 census was rigged and little is known about the ethnic and linguistic backgrounds of the 20 million citizens recruited between 1939 and 1941. It can nonetheless be said that, since Russians represented 56% of the Soviet population, Russian soldiers proportionately paid a higher price than others. Note that Jews, who constituted about 2% of the Soviet population, were considered a separate nationality according to Soviet passport classifications.

1	2	3	4	5	6	7	8	9	10
Russians 66.4%	Ukrainians 15.89%	Belorussians 2.91%	Uzbeks 2.16%	Jews 1.64%	Kazakhs 1.44%	Turkmens 1.36%	Armenians 0.96%	Georgians 0.91%	Other nationalities: 6.33%

5 • THE WOUNDED

The sick and wounded of the Red Army were twice as likely to die as those in the Wehrmacht, and four times as likely as those in the British and US armies.

The situation improved in 1943 when supplies of medicines and equipment were received from the USA.

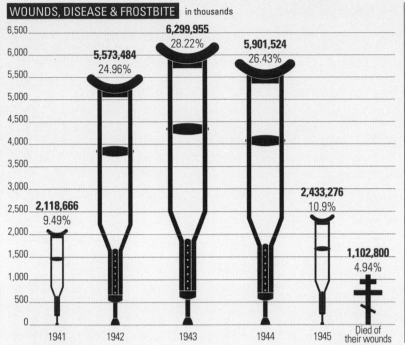

WOUNDS, DISEASE & FROSTBITE in thousands

- **5,573,484** 24.96% — 1941/1942
- **6,299,955** 28.22% — 1943
- **5,901,524** 26.43% — 1944
- **2,118,666** 9.49% — 1941
- **2,433,276** 10.9% — 1945
- **1,102,800** 4.94% — Died of their wounds

NUMBER OF WOUNDS RECEIVED

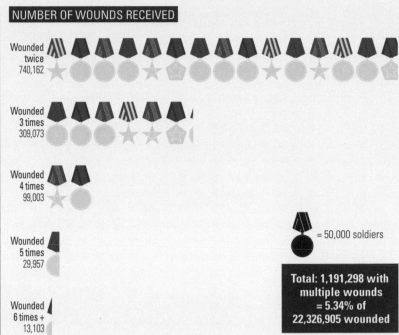

- Wounded twice 740,162
- Wounded 3 times 309,073
- Wounded 4 times 99,003
- Wounded 5 times 29,957
- Wounded 6 times + 13,103

= 50,000 soldiers

Total: 1,191,298 with multiple wounds = 5.34% of 22,326,905 wounded

TYPES OF WOUNDS as % of total

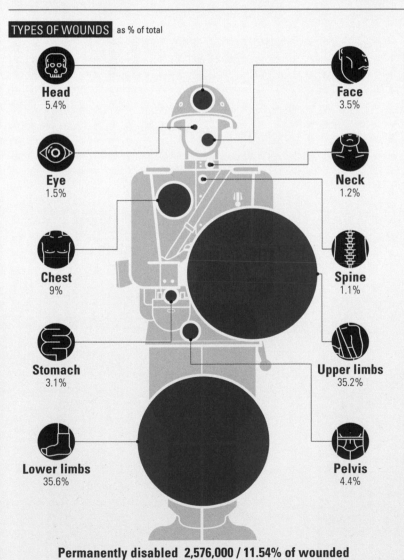

- **Head** 5.4%
- **Face** 3.5%
- **Eye** 1.5%
- **Neck** 1.2%
- **Chest** 9%
- **Spine** 1.1%
- **Stomach** 3.1%
- **Upper limbs** 35.2%
- **Lower limbs** 35.6%
- **Pelvis** 4.4%

Permanently disabled 2,576,000 / 11.54% of wounded

6 • VICTIMS OF REPRESSION

Repression was also fierce. Until Stalingrad, failure was often synonymous with treason and treated as such. Constant political surveillance and a huge number of common law offences accounted for nearly a million convicts, many of whom died in penal battalions.

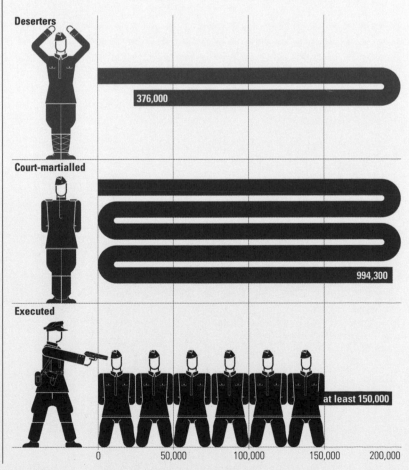

- **Deserters** 376,000
- **Court-martialled** 994,300
- **Executed** at least 150,000

SOURCES: 1. G. F. Krivosheev (ed.), *Soviet Casualties and Combat Losses in the Twentieth Century*, London, 1997.

THE NAZI CONCENTRATION CAMPS

In 1933, the SS, SA and Gestapo opened hundreds of detention centres, mostly makeshift, in which to throw opponents to the Nazi regime. But Himmler wanted to institutionalize and rationalize the system of repression, widen its scope and assign its running to the SS alone. It would also serve the 'educational' function of toughening his men up and preparing them to put the Third Reich's racial and political aims into practice. Dachau, opened in March 1933, was his prototype 'model camp', virtually a small town of 5,000 to 6,000 inhabitants, built from nothing, ruled by terror and run by forced labour. From 1936 onwards, at least one new camp sprang up every

year. In addition to political prisoners, they detained Jehovah's Witnesses, 'social misfits', 'parasites', criminals, gay men, a few priests and then, after *Kristallnacht*, a wave of German and Austrian Jews who were quickly deported elsewhere, apart from the 700 who died from mistreatment. In the summer of 1938, conditions started to deteriorate and the mortality rate increased. Both of these trends increased until 1943, then dropped somewhat, before rocketing up in 1945. The first official execution, attended by Himmler, took place at Buchenwald in June 1938, after an SS guard had been murdered. From then on, violence was uncontained. Once war had

1 • PRISONER NUMBERS IN SS CONCENTRATION CAMPS

The camp population tripled between 1934 and 1937, then tripled again in a few months from 1938 with the arrival of Austrian anti-Nazis and increasingly frequent round-ups of 'social misfits'. In 1939–40 it doubled, mainly due to the opening of Auschwitz I in Poland on 14 June 1940. From 1941 the spread of resistance in Europe and the arrival of millions

of forced labourers caused the camp population to increase tenfold. The biggest rise was in 1943. The convoys from occupied Europe, now liberated, stopped after the summer of 1944, but they were offset by the emptying out of Gestapo prisons, the crackdown after the Warsaw Uprising and in particular the transfer of Jews deported from the East.

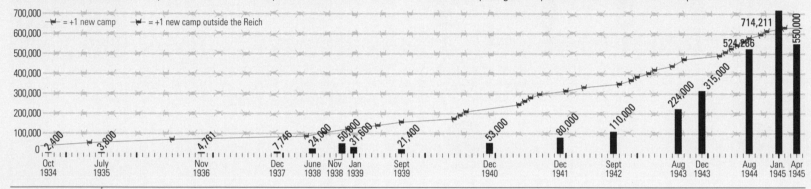

2 • LOCATIONS OF MAJOR CAMPS AND NUMBER OF VICTIMS

The older pre-war camps were by definition all located within the Reich's borders. The largest and most deadly was Auschwitz in Polish Silesia. Like Majdanek, it served a dual role as an 'ordinary' labour camp and a Jewish extermination camp. After autumn 1944,

Auschwitz was gradually wound down and Buchenwald became the largest camp. Like Flössenburg, Mauthausen in Austria owed its location to a nearby granite quarry. The unimaginable harshness of the conditions made the camp the most lethal in the West.

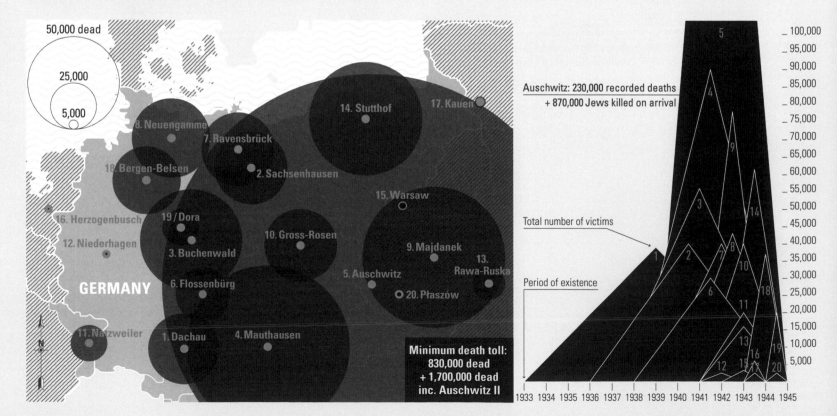

begun, foreigners were imprisoned in increasing numbers: Spanish Republicans, Poles, Czechs, Serbs, Soviets, French, Belgians, Dutch, Greek – nearly 30 different nationalities in all. Medical experiments started, killing or mutilating almost 20,000 prisoners. The first mass executions were carried out on 6,000 mentally and physically ill detainees, then on tens of thousands of Soviet prisoners of war. The periodic 'liquidation' of the weakest prisoners continued, since space had to be made for the waves of new arrivals, who were healthier and could work harder. Overcrowded and further overloaded by the evacuation of sites liberated by the Allies, the camps became

mass death camps in 1945. The distinction between extermination camps and concentration camps was blurred. The population of Bergen-Belsen tripled between 1 January and 15 April 1945, rising to 45,000 prisoners, a third of whom died in March of hunger and disease. Jewish prisoners were now everywhere and although their mortality rate was still the highest, other groups were not far behind. When the Allies arrived in Germany, the camps released their occupants on forced 'death marches' and further hundreds were killed in the panic. A third of the desperate victims who had survived up to this point went missing in that final apocalypse.

3 • THE BUCHENWALD SYSTEM

Buchenwald was the camp with the most dramatic geographical reach, with 132 external camps (out of a total of 560 in the Reich). These acted as 'branches' of the parent camp (explaining the large transfers of deportees). Its massive expansion was due to the mobilization of the German economy for 'total war' and an agreement in September 1942 between Albert Speer and Oswald Pohl, economic head of the SS. Instead of trying to attract industrialists to Buchenwald, the SS began to export its slave labour and set up

work camps close to established factories. This change, which did not apply to Jews, explained the very temporary drop in the camp mortality rate in 1943: Pohl wanted to allow the prisoners a larger calorie intake in order to make them work harder. In 1938, for every 11,000 prisoners there were 500 Kapos, inmates who acted as warders or supervisors in exchange for privileges granted by the SS. Later, there was a much higher proportion of Kapos as the number of SS guards declined steadily.

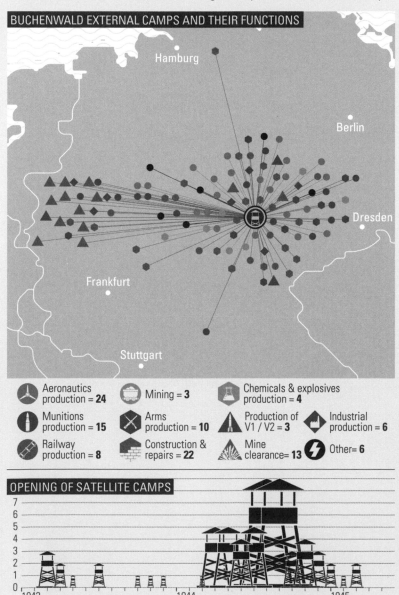

BUCHENWALD EXTERNAL CAMPS AND THEIR FUNCTIONS

- Aeronautics production = **24**
- Mining = **3**
- Chemicals & explosives production = **4**
- Munitions production = **15**
- Arms production = **10**
- Production of V1 / V2 = **3**
- Industrial production = **6**
- Railway production = **8**
- Construction & repairs = **22**
- Mine clearance = **13**
- Other = **6**

OPENING OF SATELLITE CAMPS

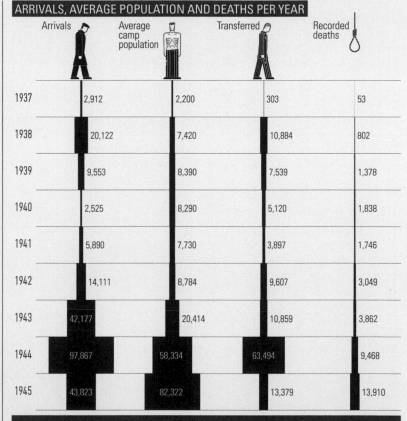

ARRIVALS, AVERAGE POPULATION AND DEATHS PER YEAR

	Arrivals	Average camp population	Transferred	Recorded deaths
1937	2,912	2,200	303	53
1938	20,122	7,420	10,884	802
1939	9,553	8,390	7,539	1,378
1940	2,525	8,290	5,120	1,838
1941	5,890	7,730	3,897	1,746
1942	14,111	8,784	9,607	3,049
1943	42,177	20,414	10,859	3,862
1944	97,867	58,334	63,494	9,468
1945	43,823	82,322	13,379	13,910

Total: at least 56,000 deaths, inc. 748 during liberation of camp, 8,000 Soviet prisoners executed, 1,100 deaths by hanging, 9,000 during final evacuation, 339 women

CAMP POPULATIONS — Czechoslovak / French / Soviet / Polish / Others

	28 August 1942	25 December 1943	15 October 1944
C	0.1%	13%	15%
F	12%	39%	27%
S	12%	20%	20%
P	6%	8%	6%
O	69.9%	20%	32%

SOURCES: 1. Steffen Grimm, *Die SS-Totenkopfverbände im Konzentrationslager Buchenwald*, Hamburg, 2011 • 2. Nikolaus Wachsmann, *KL: A History of the Nazi Concentration Camps*, London & New York, 2015 • 3. http://totenbuch.buchenwald.de/information • 4. Association Française Buchenwald Dora et Kommandos: https://asso-buchenwald-dora.com/

THE HOLOCAUST

When did Hitler or Himmler first come up with the idea of exterminating Europe's Jews? Historians disagree on this. Instead, the two Nazi leaders had multiple ideological, 'racial' and even economic reasons for wanting to get rid of them, using schemes and methods that varied according to circumstances. The original aim was to exclude Jews from the life of the Reich with a policy of extreme apartheid, culminating in emigration. But from 1938, when Germany started its territorial expansion, a growing number of Jews fell under its purview. When war broke out in 1939, it was hardly possible for those masses of human beings to emigrate outside Europe any longer. In 1940, the first steps were taken to confine the largest community, the Poles, inside ghettos, apparently until they could be expelled to the East.

The major turning point in the anti-Jewish policy was the invasion of the Soviet Union on 22 June 1941. The Nazis' aim was to destroy the 'Jewish-Bolshevik' state. A fatal connection was made: Jew = Bolshevik = threat to the security of the conquered territories. Travelling death squads, the *Einsatzgruppen*, backed by SS, police and Wehrmacht units, started executing all Jewish men of an age to carry arms. Himmler and Heydrich issued very vague instructions that were interpreted in different ways by the heads of the *Einsatzgruppen*. There was competition between the teams of killers and between

the leaders and the grassroots, constantly pushing further towards radicalization. In August, they began to slaughter women and children. In October, after the mass killing at Babi Yar, a ravine on the northern edge of Kiev, the final barrier was lifted. Local Jewish communities were exterminated right down to their last members. But the method used to wipe out these 500,000 Soviet Jews in six months was primitive and took place in public, with scattered mass graves. The system was reconfigured for the destruction of the communities in Western and Central Europe. In every country, Jews were hunted down and taken by train far into Poland. Death camps had been built there, equipped with new technology designed for mass murder using carbon monoxide or Zyklon B in gas chambers and vans; the bodies were burned in ditches or crematorium furnaces. In March 1942, convoys of Slovak and French Jews set off at the same time as the ten-times-larger convoys of Polish Jews rounded up in Operation Reinhard. In the summer of 1944, the last remaining large Jewish community in Hungary was wiped out. Jews nonetheless continued to die in their tens of thousands until the last day of the war, both in the Reich's concentration camps to which Himmler forced them to migrate and during the death marches that took place before the camps were liberated by Allied forces. By 1945, over 6 million of Europe's 11.5 million Jews were dead.

1 • EUROPE'S JEWISH POPULATIONS ABSORBED INTO THE 'GREATER REICH'

The expansion of the Third Reich was accompanied by a steep increase in its Jewish population, which rose from 500,000 to over 8 million in under four years. In 1940, Nazi anti-Jewish policy was still vague, wavering between plans to deport Jews to other parts of the world, e.g. the East or Madagascar, or to keep them in improvised ghettoes.

Extermination began in the East in countries where the Wehrmacht had destroyed the framework of the state (occupied Soviet territories, Poland), with the active participation of vassal states (Romania, Slovakia, Croatia) and nationalists (Baltic, Ukrainian). In the West, especially France, the killing of Jews had many supporters in political circles.

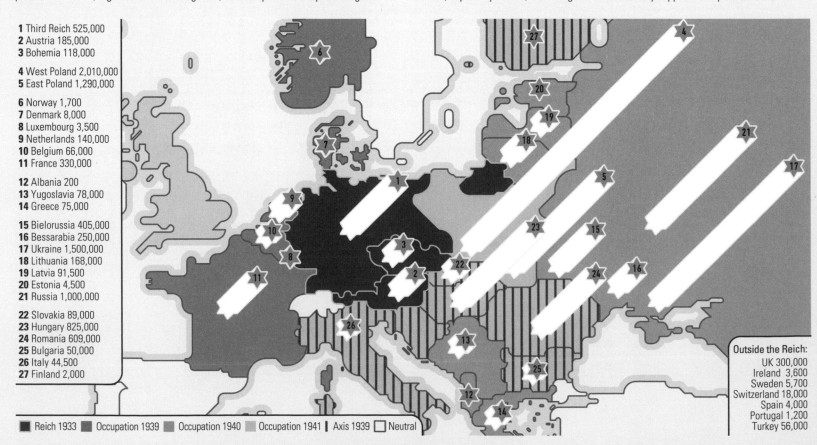

1 Third Reich 525,000
2 Austria 185,000
3 Bohemia 118,000

4 West Poland 2,010,000
5 East Poland 1,290,000

6 Norway 1,700
7 Denmark 8,000
8 Luxembourg 3,500
9 Netherlands 140,000
10 Belgium 66,000
11 France 330,000

12 Albania 200
13 Yugoslavia 78,000
14 Greece 75,000

15 Bielorussia 405,000
16 Bessarabia 250,000
17 Ukraine 1,500,000
18 Lithuania 168,000
19 Latvia 91,500
20 Estonia 4,500
21 Russia 1,000,000

22 Slovakia 89,000
23 Hungary 825,000
24 Romania 609,000
25 Bulgaria 50,000
26 Italy 44,500
27 Finland 2,000

Outside the Reich:
UK 300,000
Ireland 3,600
Sweden 5,700
Switzerland 18,000
Spain 4,000
Portugal 1,200
Turkey 56,000

■ Reich 1933 ■ Occupation 1939 ■ Occupation 1940 ■ Occupation 1941 | Axis 1939 □ Neutral

2 • A CHRONOLOGY OF GENOCIDE

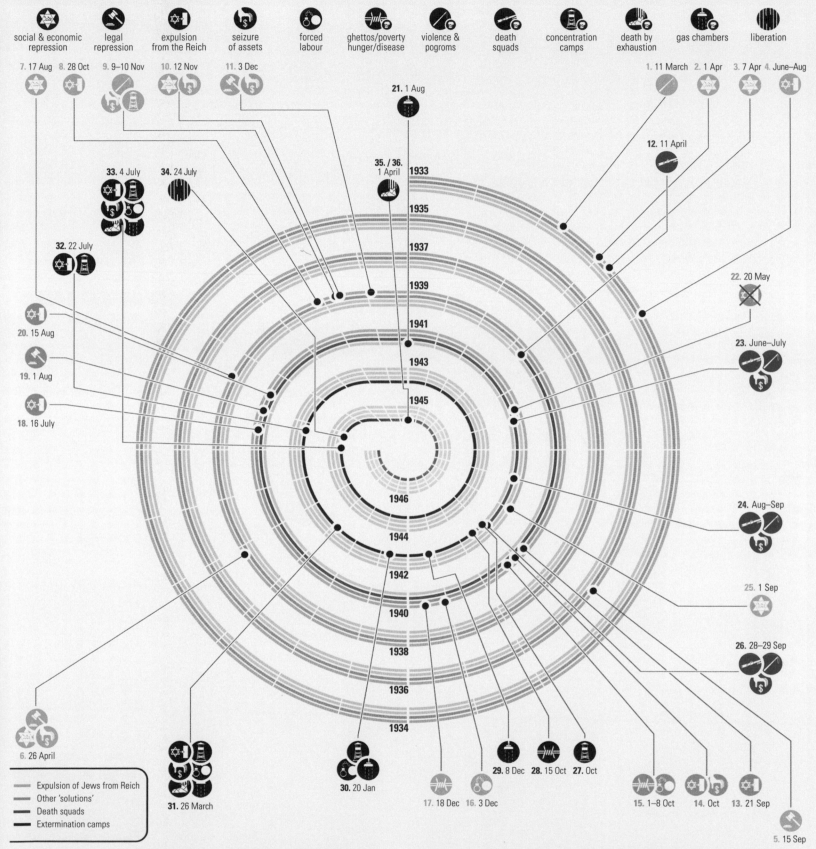

social & economic repression | legal repression | expulsion from the Reich | seizure of assets | forced labour | ghettos/poverty hunger/disease | violence & pogroms | death squads | concentration camps | death by exhaustion | gas chambers | liberation

7. 17 Aug **8.** 28 Oct **9.** 9–10 Nov **10.** 12 Nov **11.** 3 Dec

21. 1 Aug

1. 11 March **2.** 1 Apr **3.** 7 Apr **4.** June–Aug

35. / 36. 1 April

12. 11 April

33. 4 July **34.** 24 July

1933
1935
1937
1939
1941
1943
1945
1946
1944
1942
1940
1938
1936
1934

32. 22 July

22. 20 May

20. 15 Aug

23. June–July

19. 1 Aug

18. 16 July

24. Aug–Sep

25. 1 Sep

26. 28–29 Sep

6. 26 April

29. 8 Dec **28.** 15 Oct **27.** Oct

31. 26 March

30. 20 Jan

17. 18 Dec **16.** 3 Dec

15. 1–8 Oct **14.** Oct **13.** 21 Sep

5. 15 Sep

Expulsion of Jews from Reich
Other 'solutions'
Death squads
Extermination camps

1. Violence begins. 2. Boycotting of Jewish businesses. 3. Jews banned from professions. 4. Agreement with German Zionist Federation, allowing migration to Palestine. 5. Nuremberg Laws: German Jews excluded from civil life. 6. Decree allows seizure of Jewish assets. 7. Forced name changes. 8. Expulsion of 15,000 Polish-born Jews from the Reich. 9. *Kristallnacht*: mass looting, synagogues burned, 30,000 interned in camps. 10. Jews fined one billion marks to pay for *Kristallnacht*. 11. Decree: Jews removed from German economic life. 12. Polish Jews and intellectuals shot by SS *Einsatzgruppen* (50,000 victims). 13. Polish Jews expelled from areas annexed by Germany. 14. Nisko–Lublin plan to expel Austrian and Czech Jews to Poland. 15. Jewish ghettos established in Poland. 16. Forced labour enforced for all German Jews. 17. German Jews placed on starvation rations. 18. Jews expelled from Alsace, Lorraine, Saarland, the Palatinate and Baden into non-occupied France. 19. German racial laws extended to the Polish General Government. 20. Eichmann plan to deport Jews to Madagascar. 21. Start of Aktion T4: 80,000 mentally ill people killed by gas van, a test run for the extermination of the Jews. 22. German

Jews forbidden to emigrate. 23. Mass shootings of Jewish men aged 14 to 65 begin in the occupied USSR, along with dozens of pogroms, aided by local populations (at least 10,000 killed). 24. Mass shootings expanded to include women, children and the elderly; some community members spared. 25. The wearing of yellow star badges is made obligatory. 26. In the wake of the Babi Yar massacre (Kiev), entire Jewish communities are slaughtered. 27. Construction of extermination camps in Poland: Belzec, Majdanek, Chełmno, Auschwitz-Birkenau, Sobibor, Treblinka. 28. Start of deportation of German Jews to the ghettos of Poland, the Baltic countries and Bielorussia. 29. Gas vans used on Jewish communities. 30. Wannsee Conference to plan the wholesale extermination of the Jews. 31. Start of deportation of European Jews to extermination camps; start of deportation of 60,000 Slovakian Jews. 32. Start of deportation of Jews from the Warsaw ghetto. 33. The final large contingent of victims are deported from Hungary (450,000 deaths). 34. The Red Army liberates the first extermination camp, Majdanek. 35. The Red Army liberates Auschwitz. 36. The final death marches take place.

3 • THE ŁÓDŹ GHETTO

Łódź, Poland's second city and an industrial centre, was incorporated into the Reich on 8 November 1939. A campaign of harsh mistreatment, dispossession and terror was intended to force the 230,000 Jews in the city – its name germanized to Litzmannstadt – to migrate to the General Government region of occupied Poland, but its governor-general, Hans Frank, objected to the plan. A makeshift ghetto was therefore set up until a 'solution' was found. In 1940, the Jews of Łódź began to die of hunger after being starved of resources by the German authorities and the city's Germanic environment prevented the operation of a black market. Once again, a temporary 'solution' had to be found. At the instigation of Hans Biebow, a German businessman, and with the backing

of Mordechai Rumkowski, head of the Jewish Council of Elders, the ghetto was turned into a factory, where residents worked day and night in appalling conditions and for starvation wages. The hated Rumkowski managed to preserve an education and health system and an active cultural life, but the revenue from the workshops did little to slow down the rise in mortality and even then, only from 1941. The Łódź ghetto survived until 1944, although the Nazis deported 70,000 of its inhabitants to the extermination camp near Chełmno in 1942, where they were killed by gas vans. The camp was closed in 1943 but reopened in 1944 for another 7,000 Łódź Jews to be killed. Disappointed with the ghetto's 'output', the SS sent its 54,000 survivors straight to Auschwitz.

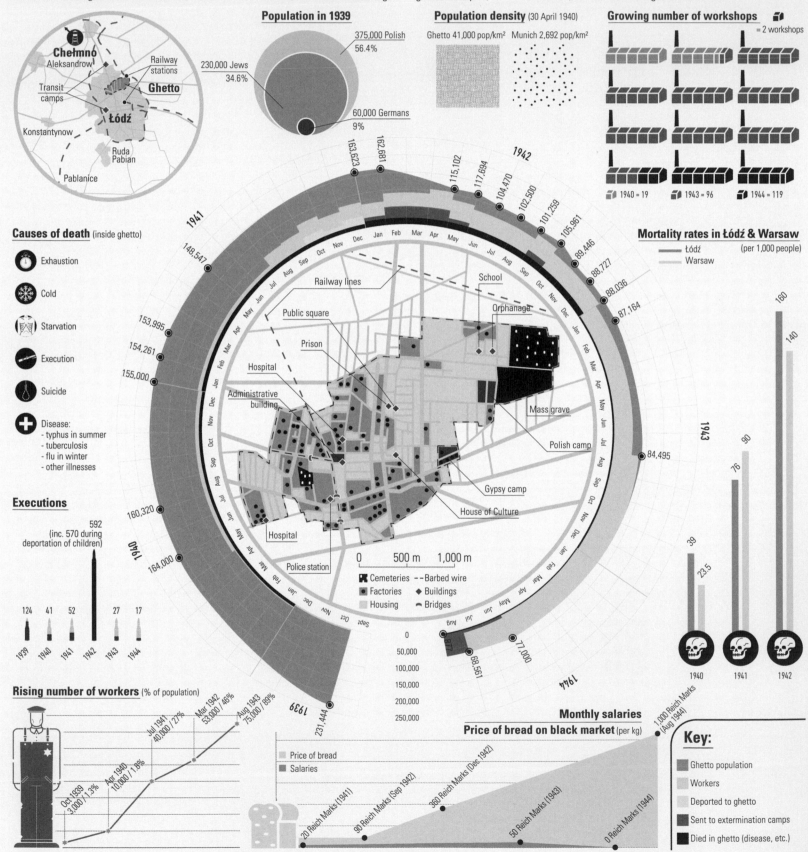

Population in 1939

375,000 Polish 56.4%
230,000 Jews 34.6%
60,000 Germans 9%

Population density (30 April 1940)

Ghetto 41,000 pop/km²   Munich 2,692 pop/km²

Growing number of workshops

= 2 workshops

1940 = 19   1943 = 96   1944 = 119

Causes of death (inside ghetto)

- Exhaustion
- Cold
- Starvation
- Execution
- Suicide
- Disease:
  - typhus in summer
  - tuberculosis
  - flu in winter
  - other illnesses

Executions

124 (1939)   41 (1940)   52 (1941)   592 (inc. 570 during deportation of children) (1942)   27 (1943)   17 (1944)

Rising number of workers (% of population)

Oct 1939 3,000 / 1.3%
Apr 1940 10,000 / 1.8%
Jul 1941 40,000 / 27%
Mar 1942 53,000 / 46%
Aug 1943 75,000 / 89%

Mortality rates in Łódź & Warsaw

Łódź (per 1,000 people)
Warsaw

1940: 39 / 23.5
1941: 76 / 90
1942: 160 / 140

Monthly salaries
Price of bread on black market (per kg)

- Price of bread
- Salaries

20 Reich Marks (1941)
90 Reich Marks (Sep 1942)
360 Reich Marks (Dec 1942)
50 Reich Marks (1943)
0 Reich Marks (1944)
1,000 Reich Marks (Aug 1944)

Key:

- Ghetto population
- Workers
- Deported to ghetto
- Sent to extermination camps
- Died in ghetto (disease, etc.)

Map labels: Chełmno, Aleksandrow, Transit camps, Railway stations, Ghetto, Konstantynow, Łódź, Ruda, Pabian, Pablanice

Central map labels: Railway lines, Public square, Prison, Hospital, Administrative building, School, Orphanage, Mass grave, Polish camp, Gypsy camp, House of Culture, Hospital, Police station

0   500 m   1,000 m

Cemeteries -- Barbed wire
Factories ◆ Buildings
Housing ⌒ Bridges

Extermination camps
Concentration camps
Transit camps
Major ghettos
Major pogroms
Jewish revolts

Countries under German occupation
Areas with Jewish partisan activity
→ Main deportation routes

4 • CAMPS, GHETTOS, POGROMS AND UPRISINGS

The vast majority of the nearly 6 million Jews killed by the Nazis were killed in what historian Timothy Snyder has termed the 'bloodlands', the region of Eastern Europe stretching from the Baltic States to the Black Sea and including most of 1939 Poland, Soviet Bielorussia and Ukraine. It was there that Europe's largest Jewish communities were to be found and there that the removal of all state authority and the existence of traditional anti-Semitism – the cause of many pogroms in the west of the USSR in the summer of 1941 – created the best possible conditions for an extermination policy. Soviet Jews were shot close to home by *Einsatzgruppe* death squads with the backing of the Wehrmacht. The Jews in Bessarabia and Odessa were annihilated by the Romanian

authorities, helped by the army. Polish Jews died of malnutrition and disease in the ghettos. Those who remained were slaughtered in extermination camps close to the largest communities (Łódź/Chełmno, Warsaw/Treblinka, Lublin/Majdanek). Many German, Austrian and Czech Jews were deported and killed on Soviet territory. Most of the Jews from Western Europe, Hungary and Greece were transported by train to the huge Auschwitz-Birkenau camp to be gassed with Zyklon B. On 7 October 1944, several hundred inmates from a *Sonderkommando* work unit planned to blow up one of the four crematorium furnaces at Auschwitz II. This was the most desperate of dozens of revolts, some of which, in the USSR, fed into long-term Jewish resistance.

5 • DEATH SQUADS: THE BLOODY PROGRESS OF *EINSATZGRUPPE* C IN 1941

By 1941, four motorized *Einsatzgruppen* ('task forces'), each made up of a thousand police and SS officers, were deployed at the rear of the Army Groups invading the USSR. They stirred up pogroms and in July executed Jewish men between the ages of 15 and 60, then, in August–September, whole communities of Soviet Jews, including women, children and the sick. This diagram shows the career of *Einsatzgruppe* C, divided into *Sonderkommando* (SK) and *Einsatzkommando* (EK) units. Commanded by Otto Rasch, the squad shot dead 100,000 Ukrainian Jews between July and October 1941. More than 33,000 were massacred in the Babi Yar ravine in Kiev in 48 hours, a horrific record.

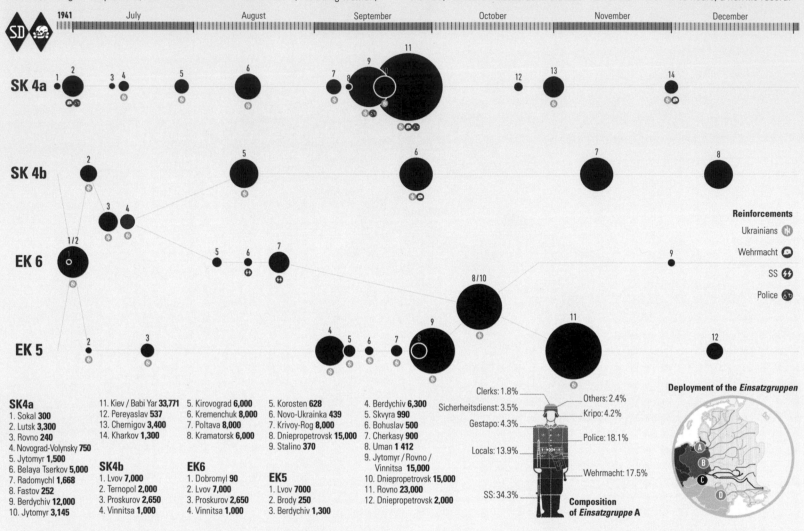

SK4a			
1. Sokal **300**	11. Kiev / Babi Yar **33,771**	5. Kirovograd **6,000**	5. Korosten **628**
2. Lutsk **3,300**	12. Pereyaslav **537**	6. Kremenchuk **8,000**	6. Novo-Ukrainka **439**
3. Rovno **240**	13. Chernigov **3,400**	7. Poltava **8,000**	7. Krivoy-Rog **8,000**
4. Novograd-Volynsky **750**	14. Kharkov **1,300**	8. Kramatorsk **6,000**	8. Dniepropetrovsk **15,000**
5. Jytomyr **1,500**			9. Stalino **370**
6. Belaya Tserkov **5,000**	**SK4b**	**EK6**	
7. Radomychl **1,668**	1. Lvov **7,000**	1. Dobromyl **90**	**EK5**
8. Fastov **252**	2. Ternopol **2,000**	2. Lvov **7,000**	1. Lvov **7000**
9. Berdychiv **12,000**	3. Proskurov **2,650**	3. Proskurov **2,650**	2. Brody **250**
10. Jytomyr **3,145**	4. Vinnitsa **1,000**	4. Vinnitsa **1,000**	3. Berdychiv **1,300**

4. Berdychiv **6,300**
5. Skvyra **990**
6. Bohuslav **500**
7. Cherkasy **900**
8. Uman **1 412**
9. Jytomyr / Rovno / Vinnitsa **15,000**
10. Dniepropetrovsk **15,000**
11. Rovno **23,000**
12. Dniepropetrovsk **2,000**

Reinforcements
Ukrainians
Wehrmacht
SS
Police

Clerks: 1.8%
Others: 2.4%
Sicherheitsdienst: 3.5%
Kripo: 4.2%
Gestapo: 4.3%
Police: 18.1%
Locals: 13.9%
Wehrmacht: 17.5%
SS: 34.3%
Composition of *Einsatzgruppe* A

Deployment of the *Einsatzgruppen*

6 • HOW WERE THEY MURDERED?

Over half of Europe's Jews were killed in gas chambers and vans. The *Einsatzgruppe* shootings in the USSR were the second largest cause of death. In addition, tens of thousands of Jewish soldiers in the Red Army were executed on the spot. Death in the ghettos and concentration camps was slow, caused by hunger, disease, cold, work exhaustion and mistreatment. The bodies of the 100,000 who died in the 1945 death marches were left on the roads and in the trains used in the emergency evacuations of Jewish deportees from the camps in the East and West to the centre of the Reich, where Hitler had hoped to make use of them in hypothetical negotiations with the Allies.

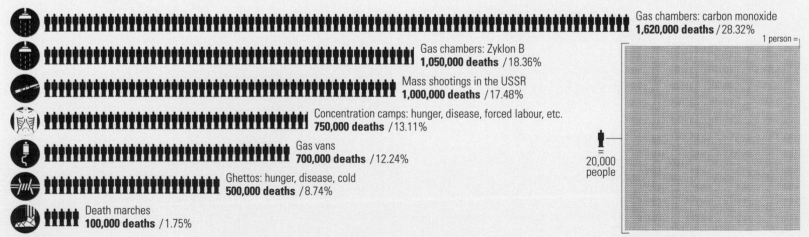

Gas chambers: carbon monoxide
1,620,000 deaths / 28.32%

1 person =

Gas chambers: Zyklon B
1,050,000 deaths / 18.36%

Mass shootings in the USSR
1,000,000 deaths / 17.48%

Concentration camps: hunger, disease, forced labour, etc.
750,000 deaths / 13.11%

Gas vans
700,000 deaths / 12.24%

Ghettos: hunger, disease, cold
500,000 deaths / 8.74%

Death marches
100,000 deaths / 1.75%

20,000 people

SOURCES: 1. I. Trunk, *Łódz Ghetto*, Bloomington, IN, 2006 • 2. L. Dobroszycki, *The Chronicle of the Łódz Ghetto, 1941–1944*, New Haven, CT, 1984 • 3. S. Spector & G. Wigoder (eds.), *The Encyclopedia of Jewish Life Before and During the Holocaust*, New York, 2001 • 4. P. Montague, *Chełmno and the Holocaust*, London, 2012 • 5. L. S. Dawidowicz, *The War Against the Jews, 1933–1945*, Harmondsworth, 1977 • 6. R. Hilberg,

7 • DEATH TOLLS BY COUNTRY: FIGURES AND PERCENTAGES

It has been established that between 5.6 and 5.8 million Jews were killed in the Holocaust, but the proportion of victims varied from country to country. In absolute and relative terms, Polish Jews paid the highest price (apart from those in Albania). It was easier to deport them since they had previously been herded into ghettos. Greek Jews accounted for a high percentage, being heavily concentrated in a single city, Salonika. Baltic Jews suffered from a hostile environment, with nationalist militias helping the Nazis to wipe them out. Large numbers of Dutch Jews lived in Amsterdam and Rotterdam and it was difficult for them to find refuge in their small, flat country, tightly controlled by *Reichskommissar* Arthur Seyss-Inquart. In France, by contrast, the size of the country and the sparseness of the German occupation in rural and mountain areas gave French Jews an advantage and they were actively assisted by thousands of their non-Jewish compatriots. That was much less true of the non-French Jews living in France, who represented two-thirds of the victims. In Italy, Mussolini's later anti-Semitic policies did not have much support and the deportations by the Germans did not start until after the fall of Mussolini in September 1943. Two-thirds of Soviet Jews escaped the *Einsatzgruppen* since they were living in areas not occupied by the Wehrmacht or were able to take refuge there in summer 1941. The relatively small percentages of German and Austrian Jews killed were due to mass emigration between 1933 and 1939.

DEATH TOLL & PERCENTAGE OF JEWISH POPULATION KILLED

Total deaths: 5,720,000
58.41% of the Jewish population of Europe

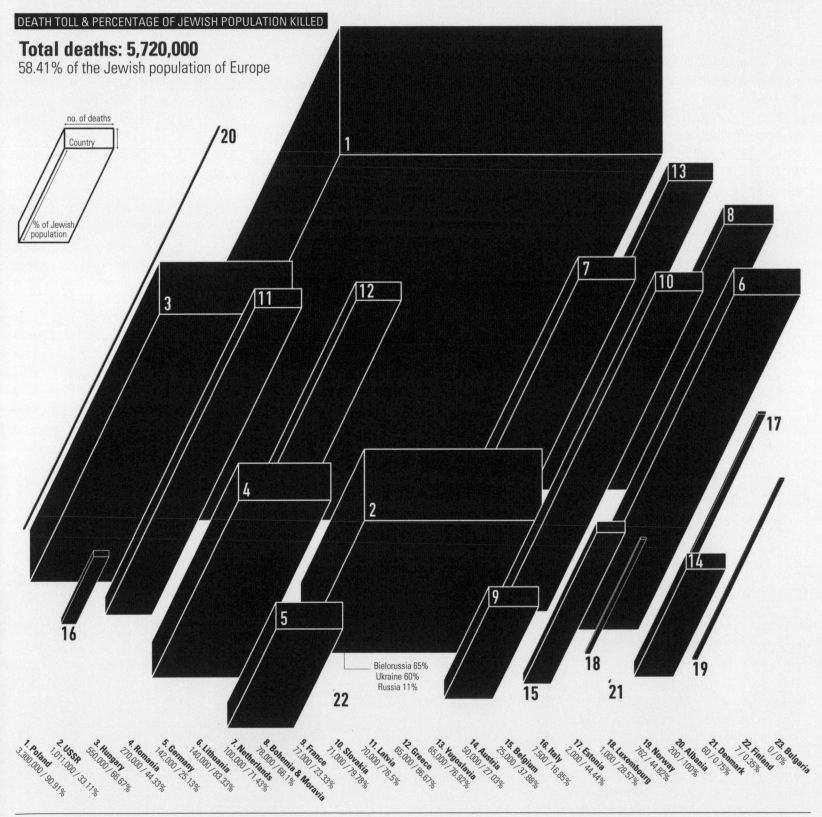

no. of deaths
Country
% of Jewish population

Bielorussia 65%
Ukraine 60%
Russia 11%

1. Poland 3,300,000 / 90.91%
2. USSR 1,011,000 / 33.11%
3. Hungary 550,000 / 66.67%
4. Romania 270,000 / 44.33%
5. Germany 142,000 / 25.13%
6. Lithuania 140,000 / 83.33%
7. Netherlands 100,000 / 71.43%
8. Bohemia & Moravia 78,000 / 66.1%
9. France 77,000 / 23.33%
10. Slovakia 71,000 / 79.78%
11. Latvia 70,000 / 76.5%
12. Greece 65,000 / 86.67%
13. Yugoslavia 65,000 / 76.92%
14. Austria 50,000 / 27.03%
15. Belgium 25,000 / 37.88%
16. Italy 7,500 / 16.85%
17. Estonia 2,000 / 44.44%
18. Luxembourg 1,000 / 28.57%
19. Norway 762 / 44.82%
20. Albania 200 / 100%
21. Denmark 60 / 0.75%
22. Finland 7 / 0.35%
23. Bulgaria 0 / 0%

The Destruction of the European Jews, London, 1961 • 7. D. Blatman, *The Death Marches*, Cambridge, MA, 2011 • 8. K. M. Mallmann *et al.* (eds.), *Die 'Ereignismeldungen UdSSR' 1941*, Darmstadt, 2011 • 9. T. Snyder, *Bloodlands*, London, 2011 • 10. https://kehilalinks.jewishgen.org/lodz/holocaust.htm • 11. http://www.yadvashem.org • 12. https://www.cairn.info/revue-les-cahiers-de-la-shoah-2003-1-page-15.htm

COLLABORATION WITH THE NAZI REGIME

By 1942, the Nazis had crushed crushed Europe and subjugated 238 million people. But Germany needed collaborators from which it could take the political, economic and human resources it needed for its war effort. Collaboration took different forms, whether voluntary, dictated by circumstances or enforced. It affected every kind of behaviour and was fed by the history and traditions of each territory. Due to its impact and the 'spirit of collaboration' that it fostered, state collaboration was the most important form. But when did it begin? Was it collaboration, for example, to sign unfair business agreements, according to which German firms bought more from abroad and made the Reich richer at the expense of its 'partners'?

In exchange for crumbs, Marshal Pétain kept order in the interests of the Reich, assisted in genocide, organized forced labour, financed Germany to the tune of 860 billion francs and encouraged 30,000 Frenchmen to join its army. Pétain claimed to be sacrificing himself to France, but in fact he sacrificed France to Germany. Why? Not just because he was blind, but because of ambition and ideological opportunism. He took advantage

1 • STATE COLLABORATION

Bulgaria, Romania, Hungary and Finland joined the Axis camp, believing that their future depended on the Reich as a shield against Communism and an arbiter of the many territorial conflicts in Eastern Europe. All of them apart from Finland became satellites. As well as military assistance, they collaborated economically and took part in acts of genocide. Woe betide anyone that kept their distance. In the spring of 1944, Hitler placed Hungary under Reich administration. Even Mussolini was just a pawn once he became head of the Italian Social Republic. All the governments in the occupied territories, apart from the Danish democracy, which had survived the invasion and preferred to step down in 1943 rather than compromise itself further, came from reactionary forces (Vichy) or Fascist backgrounds (Croatia, Slovakia) and were forced into a collaborationist spiral. 'Neutral' states trapped in the German economic sphere also submitted to the Reich's demands.

COMPENSATION AGREEMENTS

Swedish state

German state

Finances

Drawn from

Adjustment of accounts postponed until end of war

Stockholm compensation fund

Berlin compensation fund

Advances funds to cover purchases

Pays out funds to cover purchases

Producer / Vendor

Industry / Buyer

PACTS BROUGHT THE REICH 400 BILLION FRANCS

160 billion francs owed to France
(40% of total)

240 billion francs owed to other states
(60% of total)

400 billion francs of debts accumulated by the Reich under compensation agreements

MAP OF POLITICAL COLLABORATION IN 1941

Allies
Neutral
The Reich
Protectorate
Reich Commissariat & General Government

Occupied by Italy
Occupied by the Reich under military administration

Independent state: partner of the Reich
Independent state: Reich satellite
Independent state under control of the Reich

1 Belgium
2 Netherlands
3 Denmark
4 Switzerland
5 Bohemia & Moravia
6 Slovakia
7 Hungary
8 Croatia
9 Serbia
10 Albania
11 Montenegro

Norway

Swed

Ireland

UK

Third Reich

Occupied France

Vichy France

Italy

Portugal

Spain

of the crisis to start his National Revolution programme, knowing that his government could only survive in a German Europe.

Where the German occupiers had no government partners, they relied on local adminstrators. There was no shortage of volunteers greedy for the crumbs of power or wanting to serve the Nazi collective by boosting its economic and administrative system. In Belgium, a coterie of senior civil servants, legal figures and businessmen led by Alexandre Galopin emerged. In the Netherlands, the Nazis favoured civil servants over the unpopular

and incompetent local Fascists. In the east, the Nazis were able to spurn calls from Baltic and Ukrainian nationalists in order to avoid half-opening the door to the creation of states in their future eastern colonies. Collaboration was further complicated by the fact that the Reich had no dedicated plan or staff for it. It improvised, with departments competing to gain any advantages they could. Nevertheless, state collaboration had a significant impact. It greatly aided in the acquisition of a huge territory, provided 3 million troops to support the German army and stirred up anti-Semitic sentiment.

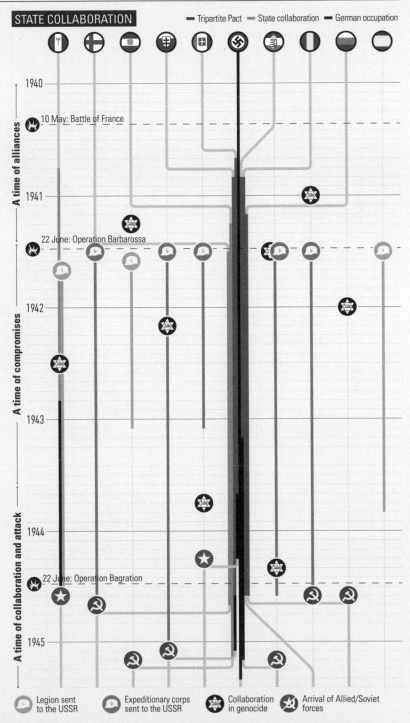

Vichy France: Pétain govt. relocated to Germany (19 Aug 1944) • **Finland:** armistice with Allies (4 Sep 1944), declaration of war on Reich (15 Sep 1944) • **Croatia:** Pavelić flees (6 Apr 1945) • **Slovakia:** Tiso flees (Feb 1945) • **Italy:** creation of RSI puppet state (Sept 1943), death of Mussolini (28 Apr 1945), fall of fascist RSI (29 Apr 1945) • **Hungary:** puppet Szálasi govt. installed (16 Oct 1944), Szálasi flees (29 Mar 1945) • **Romania:** arrest of Antonescu (23 Aug 1945), declaration of war on Reich (24 Aug 1945) • **Bulgaria:** coup d'état (9 Sep 1944), armistice with Allies, declaration of war on Reich (28 Oct 1944).

2 • MILITARY COLLABORATION

The Reich's allies, attracted by the hope of territorial expansion, took part in the invasion of Yugoslavia then responded to the call to a crusade against Bolshevism. Fighting alongside the Wehrmacht, their forces increased German manpower by a third. A few units were also provided by friendly governments, for instance the Legion of French Volunteers (LVF) and the Spanish División Azul (Blue Division). From 1942, the Wehrmacht recruited 530,000 auxiliaries known as Hiwis (short for *Hilfswilliger*, 'willing helper') from among prisoners and in the occupied Soviet territories, as well as national combat legions (including 210,000 Turkmen and Tatar troops), who even fought on the Normandy beaches. Not to be outdone, the Waffen SS had 600,000 foreign troops (half of them classed as *Volksdeutsche*, ethnic Germans resident in other countries), initially as volunteers and then conscripts. Finally, it was not possible to maintain order in Europe without the help of thousands of volunteers, who played a major role in the fight against the partisans and in the extermination of the Jews. For them, collaboration was an opportunity for horrific ethnic and political cleansing.

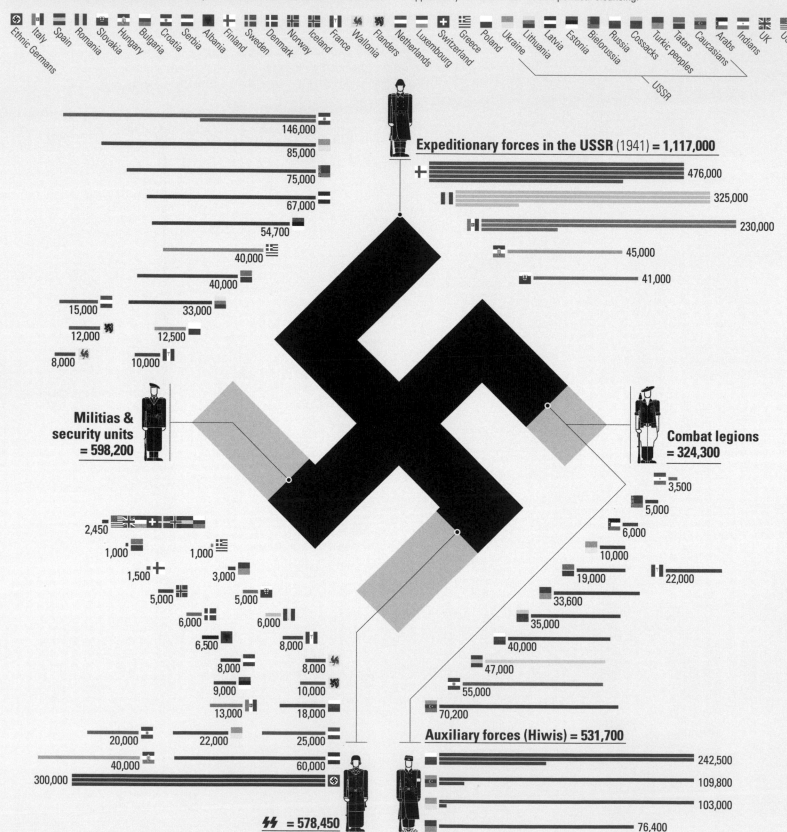

Ethnic Germans · Italy · Spain · Romania · Slovakia · Hungary · Bulgaria · Croatia · Serbia · Albania · Finland · Sweden · Denmark · Norway · Iceland · France · Wallonia · Flanders · Netherlands · Luxembourg · Switzerland · Greece · Poland · Ukraine · Lithuania · Latvia · Estonia · Bielorussia · Russia · Cossacks · Turkic peoples · Tatars · Caucasians · Arabs · Indians · UK · USA

USSR

Expeditionary forces in the USSR (1941) = **1,117,000**

476,000
325,000
230,000
45,000
41,000

146,000
85,000
75,000
67,000
54,700
40,000
40,000
15,000
33,000
12,000
12,500
8,000
10,000

Militias & security units = 598,200

Combat legions = 324,300

3,500
5,000
6,000
10,000
19,000
22,000
33,600
35,000
40,000
47,000
55,000
70,200

2,450
1,000
1,000
1,500
3,000
5,000
5,000
6,000
6,000
6,500
8,000
8,000
8,000
9,000
10,000
13,000
18,000
20,000
22,000
25,000
40,000
60,000
300,000

✠✠ = 578,450

Auxiliary forces (Hiwis) = 531,700

242,500
109,800
103,000
76,400

SOURCES: 1. Rolf-Dieter Müller, *An der Seite der Wehrmacht, Hitlers ausländische Helfer beim 'Kreuzzug gegen den Bolschewismus'*, Berlin, 2007 • 2. Jean-Luc Leleu, Françoise Passera, Jean Quellien & Michel Daeffler (eds.), *La France pendant la Seconde Guerre mondiale, Atlas historique*, Paris, 2010 • 3. François Broche & Jean-François Muracciole, *Histoire de la collaboration*, Paris, 2017 • 4. Yves Durand, *Le Nouvel Ordre européen nazi*,

3 • THE COMPLEX NATURE OF COLLABORATION

There were often more differences than similarities between collaborators. They included the desperate Soviet prisoners who joined the Wehrmacht to avoid starving to death, opportunistic day-to-day collaborators (such as entrepreneurs, volunteer workers, informers) and collaborators who truly wanted a new world order. Pétain himself chose to collaborate in good faith because he thought it would enable him to influence the Reich. His authority soon came up against internal quarrels and the growing influence of the government leaders, Laval and Darlan. A different kind of collaboration, by collaborationist parties, emerged in Paris. This movement, which had very few members (under 100,000 sympathizers), was dominated by figures who detested each other (Doriot, Déat, Bucard). Excluded from Vichy, they plotted and vied to win the support of the occupiers and snatch some crumbs of power. These rivalries, stirred up by the German ambassador, Otto Abetz, played into Germany's hands. France was a weak partner, undermined from within. There was also friction within the occupiers because of the many different interests involved. But the French were incapable of exploiting this.

THE CAUSES OF COLLABORATION — according to Werner Rings, *Life with the Enemy: Collaboration and Resistance in Hitler's Europe* (1979)

 'I cooperate because the sole alternative appears to be bankruptcy, unemployment, starvation, chaos and destruction.

 'I agree to collaborate despite my hostility to National Socialism and the Third Reich. I may do so for a variety of reasons: to throw off the foreign yoke and regain my freedom; to prevent the mass murder of innocent people whenever possible...'

 'I accept that life must go on. Knowingly and from self-interest, I directly or indirectly work for the occupying power without professing its political and ideological principles. My attitude is dictated by circumstances beyond my control. I am determined to survive the war and my country's defeat as best I can.'

 'I cooperate with the occupying power although I endorse only some, not all, of the National Socialist doctrines. Subject to that proviso, I am ready and eager to collaborate faithfully because I wish to change the circumstances that dictate my attitude.'

 'I join forces with the occupying power because I endorse its principles and ideals. My attitude is dictated, not by circumstances, but by allegiance to National Socialism.'

COLLABORATION IN FRANCE

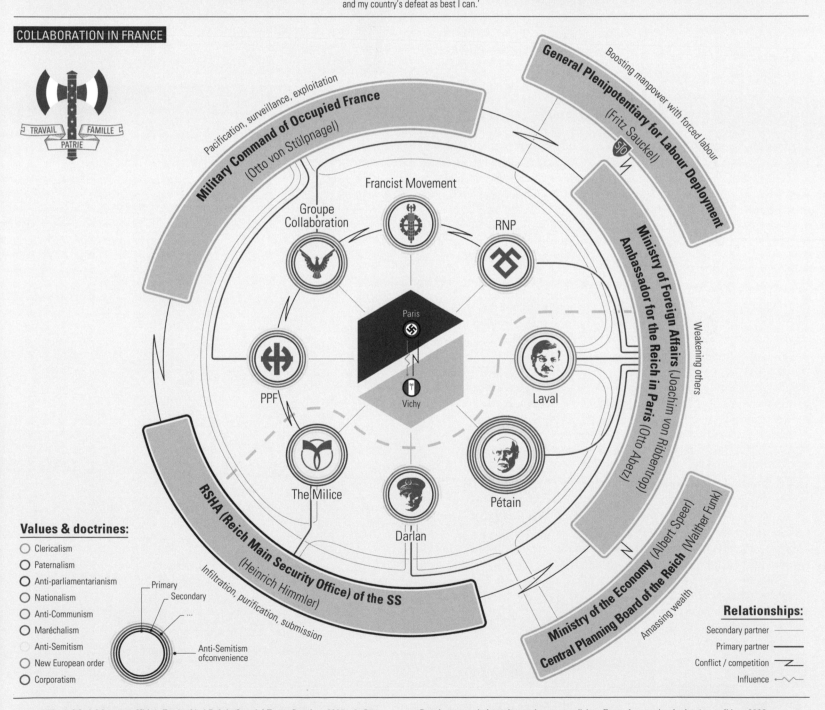

Values & doctrines:
- Clericalism
- Paternalism
- Anti-parliamentarianism
- Nationalism
- Anti-Communism
- Maréchalism
- Anti-Semitism
- New European order
- Corporatism

Primary
Secondary
....
Anti-Semitism of convenience

Relationships:
- Secondary partner
- Primary partner
- Conflict / competition
- Influence

Paris, 1990 • 5. Mark Mazower, *Hitler's Empire: Nazi Rule in Occupied Europe*, London, 2008 • 6. Götz Aly, *Hitler's Beneficiaries: Plunder, Racial War, and the Nazi Welfare State*, New York, 2007 • 7. Jérôme Blanc, *Pouvoirs et monnaie durant la seconde guerre mondiale en France: la monnaie subordonnée au politique*, 2008; https://halshs.archives-ouvertes.fr

RESISTANCE IN OCCUPIED EUROPE

France is merely one of the many countries that has idealized its history of resistance. Nowadays, historians are painting a different picture, less flattering but nonetheless deeply human, of resistance that allowed minorities to become actors in their own history, to stop resigning themselves to despair, to stand up and simply say no. Three forms of resistance emerged, shaped by local environments and also mirroring the repressive regime: a resistance of loyalty in north-west Europe, of survival in eastern and central Europe and of diversion in the USSR. In the west, where the occupation did not threaten the existence of communities (apart from the Jews), resistance remained a more individual and urban phenomenon, predominantly civilian in nature. The struggle against the occupying forces was also a fight to safeguard democratic, humanist and patriotic principles while awaiting liberation from outside. As Basil Davidson, a former member of the British SOE, wrote, 'They cleared a space for civic decency and even progress in all the brutish squalor of those years.' Actions consisted mainly of aiding fugitives, propaganda, strikes and refusal to collaborate (60% of Norwegian teachers resigned in 1942 to avoid swearing allegiance to the Nazis). Military resistance took the form of intelligence and sabotage rather than guerrilla warfare.

In east and central Europe (Czechoslovakia, Poland, Yugoslavia, Greece, Italy after 1943), where governments had ceased to exist and the Nazis and their local cronies were dismantling the whole of society with unbelievable brutality, resistance was key to the survival of individuals and the nation. Right from the start, resistance was communal (the Polish AK had 380,000 members), military and social. The resistance waged guerrilla warfare, which in 1941 turned into insurrection in Yugoslavia and in the summer of 1944 into uprisings in Warsaw and Slovakia, which were ruthlessly crushed. In the basements of houses in Poland and the mountainous areas of Yugoslavia and Greece, resistance fighters set up counter-societies with their own institutions, laws, legal systems, education and culture. However, there were profound differences. In Poland, the struggle was carried on by institutional figures, the government in exile, the military and academics, trying to preserve the pre-war structures. In southern Europe, resistance provided a tabula rasa that worked to the advantage of the Communists. The intolerable old world disappeared. In Greece, the Greek People's Liberation Army created a self-governing society in which young people and women played a role. But the war of liberation then became bound up with vicious civil wars.

In the USSR, thousands of people fleeing Nazi repression who had sought refuge in isolated regions came into the hands of the Stalinist government. It deployed them in military actions (guerrilla warfare, diverting as many of the enemy as possible) and political activities (ensuring that the population was loyal to the Communist regime). Although the former achieved very little, the latter played an important role in regaining control of the liberated territories.

1 • WAR OF THE SOVIET PARTISANS

Propaganda portrayed partisans as major players in the war; up to a million of them were responsible for the deaths of 500,000 Fascists. But records show a different reality. The partisans – lost soldiers, Communists, Jews, landless peasants, even ex-collaborators – were fewer in number. They were poorly armed and had priorities other than guerrilla fighting. Forced to survive in the marshlands of Bielorussia, they were more given to looting than to sabotage. Until 1943 they made no impact at all. After that, they were more active, but with little significant effect since they were outside the main axes. On the other hand, by creating a climate of insecurity, they disrupted the exploitation of the occupied territories and ensured that the population was loyal to Stalin. The occupying forces were unable to catch them in their forest refuges and so set about clearing the areas with a scorched earth policy. Targeting civilians rather than the partisans, they launched a scheme for massive Slav depopulation, aimed at future German colonization.

Estimated partisan troop numbers and rail attacks (Soviet archives)

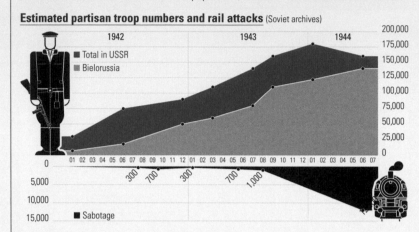

Resistance and repression in the forests of Bryansk

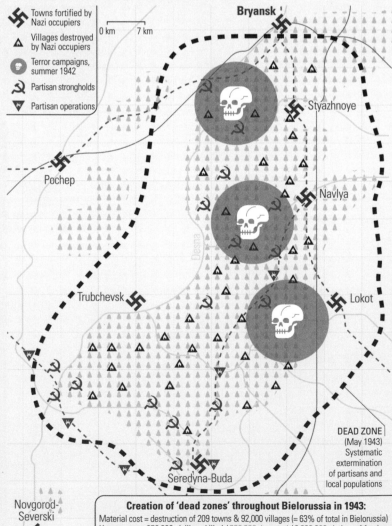

Creation of 'dead zones' throughout Bielorussia in 1943:
Material cost = destruction of 209 towns & 92,000 villages (= 63% of total in Bielorussia)
Human cost = 250,000 civilians killed / 380,000 deported / 3,000,000 victims of famine

2 • RESISTANCE IN YUGOSLAVIA
All estimates are contested since they are key to the collective memories of the Balkan countries. We have used scientifically validated estimates.

In 1941, Yugoslavia was in pieces. The Ustaše set up a regime of terror in Croatia (including Bosnia) and organized anti-Serb and anti-Semitic massacres. Elsewhere, the Nazis exterminated Jews and gypsies and germanized the annexed Banat region of Serbia and Slovenia. Resistance was a matter of survival. The first Chetnik guerrillas grew up around General Mihailović, supported by the government in exile and the British. However, being pro-Serb and anti-Communist, it compromised with the occupiers and carried out more massacres (Croats, Muslims, Communists). A second, Communist,

guerrilla force was more federal, promising 'threefold' liberation from the occupiers, from ethnic conflict and from social inequality. The hilly terrain provided refuges where partisans built an alternative society. They took over industrial towns, forcing the enemy into exhausting clearance operations. In 1943, Tito gained the upper hand and support from the Allies, who no longer wished to be associated with the Chetniks. By the time the Red Army arrived in autumn 1944, the Axis only controlled the towns in the north. However, it did not give in until April 1945, leaving a number of mass graves behind.

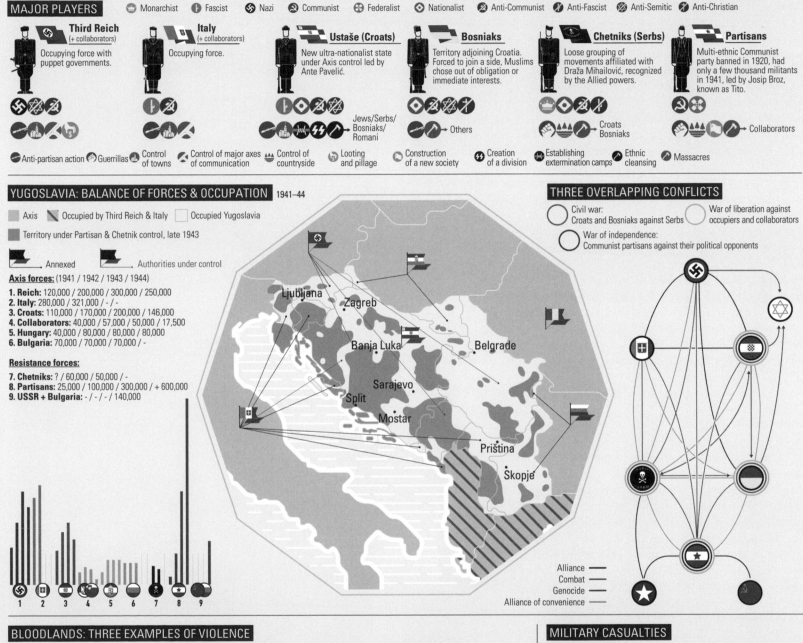

SOURCES: 1. Masha Cerovic, *Les Enfants de Staline. La guerre des partisans soviétiques (1941–1944)*, Seuil, 2018 • 2. Gael Eismann & Stefan Martens (eds.), *Occupation et répression militaire allemandes (1939–1945)*, Paris, 2007 • 3. Vladimir Geiger, 'Human losses of the Croats in World War II and the immediate post-war period', *Review of Croatian History*, no. 1, 2012, pp. 77–121 • 4. Mark Mazower, *Hitler's Empire. Nazi Rule in Occupied Europe*, London, 2008 • 5. Olivier Wieviorka, *Une histoire de la Résistance en Europe occidentale*, Paris, 2017

THE FRENCH RESISTANCE

In the summer of 1940, the Resistance did not yet exist. On 18 June, Charles de Gaulle envisaged it taking a purely military form. He called upon soldiers and engineers to 'make contact' with him. The Free French Forces were born, with a core of 10,000 volunteers, mostly professionals and nearly 20% of them foreigners. This was negligible compared with the numbers mobilized in the conflict as a whole, but it was still an invaluable contribution to the preservation of Free France. 75% of the future Free French fighters were abroad; 40% of those from mainland France were from coastal regions, especially Brittany. France's colonies (the New Hebrides, Equatorial Africa, Cameroon, possessions in the Pacific and East Indies from 1940) also rallied behind Free France, providing volunteers, natural resources, bases, tax revenue and legitimacy. However, it was not until the invasion of North Africa, the merger with the French Army of Africa, and US rearmament that the French Committee of National Liberation, renamed the Provisional Government of the French Republic in 1944, had an army worthy of the name (10% of Allied manpower in 1945). Yet the Allies relegated it to a subordinate role.

The earliest resistance initiatives were individual and improvised, by people simply wanting to 'do something': patriotic demonstrations, occasional small-scale sabotage. The first resistance organizations emerged that autumn, making contact with London before being swept aside. The first turning point came in 1941, when the French Communist Party, clandestine since 1939, shifted awkwardly towards armed resistance. However, a lack of volunteers (never more than around 50 active in Paris), the fragmented nature of the movements, tactics, amateurism, shortage of equipment and horrific repression – especially by the police in Vichy – limited the effectiveness of the 'army of shadows' in the long term. A second turning point did not come until the second half of 1943. It was both political, with unification as the National Council of the Resistance, ideological, when the Resistance was seen by the public as a credible opposition to Vichy, geographical, because having started as an urban movement, the Resistance became more rural with the establishment of the Maquis, and finally human, when the number of members exceeded a hundred thousand. Through insurrection, the contribution of the French Forces of the Interior (FFI) to the Liberation was probably more political than military, but was romanticized after the war. However, their sacrifice was not in vain. Not only did the Resistance make it possible to rebuild a national identity, it also preserved French values and prevented a dangerous power vacuum in 1944.

1 • HOW MANY?

Support for the Free French started in July–August 1940 and then grew with the victory in the Levant in summer 1941 and the victory in North Africa in 1943, where it attracted civilians and combatants immediately before it merged with the French Army of Africa. It is, however, difficult to estimate the scale of resistance within France; as the saying goes, it was most likely on the scale of 'a few thousand in 1940, tens of thousands in 1942, hundreds of millions in 1944'. Less than 4 percent of those called 'volunteer Resistance fighters' actually were so in 1940 (and the figure is also inflated by the inclusion of the Communist resistance to Vichy). The Resistance only got off the ground after the rebellion against forced labour and a change in the strategic situation. Those who joined at the last minute are not included here.

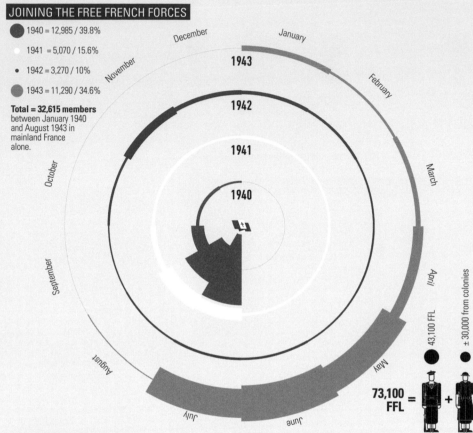

JOINING THE FREE FRENCH FORCES

- 1940 = 12,985 / 39.8%
- 1941 = 5,070 / 15.6%
- 1942 = 3,270 / 10%
- 1943 = 11,290 / 34.6%

Total = 32,615 members between January 1940 and August 1943 in mainland France alone.

43,100 FFL   ± 30,000 from colonies

73,100 FFL =   +

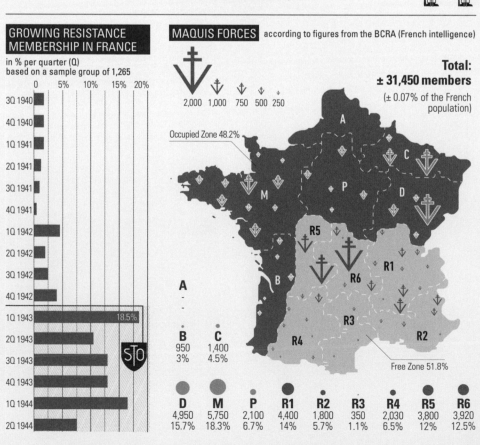

GROWING RESISTANCE MEMBERSHIP IN FRANCE

in % per quarter (Q)
based on a sample group of 1,265

	0	5%	10%	15%	20%
3Q 1940					
4Q 1940					
1Q 1941					
2Q 1941					
3Q 1941					
4Q 1941					
1Q 1942					
2Q 1942					
3Q 1942					
4Q 1942					
1Q 1943				18.5%	
2Q 1943					
3Q 1943					
4Q 1943					
1Q 1944					
2Q 1944					

MAQUIS FORCES according to figures from the BCRA (French intelligence)

2,000 1,000 750 500 250

Total: ± 31,450 members (± 0.07% of the French population)

Occupied Zone 48.2%

Free Zone 51.8%

A	B	C	D	M	P	R1	R2	R3	R4	R5	R6
-	950	1,400	4,950	5,750	2,100	4,400	1,800	350	2,030	3,800	3,920
-	3%	4.5%	15.7%	18.3%	6.7%	14%	5.7%	1.1%	6.5%	12%	12.5%

2 • WHO WERE THEY?

Resistance, especially outside France, was mainly the preserve of urban young men, The average age was 24 in the Free French Forces (FFL), 34 in the French Forces of the Interior (FFI). The FFL came from the prosperous educated classes. They tended not to be highly politicized or, if they were, they tended towards the right. The historian Jean-François Muracciole commented: 'Although the elites were conspicuous by their absence in London in 1940, their children were certainly there.' The resistance within France was of a more diverse nature but once again rural communities appear to have been under-represented, in contrast to professionals. This distortion was also found amongst the enemy in collaborationist circles. Studies also relativize the myth that the Resistance was dominated by the working classes. Although a third of deported resistance fighters had joined the Communist Party, less than 20% were manual workers, proving that the Party had attracted members from all strata of society.

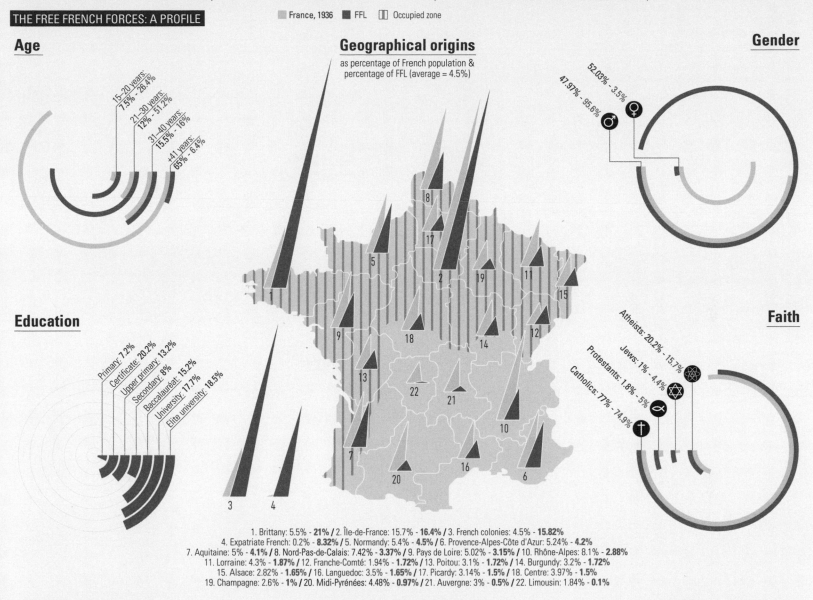

THE FREE FRENCH FORCES: A PROFILE

Legend: France, 1936 — FFL — Occupied zone

Age

- 15–20 years: 7.5% - 26.4%
- 21–30 years: 12% - 51.2%
- 31–40 years: 15.5% - 16%
- +41 years: 65% - 6.4%

Geographical origins
as percentage of French population & percentage of FFL (average = 4.5%)

Gender
- 52.03% - 3.5%
- 47.97% - 95.6%

Education
- Primary: 7.2%
- Certificate: 20.2%
- Upper primary: 13.2%
- Secondary: 8%
- Baccalauréat: 15.2%
- University: 17.7%
- Elite university: 18.5%

Faith
- Atheists: 20.2% - 15.7%
- Jews: 1% - 4.4%
- Protestants: 1.8% - 5%
- Catholics: 77% - 74.9%

1. Brittany: 5.5% - **21%** / 2. Île-de-France: 15.7% - **16.4%** / 3. French colonies: 4.5% - **15.82%**
4. Expatriate French: 0.2% - **8.32%** / 5. Normandy: 5.4% - **4.5%** / 6. Provence-Alpes-Côte d'Azur: 5.24% - **4.2%**
7. Aquitaine: 5% - **4.1%** / 8. Nord-Pas-de-Calais: 7.42% - **3.37%** / 9. Pays de Loire: 5.02% - **3.15%** / 10. Rhône-Alpes: 8.1% - **2.88%**
11. Lorraine: 4.3% - **1.87%** / 12. Franche-Comté: 1.94% - **1.72%** / 13. Poitou: 3.1% - **1.72%** / 14. Burgundy: 3.2% - **1.72%**
15. Alsace: 2.82% - **1.65%** / 16. Languedoc: 3.5% - **1.65%** / 17. Picardy: 3.14% - **1.5%** / 18. Centre: 3.97% - **1.5%**
19. Champagne: 2.6% - **1%** / 20. Midi-Pyrénées: 4.48% - **0.97%** / 21. Auvergne: 3% - **0.5%** / 22. Limousin: 1.84% - **0.1%**

Social composition
as percentage of French population & percentage of FFL

- Unemployed: 3% - 0.9%
- Farm workers: 31.6% - 2%
- Blue collar workers: 31.3% - 10%
- White collar workers: 13.8% - 10.8%
- Freelance trades: 16% - 4.3%
- Professions/students 1.5% - 37.2%
- Military: 2.8% - 33.9%

Political allegiances

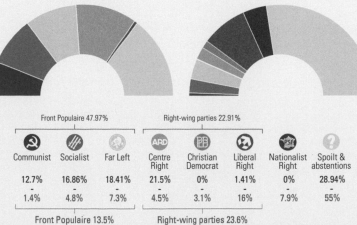

Elections 1936 — FFL 1942

Front Populaire 47.97% — Right-wing parties 22.91%

	Communist	Socialist	Far Left	Centre Right	Christian Democrat	Liberal Right	Nationalist Right	Spoilt & abstentions
	12.7%	16.86%	18.41%	21.5%	0%	1.41%	0%	28.94%
	1.4%	4.8%	7.3%	4.5%	3.1%	16%	7.9%	55%

Front Populaire 13.5% — Right-wing parties 23.6%

Origins of French army troops
November 1942–May 1945, as %

- Free French Forces - 5.7%
- Escapees from France - 1.7%
- Corsican recruits - 1.5%
- African colonies - 9.1%
- French Algerians - 20%
- Other Algerians - 15.1%
- Moroccans - 8.2%
- Tunisians - 3%
- FFI units amalgamated in 1944 - 21.5%
- Volunteers - 14.2%

3 • THE RESISTANCE IN COMBAT

The fighting started in Africa with a series of peripheral skirmishes against Vichy, from Dakar to the Levant and including West Africa. It was not until the spring of 1942 that a Free French brigade fought in the front lines (Bir Hakeim). Even with the addition of Leclerc's armoured division in North Africa, the French presence remained superficial. This situation changed at the end of 1942 when the French Army of Africa rallied in support, leading to a merger between these fraternal enemies. This combined army, 88% of whose manpower was drawn from colonized nations and French settlers in 1943, took its place alongside the Allies and was fully involved in the fighting (with a corps in Italy and a 250,000-man army in France), thus justifying France's presence at the German surrender. Within France, the Resistance was a nebulous group of movements with

different agendas: intelligence, aiding fugitives, attempts at mass mobilization. Though modest at first, these actions began to bear fruit in 1942. The same was not true of the armed resistance. Successful sabotage was rare and not crucial until 1944, supporting the Allied landing. Only 0.02% of Germans died in France between 23 August 1941, when Communist Pierre Georges killed a German soldier called Alfons Moser at Barbès metro station in reprisal for the invasion of the USSR, and 6 June 1944. The Resistance fighters killed more French people, collaborators or assumed collaborators and police officers in Vichy. Even the uprising in the summer of 1944 had little impact. Disaster was only averted by the German retreat, trapped between the Allied forces who had landed in Normandy and Provence. But in order to rebuild itself, France tried to idealize its past.

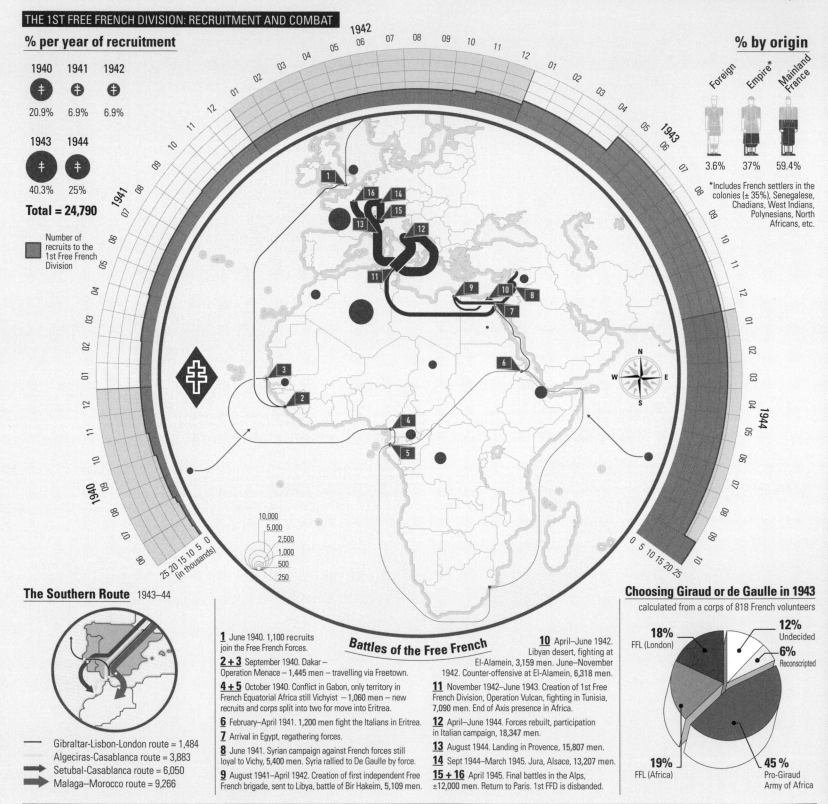

THE 1ST FREE FRENCH DIVISION: RECRUITMENT AND COMBAT

% per year of recruitment

1940	1941	1942
20.9%	6.9%	6.9%

1943	1944
40.3%	25%

Total = 24,790

Number of recruits to the 1st Free French Division

% by origin

Foreign	Empire*	Mainland France
3.6%	37%	59.4%

*Includes French settlers in the colonies (± 35%), Senegalese, Chadians, West Indians, Polynesians, North Africans, etc.

1942

10,000
5,000
2,500
1,000
500
250

25 20 15 10 5 0
(in thousands)

0 5 10 15 20 25

The Southern Route 1943–44

— Gibraltar-Lisbon-London route = 1,484
Algeciras-Casablanca route = 3,883
➡ Setubal-Casablanca route = 6,050
➡ Malaga–Morocco route = 9,266

Battles of the Free French

1 June 1940. 1,100 recruits join the Free French Forces.

2 + 3 September 1940. Dakar – Operation Menace – 1,445 men – travelling via Freetown.

4 + 5 October 1940. Conflict in Gabon, only territory in French Equatorial Africa still Vichyist – 1,060 men – new recruits and corps split into two for move into Eritrea.

6 February–April 1941. 1,200 men fight the Italians in Eritrea.

7 Arrival in Egypt, regathering forces.

8 June 1941. Syrian campaign against French forces still loyal to Vichy, 5,400 men. Syria rallied to De Gaulle by force.

9 August 1941–April 1942. Creation of first independent Free French brigade, sent to Libya, battle of Bir Hakeim, 5,109 men.

10 April–June 1942. Libyan desert, fighting at El-Alamein, 3,159 men. June–November 1942. Counter-offensive at El-Alamein, 6,318 men.

11 November 1942–June 1943. Creation of 1st Free French Division, Operation Vulcan, fighting in Tunisia, 7,090 men. End of Axis presence in Africa.

12 April–June 1944. Forces rebuilt, participation in Italian campaign, 18,347 men.

13 August 1944. Landing in Provence, 15,807 men.

14 Sept 1944–March 1945. Jura, Alsace, 13,207 men.

15 + 16 April 1945. Final battles in the Alps, ±12,000 men. Return to Paris. 1st FFD is disbanded.

Choosing Giraud or de Gaulle in 1943

calculated from a corps of 818 French volunteers

- **18%** FFL (London)
- **12%** Undecided
- **6%** Reconscripted
- **45%** Pro-Giraud Army of Africa
- **19%** FFL (Africa)

SOURCES: 1. Jean-Luc Leleu, Françoise Passera, Jean Quellien & Michel Daeffler (eds.), *La France pendant la Seconde Guerre mondiale, Atlas historique*, Paris, 2010 • 2. François Marcot (ed.), *Dictionnaire historique de la Résistance*, Paris, 2006 • 3. Jean-François Muracciole, *Les Français libres, l'autre Résistance*, Paris, 2009 • 4. Olivier Wieviorka, *The French Resistance, 1940–1945*, Cambridge, MA, 2016 • 5. Jean-Louis

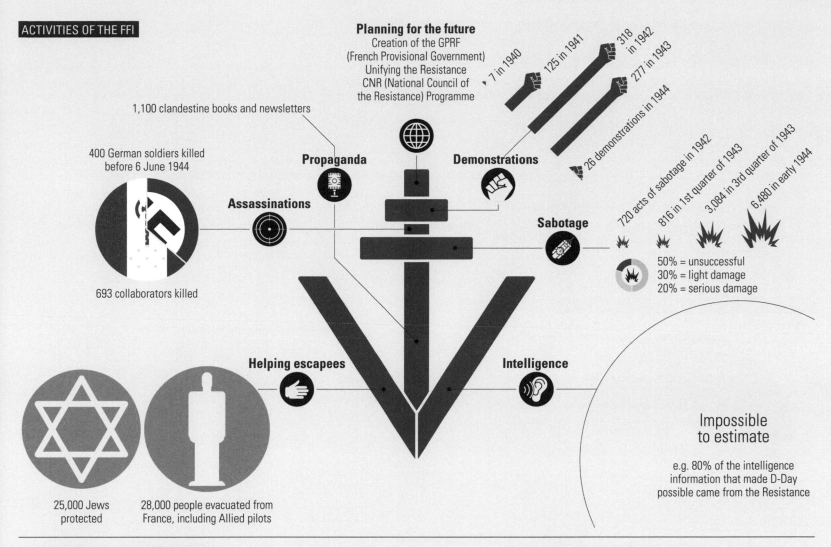

ACTIVITIES OF THE FFI

Planning for the future
Creation of the GPRF
(French Provisional Government)
Unifying the Resistance
CNR (National Council of
the Resistance) Programme

1,100 clandestine books and newsletters

7 in 1940
125 in 1941
318 in 1942
277 in 1943

26 demonstrations in 1944

Propaganda

Demonstrations

400 German soldiers killed
before 6 June 1944

Assassinations

Sabotage

720 acts of sabotage in 1942
816 in 1st quarter of 1943
3,084 in 3rd quarter of 1943
6,480 in early 1944

693 collaborators killed

50% = unsuccessful
30% = light damage
20% = serious damage

Helping escapees

Intelligence

Impossible to estimate

e.g. 80% of the intelligence
information that made D-Day
possible came from the Resistance

25,000 Jews
protected

28,000 people evacuated from
France, including Allied pilots

4 • DEATHS IN THE RESISTANCE

A martyr's death was an act of resistance in itself and true proof of patriotism after the war. The French Communist Party proudly claimed that 75,000 of its militants were shot, but this seems to be pure fabrication: according to records, there were fewer than 4,000 executions. This does not mean, however, that the occupying forces were lenient. Firstly, 50,000 French people were deported simply for listening to the BBC and about 18,000 did not survive. Secondly, compared with the small number of people involved, the losses were horrific, at least in 1941–42. Anyone who joined the Resistance early on had virtually no chance of survival. The networks were regularly decimated. The uprising in the summer of 1944 was also devastating, with around 12,000 killed.

External resistance and the Liberation Army also paid a heavy price. Some 3,200 Free French troops died between 1940 and 1942 and 25,000 members of the Liberation Army between 1943 and 1945.

THE RESISTANCE

Total = ± 500,000 recruited - 33,734 dead / 6.75%

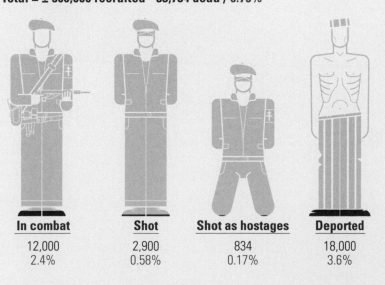

In combat	Shot	Shot as hostages	Deported
12,000	2,900	834	18,000
2.4%	0.58%	0.17%	3.6%

FRENCH LIBERATION ARMY

Total = 75,823 wounded / 25,370 dead

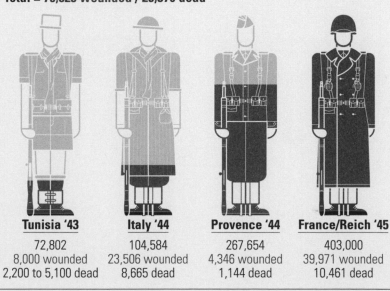

Tunisia '43	Italy '44	Provence '44	France/Reich '45
72,802	104,584	267,654	403,000
8,000 wounded	23,506 wounded	4,346 wounded	39,971 wounded
2,200 to 5,100 dead	8,665 dead	1,144 dead	10,461 dead

Crémieux-Brilhac, *La France libre, de l'appel du 18 juin à la Libération*, 2 vols, Paris, 2014 • 6. Franck Liaigre, *Les FTP. Nouvelle histoire d'une résistance*, Paris, 2016 • 7. François Broche, Georges Caïtucoli, Jean-François Muracciole, Max Gallo, *La France au combat*, Paris, 2007 • 8. Fabrice Grenard, *Maquis noirs et faux maquis*, Paris, 2013 • 9. www.francaislibres.net

MIGRATION IN POST-WAR EUROPE

The Second World War was notable for the huge number of displaced civilians: 40 million in Europe between 1939 and 1945. Realizing that they had to care for, feed and repatriate this wave of humanity but unaware of its scale, in 1943 the Allies set up an international organization, the United Nations Relief and Rehabilitation Administration (UNRRA). This had overall responsibility for aid projects but was accountable to the military. The Allies found 12 to 13 million foreign workers, prisoners of war and deportees in Germany after it surrendered. This was, of course, an approximate figure since the collapse of the Reich made it impossible

to keep records. The situation was complicated by the millions of Germans – city dwellers who had left the bombed cities (4.8 million), refugees fleeing the advance of the Red Army (between 6 and 9 million) – displaced within their own country. They were thrown onto the roads of a devastated land, swarms of people in moving columns. The UNRRA was overwhelmed, ineffective and unable to operate in the Soviet zones. At Bergen-Belsen, 140,000 deportees died after being liberated. The fact that the authorities were able to bring these refugees together and then repatriate most of them within the space of six months was something of a miracle. However, there were still

1 • THE GREAT RETURN
Figures are estimates, since the collapse of the Reich made accurate record-keeping impossible.

FOREIGNERS WITHIN THE REICH ON 30 APRIL 1945
out of a total of 12 to 13 million

By nationality

By category

1 Soviet = 6,936,000 - **2** French = 1,690,200 - **3** Polish ≈ 1,403,000 - **4** Italian ≈ 700,000
5 Belgian ≈ 500,000 - **6** Dutch ≈ 402,000 - **7** Czech ≈ 350,000 - **8** Yugoslavian ≈ 328,000
9 Anglo-American = 275,000 - **10** Baltic = 100,000 - **11** Other ≈ 315,800

1 Workers = 8,000,000 - **2** Prisoners of war = 3,584,200
(inc. 1,836,000 Soviet / 937,000 French / 300,000 Polish / 275,000 Anglo-American)
3 Political deportees = 1,000,000 - **4** Racial deportees = 100,000 - **5** Other ≈ 315,800

THE REPATRIATION OF THE FRENCH
in thousands

By month

03/45	30,000
04/45	310,000
05/45	880,000
06/45	270,000
07/45	90,000
08/45	30,000
09/45	80,200

1,690,200 displaced persons and prisoners

By category

Forced labour	618,700
Soldiers	937,000
Forced conscripts	93,000
FFI	39,000
Jews	2,500 (out of 75,000)

THE FATE OF REPATRIATED SOVIETS, 1 MARCH 1946
according to filtration camp records / total: 4,200,000

The fate of 2,800,000 people remains unknown, for a variety of reasons: files not available (in at least 800,000 cases), died before repatriation, lack of records in filtration camps, refusal to return to the USSR (half the Soviets liberated by the West avoided repatriation to the 'motherland').

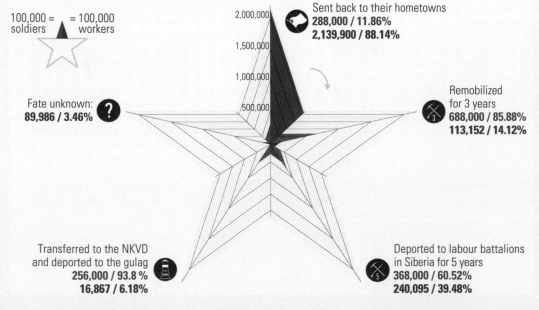

100,000 = soldiers
= 100,000 workers

Sent back to their hometowns
288,000 / 11.86%
2,139,900 / 88.14%

Fate unknown:
89,986 / 3.46%

Remobilized for 3 years
688,000 / 85.88%
113,152 / 14.12%

Transferred to the NKVD and deported to the gulag
256,000 / 93.8 %
16,867 / 6.18%

Deported to labour battalions in Siberia for 5 years
368,000 / 60.52%
240,095 / 39.48%

2 • POPULATION EXCHANGES

At the centre of this population flux was Poland, which was edging towards the West to take over German territory to compensate for territory lost to the USSR. Its people had to follow. But ethnic purification was widespread. Its methods, evolved over thirty years, were the same everywhere: intimidation, discrimination, violence, internment (over 3 million Germans in the USSR, Poland and Yugoslavia, a quarter of whom died), expulsion on foot or by train. This mostly happened before 1948, but until 1954 states were carrying out purges and dilution (forced movements within the borders of a state affecting, for instance, 140,00 Ukrainians from Poland, 250,000 Ukrainians and 82,000 Lithuanians in the USSR), then assimilation.

DISPLACEMENT OF PEOPLE OF GERMANIC ORIGIN
numbers of people registered by host authorities
? = figure unknown

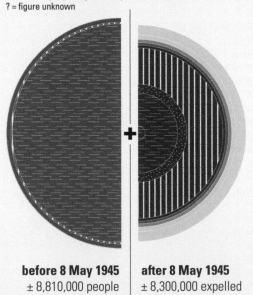

before 8 May 1945
± 8,810,000 people

after 8 May 1945
± 8,300,000 expelled

	before 8 May 1945	after 8 May 1945
ex-German provinces:	8,350,000	542,000 (USSR) / 2,500,000 (Pol.)
Poland:	?	700,000
Czechoslovakia:	120,000	2,800,000
Romania:	?	213,000
USSR:	320,000	195,000
Hungary:	20,000	253,000
Yugoslavia:	?	335,000
Rest of Europe:	?	762,000

and between 500,000 and 2,251,500 dead
Total: ± 17,110,000 displaced

1.5 million Poles, Ukrainians, Baltic people and Jews who could not be repatriated. They were re-interned in barracks and converted 'filtration' camps where they suffered from overcrowding, lack of privacy and poor sanitary conditions. The wait for visas seemed interminable – the last camp did not close until 1959. And new camps sprung up as people were expelled to Europe from the East.

In fact, the deportations by Stalin and Hitler opened the floodgates. The concept of a settled and stable community on which European societies were founded was destroyed. Populations began to shift and the Western powers rallied to Stalin in defiance of the Atlantic Charter. They hoped to base a future peace on ethnically homogenous states. There had never been repopulation on this scale. The figures were staggering: 12 to 16 million.

Although Germans were the worst affected (9 million expelled, 500,000 or more dead), at least their mother country was about to experience an economic boom. The same was not true for many others, deported to countries that were underdeveloped and ruled by dictators. The human cost of these expulsions, the bitterness they stirred up and the lasting economic chaos they caused added to the suffering of Eastern Europe.

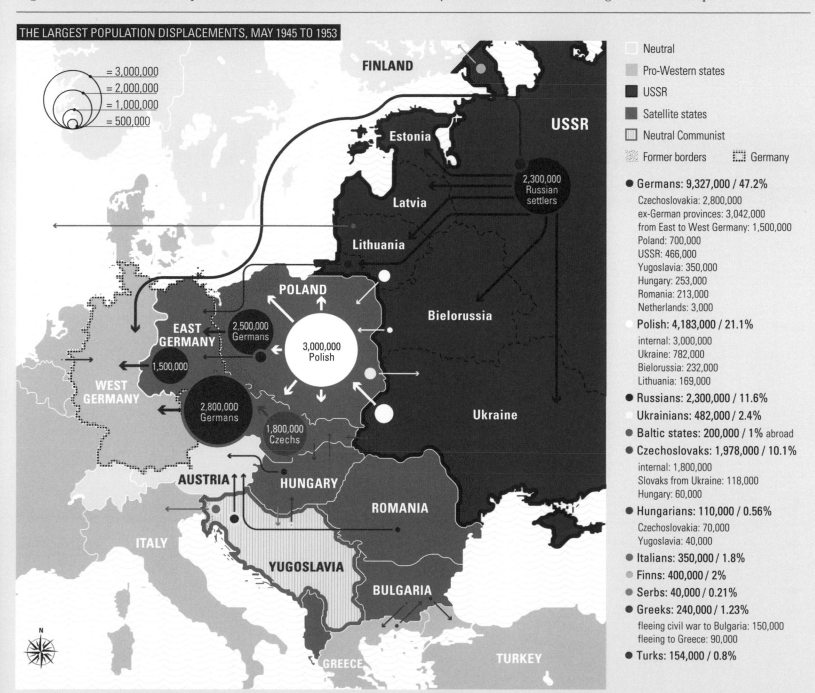

THE LARGEST POPULATION DISPLACEMENTS, MAY 1945 TO 1953

= 3,000,000
= 2,000,000
= 1,000,000
= 500,000

Neutral
Pro-Western states
USSR
Satellite states
Neutral Communist
Former borders   Germany

● **Germans: 9,327,000 / 47.2%**
Czechoslovakia: 2,800,000
ex-German provinces: 3,042,000
from East to West Germany: 1,500,000
Poland: 700,000
USSR: 466,000
Yugoslavia: 350,000
Hungary: 253,000
Romania: 213,000
Netherlands: 3,000

○ **Polish: 4,183,000 / 21.1%**
internal: 3,000,000
Ukraine: 782,000
Bielorussia: 232,000
Lithuania: 169,000

● **Russians: 2,300,000 / 11.6%**

○ **Ukrainians: 482,000 / 2.4%**

● **Baltic states: 200,000 / 1%** abroad

● **Czechoslovaks: 1,978,000 / 10.1%**
internal: 1,800,000
Slovaks from Ukraine: 118,000
Hungary: 60,000

● **Hungarians: 110,000 / 0.56%**
Czechoslovakia: 70,000
Yugoslavia: 40,000

● **Italians: 350,000 / 1.8%**

● **Finns: 400,000 / 2%**

● **Serbs: 40,000 / 0.21%**

● **Greeks: 240,000 / 1.23%**
fleeing civil war to Bulgaria: 150,000
fleeing to Greece: 90,000

● **Turks: 154,000 / 0.8%**

Map labels: FINLAND, USSR, Estonia, Latvia, Lithuania, 2,300,000 Russian settlers, POLAND, Bielorussia, EAST GERMANY, 2,500,000 Germans, 3,000,000 Polish, 1,500,000, WEST GERMANY, 2,800,000 Germans, 1,800,000 Czechs, Ukraine, AUSTRIA, HUNGARY, ROMANIA, ITALY, YUGOSLAVIA, BULGARIA, GREECE, TURKEY

N

SOURCES: 1. Timothy Snyder, *Bloodlands: Europe between Hitler and Stalin*, New York, 2010 • 2. Catherine Gousseff, *Échanger les peuples: le déplacement des minorités aux confins polono-soviétiques*, Paris, 2015 • 3. Nicolas Werth, 'Le grand retour, URSS 1945–1946', *Histoire@politique. Politique, culture, société*, no. 3, 2007 • 4. Ben Shephard, *The Long Road Home: The Aftermath of the Second World War*, London, 2010 • 5. Keith Lowe, *Savage Continent: Europe in the Aftermath of World War II*, London, 2012 • 6. Malcolm J. Proudfoot, *European Refugees (1939–1952): A Study in Forced Population Movement*, Evanston, IL, 1956 • 7. Jessica Reinisch & Elizabeth White (eds.), *The Disentanglement of Populations: Migration, Expulsion and Displacement in Post-War Europe, 1944–49*, London, 2011 • 8. Mark Wyman, *DPs: Europe's Displaced Persons, 1945–1951*, Ithaca, NY, 1998 • 9. Gerhard Reichling, *Die deutschen Vertriebenen in Zahlen*, Bonn, 1985 • 10. R. M. Douglas, *Orderly and Humane: The Expulsion of the Germans After the Second World War*, New Haven & London, 2012.

THE ECONOMIC TOLL OF THE WAR

'Europe in the aftermath of the Second World War offered a prospect of utter misery and desolation. Photographs and documentary films of the time show pitiful streams of helpless civilians trekking through a blasted landscape of broken cities and barren fields.'
– Tony Judt, *Postwar: A History of Europe Since 1945*

Germany had no government, money was worthless, there was nothing to sell, nothing to eat, no work. A disaster on this scale, unique in human history, raised fears of twenty years of misery, punctuated by civil wars. The picture in Asia was no better. Japan was in ashes and famine had broken out. Astonishingly, both Japan

1 • OUT OF THE RUINS

Paris and Rome had miraculously survived, but Berlin, Warsaw, Minsk and many other cities had been reduced to rubble. In Eastern Europe, the destruction was unimaginable. From Prussia to Moscow, settlements of all sizes had been damaged or razed to the ground; 70,000 villages and 1,700 towns were destroyed in the USSR alone as well as 32,000 factories. Even places on the margins of the fighting had suffered; 1,000 Greek villages were reduced to ashes by the occupying forces. By comparison, the West seemed relatively well preserved, but in fact this was far from the case. Exterminations and the scorched earth policy had created far more destruction than Allied bombs or fighting in Europe. Transport systems were severely affected. There was not a single bridge left across the Seine downstream from Paris and only one left on the Rhine. The French had lost 12,800 trains and the Soviets 15,000, paralysing their economies.

COST TO GDP AND DAMAGE TO TRANSPORT NETWORKS

540% of GDP

300% of GDP

300% of GDP

150% of GDP

150% of GDP

50% of GDP

50% of GDP

33% of GDP

10% of GDP

Belgium — Netherlands — UK — Italy — Third Reich — France — Yugoslavia — Poland — USSR

40% remaining — 40% remaining? — 70% remaining? — 50% remaining — 50% remaining — 55% remaining — 2% remaining? — 2% remaining? — 40% remaining

95% remaining?

PROPORTION OF HOUSING DESTROYED AND PEOPLE LEFT HOMELESS in 1945

= 10% unaffected
= 10% damaged
= 10% totally destroyed

= 1,000,000 people

USSR: 25,000,000
(14.3% of the population)

7% damaged / 15% destroyed

2 • STARVATION

Rural areas also suffered. In the Netherlands, 11% of agricultural land was flooded and salinized. Yugoslavia lost 25% of its vineyards, 50% of its livestock and 75% of its ploughs. Huge numbers of draught animals had been killed and distribution systems no longer functioned. Europe was reliant on grain supplies from America. 'Better to make the most of the war, peace is going to be terrible' was a standard joke in Berlin in 1944.

In the winter of 1945–46, rations were effectively lower than they had been in 1943. The following summer, infant mortality rose to 66% in one quarter. Epidemics broke out in the East, fueled by massive population movements. Up to 1948, 100,000 Japanese starved to death. The worst situation was in the USSR in 1946–47, when a famine in the newly annexed western regions for which the government bore responsibility resulted in a million and a half deaths and killed off the hope of an eastern baby boom. In most locations, it was three to five years before rationing came to an end.

AVERAGE CALORIE CONSUMPTION

= minimum daily threshold for a worker 2,150 Kcal

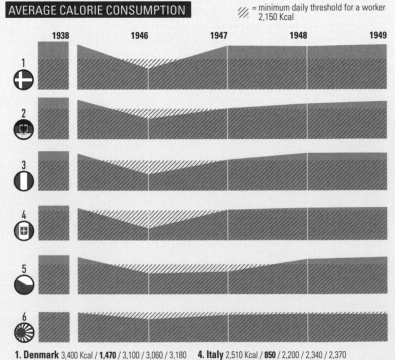

| | 1938 | 1946 | 1947 | 1948 | 1949 |

1. **Denmark** 3,400 Kcal / **1,470** / 3,100 / 3,060 / 3,180
2. **Germany** 2,960 Kcal / **1,450** / 2,190 / 2,530 / 2,690
3. **France** 2,830 Kcal / **1,160** / 2,210 / 2,690 / 2,680
4. **Italy** 2,510 Kcal / **850** / 2,200 / 2,340 / 2,370
5. **Czechoslovakia** 2,700 Kcal / **1,510** / 1,629 / 2,441 / 2,690
6. **Japan** 2,180 Kcal / **1,581** / 1,960 / 2,050 / 2,000

and Europe managed to pull themselves out of the mire within ten years or so and became places of prosperity. A few factors made this possible. Firstly, the existence of an industrial fabric as a foundation for rebuilding. Secondly, the huge scale of the disaster meant that fresh perspectives were needed. In the UK, France, Italy, Czechoslovakia and elsewhere, democracies became welfare states. If democracies were to survive, they saw it was a priority to overcome the poverty, lack of education, and social injustice that had sowed the seeds of totalitarianism. Governments widened their scope to economic and social action. The fight against war profiteering was an opportunity for agrarian reform in Eastern

Europe and for wide-ranging nationalization everywhere else. States made up for the lack of private capital while having leverage to plan and act on growth. Social legislation and expenditure increased. Reconstruction was a chance to provide a higher standard of living. These proactive states restored cohesion and gave reassurance, but the dynamic could not continue unless supply could meet the rise in demand. It took five years for that to happen. These ambitious plans would probably have foundered in the social crisis of 1947 without financial and material contributions from the powerful USA and the new international agencies, UNRRA and the International Bank for Reconstruction and Development (IBRD).

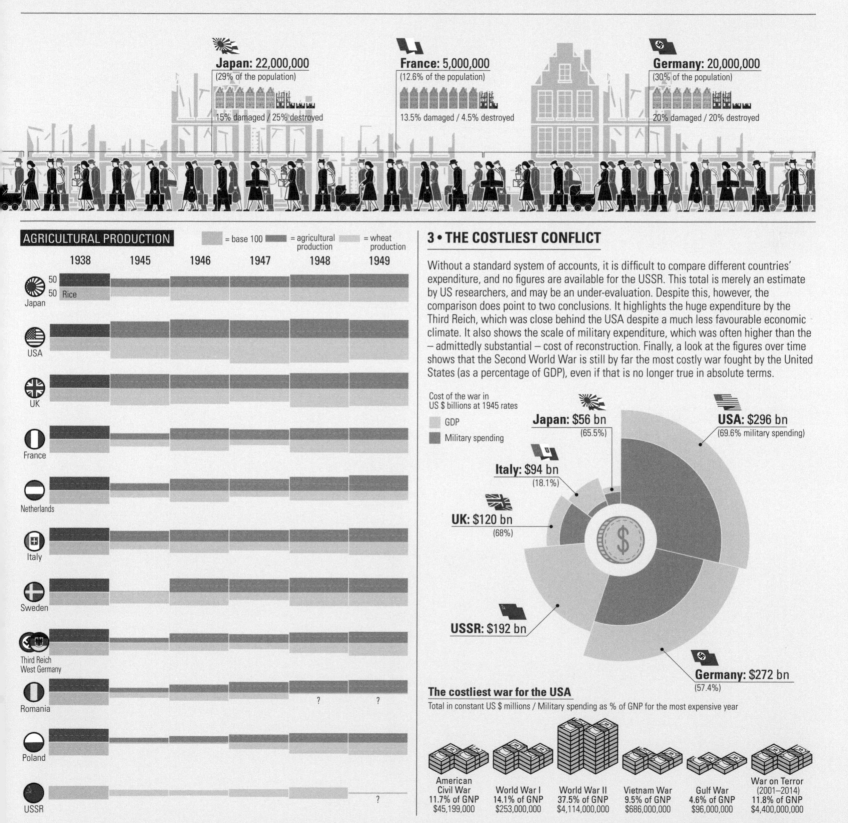

Japan: 22,000,000
(29% of the population)
15% damaged / 25% destroyed

France: 5,000,000
(12.6% of the population)
13.5% damaged / 4.5% destroyed

Germany: 20,000,000
(30% of the population)
20% damaged / 20% destroyed

AGRICULTURAL PRODUCTION

= base 100   = agricultural production   = wheat production

	1938	1945	1946	1947	1948	1949
Japan	50 / 50 Rice					
USA						
UK						
France						
Netherlands						
Italy						
Sweden						
Third Reich West Germany						
Romania					?	?
Poland						
USSR						?

3 • THE COSTLIEST CONFLICT

Without a standard system of accounts, it is difficult to compare different countries' expenditure, and no figures are available for the USSR. This total is merely an estimate by US researchers, and may be an under-evaluation. Despite this, however, the comparison does point to two conclusions. It highlights the huge expenditure by the Third Reich, which was close behind the USA despite a much less favourable economic climate. It also shows the scale of military expenditure, which was often higher than the – admittedly substantial – cost of reconstruction. Finally, a look at the figures over time shows that the Second World War is still by far the most costly war fought by the United States (as a percentage of GDP), even if that is no longer true in absolute terms.

Cost of the war in US $ billions at 1945 rates

GDP
Military spending

Japan: $56 bn
(65.5%)

USA: $296 bn
(69.6% military spending)

Italy: $94 bn
(18.1%)

UK: $120 bn
(68%)

USSR: $192 bn

Germany: $272 bn
(57.4%)

The costliest war for the USA

Total in constant US $ millions / Military spending as % of GNP for the most expensive year

American Civil War	World War I	World War II	Vietnam War	Gulf War	War on Terror (2001–2014)
11.7% of GNP	14.1% of GNP	37.5% of GNP	9.5% of GNP	4.6% of GNP	11.8% of GNP
$45,199,000	$253,000,000	$4,114,000,000	$686,000,000	$96,000,000	$4,400,000,000

4 • DISASTER AND ECONOMIC RECOVERY

In 1945, industry was at a standstill in the defeated countries. France was not even producing half of its pre-war output. Fortunately, not more than 20% of the industrial fabric had been destroyed anywhere. Czechoslovakia and Hungary even came out of the war with greater industrialization, while in Germany equipment had been updated. To start reconstruction, industries were most in need of workers, raw materials, energy and, as an absolute priority, the restoration of the transport network. This started working again in a year or two, including in Eastern Europe where the Red Army made a substantial – and self-interested – contribution. However, recovery was delayed in 1947 by the Allied occupation of Germany, around which European trade had traditionally revolved, coupled with the Allies' reservations about reviving German industry. In addition, Europeans no longer had the financial resources to pay for US imports.

Having tolerated many sacrifices, the people of Europe lost their new-found hope and slipped into recession. Destruction was still everywhere and supplies were scarce. Strong social movements began to appear. Socially, Europe was vacillating, but the announcement of the Marshall Plan and the decision to settle the German question by forming a new state in the west averted the worst. The Marshall Plan was a $13 billion growth plan spread over several years. The aid was dependent on the establishment of a proper industrial investment programme shared by the nations of Europe and the requirement to import US goods of equivalent value. It is true that, as Alan Milward has pointed out (confirmed by the figures shown here), economic recovery began earlier than the Plan. Nevertheless, the Plan accelerated recovery and stimulated reconstruction. Western Europe moved into a period of prosperity such as it had never known.

CHANGING GDPS
in $ billions at 1990 rates

GDP in 1938 ▪ GDP < that of 1938 ▪ GDP = or > that of 1938

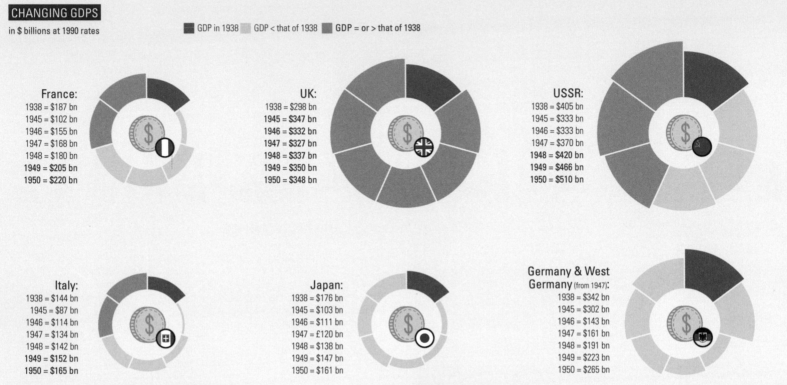

France:
1938 = $187 bn
1945 = $102 bn
1946 = $155 bn
1947 = $168 bn
1948 = $180 bn
1949 = $205 bn
1950 = $220 bn

UK:
1938 = $298 bn
1945 = $347 bn
1946 = $332 bn
1947 = $327 bn
1948 = $337 bn
1949 = $350 bn
1950 = $348 bn

USSR:
1938 = $405 bn
1945 = $333 bn
1946 = $333 bn
1947 = $370 bn
1948 = $420 bn
1949 = $466 bn
1950 = $510 bn

Italy:
1938 = $144 bn
1945 = $87 bn
1946 = $114 bn
1947 = $134 bn
1948 = $142 bn
1949 = $152 bn
1950 = $165 bn

Japan:
1938 = $176 bn
1945 = $103 bn
1946 = $111 bn
1947 = £120 bn
1948 = $138 bn
1949 = $147 bn
1950 = $161 bn

Germany & West Germany (from 1947):
1938 = $342 bn
1945 = $302 bn
1946 = $143 bn
1947 = $161 bn
1948 = $191 bn
1949 = $223 bn
1950 = $265 bn

CHANGES IN INDUSTRIAL PRODUCTIVITY

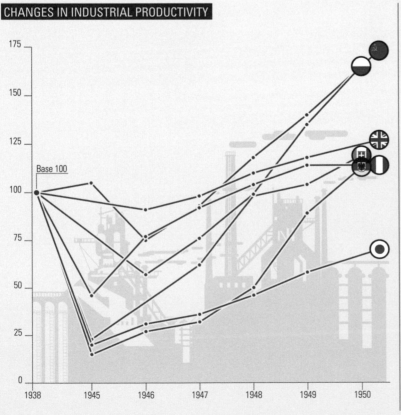

UNEMPLOYMENT FIGURES in thousands

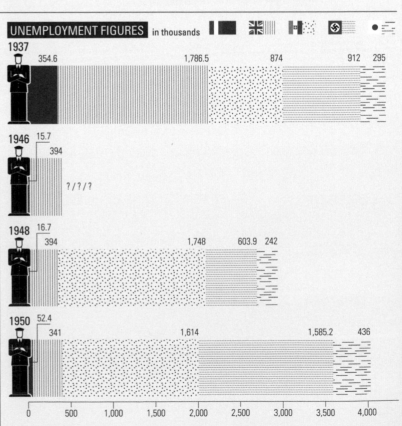

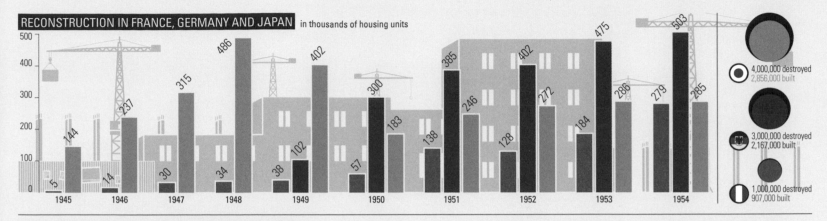

RECONSTRUCTION IN FRANCE, GERMANY AND JAPAN in thousands of housing units

4,000,000 destroyed
2,856,000 built

3,000,000 destroyed
2,167,000 built

1,000,000 destroyed
907,000 built

CHANGES IN PRODUCTION OF GOODS AND MATERIALS between 1938 and 1950

Coal extraction
(in thousands of tonnes)

Iron ore extraction
(in thousands of tonnes)

Steel production
(in thousands of tonnes)

Electricity production
(in MW)

Car production

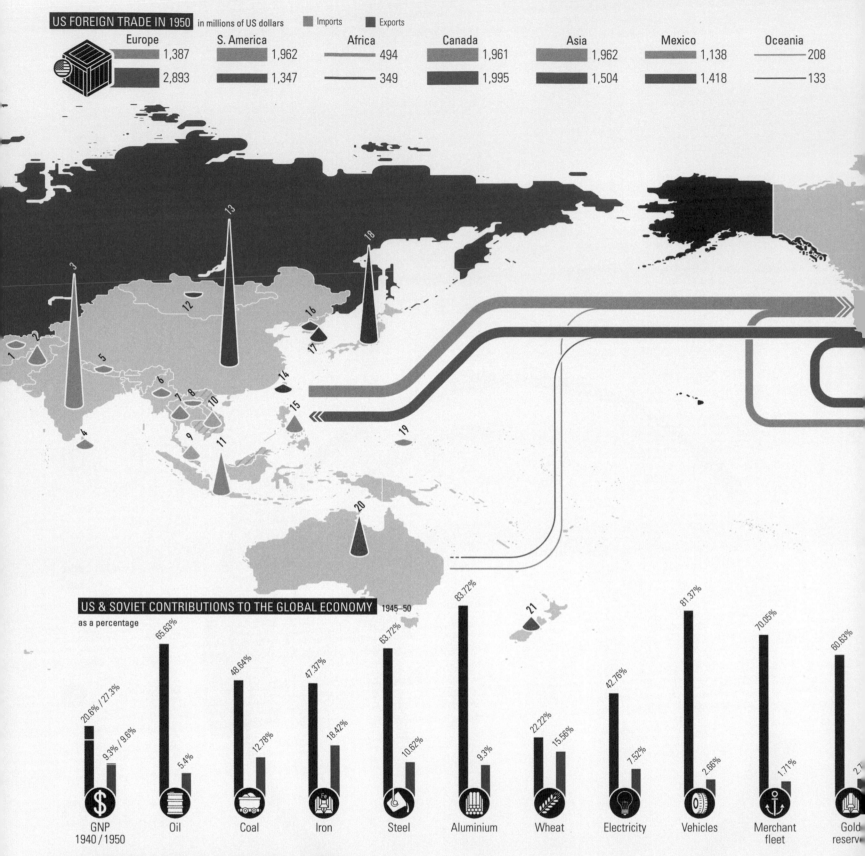

	Europe	S. America	Africa	Canada	Asia	Mexico	Oceania
Imports	1,387	1,962	494	1,961	1,962	1,138	208
Exports	2,893	1,347	349	1,995	1,504	1,418	133

US & SOVIET CONTRIBUTIONS TO THE GLOBAL ECONOMY 1945–50
as a percentage

GNP 1940 / 1950	20.6% / 27.3%	9.3% / 9.6%	
Oil	65.63%	5.4%	
Coal	48.64%	12.76%	
Iron	47.37%	18.42%	
Steel	63.72%	10.62%	
Aluminium	83.72%	9.3%	
Wheat	22.22%	15.56%	
Electricity	42.76%	7.52%	
Vehicles	81.37%	2.66%	
Merchant fleet	70.05%	1.71%	
Gold reserve	60.63%	2.7	

5 • THE US WORLD-ECONOMY REACHES ITS PEAK

In 1949, the historian Fernand Braudel defined a world-economy as 'an economically autonomous section of the planet [with a ruling centre and ruled peripheries] ...to which its internal links and exchanges give a certain organic unity'. At the beginning of the 20th century, the US world-economy began to take over from the British one, but it was not until the Second World War that the transition became definite. In 1945, the USA had greater status and influence in the world than any other country. It held 60% of gold reserves, possessed over 50% of the world's wealth (but only 6% of its population) and only left crumbs to the others, including the USSR. It was the beating heart of globalization and still growing, primarily because Europe and Asia were in ruins and were forced to import on a massive scale. At the Bretton Woods Conference (1944), the dollar was established as the currency for international trade and the GATT Agreement (1947) marked the start of free trade. The 'American way' became global. In 1947, Europe imported six times more from the US than it exported, and the UK acquired half its imports from there. Coal and grain could only be purchased with the help of substantial loans from the superpower ($4.4 billion to the UK, $1.9 billion to France and hundreds of millions to the USSR). In 1947, the trade deficit doubled. As tensions with the USSR mounted, Europe was on the verge of bankruptcy. Marshall offered a way out of the crisis with a well-thought-out plan. It had the advantage that it resolved the social crisis in the short term and embedded Western Europe and its colonies firmly within the US world-economy, while benefiting American business. In the long term, the Americans took the risk of encouraging the emergence of trade competitors because they were confident that their innovations would keep them in the lead. They entered the Cold War with a masterstroke. Over the next few years, the building of a US-centric Western bloc was completed with a network of military alliances.

SOURCES: 1. *Yearbook of the United Nations*, 1948–53 • 2. *Statistical Abstract of the United States*, 1953 • 3. *World Economic Report*, UN, 1949 • 4. Dominique Barjot, Rémi Baudouï & Danièle Voldman (eds.),

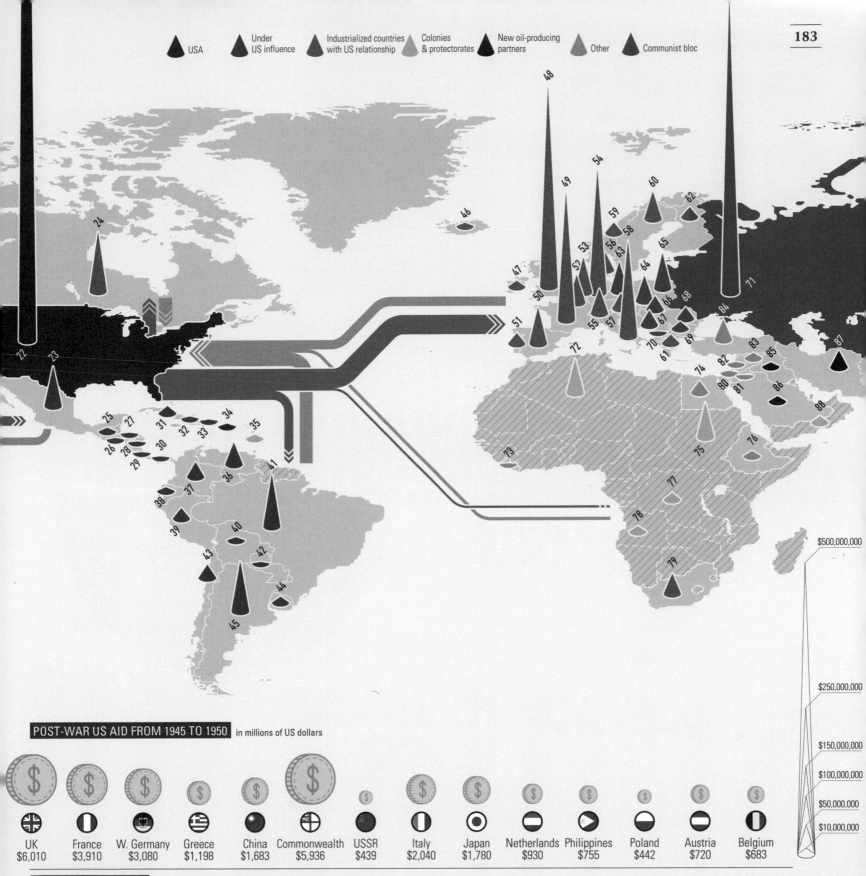

USA | Under US influence | Industrialized countries with US relationship | Colonies & protectorates | New oil-producing partners | Other | Communist bloc

POST-WAR US AID FROM 1945 TO 1950 in millions of US dollars

| UK $6,010 | France $3,910 | W. Germany $3,080 | Greece $1,198 | China $1,683 | Commonwealth $5,936 | USSR $439 | Italy $2,040 | Japan $1,780 | Netherlands $930 | Philippines $755 | Poland $442 | Austria $720 | Belgium $683 |

$500,000,000
$250,000,000
$150,000,000
$100,000,000
$50,000,000
$10,000,000

GLOBAL GDPS IN 1950 in millions of US dollars at 1990 rates

1. Afghanistan: 5,255 - 2. Pakistan: 25,366 - 3. India: 222,222 - 4. Sri Lanka: 9,438 - 5. Nepal: 4,462 - 6. Burma: 7,711 - 7. Thailand: 9,438 - 8. Laos: 1,156 - 9. British colonies in Asia: 17,262 - 10. Indochina: 18,836 - 11. Indonesia: 5,255 - 12. Mongolia: 339 - 13. China: 244,985 - 14. Taiwan: 7,378 - 15. Philippines: 66,358 - 16. North Korea: 8,087 - 17. South Korea: 17,800 - 19. Japan: 160,966 - 20. Rest of Asia: 3,871 - 21. Australia: 61,274 - 22. New Zealand: 16,136 - 22. USA: 1,455,916 - 23. Mexico: 67,368 - 24. Canada: 102,164 - 25. Guatemala: 6,190 - 26. El Salvador: 2,888 - 27. Honduras: 1,880 - 28. Nicaragua: 1,774 - 29. Costa Rica: 1,702 - 30. Panama: 1,710 - 31. Cuba: 11,837 - 32. Haiti: 3,254 - 33. Dominican Republic: 2,416 - 34. Puerto Rico: 4,755 - 35. Rest of Caribbean: 8,242 - 36. Venezuela: 37,377 - 37. Ecuador: 6,728 - 38. Colombia: 24,955 - 39. Peru: 17,613 - 40. Bolivia: 5,309 - 41. Brazil: 89,342 - 42. Paraguay: 2,338 - 43. Chile: 22,352 - 44. Uruguay: 10,224 - 45. Argentina: 85,524 - 46. Rest of Europe: 5,880 - 47. Ireland: 10,231 - 48. UK: 347,850 - 49. France: 220,492 - 50. Spain: 61,429 - 51. Portugal: 17,615 - 52. Belgium: 47,190 - 53. Netherlands: 60,642 - 54. West Germany: 213,942 - 55. Switzerland: 42,545 - 56. Denmark: 29,654 - 57. Austria: 25,702 - 58. Italy: 164,957 - 59. Norway: 17,728 - 60. Sweden: 47,269 - 61. Greece: 14,489 - 62. Finland: 17,051 - 63. East Germany: 51,412 - 64. Czechoslovakia: 43,368 - 65. Poland: 60,742 - 66. Hungary: 23,158 - 67. Yugoslavia: 25,277 - 68. Romania: 19,279 - 69. Bulgaria: 11,971 - 70. Albania: 1,229 - 71. USSR: 510,243 - 72. French colonies in Africa: 57,828 - 73. Liberia: 869 - 74. Egypt: 19,923 - 75. British colonies in Africa: 59,204 - 76. Ethiopia: 8,417 - 77. Belgian colonies in Africa: 9,916 - 78. Portuguese colonies in Africa: 11,696 - 79. South Africa: 34,465 - 80. Israel: 3,623 - 81. Jordan: 1,233 - 82. Lebanon: 3,313 - 83. Syria: 8,418 - 84. Turkey: 34,279 - 85. Iraq: 7,041 - 86. Saudi Arabia: 8,610 - 87. Iran: 28,128 - 88. British protectorates: 17,262

Les Reconstructions en Europe (1945–1949), Brussels, 1997 • 5. Jean Chardonnet, *Les Conséquences économiques de la guerre (1939–1946)*, Paris, 1947 • 6. Tony Judt, *Postwar: A History of Europe since 1945*, London, 2010.

THE MANHATTAN PROJECT

The leading world powers all had atomic research programmes in 1939. The French and German programmes were relatively advanced, but had to contend with limited budgets and lack of progress, particularly in isotope enrichment. The Nazis showed little interest given the lack of short-term results, but it has been suggested in recent years that a limited German nuclear test might have been carried out before the end of the war. The French programme started by Frédéric Joliot-Curie continued in Britain, using heavy water from Norway, but made very little headway. The British programme under the codename 'Tube Alloys' was also limited, but was later secretly incorporated into the US programme. Not initially involved, the Americans, alerted by a famous letter written by Albert Einstein in 1939, embarked belatedly but determinedly on atomic research with the resources they had available. A secret programme named the 'Manhattan

1 • 'I AM BECOME DEATH': A MODESTLY MASSIVE UNDERTAKING

The Manhattan Project employed up to half a million people in total at its various American sites and as far away as Canada. Some 400 scientists at Los Alamos and 6,000 servicemen were working on it in 1945. Although the total cost seemed enormous for just a handful of bombs – $1.9 billion at the time, $25 billion at current rates – the investment in the Manhattan Project seems relatively small compared with the overall American expenditure on the war, at about 0.6%. The atomic programme ushered in a new era of military and civilian technology, which soon became unstoppable and paved the way for a new global balance of power.

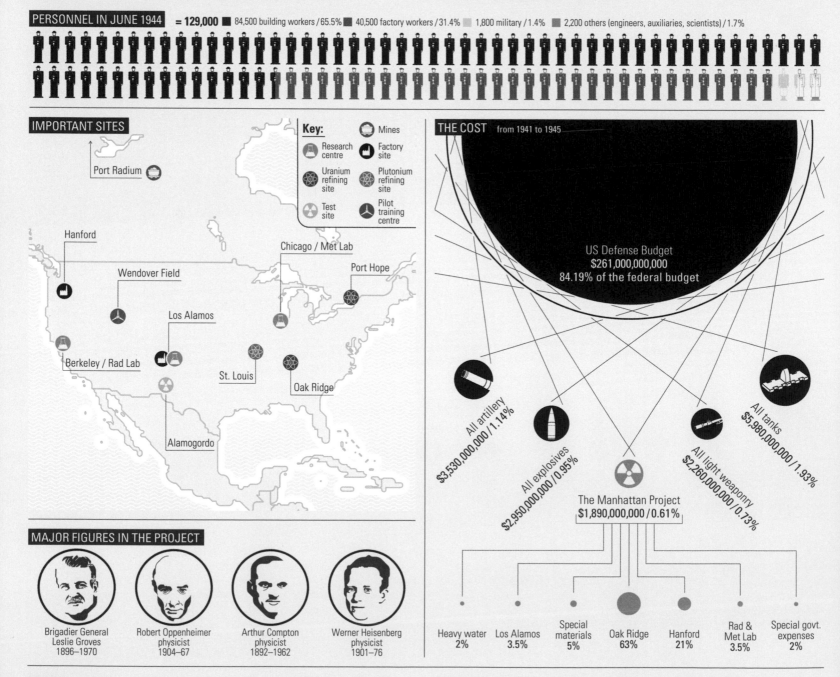

PERSONNEL IN JUNE 1944 = 129,000 ■ 84,500 building workers / 65.5% ■ 40,500 factory workers / 31.4% ■ 1,800 military / 1.4% ■ 2,200 others (engineers, auxiliaries, scientists) / 1.7%

IMPORTANT SITES

Key:
- Research centre
- Mines
- Uranium refining site
- Factory site
- Test site
- Plutonium refining site
- Pilot training centre

Port Radium

Hanford
Wendover Field
Chicago / Met Lab
Port Hope
Los Alamos
Berkeley / Rad Lab
St. Louis
Oak Ridge
Alamogordo

THE COST from 1941 to 1945

US Defense Budget
$261,000,000,000
84.19% of the federal budget

All artillery
$3,530,000,000 / 1.14%

All explosives
$2,950,000,000 / 0.95%

All tanks
$5,980,000,000 / 1.93%

All light weaponry
$2,260,000,000 / 0.73%

The Manhattan Project
$1,890,000,000 / 0.61%

| Heavy water 2% | Los Alamos 3.5% | Special materials 5% | Oak Ridge 63% | Hanford 21% | Rad & Met Lab 3.5% | Special govt. expenses 2% |

MAJOR FIGURES IN THE PROJECT

Brigadier General Leslie Groves 1896–1970

Robert Oppenheimer physicist 1904–67

Arthur Compton physicist 1892–1962

Werner Heisenberg physicist 1901–76

SOURCES: 1. *Statistical Review, World War II: A Summary of ASF Statistics*, US War Department, 1946 • 2. *United States Strategic Bombing Survey (Pacific War)*, Washington, DC, 1946 • 3. *Historical Statistics of the United States from Colonial Times to 1970*, US Census Bureau, 1975 • 4. Stephen I. Schwartz, *Atomic Audit: The Costs and Consequences of U.S. Nuclear Weapons since 1940*, Washington, DC, 1998.

Project', brought together experts from all over the world and was allocated over a billion dollars in financing, a thousand times the amount of UK investment. Between 1939 and 1945, the project, headed by Robert Oppenheimer, led to the development of two different types of bomb. The first, using uranium 235, was simple and reliable but difficult to make. This was 'Little Boy', dropped on Hiroshima on 6 August 1945. The other, using plutonium 239, was more complex but could be produced in larger numbers. That bomb, 'Fat Man', was tested in the New Mexico desert on 16 July 1945 and dropped on Nagasaki, devastating it on 9 August 1945. As the war ended, the world fearfully entered the nuclear age.

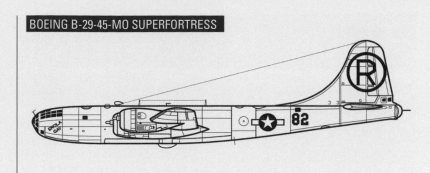

BOEING B-29-45-MO SUPERFORTRESS

2 • 'THE DESTROYER OF WORLDS': HIROSHIMA AND NAGASAKI

Combined casualty figures for the atomic bombings of Hiroshima and Nagasaki on 6 and 9 April 1945 vary from more than 100,000 to 250,000 deaths (between August and December 1945). Although of a different kind, the total death toll was comparable to those of regular deadly raids during the war (e.g. Hamburg 1943: 60,000 dead, Dresden 1945: 40,000, Tokyo 1945: 100,000). In the context of widespread strategic bombing, the effect of the bombs on the Japanese decision to surrender has perhaps been overestimated. Even so, the horror of the atomic bomb opened up a new strategic age of terror in which a single weapon could destroy a city or a whole region.

1. The bomb explodes at an altitude of around 600 m. The heat pushes the air outwards, causing massive pressure and an enormous blast.
2. Air pressure collapses in the centre, reversing the flow of air and creating a devastating shockwave.

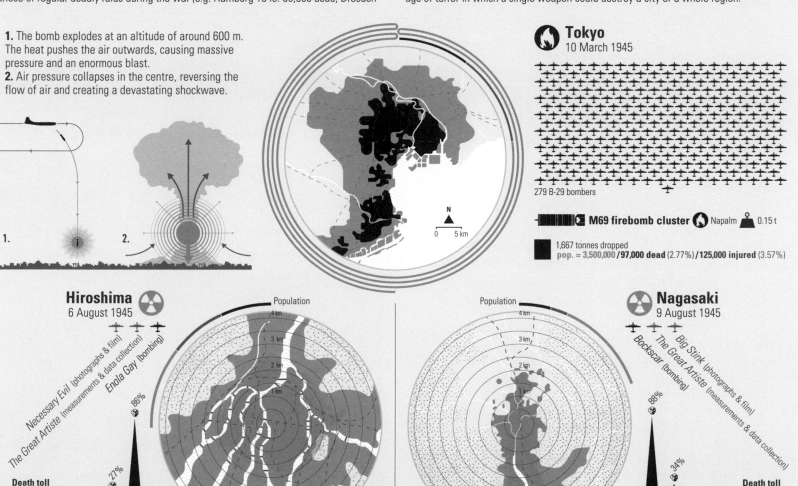

Tokyo
10 March 1945

279 B-29 bombers

M69 firebomb cluster — Napalm — 0.15 t

1,667 tonnes dropped
pop. = 3,500,000 / **97,000 dead** (2.77%) / **125,000 injured** (3.57%)

N
0   5 km

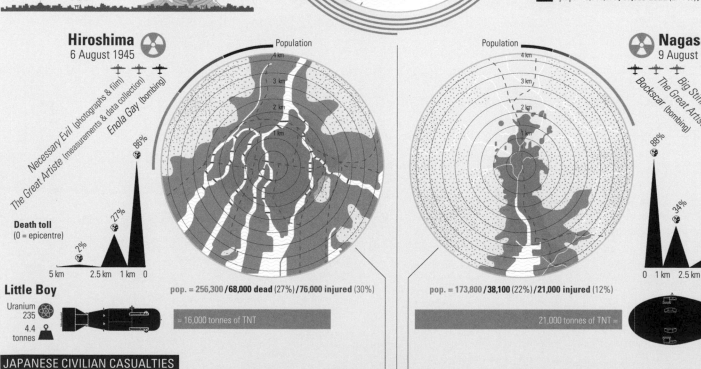

Hiroshima
6 August 1945

Necessary Evil (photographs & film)
The Great Artiste (measurements & data collection)
Enola Gay (bombing)

Population
4 km
3 km
2 km
1 km

86%

27%

2%

Death toll
(0 = epicentre)

5 km   2.5 km   1 km   0

Little Boy
Uranium 235
4.4 tonnes

= 16,000 tonnes of TNT

pop. = 256,300 / **68,000 dead** (27%) / **76,000 injured** (30%)

pop. = 173,800 / **38,100** (22%) / **21,000 injured** (12%)

Population
4 km
3 km
2 km
1 km

86%

34%

11%

Death toll
(0 = epicentre)

0   1 km   2.5 km   5 km

Nagasaki
9 August 1945

Big Stink (photographs & film)
The Great Artiste (measurements & data collection)
Bockscar (bombing)

21,000 tonnes of TNT =

Fat Man
Plutonium 239
4.67 tonnes

JAPANESE CIVILIAN CASUALTIES

| **300,000 dead** (37.5%) Overseas (Okinawa, Taiwan, Manchuria, Korea, Philippines, etc.) | **100,000 dead** (12.5%) Tokyo | **± 110,000** (13.75%) Hiroshima & Nagasaki | **290,000 dead** (36.25%) Rest of mainland Japan, strategic bombing and famine |

THE DAWN OF THE COLD WAR IN EUROPE

The confrontation between Western democracies and the USSR that took place between 1947 and 1989 was not a consequence of the Second World War. The conflict of ideology and the global ambitions of both Communism (proletarian internationalism) and free market capitalism (globalization) had already made confrontation inevitable.

It started as long ago as 1920, when Western forces became involved in the Russian Civil War. The Nazis, a deadly enemy of both sides, merely disrupted the duel for a time and obliged them to form a temporary Great Alliance. But although the Second World War did not cause the Cold War, it undoubtedly reshuffled the cards. Without the war, the USSR would have become a great power in any case, but its victory over Hitler lent it considerable prestige, elevated it to the rank of a superpower and allowed it to expand its territories in a way that would have been unthinkable before the war, when the French and the British considered it to be less powerful than Poland. The war also changed the status of the USA. Its economic and financial dominance was absolute, it reigned supreme in the air and at sea and was the only country with nuclear weapons (albeit still on a small scale). With Germany neutralized, France outclassed and Britain financially drained, the USA led the world. To an extent, the overlapping wars in Yugoslavia, Greece and the Baltic states prolonged the fighting after May 1945, creating a continuity between the Second World War and the Cold War.

Were the parties involved aware of this? Roosevelt died still nursing his dream of cooperation between the 'Big Four' to guarantee security and allow the USSR time to soften its attitude. This strategy meant reassuring Stalin by giving way to his territorial claims and his hunger for security, as illustrated by Yalta and Potsdam. Far from sharing Europe, the Americans established the principle of a new European order founded on democracy and agreement between the ruling powers. In a similar spirit, Germany was controlled by a four-nation committee with a view to democratization. In Eastern Europe, Roosevelt thought he had managed to establish countries that were friendly to the USSR but still possessed a certain amount of national freedom via coalition governments (a model that ultimately would only be successful in Finland). But Stalin wanted to push his advantage as far as possible. In the words of historian Georges-Henri Soutou: 'Stalin's goal was in fact to establish a hegemonic system throughout the continent, within a very left-wing political landscape ... wherever the correlation of forces and in particular the crisis of capitalism allowed.' In Western Europe, the political landscape had shifted to the left after the conservative parties had been discredited in the war. Three parties dominated: the revitalized Christian Democrats, the old Social Democrats and the Communist Party, representing between 10 and 30% of the electorate.

Aware of Britain's weakened state, expecting a quick withdrawal by US forces and a worsening of the socio-economic situation, Stalin made his move, quickly when he could and otherwise slowly, always keeping up appearances. This was the strategy for the democratic fronts. Stalin was more aggressive in China and Iran, and even sounded out Turkey. Although he pulled back as soon as he sensed resistance, as he did in Greece, Turkey and Iran, he did not prevent the building of tension. The Americans reacted, but their reactions were selective. Their firm response in Iran contrasted with their resigned approach in the Balkans and this led to the creation of the Iron Curtain. In March 1947, the Truman Doctrine was announced, a policy whose aim was to counter the spread of Communism. The Cold War had begun.

1 • EUROPE AFTER THE WAR

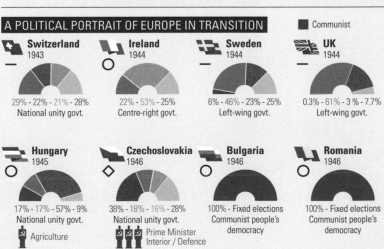

A POLITICAL PORTRAIT OF EUROPE IN TRANSITION

■ Communist

Switzerland 1943
29% - 22% - 21% - 28%
National unity govt.

Ireland 1944
22% - 53% - 25%
Centre-right govt.

Sweden 1944
6% - 46% - 23% - 25%
Left-wing govt.

UK 1944
0.3% - 61% - 3 % - 7.7%
Left-wing govt.

Hungary 1945
17% - 17% - 57% - 9%
National unity govt.
Agriculture

Czechoslovakia 1946
38% - 18% - 16% - 28%
National unity govt.
Prime Minister Interior / Defence

Bulgaria 1946
100% - Fixed elections
Communist people's democracy

Romania 1946
100% - Fixed elections
Communist people's democracy

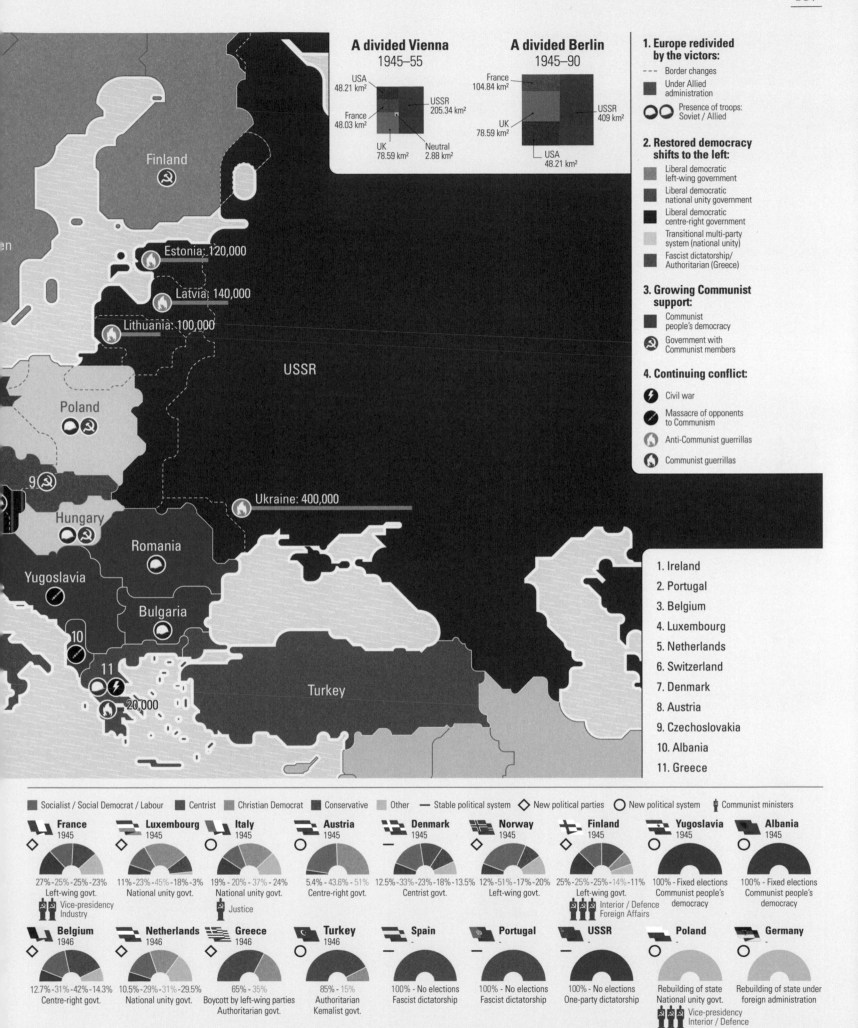

A divided Vienna 1945–55

USA 48.21 km²
USSR 205.34 km²
France 48.03 km²
UK 78.59 km²
Neutral 2.88 km²

A divided Berlin 1945–90

France 104.84 km²
USSR 409 km²
UK 78.59 km²
USA 48.21 km²

1. Europe redivided by the victors:

- - - Border changes

Under Allied administration

◯◯ Presence of troops: Soviet / Allied

2. Restored democracy shifts to the left:

Liberal democratic left-wing government

Liberal democratic national unity government

Liberal democratic centre-right government

Transitional multi-party system (national unity)

Fascist dictatorship/ Authoritarian (Greece)

3. Growing Communist support:

Communist people's democracy

Government with Communist members

4. Continuing conflict:

Civil war

Massacre of opponents to Communism

Anti-Communist guerrillas

Communist guerrillas

Finland

Estonia: 120,000

Latvia: 140,000

Lithuania: 100,000

USSR

Poland

9

Hungary

Romania

Yugoslavia

Bulgaria

10

11

20,000

Ukraine: 400,000

Turkey

1. Ireland
2. Portugal
3. Belgium
4. Luxembourg
5. Netherlands
6. Switzerland
7. Denmark
8. Austria
9. Czechoslovakia
10. Albania
11. Greece

■ Socialist / Social Democrat / Labour ■ Centrist ■ Christian Democrat ■ Conservative ■ Other — Stable political system ◇ New political parties ◯ New political system ⚒ Communist ministers

France 1945
◇
27% - 25% - 25% - 23%
Left-wing govt.
Vice-presidency Industry

Luxembourg 1945
◇
11% - 23% - 45% - 18% - 3%
National unity govt.

Italy 1945
◯
19% - 20% - 37% - 24%
National unity govt.
Justice

Austria 1945
◯
5.4% - 43.6% - 51%
Centre-right govt.

Denmark 1945
—
12.5% - 33% - 23% - 18% - 13.5%
Centrist govt.

Norway 1945
◇
12% - 51% - 17% - 20%
Left-wing govt.

Finland 1945
◇
25% - 25% - 25% - 14% - 11%
Left-wing govt.
Interior / Defence Foreign Affairs

Yugoslavia 1945
◯
100% - Fixed elections
Communist people's democracy

Albania 1945
◯
100% - Fixed elections
Communist people's democracy

Belgium 1946
◇
12.7% - 31% - 42% - 14.3%
Centre-right govt.

Netherlands 1946
◇
10.5% - 29% - 31% - 29.5%
National unity govt.

Greece 1946
◇
65% - 35%
Boycott by left-wing parties
Authoritarian govt.

Turkey 1946
85% - 15%
Authoritarian Kemalist govt.

Spain
100% - No elections
Fascist dictatorship

Portugal
100% - No elections
Fascist dictatorship

USSR
100% - No elections
One-party dictatorship

Poland
◯
Rebuilding of state
National unity govt.
Vice-presidency Interior / Defence

Germany
◯
Rebuilding of state under foreign administration

2 • SATELLIZATION SPLITS EUROPE IN TWO

In 1944, Stalin told Yugoslav Communist Milovan Djilas that the war was different from previous wars; everyone imposed their social system as far as their army could advance. In fact, this was not new, nor was it so simple. Communist parties in liberated countries were small. They had little legitimacy and the population was fairly hostile to them. But this did not stop them starting to take control in 1944. The principle was simple. In the words of Walter Ulbricht, head of the German Communist party, in 1945: 'It must look democratic but everything must be under our control.' The process had five stages: 1. win over with conciliatory and populist language, mass recruitment (with lax conditions) to give the illusion of numbers; 2. control the levers of political and administrative power; 3. use these to create a hostile climate to justify the fourth stage;

THE STAGES OF SATELLIZATION

1. Convince & reassure
• Promote national unity: create democratic fronts bringing together a wide range of anti-Fascist parties; join national unity governments to secure strategic ministries (justice, agriculture, ideally interior).
• Encourage popular reforms (e.g. agrarian reforms redistributing land to the poorest).

2. Infiltrate
• Communist infiltration of the government and police; create state police under NKVD control.
• Infiltrate other parties.
• Initiate and control purges.
• USSR takes over Allied Control Council (Westerners neutralized, right of scrutiny of ministers' portfolios, laws, etc.); the NKVD infiltrates and carries out arrests.

3. Discredit
• Organize strikes and create a climate of chaos.
• Campaign to discredit opponents.
• Pressure from USSR for immediate payment of war reparations, crippling the government.

4. Break down the rule of law
• Purge the judiciary and the police.
• Acts of terror against other parties (violence, assassination, arbitrary arrests for conspiracy, political processes, ban on opposition press).
• Use 'salami' tactics to gradually eliminate political opponents from right and left. Use infiltrated organizations to provoke schisms: one side supports the CP, the other is eliminated.

5. Stalinize
• New constitution: Soviet type or similar.
• Absorb or ban any remaining parties.
• Destroy civil society: purge of knowledge (teachers and libraries) + destruction of peasantry + control over clergy + ban on organizations.
• Nationalization and collectivization.
• Purge of CP (June 1948: Cominform conference condemns Titoism and calls for standardization of CPs + elimination of leading Communist figures.

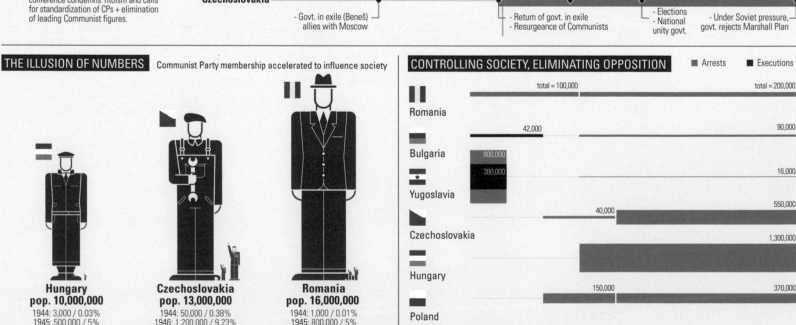

SOURCES: 1. Masha Cerovic, *Les Enfants de Staline. La guerre des partisans soviétiques (1941–1944)*, Seuil, 2018 • 2. Gael Eismann & Stefan Martens (eds.), *Occupation et répression militaire allemandes (1939–1945)*, Paris, 2007 • 3. Vladimir Geiger, 'Human losses of the Croats in World War II and the immediate post-war period', *Review of Croatian History*, no. 1, 2012, pp. 77–121 • 4. Mark Mazower, *Hitler's Empire. Nazi Rule in Occupied Europe*, London, 2008 • 5. Olivier Wieviorka, *Une histoire de la Résistance en Europe occidentale*, Paris, 2017.

4. break down the rule of law (arbitrary arrests, rigged elections); 5. Stalinize society. In some places, the slaughter of the intelligentsia during the war made the task easier.

Moscow's influence was essential. Governments were overseen by the Soviet Control Commission, which had a right of scrutiny and a veto over national policy. The NKVD advised and trained local Communists, particularly the future security services. The Red Army maintained 'orderly disorder' that favoured the Communists. Without this presence, Stalin failed in Greece and Finland and had to take Czechoslovakia by force. The USSR eventually satellized Eastern Europe via Cominform (a link between Moscow and local Communist parties) and Comecon (Council for Mutual Economic Assistance), an economic body promoting socialist labour principles that benefited the USSR. Only Tito, who had genuine public support and adopted Stalinist methods, resisted satellization and took his own route to socialism. The result was the bipolarization of Europe.

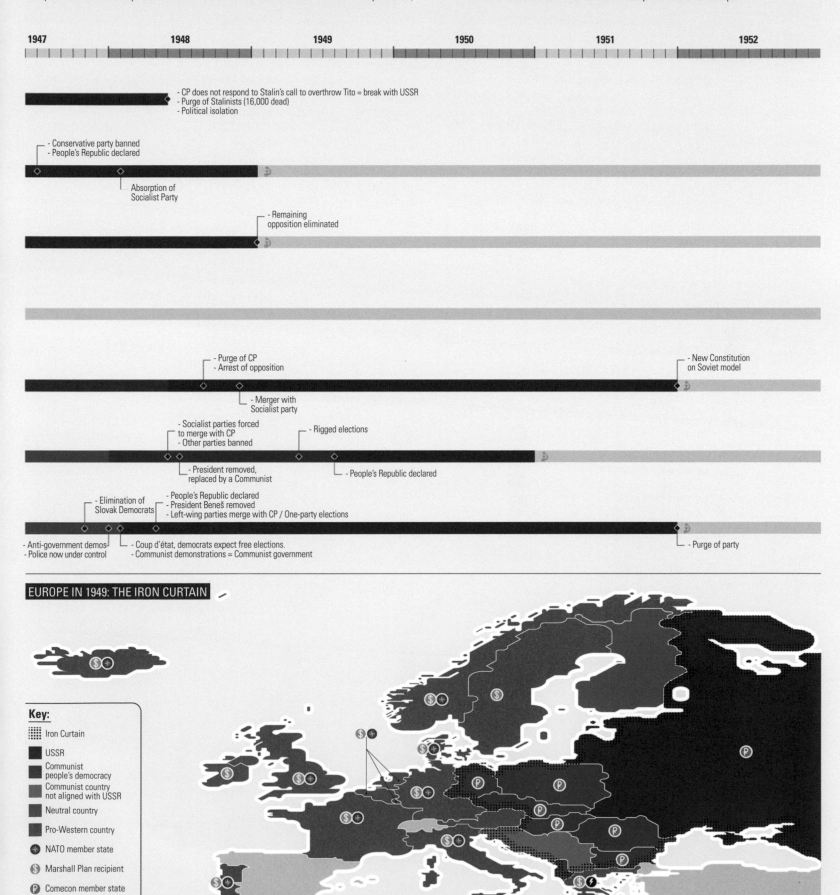

| 1947 | 1948 | 1949 | 1950 | 1951 | 1952 |

- CP does not respond to Stalin's call to overthrow Tito = break with USSR
- Purge of Stalinists (16,000 dead)
- Political isolation

- Conservative party banned
- People's Republic declared

Absorption of Socialist Party

- Remaining opposition eliminated

- Purge of CP
- Arrest of opposition

- New Constitution on Soviet model

- Merger with Socialist party

- Socialist parties forced to merge with CP
- Other parties banned

- Rigged elections

- President removed, replaced by a Communist

- People's Republic declared

- Elimination of Slovak Democrats

- People's Republic declared
- President Beneš removed
- Left-wing parties merge with CP / One-party elections

- Anti-government demos
- Police now under control

- Coup d'état, democrats expect free elections.
- Communist demonstrations = Communist government

- Purge of party

EUROPE IN 1949: THE IRON CURTAIN

Key:
- Iron Curtain
- USSR
- Communist people's democracy
- Communist country not aligned with USSR
- Neutral country
- Pro-Western country
- NATO member state
- Marshall Plan recipient
- Comecon member state
- Civil war ends: monarchist victory

COLONIAL UNREST: THE FALL OF EMPIRES

Already shaken by the First World War and the heavy losses of indigenous troops (from North Africa, India, etc.), Europe's colonial empires did not remain immune from the radical changes resulting from the Second World War. Although serious conflicts were already breaking out in Africa, especially Algeria and Madagascar, it was in South-East Asia, devastated by the Japanese occupation, that the break-up happened fastest, leading to the first major wave of post-war decolonization. Korea, neighbour to a China that was falling into civil war, was divided into two independent states that soon became enemies. Wars of independence broke out in the Dutch East Indies (led by Sukarno) and Indochina (led by Ho Chi Minh), leading to the creation of Indonesia and Vietnam respectively. British India, already on the way to a planned 'enfranchisement' in 1939, was partitioned into India and Pakistan, with disastrous consequences. These countries were only among the first to win their independence in a process that was to continue for several decades.

1 • COLONIAL EMPIRES IN THE WAR

The contribution of colonial troops to the European war effort and the poor recompense they received were important factors in independence movements at the end of the war. In France, the Minister for the Colonies, Georges Mandel, promised to bring two million soldiers and half a million workers from the colonies. The eventual number was nowhere close to that. Europe as a whole and in particular the British, French and Italians and the Dutch in Asia were supported by over a million colonial soldiers who made up most of the manpower in the garrisons and combat forces in the sub-Saharan theatre and formed a major contingent in the North Africa campaign. With fewer than 200,000 men in 1939, one-third of them British officers and men, the Indian Army was a particularly notable example of a phenomenon that already foreshadowed the sub-continent's independence. Up to two and a half million men were mobilized there, forming around thirty divisions, of whom many fought in South-East Asia as well as in the Middle East and Italy.

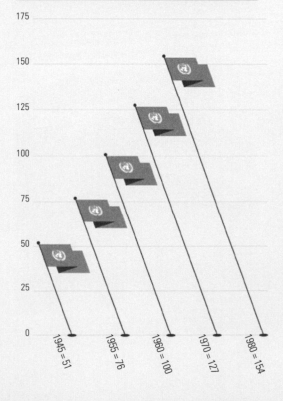

INDEPENDENT SOVEREIGN STATES IN THE UN

1945 = 51
1955 = 76
1960 = 100
1970 = 127
1980 = 154

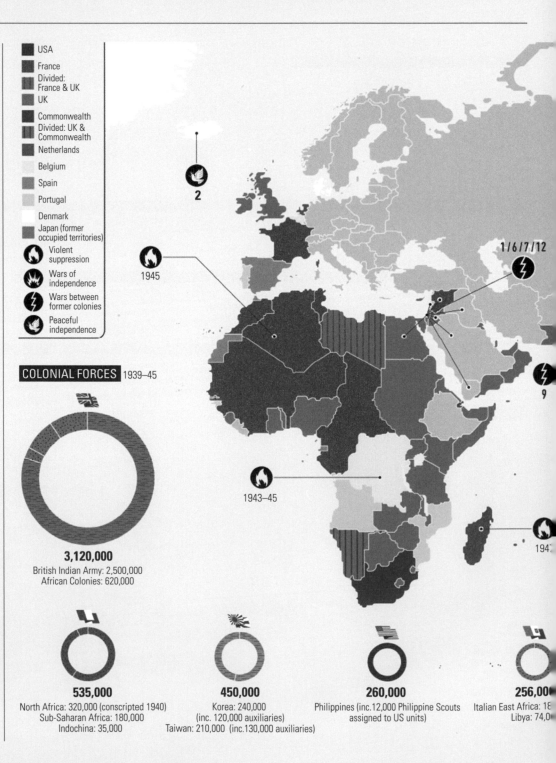

Legend:
- USA
- France
- Divided: France & UK
- UK
- Commonwealth
- Divided: UK & Commonwealth
- Netherlands
- Belgium
- Spain
- Portugal
- Denmark
- Japan (former occupied territories)
- Violent suppression
- Wars of independence
- Wars between former colonies
- Peaceful independence

2

1945

1/6/7/12

1943–45

9

194?

COLONIAL FORCES 1939–45

3,120,000
British Indian Army: 2,500,000
African Colonies: 620,000

535,000
North Africa: 320,000 (conscripted 1940)
Sub-Saharan Africa: 180,000
Indochina: 35,000

450,000
Korea: 240,000
(inc. 120,000 auxiliaries)
Taiwan: 210,000 (inc.130,000 auxiliaries)

260,000
Philippines (inc.12,000 Philippine Scouts assigned to US units)

256,00...
Italian East Africa: 18...
Libya: 74,0...

2 • SÉTIF, GUELMA AND KERRATA: A DECADE OF PEACE TURNS TO BLOODSHED

As soon as the war ended in Europe, violence broke out in French Algeria, which had had a strong independence movement since the 1920s. In May and June 1945, demonstrations in Sétif, Guelma and Kerrata degenerated into a massacre of around a hundred Europeans, followed by blind and extremely bloody repression resulting in thousands of deaths and arrests. At the time, General Duval reported that he had won a decade of peace for Algeria, while calling on the government for radical reforms. The Algerian War broke out less than ten years later in 1954, and eventually led to independence in 1962.

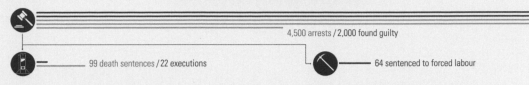

Casualties of the riots:

Europeans killed = 102 (inc. 90 at Sétif) / Injured = 110

State suppression by 28 February 1946:

4,500 arrests / 2,000 found guilty

99 death sentences / 22 executions

64 sentenced to forced labour

The toll of military oppression: competing claims (by source) ▮ = 1,000 Algerian deaths ● French state = 1,000 dead ◓ Historians = from 3,000 to 8,000 dead ● FLN and Algerian state = 45,000 dead

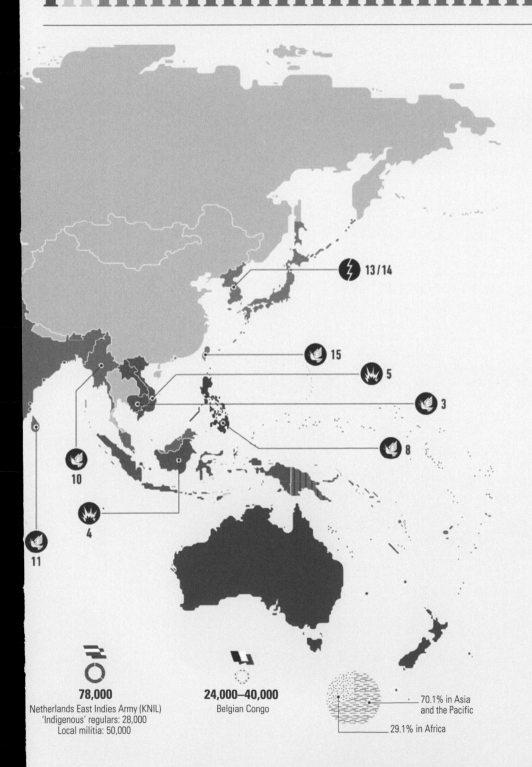

1. Lebanon
22 November 1943
Arab–Israeli War
1948–49

3. Laos
8 April 1945
recognized in 1953

5. Vietnam
2 September 1945
Indochina War
1946–54

7. Jordan
25 May 1946
Arab–Israeli War
1948–49

9. India & Pakistan
15 August 1947
partition and war
1947–48

11. Ceylon
4 February 1948

13. South Korea
(ex-Japan)
15 August 1948
Korean War
1950–53

15. Taiwan (ex-Japan)
7 December 1949

INDEPENDENCE DAYS

2. Iceland
17 June 1944

4. Indonesia
17 August 1945
war 1945–49

6. Syria
17 April 1946
Arab–Israeli War
1948–49

8. Philippines
4 July 1946
de facto since 1936

10. Burma
4 January 1948

12. Israel
14 May 1948
Arab–Israeli War
1948–49

14. North Korea
(ex-Japan)
9 September 1948
Korean War
1950–53

Mahatma Gandhi
1869–1948

Sukarno
1901–70

Ho Chi Minh
1890–1969

Messali Hadj
1898–1974

78,000
Netherlands East Indies Army (KNIL)
'Indigenous' regulars: 28,000
Local militia: 50,000

24,000–40,000
Belgian Congo

70.1% in Asia
and the Pacific

29.1% in Africa

SOURCES: 1. Bernard Droz, *Histoire de la décolonisation au XXe siècle*, Paris, 2006 • 2. *Encyclopedia of World War II*, eds. Alan Axelrod & Jack A. Kingston, New York, 2007 • 3. Jean-François Muracciole & Guillaume Piketty (eds.), *Encyclopédie de la Seconde Guerre mondiale*, Paris, 2015 • 4. David Killingray, *Fighting for Britain: African Soldiers in the Second World War*, Woodbridge, Suffolk, 2012 • 5. Jean-Louis Planche, *Sétif 1945: histoire d'un massacre annoncé*, Paris, 2006 • 6. *1940: Des coloniaux dans l'armée régulière et la Résistance*, Musée de l'Histoire de l'Immigration, Palais de la Porte-Dorée, Paris.

On the front cover: Graphic illustrating the changing numbers of British
and German fighter pilots and planes during the Battle of Britain,
July to November 1940 (see page 91).

Translated from the French *Infographie de la seconde guerre mondiale* by Lorna Dale

Original edition © 2018 Perrin, an imprint of Place des Éditeurs
This edition © 2019 Thames & Hudson Ltd, London

First published in 2019 in the United States of America by
Thames & Hudson Inc., 500 Fifth Avenue, New York, New York 10110

www.thamesandhudsonusa.com

Library of Congress Control Number 2019932293

ISBN 978-0-500-02292-4

Printed in Slovenia